Globalization and Growth

Implications for a Post-Crisis World

Commission on Growth and Development

Globalization and Growth
Implications for a Post-Crisis World

Edited by Michael Spence and Danny Leipziger

Contributions by
Michael Spence
Danny Leipziger
Daron Acemoglu
Philippe Aghion
David E. Bloom
Charles W. Calomiris
David Canning
William R. Cline
Richard N. Cooper
Antonio Estache
Marianne Fay
Günther Fink
David Hemous
Ravi Kanbur
Enisse Kharroubi
Robert Mendelsohn
Dani Rodrik
Andrew Sheng
David Wheeler

COMMISSION ON GROWTH AND DEVELOPMENT

© 2010 The International Bank for Reconstruction and Development /
The World Bank
On behalf of the Commission on Growth and Development
1818 H Street NW
Washington, DC 20433
Telephone: 202-473-1000
Internet: www.worldbank.org
         www.growthcommission.org
E-mail: info@worldbank.org
         contactinfo@growthcommission.org

All rights reserved

1 2 3 4 13 12 11 10

This volume is a product of the Commission on Growth and Development, which
is sponsored by the following organizations:

Australian Agency for International Development (AusAID)
Dutch Ministry of Foreign Affairs
Swedish International Development Cooperation Agency (SIDA)
U.K. Department for International Development (DFID)
The William and Flora Hewlett Foundation
The World Bank Group

The findings, interpretations, and conclusions expressed herein do not necessarily
reflect the views of the sponsoring organizations or the governments they represent.

    The sponsoring organizations do not guarantee the accuracy of the data
included in this work. The boundaries, colors, denominations, and other
information shown on any map in this work do not imply any judgment on the
part of the sponsoring organizations concerning the legal status of any
territory or the endorsement or acceptance of such boundaries.

    All queries on rights and licenses, including subsidiary rights, should be
addressed to the Office of the Publisher, The World Bank, 1818 H Street
NW, Washington, DC 20433, USA; fax: 202-522-2422; e-mail: pubrights@
worldbank.org.

ISBN: 978-0-8213-8220-2
eISBN: 978-0-8213-8221-9
DOI: 10.1596/978-0-8213-8220-2

Library of Congress Cataloging-in-Publication Data
Globalization and growth: implications for a post-crisis world / Michael Spence
and Danny Leipziger.
    p. cm.
 Includes bibliographical references and index.
 ISBN 978-0-8213-8220-2—ISBN 978-0-8213-8221-9 (electronic)
 1. Financial crises—History—21st century. 2. Economic history—History—
21st century. 3. Globalization. I. Spence, Michael, 1943– II. Leipziger, Danny M.
 HB3722.G598 2010
 338.9—dc22
                                                       2009054247

Cover design: Naylor Design

Contents

Figures

Tables

Preface

The Commission on Growth and Development was established in April 2006 as a response to two observations. While we felt that the benefits of growth were not fully appreciated, we recognized that the causes of growth were not fully understood. Growth is often overlooked and underrated as an instrument for tackling the world's most pressing problems, such as poverty, illiteracy, income inequality, unemployment, and pollution. At the same time, our understanding of economic growth is less definitive than commonly thought—even though advice sometimes has been given to developing countries with greater confidence than perhaps the state of our knowledge would justify. Consequently, the Commission's mandate was to "take stock of the state of theoretical and empirical knowledge on economic growth with a view to drawing implications for policy for the current and next generation of policy makers." This mandate has even more significance in the aftermath of the financial and economic crisis of 2008. As developing countries seek to repair the damage to their economies and to relaunch themselves on a sustained high-growth path, there has never been a greater need for fresh new ideas and approaches to achieving sustained high growth.

To help gauge the state of knowledge, the Commission invited leading academics and policy makers from around the world to a series of 13 workshops, held from 2007 to 2009 in Washington, DC; New York; New Haven, CT; and Cambridge, MA and commissioned a series of thematic papers. These papers reviewed subjects such as the causes and consequences of the financial crisis, monetary and fiscal policy, climate change, inequality, growth, and urbanization. In addition, 25 case studies were commissioned to explore the dynamics of growth in specific countries. Each presentation benefited from comments by members of the Commission and other workshop participants from the worlds of policy, theory, and practice.

The workshops were intense and lively affairs. It became clear that experts do not always agree, even on issues that are central to growth. The Commission had no wish to disguise or gloss over these uncertainties and differences; it did not want to present a false confidence in its conclusions beyond that justified by the evidence and accumulated experience. Researchers do not always know the correct "model" that would explain the world they observe, and even if they know the factors that matter, they cannot always measure them convincingly.

While researchers will continue to improve our understanding of the world, policy makers cannot wait for scholars to satisfy all of their doubts or resolve their differences. Decisions must be made with only partial knowledge. One consequence is that most policy decisions, however well informed, take on the character of experiments, which yield useful information about the way the world works, even if they do not always turn out the way policy makers hoped. It is best to recognize this fact, if only so that policy makers can be quick to spot failures and learn from mistakes.

The workshops from which we drew much of the inspiration for this volume, "Global Trends and Challenges" and "The Financial Crisis and Its Impact on Developing Countries' Growth Strategies and Prospects," were held in September 2007 and April 2009 in New Haven, CT, and Cambridge, MA, respectively. We were immensely fortunate to benefit from the wisdom and insights of outstanding researchers and experienced practitioners, and we are grateful to all of the participants, who are listed further in the volume. Globalization is an overarching theme that is relevant to the way we think of growth in open economies, and a volume on globalization and growth is particularly relevant given the current environment. The remainder of this preface is not an exhaustive summary of the workshops or the chapters; rather, it outlines the main goals and themes of this volume as well as the position and recommendations of the Commission with regard to the crisis.

Faced with increasing skepticism about the fate of globalization and the prospects for developing-country growth in the wake of the crisis, the Commission outlined its views in *Post-Crisis Growth in Developing Countries: A Special Report of the Commission on Growth and Development on the Implications of the 2008 Financial Crisis* (December 2009). The current crisis has raised numerous questions about the best strategies for achieving sustained growth and poverty reduction in developing countries, foremost among them whether the failure of the financial system also signifies a broader failure of market-oriented capitalist systems. Practically speaking, this raises questions as to whether the growth strategies that are understood to have worked in the past are still valid in the post-crisis world.

The Commission believes that the crisis was a failure of the financial system. The lightly and incompletely regulated model that characterized the advanced-country systems, especially in the United States and United Kingdom, is fundamentally flawed and in need of change. Regulators, central banks, market participants, and researchers (with a few notable exceptions) failed to appreciate the full dangers of this financial fragility. Going forward, they cannot afford to maintain their narrow focus on consumer prices and employment, leaving asset prices and balance sheets to their own devices. Certain entities in the regulatory system will have to take responsibility for the stability and sustainability of asset prices, leverage, and balance sheets. The alternative, which is to go back to the pre-crisis status quo, is neither economically nor politically acceptable.

That said, we have not found any evidence of a more broad-based failure of the market and capitalist economies. While the real economy has been damaged globally, private sector responses have generally been appropriate to the diminished circumstances. In the Commission's view, an outward-looking, market-driven strategy, as suggested in the original *Growth Report*, remains broadly valid. However, while this strategy remains the best alternative, it may not be as rewarding as it was in the years before the crisis, as the world economy that emerges from the recent upheaval is likely to be marked by slower growth in trade, costlier capital, and a more inhibited American consumer.

In the view of the Commission, the policy debate should be focused on the financial sectors' stability and performance. The nature of this crisis has inevitably strengthened the hands of those who prefer a more expansive role for the state. Properly channeled, this is not necessarily a bad outcome, but there are ample opportunities to make mistakes or to go too far. A substantial expansion of the government into the broader economy might disrupt the private dynamism that has contributed to all the successful high-growth cases of which we are aware. In our view, the state's expansion needs to be reversed as the crisis subsides. Central banks need to withdraw their support as private credit channels return, while in the meantime retaining the independence to do this when the time is right. The government should, however, be more involved in protecting people in the face of extreme economic turbulence, which would complement efforts to achieve greater economic and financial stability.

Internationally, some of the poorer countries only recently adopted fledgling growth-oriented policies, and the consensus in their favor, which was somewhat fragile going into the crisis, may break down as a result of it. If so, it may be the poorer, small countries that suffer the most lasting consequences. Meanwhile, their future depends greatly on developments beyond their borders: on how quickly foreign financing returns and on how soon their export markets revive. It would be morally unacceptable to leave these countries stranded by a crisis that was caused elsewhere. That is why the resources of the International Monetary Fund (IMF) must be equal to the crises that it and the global economy face. Lingering doubts about its governance need to be resolved so that the institution can act authoritatively and speedily. Resources and reform go hand in hand. Developing countries should be given a greater say in the institution, commensurate with their new prominence in the world economy.

On the positive side, there are countervailing forces. Some of the fundamental determinants of growth are relatively crisis proof: demography, for example, or human ingenuity. Wealth has been destroyed, but the stock of know-how from which developing countries can learn is undiminished. In principle, the potential for "catch-up" growth depends only on the gap between the developing country and the technological frontier. Thus developing countries still have the opportunity to set and modify policies and resume progress toward sustained high levels of growth, despite the multitude of pitfalls that remain as a result of the crisis.

It is clear that there will be a wide variety of policy implications to be drawn from the crisis, unique to each country's stage of development. With regard to two of the most important policy issues—the structure of financial sectors in developing countries and the macroeconomic policy framework—the Commission strongly recommends that developing countries adopt a more conservative, if more costly, financial model and position themselves favorably to withstand external shocks by maintaining low levels of public debt, ample foreign exchange reserves, and high domestic savings. In times of stability and relatively high growth, policy should lean in the countercyclical direction. The individual chapters in this volume provide more in-depth analysis of specific policy issues germane to developing-country growth in the post-crisis world, touching on aspects of fiscal policy, employment, inequality, demographics, and climate change, to name a few.

As an introduction, Danny Leipziger provides in chapter 1 a timely and comprehensive overview of the state of the world economy and the debates surrounding the future of globalization and economic growth once the crisis has passed. He concludes that, while multiple outcomes to the current crisis are possible, the post-crisis environment will hinge largely on the leadership displayed by governments in the present, most notably the United States, the European Union, and large emerging markets. This leadership will be shaped and influenced in no small part by the domestic political debates surrounding the benefits of globalization as well as the very real long-term fiscal and monetary consequences of present action. The remainder of the volume provides an in-depth analysis of the specific causes and effects of the crisis and their consequences for short-term, medium-term, and long-term growth in the developing world.

Contributions to part 1—The Global Financial Crisis: Causes, Mitigation, and Reform—meticulously detail the events and actions that contributed to and flowed from the current crisis. Part 1 takes us from the onset of the subprime crisis, highlighting the shortcomings of financial supervision, to the implosion of large financial institutions resulting in the near-collapse of credit markets and the entire financial system. Authors Daron Acemoglu, Charles Calomiris, Andrew Sheng, Richard Cooper, and Ravi Kanbur provide their insights into the intellectual and policy mistakes that contributed to the crisis as well as the enabling environment of broader macroeconomic and financial trends. Part 1 concludes by highlighting areas of potential reform, with ā focus on mitigating the effects of the crisis on the poor.

Following the description of the anatomy of the financial crisis and its far-reaching effects in part 1, part 2—How to Foster Real Growth—provides specific insight into the way forward for emerging and developing-market economies (EDMEs), highlighting specific issues and policy options to promote real growth in their economies. Authors Dani Rodrik; Antonio Estache and Marianne Fay; William Cline; and Philippe Aghion, David Hemous, and Enisse Kharroubi provide valuable insight into new ideas that have come to the surface in light of the crisis that have important implications for medium- and long-term growth. These topics touch on issues related to the government's role in promoting sustainable economic growth, new ideas on the viability of the export-led growth model, the importance of infrastructure for long-term growth, and the appropriate role of countercyclical fiscal policy.

Finally, no volume on growth would be complete without taking account of the long-term challenges. Part 4 of *The Growth Report: Strategies for Sustained Growth and Development* (May 2008) provides a comprehensive overview of these challenges; however, the crisis has imbued them with a greater sense of urgency. While all countries face long-term challenges to their growth, developing countries face a unique set of obstacles due to their geographic and demographic circumstances. In part 3—Long-Term Challenges to Growth—authors David Wheeler; Robert Mendelsohn; and David Bloom, David Canning, and Günther Fink explore the issues of climate change and demographics and their implications for the growth of EDMEs. While these topics may seem a measure removed from the current crisis and long-term economic growth, they are, in fact, profoundly connected. Demographic trends will have an enormous impact on fiscal policy and economic geography in the years to come. Likewise, climate change will be one of the most significant challenges facing EDMEs, which, according to some estimates, will incur 80 percent of the associated damages. In prompting a rethinking of fiscal priorities in many countries, the crisis has forced EDMEs to confront climate change and demographic issues earlier than they might otherwise have.

To conclude, this volume endeavors to provide an overview of the current debates surrounding the impact of the financial crisis on the growth trajectory of EDMEs as well as new ideas and fresh approaches for dealing with future growth challenges. The scale and scope of the downturn leave no doubt that the economic environment post-crisis will differ markedly from that preceding it. While the Commission on Growth and Development does not seek to make specific predictions as to the future of the economic landscape, our goal is to present ideas at the forefront of the debate on what that landscape may resemble and how developing countries can best adapt. On behalf of the Commission Secretariat, commissioners, and participants, we hope that you enjoy this volume.

Workshop Participants

Global Trends and Challenges
September 29–30, 2007

Ahluwalia, Montek, Commissioner and Deputy Chairman, Planning Commission, India

Aninat, Cristobal, Ministry of External Affairs, Chile

Annez, Patricia, World Bank

Barr, Nicholas, London School of Economics

Bhattacharya, Amar, G-24 Secretariat

Birdsall, Nancy, Center for Global Development

Bloom, David, Harvard University

Bosworth, Barry, Brookings Institution

Buckley, Robert, Rockefeller Foundation

Canning, David, Harvard University

Cline, William, Peterson Institute for International Economics and the Center for Global Development

Cooper, Richard, Harvard University

Dadush, Uri, World Bank

Darlington, Muriel, Commission on Growth and Development Secretariat

Derviş, Kemal, Administrator, United Nations Development Programme

Engel, Eduardo, Yale University

Fay, Marianne, World Bank

Frankel, Jeffrey, Harvard University

Gómez-Ibáñez, José, Kennedy School of Government, Harvard University

Hanson, Gordon, University of California, San Diego

Harrison, Ann, University of California-Berkeley

Hesse, Heiko, International Monetary Fund

Hoekman, Bernard, World Bank

Holzmann, Robert, World Bank

Joshi, Manosh, Embassy of India, Washington, DC

Jousten, Alain, International Monetary Fund

Kharas, Homi, Brookings Institution

Leipziger, Danny, Vice Chair of the Commission on Growth and Development, Washington, DC, and Vice President and Head of Poverty Reduction and Economic Management Network, World Bank

Lewis, Maureen, World Bank

Lim, Edwin, China Economic Research and Advisory Program

Mahovsky, Madeleine, European Commission

Manevskaya, Diana, Commission on Growth and Development Secretariat

Mattoo, Aaditya, World Bank

Meadows, Graham, European Research Institute, University of Sussex

Mendelsohn, Robert, Yale University

Montiel, Peter, Williams College

Nabli, Mustapha, World Bank

Nankani, Gobind, Global Development Network

Nordhaus, William, Yale University

Nowak, Dorota, Commission on Growth and Development Secretariat

Okonjo-Iweala, Ngozi, Commissioner and Managing Director, World Bank

Ozer, Ceren, World Bank

Perry, Guillermo, World Bank

Pritchett, Lant, Harvard University

Rajan, Raghuram, University of Chicago

Rosenzweig, Mark, Yale University

Shiller, Robert, Yale University

Sjoblom, Mirja, World Bank

Spence, Michael, Chair of the Commission on Growth and Development, Nobel Laureate, and Professor Emeritus, Stanford University

Venables, Anthony, University of Oxford, United Kingdom

Viveros, Alejandra, World Bank

Wacziarg, Romain, Graduate School of Business, Stanford University

Wheeler, David, Center for Global Development

Zagha, Roberto, Commission on Growth and Development Secretariat and World Bank

Zedillo, Ernesto, Commissioner and Director, Yale Center for Study of Globalization

The Financial Crisis and Its Impact on
Developing Countries' Growth Strategies and Prospects
April 20–21, 2009

Acemoglu, Daron, Massachusetts Institute of Technology

Acharya, Viral, New York University

Aghion, Philippe, Harvard University

Ahluwalia, Montek, Commissioner and Deputy Chairman, Planning Commission, India

Akerlof, George, Nobel Laureate in Economics, University of California, Berkeley

Athayde, Christopher, U.K. Treasury

Aziz, Jahangir, J. P. Morgan, Mumbai, India

Bacha, Edmar, Commissioner and Director, Casa Das Garças Institute for Economic Policy Studies, Brazil

Banerjee, Abhijit, Massachusetts Institute of Technology

Bates, Jennifer, British Embassy, Washington, DC

Blejer, Mario, Macroeconomic Advisory Group, Argentina

Boediono, Dr., Commissioner and Governor, Central Bank of Indonesia

Brahmam, Maya, World Bank

Brahmbhatt, Milan, World Bank

Brunnermeier, Markus, Princeton University

Calomiris, Charles, Columbia University

Canuto, Otaviano, World Bank

Cooper, Richard, Harvard University

Cox, Simon, *The Economist*

Cran, William, PITV Productions, London

Darlington, Muriel, Commission on Growth and Development Secretariat

Derviş, Kemal, Commissioner and Former Executive Head of the United Nations Development Programme; Vice President and Director, Global Economy and Development, Brookings Institution, Washington, DC

Feldstein, Martin, Harvard University

Frankel, Jeffrey, Harvard University

Giugale, Marcelo, World Bank

Goldfajn, Ilan, Pontifical Catholic University of Rio de Janeiro, Brazil

Han, Duck-soo, Commissioner and Ambassador of the Republic of Korea to the United States

Hausmann, Ricardo, Center for International Development and Harvard University

Ito, Takatoshi, University of Tokyo

Johnson, Robert, Former Chief Economist for the U.S. Senate Banking and Budget Committees

Kanbur, Ravi, Cornell University

Kenen, Peter, Princeton University

Khalaf-Hunaidi, Rima, Former Assistant Secretary General and Director of the Regional Bureau for Arab States at the United Nations Development Programme; Former Deputy Prime Minister of Jordan

Kharas, Homi, Wolfensohn Center for Development, Brookings Institution

Lee, Kwang suk, Embassy of the Republic of Korea, Washington, DC

Leipziger, Danny, Vice Chair of the Commission on Growth and Development, Washington, DC, and Vice President and Head of Poverty Reduction and Economic Management Network, World Bank

Lewis, Jeffrey, World Bank

Lim, Edwin, China Economic Research and Advisory Program

Lin, Justin, World Bank

Loewald, Christopher, Ministry of Finance, South Africa

Mahovsky, Madeleine, European Commission

Malan, Pedro, Former Minister of Finance, Brazil

Marchal, Wijnand, Royal Netherlands Embassy, Washington, DC

Miller, Callum, Department for International Development, Growth and Investment Group

Mohieldin, Mahmoud, Commissioner and Minister of Investment, Arab Republic of Egypt

Monfort, Philippe, European Commission

Nankani, Gobind, International Growth Center, United Kingdom

Nowak, Dorota, Commission on Growth and Development Secretariat

Okonjo-Iweala, Ngozi, Commissioner and Managing Director, World Bank Group

O'Neill, Jim, Goldman Sachs

Oya, Shin, Japan Bank for International Cooperation

Pinto, Brian, World Bank

Portes, Richard, London School of Economics

Richardson, Matthew, Stern School of Business, New York University

Rodrik, Dani, Harvard University

Romer, Paul, Stanford Center for International Development and Stanford Institute for Economic Policy Research

Rostom, Ahmed, Ministry of Investment, Arab Republic of Egypt

Scholes, Myron, Nobel Laureate in Economics, Stanford University

Serven, Luis, World Bank

Shah, Ajay, National Institute for Public Finance and Policy, India

Sheel, Alok, Economic Advisory Council to the Prime Minister, India

Sheng, Andrew, China Banking Regulatory Commission

Singh, Pavneet, Commission on Growth and Development Secretariat

Söderbäck, Mikael, Financial Systems Development, Swedish International Development Cooperation Agency

Solow, Robert, Commissioner and Professor Emeritus, Massachusetts Institute of Technology, and Nobel Laureate in Economics

Spence, Michael, Chair of the Commission on Growth and Development and Professor Emeritus, Stanford University, and Nobel Laureate in Economics

Steer, Cynthia, Rogerscasey, United States

Thompson, SueLena, Independent Producer and Consultant

Thunell, Lars, Executive Vice President and CEO, International Finance Corporation, World Bank Group

Venner, Dwight, Commissioner and Governor, Eastern Caribbean Central Bank, St. Kitts and Nevis

Watanabe, Hiroshi, Commissioner and President and CEO, Japan Bank for International Cooperation

Wolfson, Mark, Stanford University

Zagha, Roberto, Commission on Growth and Development Secretariat

Zappala, Cara, World Bank

Biographies of the Editors and Contributors

Daron Acemoglu is Charles P. Kindleberger Professor of Applied Economics at Massachusetts Institute of Technology (MIT) and winner of the 2005 John Bates Clark Medal. He is a member of the Economic Growth Program of the Canadian Institute of Advanced Research. He is also affiliated with the National Bureau of Economic Research, the Center for Economic Performance, and the Centre for Economic Policy Research (London). His principal interests are political economy, economic development, economic growth, technology, income and wage inequality, human capital and training, and labor economics. His most recent works concentrate on the role of institutions in economic development and political economy.

Philippe Aghion is Robert C. Waggoner Professor of Economics at Harvard University, having previously been Professor at University College London, an Official Fellow at Oxford's Nuffield College, and an Assistant Professor at MIT. His main research work is on growth and contract theory. With Peter Howitt, he developed the so-called Schumpeterian Paradigm and extended the paradigm in several directions; much of the resulting work is summarized in his book with Howitt entitled *Endogenous Growth Theory*.

David E. Bloom is Clarence James Gamble Professor of Economics and Demography and Chair of the Department of Global Health and Population at the Harvard School of Public Health and Director of Harvard University's Program on the Global Demography of Aging. He is also an

Adjunct Trustee of amfAR (the Foundation for AIDS Research) and a Faculty Research Associate at the National Bureau of Economic Research. Professor Bloom is a Fellow of the American Academy of Arts and Sciences and an Ambassador in the Paul G. Rogers Society for Global Health Research. He has served on the public policy faculty at Carnegie-Mellon University and on the economics faculties at Harvard University and Columbia University. He served as Chair of the Department of Economics at Columbia University and as Deputy Director of the Harvard Institute for International Development. His current research focuses mainly on the links among health, demography, and economic growth.

Charles W. Calomiris is Henry Kaufman Professor of Financial Institutions at Columbia University's Graduate School of Business and Professor at Columbia's School of International and Public Affairs. His research spans several areas, including banking, corporate finance, financial history, and monetary economics. He is a member of the Shadow Financial Regulatory Committee, the Shadow Open Market Committee, and the Financial Economists Roundtable, a Research Associate of the National Bureau of Economic Research, and a member of the Hoover Institution's Task Force on Property Rights. Professor Calomiris was Co-Director of the Project on Financial Deregulation and also a Senior Fellow at the Council on Foreign Relations. Professor Calomiris served on the International Financial Institution Advisory Commission, a congressional commission to advise the U.S. government on the reform of the International Monetary Fund (IMF), the World Bank, the regional development banks, and the World Trade Organization (WTO). He has published numerous books, journal articles, and chapters in scholarly volumes, served on numerous journal editorial boards, and advised a broad array of government and private organizations.

David Canning is Professor of Economics and International Health in the Department of Global Health and Population, Harvard School of Public Health. He has served on the faculty of the London School of Economics, Cambridge University, Columbia University, and Queen's University Belfast. His research focuses on the role of health as a form of human capital and the effect of demographic change on economic development.

William R. Cline is Senior Fellow jointly at the Peterson Institute for International Economics and the Center for Global Development in Washington, DC. During 1996–2001, while on leave from the Peterson Institute, Dr. Cline was Deputy Managing Director and Chief Economist of the Institute of International Finance (IIF) in Washington, DC. He has been Senior Fellow at the Peterson Institute for International Economics since its inception in 1981. Previously he was Senior Fellow at the Brookings Institution (1973–81); Deputy Director of Development and Trade Research in the Office of the Assistant Secretary for International Affairs, U.S. Treasury Department (1971–73); Ford Foundation Visiting Professor in Brazil (1970–71); and Lecturer and Assistant Professor of Economics at Princeton University (1967–70). He is the author of 22 books, including *Trade and Income Distribution* (1997) and *Trade Policy and Global Poverty* (2004).

Richard N. Cooper is Maurits C. Boas Professor of International Economics at Harvard University. He was formerly Vice Chairman of the Global Development Network and a member of the Trilateral Commission, the Council on Foreign Relations, the Executive Panel of the U.S. Chief of Naval Operations, and the Brookings Panel on Economic Activity. He has served on several occasions in the U.S. government, as Chairman of the National Intelligence Council (1995–97), Undersecretary of State for Economic Affairs (1977–81), Deputy Assistant Secretary of State for International Monetary Affairs (1965–66), and Senior Staff Economist at the Council of Economic Advisers (1961–63). He was also Chairman of the Federal Reserve Bank of Boston (1990–92). His most recent books, which he co-authored, include *Boom, Crisis, and Adjustment*; *Macroeconomic Management in Korea, 1970–1990*; *Environment and Resource Policies for the World Economy*; and *What the Future Holds*.

Antonio Estache is Professor of Economics at the Université Libre de Bruxelles, where he holds the Bernard Van Ommeslaghe Chair and is a member of the European Center for Advanced Research of Economics. Prior to that, he was Chief Economist for the Sustainable Development Network of the World Bank, where he spent 25 years (1982–2007) working across regions on various dimensions of public sector reform. He has published widely on the regulation of network industries (electricity, telecommunications, transport, and water and sanitation), assessment of the performance of the public sector, and the growth and distributional effects of environmental, fiscal, and sectoral policies in developing countries.

Marianne Fay is Chief Economist for the Sustainable Development Network of the World Bank and Co-Director of the *World Development Report 2010* on climate change. She has held positions in different regions of the World Bank (Europe and Central Asia, Latin America and the Caribbean, Africa) working on infrastructure, urbanization, and more recently adaptation to climate change. Her research has focused mostly on the role of infrastructure and urbanization in development, with a particular interest in issues related to urban poverty. She is the author of numerous articles and books on these topics.

Günther Fink is Assistant Professor of International Health Economics at the Department of Global Health and Population, Harvard School of Public Health. His research has covered a wide range of topics related to economic development, with a particular focus on the interactions between health and human capital, on one side, and economic growth, on the other. He is currently conducting a longitudinal household health and wealth survey in Accra, Ghana, that investigates the daily burden of disease in urban Sub-Saharan Africa with a special focus on malaria. He is also working on a broad socioeconomic evaluation of the large-scale anti-malaria program rolled out in Zambia since 2006.

David Hemous is currently in a Ph.D. program in economics at Harvard University. His research interests include growth, trade, and environmental economics.

Ravi Kanbur is T. H. Lee Professor of World Affairs, International Professor of Applied Economics and Management, and Professor of Economics at Cornell University. He has taught at the universities of Oxford, Cambridge, Essex, Warwick, Princeton, and Columbia. Ravi Kanbur has held numerous positions at the World Bank, including Senior Economic Adviser, Resident Representative in Ghana, and Chief Economist of the Africa Region. He has also served as Director of the World Bank's *World Development Report*. Professor Kanbur's main areas of interest are public economics and development economics. His work spans conceptual, empirical, and policy analysis. He is particularly interested in bridging the worlds of rigorous analysis and practical policy making. He is the author of more than 150 publications, covering topics such as risk taking, inequality, poverty, structural adjustment, debt, agriculture, and political economy. He has published in leading economics journals such as *American Economic Review*, *Journal of Political Economy*, *Review of Economic Studies*, *Journal of Economic Theory*, and *Economic Journal*.

Enisse Kharroubi is Senior Economist in the International Affairs Department at the French Central Bank. He received a Ph.D. from DELTA (now called the Paris School of Economics) in 2003. He then joined the French Central Bank in the Economic Studies Department, where he worked on various topics, including macroeconomic volatility, financial integration, and labor market institutions. He joined the International Affairs Department in 2007, conducting research on three main topics: international finance and capital flows, liquidity crises and banking, and open economy monetary economics. His recent publications include an article in the *International Journal of Central Banking* titled "Liquidity, Moral Hazard, and Inter-Bank Market Collapse."

Danny Leipziger is Professor of International Business at the George Washington University and Vice Chair of the Commission on Growth and Development. He is former Vice President of the Poverty Reduction and Economic Management Network (2004–09) at the World Bank. As Vice President, he provided leadership for the Bank's strategic initiatives on growth and poverty reduction, directing work on economic policy, debt, trade, gender, and governance issues as well as the Bank's dialogue with key partner institutions, including the International Monetary Fund, the World Trade Organization, the Organisation for Economic Co-operation and Development (OECD), and the European Union. Over the course of his 28-year career at the World Bank, he has held management positions in the East Asia and Pacific Region and the Latin America and Caribbean Region as well as in the World Bank Institute. Prior to joining the Bank, Dr. Leipziger served in senior positions at the U.S. Agency for International Development and the U.S. Department of State.

Robert Mendelsohn is Edwin Weyerhaeuser Davis Professor in the Yale School of Forestry and Environmental Studies, Yale University. Professor Mendelsohn has focused his research on measuring the benefits of protecting the environment. He has studied a wide range of topics from measuring the damages from hazardous waste and traditional air pollution to estimating the economic value of wildlife and nontimber forest products. Over the last 15 years, he has quantified the impacts of global warming and studied climate adaptation.

Dani Rodrik is Rafiq Hariri Professor of International Political Economy at the John F. Kennedy School of Government, Harvard University. He has published widely in the areas of international economics, economic development, and political economy. His research focuses on what constitutes good economic policy and why some governments are better than others in adopting it. He is affiliated with the National Bureau of Economic Research, the Centre for Economic Policy Research (London), the Center for Global Development, and the Council on Foreign Relations. He was awarded the inaugural Albert O. Hirschman Prize by the Social Science Research Council in 2007. He has also received the Leontief Award for Advancing the Frontiers of Economic Thought, an honorary doctorate from the University of Antwerp, and research grants from the Carnegie Corporation, Ford Foundation, and Rockefeller Foundation. Professor Rodrik is an editor of the *Review of Economics and Statistics* and the *Journal of Globalization and Development*.

Andrew Sheng is a Chartered Accountant and has served in various positions with Bank Negara Malaysia, the World Bank, and the Hong Kong Monetary Authority. From October 1998 to September 2005, he was Chairman of the Securities and Futures Commission, Hong Kong, China. From October 2003 to September 2005, he was Chairman of the Technical Committee of the International Organization of Securities Commissions. Since December 2005, he has been Chief Adviser to the China Banking Regulatory Commission. In addition to chairing the annual OECD–Asian Development Bank Institute Roundtable on Capital Markets in Asia, he is a Board Member of Qatar Financial Centre Regulatory Authority and of Sime Darby Berhad, Khazanah Nasional Berhad, as well as a Member of the Council of the International Center for Education in Islamic Finance. He is also concurrently Adjunct Professor in the Graduate School of Economics and Management, Tsinghua University, Beijing, and Adjunct Professor of Financial and Monetary Economics, University of Malaya. He writes a regular column on investor education for *Caijing Magazine*. He is the author of *Bank Restructuring: Lessons from the 1980s* (Oxford University Press and the World Bank 1995), and *From Asian to Global Financial Crisis* (Cambridge University Press 2009).

Michael Spence is Senior Fellow at the Hoover Institution and Philip H. Knight Professor Emeritus of Management in the Graduate School of Business, Stanford University. He was awarded the Nobel Memorial Prize in Economic Sciences in 2001. Dr. Spence was Philip H. Knight Professor and Dean of the Stanford Business School from 1990 to 1999. Since 1999, he has been a Partner at Oak Hill Capital Partners. From 1975 to 1990, he served as Professor of Economics and Business Administration at Harvard

University. Dr. Spence was awarded the John Kenneth Galbraith Prize for Excellence in Teaching in 1978 and the John Bates Clark Medal in 1981 for a "significant contribution to economic thought and knowledge." He was appointed Chairman of the Economics Department at Harvard in 1983 and served as Dean of the Faculty of Arts and Sciences from 1984 to 1990. At various times, he has served as a Member of the editorial boards of the *American Economics Review*, *Bell Journal of Economics*, *Journal of Economic Theory*, and *Public Policy*. Professor Spence is Chair of the Commission on Growth and Development.

David Wheeler is Senior Fellow at the Center for Global Development, where he works on issues related to climate change and natural resource conservation. From 1993 to 2006, as a Lead Economist in the World Bank's Development Research Group, he directed a team that worked on environmental policy and research issues in collaboration with policy makers and academics in Bangladesh, Brazil, China, Colombia, Ghana, India, Indonesia, Mexico, the Philippines, Vietnam, and other countries. After completing his doctorate in 1974, Wheeler taught economics for two years at the National University of Zaire in Kinshasa. He joined the economics faculty at Boston University in 1976 and taught there until he joined the World Bank in 1990.

Acknowledgments

The editors are most grateful for the strong support provided by the sponsors of the Commission on Growth and Development: the governments of Australia, the Netherlands, Sweden, and the United Kingdom; the William and Flora Hewlett Foundation; and the World Bank. In particular, the Poverty Reduction and Economic Management Network at the World Bank was generous in providing resources for this effort. We are much obliged to the participants in the workshops on "Global Trends and Challenges" and the "Financial Crisis and Its Impact on Developing Countries' Growth Strategies and Prospects," sponsored by the Commission and held at Yale's Center for the Study of Globalization and Harvard's Kennedy School of Government, respectively. We would especially like to thank the chapter authors for their numerous and diverse insights and the time they dedicated to engaging in discussions of the issues. Roberto Zagha, Secretary of the Commission, was a constant source of good ideas, encouragement, and stimulation. Roberto brings out the best in others, while keeping a sharp focus on the driving issues at hand. The level of discussion and the quality of the papers that follow reflect his enthusiasm and wisdom. Luis Serven dedicated his time and expertise to reviewing the thematic papers and helped to shape the workshops. William O'Boyle, a consultant for the World Bank, also deserves special thanks for his dedication to all aspects of the volume. His research, editing, and organizational efforts were instrumental in its timely completion.

A team of colleagues in the Commission Secretariat—Muriel Darlington, Diana Manevskaya, and Dorota Nowak—was dedicated to making every aspect of the Commission's work successful. They gave us what felt like undivided attention in organizing the workshops and producing this book—one of many of the Commission's activities with pressing deadlines and low tolerance for error. The whole process was only possible due to their marvelous organization and steady hard work. Aziz Gökdemir was pragmatic, accommodating, and rigorous in preparing the manuscript for publication. He never missed his deadlines and was more than understanding when we occasionally needed to shift ours. Stephen McGroarty oversaw the publication process with great skill, and Nora Ridolfi managed the printing of the book to ensure the highest quality.

Michael Spence
Danny Leipziger

Abbreviations

AIG	American International Group
CCC	contingent capital certificate
CDO	collateralized debt obligation
CDS	credit default swap
CO_2	carbon dioxide
EDME	emerging and developing market economy
EU	European Union
FC	fallacy of composition
FDICIA	Federal Deposit Insurance Corporation Improvement Act
FHA	Federal Housing Administration
G-8	Group of Eight
G-20	Group of Twenty
GATT	General Agreement on Tariffs and Trade
GDP	gross domestic product
GSE	government-sponsored enterprises
Gt	gigatons
GtC	gigatons of carbon
ILO	International Labour Organization
IMF	International Monetary Fund
IPCC	Intergovernmental Panel on Climate Change
ISIC	International Standard Industrial Classification
LFPR	labor force participation rate
LFTP	labor force to population
LGD	loss given default

MDG	Millennium Development Goal
MIS	management information system
Mt	megaton
NEP	new economic power
NGO	nongovernmental organization
NIIP	net international investment position
NRSRO	nationally recognized statistical rating organization
OECD	Organisation for Economic Co-operation and Development
OLS	ordinary least squares
OPEC	Organization of the Petroleum-Exporting Countries
OTC	over-the-counter
PD	probability of default
PPI	Private Participation in Infrastructure
ppm	parts per million
R&D	research and development
SDR	special drawing rights
SITC	Standard Industrial Trade Classification
TFP	total factor productivity
TSLS	two-stage least squares
UN	United Nations
WTO	World Trade Organization

Introduction

CHAPTER 1
Globalization Revisited

Danny Leipziger

Since the May 2008 release of *The Growth Report*, the world economy has been hit by an extraordinary series of shocks. These shocks have threatened the economic security of many poor countries and imperiled the strong macroeconomic progress recorded by others. Among other things, these shocks will provide an important test for the recommendations of *The Growth Report*. At the time of its writing, the connection between the report's recommendations and the twin crises was apparent, but not the extent to which long-term, sustainable growth would be imperiled. A mere few months later, however, with the advent of the housing, banking, and stock market crises, the situation changed radically. As Claessens, Kose, and Terrones (2008) note, although the combination of distress in these three segments of the financial system is rare, it is associated with deeper and longer recessions.[1]

Thanks are due to William G. O'Boyle for his assistance and to Philippe Aghion, Milan Brahmbhatt, Antonio Estache, José Antonio Ocampo, and Andre Sapir for useful comments.

1   Claessens, Kose, and Terrones (2008) examine evidence of 122 recessions in 21 industrial countries in the period 1960–2007. Reinhart and Rogoff (2009) catalogue severe crises and quantify the depth and duration of the following slump. See also Freund (2009) for data on the increase in trade elasticity to gross domestic product (GDP) over the last 50 years.

New in this equation are the extent of globalization, which is much wider than in earlier crises, and the extent to which increased integration will magnify the losses.[2]

Globalization as an economic phenomenon has been the dominant force for economic integration and the main driver of growth worldwide for many decades, although the speed of globalization—taken to include trade, finance, flows of information and technology, and offshoring—is unprecedented in modern economic history. The increased economic interconnections between countries are widely credited as one of the driving forces that significantly reduced poverty in China and Vietnam, enabled the poorer nations of Europe to ride the European Union train to higher incomes, and gave hope to some African countries that Collier's prognosis that globalization is biased against latecomers might be too pessimistic (Collier 2007). The extent of financial flows, reaching 8.6 percent of the combined GDP of emerging and developing market economies (EDMEs) in 2007, seemed to supplement national shortages of capital and to promote domestic investment in some cases.[3] The export drive of the EDMEs in the period 2000–07 contributed about two-thirds of the growth in total world trade and 60 percent of the growth in total world output. This is remarkable when compared even to the decade of the 1990s, when the EDMEs accounted for only a quarter of the growth in world trade and about 40 percent of the growth in world output (World Bank 2008b, 2009a).

The 2009 collapse of the bubble changed the landscape considerably. Talk of decoupling disappeared, and discussion centered on the future, not only of globalization, but also of capitalism as we know it (Wolf 2009). The startling fact that global output shrank in 2009 for the first time in modern postwar history is reinforced by the size of the decline—now variously estimated by institutional pundits to be between negative 2.5 and negative 2.9 percent. Using the steeper decline would mean that world income in 2009 has been set back at least to the level of 2007, a two-year loss. World trade has fallen by at least 10 percent in volume, and prospects for 2010 portend an anemic recovery (IMF 2009; OECD 2009b; World Bank 2009a).

Average changes in world incomes are illuminating, but, as is usually the case, the distribution of these welfare losses is asymmetric. The early concerns raised by Stiglitz (2002) and others about the unequal gains and losses from globalization become more starkly relevant when the losses begin to mount. The argument pre-crisis was that public policy was at fault for not dealing sufficiently with the losers from globalization, whereas the issue now is how much of the loss should be allocated to which segment of society. Given the expansion of national indebtedness in the United States,

---

2 Freund (2009) calculates that the elasticity of world trade to GDP rose from under 2.0 in the 1960s to a high of 3.5 before the crisis. She also finds that the decline in the growth rate of trade following a decline in GDP is sudden and, on average, more than four times as large as the growth of income.

3 See Rodrik and Subramanian (2008b) for an explanation of why foreign capital failed to be channeled to productive investment in other cases. See Bresser-Pereira and Gala (2007) for a similar argument.

for example, the fiscal incidence burden becomes increasingly intergenerational as well (Barr and Diamond 2009; Burman 2009; OECD 2009a). Recent work on fiscal incidence policy by Estache and Leipziger (2009) and their collaborators points to the importance of measuring the beneficiaries for all types of expenditures, in particular, because middle-class interests may not be appropriately protected, with adverse consequences for the conduct of economic policy (Estache and Leipziger 2009; Leipziger and Spence 2007; Stiglitz 2002).

For emerging and developing countries, the question becomes one of whether the landscape has changed so fundamentally that economic policy needs to be redesigned. In *Post-Crisis Growth in Developing Countries: A Special Report of the Commission on Growth and Development on the Implications of the 2008 Financial Crisis* (hereinafter, the special report), the Commission argues that the basic direction of policy that aims to achieve long-term growth remains unaltered, but that the gains from leveraging the international trading system may be smaller than in recent decades and that past reliance on foreign flows may need to be rethought (Commission on Growth and Development 2009). Issues surrounding globalization are here to stay, and this volume of papers, prepared for Commission workshops held from 2007 to 2009, is intended to help us to navigate various elements of the globalization debate.

There has been no dearth of commentary about what the crisis may mean, but in reality, until the bottom has been reached and the path to recovery is clear, it will be difficult to draw general lessons for the future. This collection of essays encompasses a variety of viewpoints and covers both medium- and long-term policy issues. It is said that more textbooks have become obsolete in 2009 than in any year since the Great Depression. As a corollary, much has been written that is worth reviewing in a volume on globalization. The papers look at the issue of globalization from diverse points of view and add insights and perspective to the recommendations of the *The Growth Report*.

The State of the Current Debate

There is no shortage of commentary on the implications of the current crisis for the future. Some see it as a temporary setback to the open and integrated system of both trade and finance that has ushered in two decades of spectacular world growth and monumental gains for those most integrated in the global system. To the globalizers—and here I would put prominently Bhagwati, Cooper, and Mishkin—there is much work to be done to restore the system's health, and governments need to show statesmanship in resisting nationalistic solutions that are globally welfare reducing. Globalization still offers the best outcome for the most people, even though some distributional questions remain. The efficiency arguments of globalization and the political necessity of pulling together to keep the system functioning are seen to be of paramount importance (Bhagwati 2004; Mishkin 2006; see Cooper in chapter 5 of this volume).

For others, like Stiglitz, Rodrik, and Subramanian, the system is broken to some degree, and the future should not and cannot resemble the past in many fundamental ways. Stiglitz focuses on the governance requirements of the system and its basic inequities as well as the market failures that are not easily remedied. In fact, Stiglitz would argue that "market fundamentalism" is dead, and his view that urgent reform is needed certainly has more adherents than before. Others would rely more on markets to fix themselves, stressing incentives and incentive-compatible regulation (Barth, Caprio, and Levine 2006; Calomiris in chapter 3 of this volume). Rodrik has argued that the goal should no longer be maximum openness in trade and finance, but levels that leave sufficient room for the pursuit of domestic social and economic aims. With Subramanian, he argues that the days of unquestionably open capital markets in EDMEs, and the accompanying volume of cross-border flows, are gone and that this is, on balance, a good thing (Rodrik and Subramanian 2008a; Barth, Caprio, and Levine 2006; Commission of Experts 2009; Rodrik 2009; Stiglitz 2009).

Where we will emerge from these debates remains to be seen; however, a strict return to the status quo ante is unlikely. For one, the regulatory environment will not allow it, and, as has been noted by Rajan and others, the shape of corporate finance will change and with it the nature of international flows (Dell'Ariccia, Detragiache, and Rajan 2005; Rajan 2009). Second, the tradeoff between domestic job losses and industry profits that has driven offshoring, at least in the United States, will need reexamination. We refer below to the thinking of Blinder (2007, 2009) on this important issue. Third, the future of the open, globalized system will depend a lot on how the new economic powers (NEPs) manage themselves and how they influence the system going forward (Leipziger and O'Boyle 2009).

There is considerable uncertainty about the nature of globalization post-crisis. If, for example, the switch in demand in the NEPs from exports to nontradables is permanent, then poorer developing (for example, African) countries may be able to assume the mantle of cheap manufacturer to the world. Whether this will be enough to offset the overall decline in exports to advanced countries remains to be seen. If, however, a new kind of industrial policy begins to permeate, and national industries and banks are given government preferences in countries of the Organisation for Economic Co-operation and Development (OECD) as well as the NEPs, then the system itself will undergo major transformation, and not for the better. One thing is certain, as Dominique Strauss-Kahn said at the G-8 Summit in July 2009, "Globalization is not just a topic for the FT editorial pages" (Financial Times 2009).

One of the drivers of growth in world trade in recent decades has been the demand for offshore services in the United States, arguably the growth engine for much of global demand. This offshoring, which has all the efficiency-enhancing characteristics of trade that are eloquently noted by Bhagwati, Panagariya, and Srinivasan (2004), also comes with strings attached. Blinder (2007) persuasively argues that the expansion of offshoring by U.S. firms has dramatically altered the employment landscape and will do so even more in the future. This observation was rendered before the current crisis and therefore has potentially even greater significance now for the future of globalization. Blinder sees the offshoring trend as a large, potentially disruptive force in the United States, equivalent to an industrial revolution in its impact on jobs. He argues that it is significant because it could affect between 20 and 30 percent of jobs in the United States, particularly those that are "impersonal," not requiring either face-to-face or customized interactions.[4]

This is not good news for the future of world commerce because we have now seen a conflagration of all three developments that Blinder predicts for the American labor market, namely (a) an increase in frictional unemployment due to job churning, which is unprecedented because of firm closings in the current crisis; (b) an increase in structural unemployment because of a mismatch of skills caused by the export of impersonal jobs, which, according to Blinder, is a continuing trend;[5] and (c) an increase in unemployment during cyclical downturns, which has reached historic proportions because of the sharp drop in personal income, spending, and confidence in the U.S. economy in 2009. While these phenomena are not new, they have gained considerable traction at a time of rapidly increasing unemployment. Taken as a package, the political economy consequences are inevitably going to be on the side of creating and preserving (through whatever means) domestic jobs. Even more important to the future is that, whether this will be seen as formal protectionism or not, globalization will no doubt be put at odds with national economic goals in a highly politicized fashion.

Trends and Inflection Points

A useful starting point for discussing whether or not we can expect a paradigm shift in the globalization model of recent decades is to review where we are with respect to economic integration and then to overlay both the recent unprecedented crisis and the longer-term trends that are fairly certain. The World Bank's 2007 *Global Economic Prospects* (World Bank 2007) serves as a useful guide, since it correctly portrayed a world of increasing interdependence in which trade outpaced economic growth and in which, as a result, the average trade to GDP ratio rose from 13 percent in 1970 to 25 percent in 2005. The report predicted a trebling of world trade to $27 trillion by 2030, including both rapid gains by EDMEs and

---

4 Blinder (2007) sees offshoring going far beyond billing, booking, and information technology support and observes that, even in a field such as medicine, radiology is more likely to be offshored, subject to regulatory issues, than is pediatrics.

5 Blinder (2009) posits two big shocks that will allow this phenomenon to continue: (a) adding labor previously outside the global economy will put downward pressure on wages and upward pressure on returns to capital, and (b) increases in technology will make previously personal services impersonal.

major increases in trade in services. Will these trends, which were so pronounced over the 2000–07 period, in which developing country exports more than doubled (an increase of 127 percent) and South-South trade grew at an even faster clip (150 percent), continue despite the current setbacks (WTO 2008)?

The unprecedentedly high unemployment rates in the advanced countries, particularly in the United States where social safety nets are weaker than those in much of Europe, will put enormous political pressure on policy makers to deal with job losses. Of course, a key driver of the increase in trade in services is offshoring—between 1994 and 2003 in India alone, trade in services grew more than 700 percent! We already have witnessed several protectionist measures in the context of stimulus packages in many countries, not least in the U.S. "buy American" and Chinese "buy Chinese" provisions. The future trajectory of growth with its consequences for world trade is closely connected to the issue of jobs and public policy to protect or create domestic employment (Anderlini 2009; World Bank 2007).

Taking a step back, the Pew Global Attitudes Survey of 2008, conducted prior to the crisis, found a sharp decline in positive views among Americans toward international trade. Compared to five years earlier, only 53 percent of respondents thought trade was a good thing, a drop of 25 percentage points (Pew Global Attitudes Project 2008). This reflects the increasing polarization of the globalization issue between advanced economies and emerging markets, which still largely view globalization as a positive force. Much of the disenchantment with free trade stems from the perception that it is the main cause of job losses in industrialized countries. Whether this is true or not is debatable, as is the question of what is driving job losses: lack of education, wage differentials, or technological innovation (Blinder 2009; Goldin and Katz 2007; IMF 2007; Lawrence 2008). However, one point is quite clear: in the public perception, jobs in the United States are being exported, a phenomenon that is politically untenable when combined with housing foreclosures, impaired stock market assets, and record high unemployment. Since it can be argued that the United States set the bar for globalization efforts, the current state of the economy may presage a return to economic nationalism, a trend seen worldwide these days. Recent evidence shows that 17 of the 19 individual members of the G-20 instituted some form of protection in 2009 and also that the frequency of antidumping suits increased (Gamberoni and Newfarmer 2009). Antidumping actions are frequently seen as a tactic to slow down imports and protect domestic industries under stress (Leipziger and Shin 1991). Despite general admonitions to avoid protectionism, such as those contained in G-20 and G-8 communiqués, domestic political pressures are fiercely protectionist, especially during downturns.

This brings the issue of distribution front and center. In the United States, still the largest trading nation, we see a disturbing trend regarding inequality, and it is probably connected to the finding that America's middle class reports the lowest satisfaction with international trade as a positive phenomenon (Pew Global Attitudes Project 2008). The overall Gini coefficient for the United States, flat during the 1960s and 1970s, began to rise in the 1980s and continued to climb between 1990 and 2005 to about 0.47. This places it not only among the more unequal ex ante (that is, before redistribution) of OECD countries, but, which is more important, among the most unequal ex post as well.[6] More important, however, according to the U.S. Census Bureau (2009), most of the increase in inequality has come from the unevenness between the top 5 percent and the median income earner. Most dramatically, only the top 7.5 percent of U.S. households increased their real earnings in the 2001–05 period. The coincidence of very rapid growth in incomes, a highly skewed sharing of these gains, and the high point in globalization reached in the period between 2001 and the current crisis gives rise to a great deal of cynicism in the United States toward globalization (Subramanian 2009a).

Andre Sapir observed that, among European social models, increased use of employment protection legislation is associated with lower rates of employment. He noted that the continent's most efficient and equitable social model, the Nordic model, has achieved this result through a high degree of labor market flexibility combined with a robust social safety net, although the long-term sustainability of this model and the degree to which it can be transplanted to other countries is in doubt. In a synchronized collapse such as the one experienced in 2008–09, however, these tradeoffs may recede in importance, and employment-protecting policies may well emerge across-the-board when faced with the possibility of a slow recovery.[7]

The second main concern surrounding the future of globalization centers on the capital market, where wholesale deleveraging and unprecedented actions on the part of central banks and governments have ushered in a period of extreme volatility and uncertainty (Kashyap, Rajan, and Stein 2008; Rajan 2005). Flows have dried up in response to the deleveraging of the financial sector; however, the concern is a medium-term one. As pointed out by the International Monetary Fund (IMF), the refinancing needs of the corporate sectors in EDMEs will total about $1.5 trillion for 2010, and the sources of finance are not apparent (IIF 2009; IMF 2009; World Bank 2009a). Does this imply that countries will need to be more self-sufficient in providing credit? In 2009 we have already seen that governments in the major NEPs, such as Brazil and India, have relied on state development banks to provide credit that normally would be accessed abroad. Such a reversal in financing sources can bring with it concerns about government

---

6   Jesuit and Mahler (2004) show that, after fiscal redistribution, the picture changes entirely, and most OECD countries have Gini coefficients below 0.30, while only the United States (0.345) and the United Kingdom (0.323) exceed that level.

7   Sapir (2005) observes that the Anglo-Saxon model is efficient, but lacks equity. The continental and Mediterranean models are not efficient and are therefore unsustainable in the long term. He finds an inverse relationship between the strictness of employment protection legislation (used more in continental and Mediterranean models) and the employment rate. See Aghion and others (2008) for the implications of trust on labor market regulation. See also Algan and Cahuc (2006) for an anlysis of the adaptability of social models.

intervention in sectors and can revive old debates about industrial policy (Exman 2009).

More generally, the debate has shifted recently to discussions about not only the regulatory failures but also the appropriate role of foreign capital in the development process. Subramanian has argued that the "fetish" of relying on foreign capital may have ended. Past debates about controlling the quality of capital inflows (for example, the Chilean reserve tax, which discouraged short-term inflows, and even the Malaysian response to the East Asia crisis) are being reopened as commentators wonder about the advisability of open capital accounts and the inherent riskiness of reliance on external capital (Demirgüç-Kunt and Serven 2009; SAIS 2009; Subramanian 2009a). While some, like Cooper in chapter 5 of this volume, are not swayed in their confidence in markets, others like Rodrik and Subramanian see the end of an era of open capital accounts and the advent of much greater management of exchange rates, imbalances, and, by implication, other policy variables. There is a consensus on the need for financial reform, if not on the schemes to be chosen.[8] Of course, the nature of the chosen regulatory path will have major implications for the future of capital flows and, therefore, for the future of globalization.

With a smaller pool of available capital—a consequence of smaller imbalances in the medium term—the cost of capital will be higher, especially if risk premia are more pronounced in the future and more conservative capital adequacy becomes the norm. One wild card is the existing stock of international reserves, prominently in China, which has no attractive alternative use other than to purchase U.S.-denominated assets. Despite talk of the emergence of SDRs (special drawing rights), a unit of account available in very limited quantities since the 1970s, there is as yet no practical proposal that would diminish greatly the role of the dollar (Eichengreen 2009). That said, in many countries, there are significant savings, but much of it rests offshore because of governance concerns. In the case of Argentina, for example, at least $45 billion in domestic savings has left the country in the past two years alone (Leipziger 2009). The implication of less plentiful external flows is that domestic capital markets can be given a boost; however, this requires not only technical market development, but also assurances of greater governance in some cases (Rodrik and Subramanian 2008a).

One thing for certain is that the crisis will accelerate a rethinking of the merits of increased globalization. In this context, Stiglitz was prescient in drawing attention to the question of winners and losers and to the necessity of using the instruments of public policy to deal with the consequences of globalization and also the concentration of economic power (Stiglitz 2006). Moreover, those such as Eichengreen, who pointed to the unsustainability of the large imbalances run by China and the United States, were also correct (Eichengreen and Park 2008). The paradigm of a consumer in the United States who does not save but instead consumes cheap goods that are

---

8   Commission of Experts (2009). See also G-20 (2009) for the joint declaration on strengthening the financial system.

produced in China by low-wage workers and sold at Wal-Mart, aided by a favorable exchange rate, only works in a growing economy with abundant credit. But when the bubble, fueled by an abundant supply of money and abnormally low interest rates, bursts and global demand falters, this model fails.[9] This raises interesting questions about the role of monetary policy, an issue seized upon by politicians on both sides of the Atlantic.

A related and interesting emerging debate concerns the nature of capitalism and markets and the respective roles to be played by government and the private sector. Many in Europe lay blame on Anglo-Saxon capitalism and put forward a supposedly superior model of state capitalism (Davies 2009). It is clear that markets in the United States and the United Kingdom were underregulated, causing extreme consequences and large public bailouts—the balance sheets of both the U.S. Fed and the Bank of England have more than doubled in the 2008–09 crisis. Whether state capitalism is the answer is not at all clear in light of concerns about both efficiency and governance. Continental European banks have also suffered huge subprime losses and are expected to be hard-hit by impending losses in their Central and Eastern European portfolios (Gros 2009). What is manifest, however, is that developing countries with neither the regulatory structures nor the institutions face a difficult dilemma regarding the role of government going forward.

Governments in all countries have been thrust back onto center stage as markets have either failed to function or gyrated greatly, making it difficult for businesses to operate. Policy responses to the crisis have varied considerably, although in most countries with fiscal space, some supplementation of aggregate demand has been adopted. Exactly what has been done and what government's role has been exert an important influence on the future conduct of economic policy. In this context, some economic policy decisions taken in the crisis will constrain future public choices and will affect future growth policies. It is worth taking a look, even in a speculative fashion, at the implications of the crisis and its management for the future.

How Crisis Management Will Shape Future Growth

Although *The Growth Report* placed governments at the center of the growth and development process, the report brought together experience and judgment applicable to sustain long-term levels of high economic growth rather than advice on crisis management. Nevertheless, it is crisis management that preoccupies policy makers at present, and it is no exaggeration to claim that the conduct of these short-term measures will have lasting implications. This is true in both the advanced and the emerging market economies.

---

9   IMF (2009) shows that the actual Fed funds rate was 4.6 percent below Taylor rule guidance in the second quarter of 2004.

One worry is that the boosts to aggregate demand may not be transitory. Reductions in tax rates are difficult to reverse, and supplements and extensions of coverage in social safety nets, although well advised, are equally hard to retract. Somewhat easier to manage may be the pure expenditure side of fiscal stimulus packages, although even here multiyear infrastructure plans, such as those being implemented in the Republic of Korea, or shifts to domestic construction, as in China, will be around for many years. For countries expected to experience renewed high growth in coming years, these shifts in fiscal stances may be sustainable. In others, particularly the more advanced economies, the fiscal burden of bailouts and increased spending will exact a future price, and that price is a lower growth trajectory.

Related to the conduct of fiscal policy is, of course, the conduct of monetary policy. The custodians of monetary policy in the United States and the United Kingdom have taken a different approach from the European Central Bank, with the latter focusing on inflation and resisting demands to prime the pump. This is a conscious tradeoff. In the so-called Anglo-Saxon economies, a sobriquet not used in an endearing fashion by critics, central banks have taken on the Herculean task of bailing out the financial sector and attempting to restore confidence and liquidity to scared and, in some cases, dysfunctional capital markets. This has led some commentators, such as El-Erian, to speak of the "new normal." He refers to a financial system laid low by deleveraging, deglobalization, and reregulation, in which price formation in many markets will be influenced by the legacy and, in some cases, the continuation of direct government involvement (El-Erian 2009). Concretely, this can be seen as diverting the U.S. Fed from one of its two roles—the price stability role—with effects on intertemporal fiscal decisions that raise debt levels in the United States and therefore constrain future growth.

Most important for EDMEs, as the role of government has changed in the advanced economies, the emerging market policy makers have taken on a revised role as well. Much in the spirit of *The Growth Report*, policy makers now see themselves as much more empowered to manage growth, to create stronger ties between business and government, to direct credit to corporates who are shut out of international markets, and, by implication, to articulate a stronger trade policy, especially in light of rising protectionist sentiment. Rodrik, in chapter 7 of this volume, points to the need for governments to be much more hands-on with respect to management of post-crisis growth, and the counterargument that this should be left to markets is clearly resonating less. Whether governments are well equipped to undertake this expanded role is a separate question, but ideology has shifted as a result of the meltdown of markets and the necessity of public sector action.

As a result of faltering demand and slower growth, attention is also shifting to the need for large-scale reallocation of resources and new forms of innovation. Schumpeterian economics, now coming back into the debate, is seen as a positive force when churning of firms and ensuing job losses can be more than compensated for (at least in the aggregate) by the creation of new firms and new jobs (Schumpeter 1942). Romer has written persuasively about this churning in his contributions to *The Growth Report*, and Romer and Aghion independently have pointed to the great benefit of innovation as a driver of growth (Aghion and Howitt 1992; Romer 1990). In recent work, Aghion has stressed the differing policy choices facing imitators and innovators as well as the complementarities among growth policies, technological innovation, and institutions (Acemoglu, Aghion, and Zilibotti 2002; Aghion and others 2009). This has been the story in the United States throughout the twentieth century; however, current political economy realities in most of the advanced countries no longer are able to accept creative destruction on a large scale. This is because of the sizable job losses associated with the current slowdown as well as the unavailability of credit at a time when lenders are conserving capital and are extremely risk averse. The former creates tremendous pressure to preserve firms with government bailouts, while the latter makes it difficult for new firms to get started or expand. It can be argued that Schumpeterian economics works less well in a global meltdown, the alternative being to protect current industries to the detriment of innovation and change. Inevitably, however, less creative destruction means less innovation and, ultimately, slower long-term growth.

Many commentators have opined on policy lessons due to the crisis. Subramanian draws lessons for Indian policy makers, and Lin and Wang draw lessons from Chinese policy for other countries (Lin and Wang 2008; SAIS 2009; Subramanian 2009b). Krugman (2009), writing in the *New York Times*, sees a widening schism between the market fundamentalists and a more pragmatic new group of influential economists who see market flaws as systemically dangerous. At the United Nations, the Commission of Experts led by Joseph Stiglitz has proposed radical changes to the global financial architecture, going so far as to include a proposal for the development of a new global reserve system and entities for global financial supervision (Commission of Experts 2009). As Mike Spence notes in the special report of the Commission, this crisis has embarrassed a lot of theories and theorists, and the question is how much can be amended yet salvaged and how much needs fundamental rethinking (Commission on Growth and Development 2009).

One area of past controversy is the role of public sector banks, often the source of huge nonperforming loans and political influence. In the aftermath of the crisis, we have seen public banks in India being shored up with a major influx of capital (partly financed by World Bank loans) to increase credit and finance infrastructure; large increases in lending by the Banco Nacional de Desenvolvimento Economico e Social, Brazil's large public development bank; and, of course, large expansions of credit through Chinese government-sponsored banks (Economist 2009; Exman 2009). Are these actions any less reasonable than the Fed's bailouts? Only time will tell, but the resurgence of public sector banks and the public takeover of private banks are realities and cannot be seen as benign for the future of globalization as we have come to know it.

The basic connection with globalization is that the reemergence of national policies—in the areas of credit for the private sector, public infrastructure investment, and use of tax credits and other means to foster demand in a particular sector (for example, autos in Brazil)—has wide-reaching implications for the international economy. Whereas the past couple of decades saw national governments taking major cues from global markets, that epoch appears to be over, at least for the largest EDMEs. For the poorer and smaller economies, the paradigm shift may be of smaller magnitude (Brahmbhatt 2008); however, the ideological shift is palpable, and international financial institutions will have a more difficult time arguing for pure market solutions.

There are some final implications to be drawn regarding the exigencies of crisis management and the attainment of longer-term goals. The debate around "decoupling" has taken an interesting turn, with a greater reliance on the positive growers for 2009 (Economist 2009; Kose, Otrok, and Prasad 2008). With this has come a shift in perceptions as to which countries are responsible custodians of the global system, and the G-20 has emerged as an important new forum, highlighting the future economic importance of the NEPs (Leipziger and O'Boyle 2009). As large emerging economies are increasingly regarded as the growth engines that will lead the world out of recession, a long overdue debate is taking place about their representation in financial and economic decision-making bodies. Over the long term, large emerging and developing economies will be more involved in systemic initiatives and will have the opportunity to take leadership roles in the international system.

In the wake of slowing growth as a result of the crisis, preserving and promoting trade will be a critically important challenge to the world economic system. Despite global rhetoric in opposition to increased protectionism, recent evidence has shown that protectionist measures have increased among the world's largest trading nations (Bown 2009 for countries for which data were available). The revival of the Doha Round is an important step, in no small part due to its symbolic importance as a test of the world's commitment to a multilateral trading system (Commission on Growth and Development 2008). However, this current wave of protectionism is occurring both within the legal bounds of World Trade Organization (WTO) rules and outside the scope of the Doha agreement. This post-crisis period presents a unique opportunity for the major trading nations, both developed and developing, to resist protectionism and strengthen the trading system from which they have greatly benefited (Mattoo and Subramanian 2009).

Reform of the global financial architecture is another issue that is being reshaped as a result of the crisis, with major developing countries playing a larger role. Given the historic debate over the opportunities versus the threats of financial globalization, this crisis has precipitated yet another reevaluation of its merits. Economists doubting the positive effects of external finance on growth have been at the forefront of this debate (Rodrik and Subramanian 2008b), and political action has led to increased regulatory scrutiny over cross-border financial flows and multinational financial institutions. The transformation of the Financial Stability Forum to include large emerging market countries has been a concrete step toward more effective cross-border regulation. The new group, the Financial Stability Board, will work closely with the IMF on identifying and addressing transnational macroeconomic and financial risks (Economist 2009) and expanding its mandate to include assessment, oversight, coordination, and information exchange capabilities (G-20 2009).

In addition to posing immediate challenges, the crisis has major implications for long-term trends, many of them correctly identified in *The Growth Report*. Urbanization is an easily identified secular trend. We have also seen governments trying to marry the need for immediate fiscal stimulus with a longer-term desire to foster "green investment," and in some cases, such as Korea, the linkage has been strongly visible in the government's stimulus program (Watts 2009). One arena in which the needs of short-term policy and longer-term trends do not necessarily coincide is in labor market issues, perhaps one of the thorniest aspects of globalization, made more complex by shifts in demographics and income inequality.

The Implications of Longer-Term Trends

Changing demographics will be an important feature of the global environment in the next few decades—one that will have impacts on saving behavior, pension systems, and fiscal stability. As *The Growth Report* documents, we will witness a continuous increase in world population, although more than 90 percent of the increase will be in EDME cities. At the same time, in the richest countries, populations will age (World Bank 2007). In fact, the proportion of the world's population above the age of 60 in 2050 compared to 100 years earlier will more than double, to 22 percent. This has major implications for the financing of safety nets and for the dependency pyramid, as Bloom, Canning, and Fink describe in chapter 13 of this volume.

According to the IMF, demographic change is the major threat to long-term fiscal solvency. In addition to population aging, potential government funding obligations of pension liabilities as a result of falling asset prices will further jeopardize fiscal stability and long-term growth. The primary risks to governments arise both from the direct effects of investments in assets affected by the crisis and from explicit guarantees covering private assets. Political pressure to make up for the losses suffered by pensioners covered by private plans will also be substantial. In the United States, for example, government defined-benefit plans have lost 25 percent of their value since the end of 2009. Such a decline in equity prices triggers a requirement to close the funding gap over the following five years, a burden that is likely to fall on government, employers, and ultimately the taxpayer. As Barr (2009) points out, there are four possible ways forward for pension systems: (a) people pay higher contributions, (b) people receive lower monthly pensions, (c) people retire later, and (d) governments find policies that increase national output (Barr 2009; Giles 2009; IMF, Fiscal Affairs Department 2009; OECD 2009a).

Such increases in age-related costs, in addition to the costs of the bailouts and stimulus packages, will have to be borne by the fiscal side, which can only be expected to be less robust. In advanced economies, the weakening in public sector accounts over 2008–09 will be the most pronounced of any in the past three decades.[10] With no further infusions of finance from surplus countries, this implies a lower-level equilibrium growth rate for the advanced economies. Translated into demand for imports from the EDMEs, one can generally expect less momentum for externally driven growth, with a greater role for domestic demand, even once the recovery has begun. Thus the components of aggregate demand will likely shift in advanced and emerging market economies to favor government spending. This is a major shift indeed.

Governments will be challenged to spend wisely in the short term to avoid giving up gains in long-term growth. In the aftermath of a crisis, the real value of government debt tends to explode, rising by an average of 86 percent in the major post–World War II episodes (Reinhart and Rogoff 2009). For this reason, fiscal measures should be largely reversible or have clear sunset clauses contingent on economic conditions and precommitment to future corrective measures. Smoothly unwinding fiscal stimulus measures either at a specific date or on a contingent basis is important to regaining fiscal positions (IMF, Fiscal Affairs Department 2009). Tax breaks and subsidies granted during the crisis will have to be unwound eventually, which is never a politically attractive option. Once economies have stabilized, governments would do well to increase tax collection efforts, given lower government revenues and the pullback in foreign flows of private capital. While volatile, foreign flows have averaged only about 1.5 percent of recipient country GDP over the 1990–2008 period, and an increased tax effort of this size is within the realm of possibility (World Bank 2009a). Research conducted by the World Bank has shown that among a sample of 104 countries, 38 percent have the capacity to increase tax revenue collection significantly without jeopardizing medium-term growth (Le, Moreno-Dodson, and Rojchaichaninthorn 2008).

Contrary to popular belief, the main cause of rapidly expanding government debt is not the widely feared cost of bailing out and recapitalizing the banking system, but rather the collapse of future tax revenues in the wake

---

10 IMF, Fiscal Affairs Department (2009). IMF data show that in 2007, 54.5 percent of countries for which data were available had fiscal surpluses and those that did not were in deficit by an average of 1.68 percent of GDP. In 2010 only 3 percent of these countries are projected to be in surplus, and the average balance of those that are projected to be in deficit will be negative 5.38 percent of GDP.

of deep and prolonged economic contractions. Therefore, governments will be challenged to ensure that programs promoting future growth are not cut for lack of resources (IMF, Fiscal Affairs and Research Departments 2008). Such cuts in growth-promoting spending have been shown to lower the present value of future tax revenues to a degree that more than offsets the improvement in the present cash deficit for which the cuts were made (Easterly, Irwin, and Serven 2007).

At present, the outlook for advanced economies is somber: the IMF projects a 56 percentage point increase in debt ratios by 2030. Emerging markets should fare somewhat better because of lower crisis costs, lower primary deficits, and lower expected age-related costs combined with a stronger growth outlook. Developing countries, however, have seen a significant falloff in private participations in infrastructure, and it is unclear whether the public sector will be able to fill the void. The August–November 2008 period alone witnessed a 26 percent decline in project completions due to delays and cancellations as a result of higher costs of financing and slackening demand (World Bank 2009b). Infrastructure spending, however, has been prominent in the G-20 stimulus packages to date, suggesting that advanced and large developing countries realize the importance of maintaining investments in the future. Of the roughly 50 percent of discretionary fiscal stimulus enacted through expenditure measures, approximately two-thirds has gone or will go toward infrastructure spending in 2008 and 2009. This represents 0.7 percent of 2008 GDP of G-20 countries (IMF, Fiscal Affairs Department 2009).

As mentioned, the vast majority of population growth in the coming decades will occur in developing-country cities, implying a rapidly increasing pace of urbanization across the globe. In 2008, the world reached an invisible but momentous milestone: more than half the world's population— 3.3 billion people—was living in urban areas. By 2030, this number is expected to swell to almost 5 billion, an increase of more than 65 million people a year. The developing world in particular will see an unprecedented scale of urban growth, with urban populations in Africa and Asia doubling between 2000 and 2030. Despite this rapid change, urban population growth rates have actually slowed in the past 30 years, peaking at 3.7 percent a year in 1950–75. However, given the growing base of people living in cities, annual population increments in absolute numbers are very large and, to many, alarming (Spence, Clarke Annez, and Buckley 2009; United Nations Population Fund 2007).

The evidence to date clearly supports the conclusion that cities are important facilitators of economic growth, increased productivity, and rising incomes in poor and rich nations alike (Quigley 2009). In all known cases of high and sustained growth, urban manufacturing and services led the process, while increases in agricultural productivity freed up labor that moved to the cities. In the high-growth cases examined by the Commission, the average productivity of a worker in manufacturing or services is on the order of three to five times that of a worker in traditional sectors and sometimes much more. There is also a robust relationship between urbanization and per capita income: nearly all countries become at least 50 percent urbanized before reaching middle-income status, and all high-income countries are 70–80 percent urbanized. In fact, we know of no countries that either achieved high incomes or rapid growth without substantial, and often rapid, urbanization (Spence, Clarke Annez, and Buckley 2009).

Urbanization poses major challenges to developing-country policy makers. While urbanization has some potentially major benefits in terms of agglomeration economies and innovation, it also has negative consequences in terms of congestion, lack of service delivery, and sheer unmanageability. The first challenge is to foster the growth of high-productivity activities that benefit from agglomeration and scale economies in developing-country cities. The second challenge involves managing the likely side effects of the economic success of cities—pollution, regional inequality, and high prices of land and housing—critical to mitigating the divisive impacts of successful economic growth. Empirical studies of livability and GDP per capita suggest that long-term growth is only feasible if city attributes regarding congestion, pollution, and safety are improved alongside urban economic management. Infrastructure and public services will be a key piece of the puzzle, perhaps the most important. According to some estimates, $40 trillion of infrastructure spending is required to meet the needs of cities in developing countries. Devising means of financing such vast expenditures is probably the biggest challenge for urbanization policy in the developing world (Gill and Kharas 2007; Gómez-Ibáñez 2008; Spence, Clarke Annez, and Buckley 2009; see also Estache and Fay in chapter 8 of this volume).

While urbanization will drive the location of industry and people, particularly in the developing world, these agglomerations of economic activity will be the focal points of increasing greenhouse gas emissions. On climate change, *The Growth Report* stakes out a view energized by the Commission's chairman, Nobel laureate Michael Spence, as well as that of his own mentor, Nobel laureate Thomas Schelling, namely, that growth in the developing world should not be curtailed in order to reach emissions goals (Schelling 2007; also see part 4 of World Bank 2008a). However, developing countries need to be deeply involved in the climate change conversation given their collective status as major global emitters. The realities are such that (a) even if the OECD countries curtailed all emissions tomorrow, we would still be on a collision course with respect to global temperatures; (b) the major incremental emitters will be the EDMEs; and (c) the carbon intensity of growth in some EDMEs far exceeds that in the advanced world (Energy Information Administration 2009; World Bank 2008a).

What conclusions can one draw from this evidence, and what does it imply for global growth and sustainability? First, *The Growth Report* makes the important point that from an economic perspective, the correct policy is to reduce emissions efficiently, namely, at the lowest cost per ton, regardless of where the pollution takes place. Of course, because of national borders, one has to distinguish among emitters, and here the second principle kicks in—namely, that the cost of this efficient abatement needs to be distributed fairly. This means taking into account not only ability to pay, but also the record of what got us to this point. The report is careful, however, not to place an exclusive burden on the rich countries either, since much of the past growth (although not environmentally sound) is also responsible for massive income gains in the poorer parts of the world. Thus the burden-sharing formulas need to be internationally negotiated, and in these conversations, the efficiency of the global growth generation machinery also needs to be considered.

The Growth Report discusses decision making under extreme uncertainty; although global damage is expected from climate change, there is still major uncertainty as to the degree and the exact tipping point (Nordhaus 2006; see also Wheeler and Mendelsohn in chapters 11 and 12, respectively, of this volume). This uncertainty argues for a robust feedback loop based on the gathering of new information and, as a corollary, an option for dealing with the problem, but not in so drastic a fashion as to compromise longer-term growth that might offer better solutions. Again, if the approach is to attack the major sources of pollution, then one must do this in an economically efficient and affordable way.

The fourth major trend that is fairly evident is the increasing intranational inequality (for data on inequality trends between countries, see United Nations 2006). This is reported in a variety of country circumstances and, as expected, with different policy responses. As reported by Bourguignon for the World Bank, an increasing number of developing countries have seen positive growth in the last 10 years, but an overwhelming proportion (42 out of Bourguignon's sample of 59) have also experienced a decline in income equality since 1990 (Bourguignon 2007). If, as in the case of Vietnam, these twin phenomena of high growth rates and rising inequality (from a low base) are combined with rapid reductions in measured poverty, this can be seen as a positive development, probably inevitable in the development process. However, in some regions like Latin America, the underlying inequality is substantial, with the top quintile capturing more than 60 percent of national income and, in Brazil, for example, outpacing the lowest 40 percent by a factor of 8 to 1 in 2003. In other regions like East Asia, the underlying inequality is less pronounced; however, the change in income shares between 1996 and 2004 are stark, with each higher quintile outearning the previous one by a significant margin (IMF 2007).

In the advanced countries, the OECD reports that the middle three quintiles of the distribution lost ground between 1995 and 2005 in terms of income shares in Canada, Denmark, Finland, France, Germany, Italy, Norway, Sweden, and the United States. The bottom quintile was either stable or lost ground in all 26 countries surveyed except Italy and Mexico. In their book on the middle class, Estache and Leipziger (2009) urge a closer look at the impact of government's fiscal policy on the entire spectrum of income groups. Ignoring the middle class and the downsides of globalization has, in the past, threatened the political support for domestic and internationally welfare-improving policies and could do so again. This is due to the fact that income determinants are many, and distributional concerns are a matter of local politics. This has never been more true than in the aftermath of the current crisis, which has claimed millions of jobs worldwide (Estache and Leipziger 2009; OECD 2008).

Increasing inequality is seen as a corollary of globalization in nations as diverse as China, India, and the United States. In reality there are many explanations for this rise. The IMF points to technology as the main driver, ascribing the bulk of change to this factor and very little to globalization per se (IMF 2007). And there are no doubt differences between the rise in China's Gini coefficient from 0.28 in 1981 to 0.42 in 2004, which accompanied tremendous urbanization and new job creation, from the situation in the United States, where, according to Goldin and Katz (2007), the wage premium to education rose dramatically after 1980, exacerbating inequality. In the case of the United States, according to Lawrence (2008), wages of blue-collar occupations rose by just 4.4 percent between 1981 and 2006, while output per hour was up 70 percent.[11] Following the views of Blinder (2009) would lead one to believe that it is no longer investment in education broadly speaking that matters, but rather investment in education that personalizes services and discourages their offshoring. The bottom line, however, is that income has become more uneven in recent decades, and the public believes that this is largely due to globalization—which is not good news for globalizers.

As ardent globalizers like Jagdish Bhagwati argue, the benefits of globalization, particularly in trade, are enormous, but there is a problem of transition and compensation. Bhagwati argues for adjustment assistance for poorer countries, while Blinder points out that adjustment assistance has never worked in the United States. Those who see fundamental flaws with the path of globalization, like Stiglitz (2002, 2006, 2009), point to the inadequacy of compensation mechanisms, the inherent asymmetry of economic power, and yes, the failure of financial regulation. As Leipziger and Spence argued in 2007, the concern about winners and losers is less about fairness than it is about the practical need to maintain political support for policies and international agreements that advance openness in the global economy (Commission of Experts 2009; Leipziger and Spence 2007; Stiglitz 2002, 2006).

The future shape of globalization is, according to some, very much in doubt. What is certain, though, is that developing countries will face new challenges to growth and must approach the current environment in anything but a business-as-usual manner. The papers assembled for this volume seek to sketch the outlines of the future growth dynamics, particularly for developing countries, as well as to stimulate debate and suggest possible ways forward.

---

11 Goldin and Katz (2007); Lawrence (2008). Lawrence finds that, while wage inequality did increase, a larger portion of the wage gap was due to measurement issues and education of non-blue-collar workers.

The Distinct Contributions of the Volume

In chapter 2 of this volume, Daron Acemoglu provides an ideal opening to a volume on globalization, elaborating on the intellectual errors economists have made in view of the crisis and what lessons these errors offer us moving forward. More important, he argues that key economic principles related to the most important goal of economic performance, the long-run growth of nations, are still valid and hold important lessons for intellectual and practical deliberations on policy. Acemoglu emphasizes the importance of technological innovation for the prosperity and success of the capitalist economy. However, despite their positive impacts on long-run economic growth, innovation and reallocation have been conspicuous in their absence from the political debate and have played little role in the design of crisis management responses. Acemoglu highlights why a focus on economic growth is essential. Barring a complete meltdown of the global system, the possible loss of GDP for most countries is in the range of a couple of percentage points. In contrast, modest changes in economic growth will accumulate to much larger numbers within one decade or two. Thus, from a policy and welfare perspective, sacrificing economic growth to deal with the current crisis is a bad option. Economic growth ought to be a central part of the discussion, not an afterthought.

Acemoglu also addresses the dangers posed by growing skepticism toward globalization and the political economy of growth. He reminds us that, because of the reallocation and creative destruction brought about by economic growth, there will always be parties, often strong parties, opposed to certain aspects of economic growth. Thus one of the major risks facing globalization is one of consumers and policy makers becoming pessimistic about future growth and the promise of markets. Ultimately, the crisis should be regarded as a failure not of capitalism or free markets, but, according to Acemoglu, of unregulated markets.

In chapter 3, Charles Calomiris elaborates on the regulatory failures that contributed to the onset of the financial crisis. While he, like many others, acknowledges that regulation was a primary contributor, he argues that the problem was less a lack of regulation than bad regulation. Calomiris does not agree with those who argue that the subprime crisis is mainly a story of government "errors of omission," which allowed banks to avoid regulatory discipline due to the insufficient application of bank capital regulations. Instead, the main story of the subprime crisis, in his view, is one of government "errors of commission," which were far more important in generating the huge risks and large losses that brought down the U.S. financial system. Government actions were the root problem, not government inaction. Calomiris references the literature to make his point that in times and places where these government interventions were absent, financial crises were relatively rare and not very severe.

However, realizing the need for appropriate regulation given the complexity of today's system, Calomiris details six categories of policy reform that would address the weaknesses that gave rise to the subprime crisis, including (a) smarter "micro prudential" regulation of banks, (b) new ideas for "macro prudential" regulation of bank capital and liquidity standards, (c) the creation of detailed and regularly updated prepackaged "bridge bank" plans for large, complex financial organizations, (d) reforms to eliminate the distortions in housing finance induced by government policies that encourage high risk and leveraging, (e) reforms to improve stockholder discipline of banks, and (f) initiatives to encourage greater transparency in derivatives transactions.

In chapter 4, Andrew Sheng applies network theory to the behavior of global financial markets and draws implications for supervision and governance. Sheng suggests that new insights in this area could assist theoreticians and practitioners in understanding better how markets work and how to improve current policies. Sheng begins with the premise that a system cannot be regulated unless policy makers have a complete understanding of how it works. The collapse of Lehman Brothers highlighted the nature of modern financial crises in terms of their complexity, depth, speed of contagion, and transmission. The scale of loss was unprecedented—a painful demonstration that financial regulators and policy makers did not understand the animal with which they were dealing.

Sheng highlights the need for a framework to simplify the understanding of such complex markets, in which the interaction between market participants operating under asymmetric information is dynamic, but not always stable. Such a framework needs to deal not only with a systemwide perspective, but also with vulnerabilities at the detail level—that is, the weakest link. While the network analysis does not have predictive capacity, it is useful in laying out an organizational framework to decipher current behavior, revealing our lack of appreciation of the problems of externalities, wrong incentives, weak structures, and flawed processes. The major insight of network analysis is that the process of change is not linear. In fact, it is interactive, interconnected, and the outcome of experimentation, accident, and manipulation by system participants, including financial institutions, investors, regulators, and policy makers.

In chapter 5, Richard Cooper argues that global imbalances in current account positions are a natural consequence of the globalization of financial markets and demographic trends, particularly in Europe and East Asia. Those societies are aging rapidly, with declining numbers of young adults. In both regions, savings should be high and investment weak, resulting in excess saving. With globalization of capital markets, this excess saving will naturally seek secure investment opportunities abroad. The U.S. economy, where demographic trends are markedly different (due in part to immigration of young adults), offers a good combination of yield, liquidity, and security for this excess savings, which in time will be liquidated to finance consumption in old age. Thus the large "imbalance" does not obviously reflect disequilibria in the world economy, but rather a current phase of intertemporal trade.

Speaking at the World Bank in 2009, Cooper gave positive views on the future of globalization, despite the crisis, crediting the growth and integration of the world economy in the past half century, and especially in the past two decades, for driving the biggest reduction in both relative and absolute poverty in history. However, he was careful to mention that the current crisis does pose serious dangers, foremost among them the potential popular backlash against globalization and trade in particular. A significant protectionist reaction on the part of large trading nations would have a major negative impact on long-term growth. Cooper regards financial crises as inevitable in any modern economy; the challenge to policy makers is not to prevent crises, but to limit the real damage and to be ready to take advantage of the post-crisis environment in proposing effective regulatory reforms. Cooper argues that thus far post-crisis management has failed on both these counts (Cooper 2009: 320–32).

In chapter 6, Ravi Kanbur addresses a question that is central for policy makers concerned with helping the poor during macroeconomic crises, namely, how to target scarce resources at a time of greater need. Technical arguments have suggested that finer targeting of anti-poverty initiatives, through tightening individual programs or reallocating resources toward more tightly targeted programs, leads to more efficient resource use—even when the greater information costs and the incentive effects of finer targeting are taken into account. However, political economy arguments suggest that finer targeting that results in fewer overall resources being allocated is short-sighted and that looser targeting, because it knits together the interests of the poor and the near-poor, may well be preferable. The snowballing effects associated with the near-poor being pushed into poverty by the crisis and the general desire to uphold basic consumption levels among groups in the lower part of the distribution imply that leakier programs may well be preferred in times of dramatic economic downturns.

Kanbur's chapter is particularly appropriate in the current environment because no volume on globalization, growth, and the financial crisis would be complete without a discussion of the effects of the crisis on the poor. While the crisis has dominated headlines for bringing down some of the world's most storied financial institutions, its effect on the poor has received less attention. According to the World Bank, 90 million more people lived in extreme poverty in 2009 as a result of the crisis. In the post-crisis environment, strategies and policies to mitigate the effects of the crisis on the poor are sorely needed. While distributional concerns always matter, they become even more relevant in periods of declining income. How one mitigates the worst consequences of crises also plays an important role in shaping the future path of recovery, and indeed, the future role of globalization in developing economies, a topic addressed in part 2.

Part 2 of the volume shifts focus from the immediate crisis to the impact of the crisis on developing-country growth. In chapter 7, Dani Rodrik examines the global environment for economic growth in the developing world as it emerges from the present financial crisis. For Rodrik, the answer depends on how well the following tensions are managed. On the one hand, global macroeconomic stability requires that we prevent external imbalances from getting too large; on the other hand, growth in poor nations requires that the world economy be able to absorb a rapid increase in the supply of tradables they produce.

Rodrik's views have major policy implications. He argues that it is possible to render these two requirements compatible, but that doing so will require greater use of explicit industrial policies in developing countries that have the potential for encouraging modern tradable activities without spilling over into trade surpluses. He asserts that the key to growth is the domestic output of modern tradables, not the excess supply thereof. The implication for developing nations that have gotten hooked on trade surpluses as their engine of growth should be clear: there is no need to sacrifice growth as long as domestic demand for tradables can be increased alongside domestic supply.

In chapter 8, Antonio Estache and Marianne Fay provide an overview of the major current debates on infrastructure policy given the relationship between infrastructure development and economic growth. They review the evidence on the macroeconomic significance of the sector in terms of growth and poverty alleviation and discuss the major institutional debates, including the relative comparative advantage of the public and the private sectors in the various stages of infrastructure service delivery as well as the main options for changing the role of government (that is, regulation and decentralization).

While the heterogeneity of the infrastructure business is such that it is difficult to draw specific conclusions for any given subsector or country, Estache and Fay find that some general conclusions can be drawn. First, while the literature on infrastructure and growth teaches us that infrastructure is important, its importance varies across countries, within countries, and over time, as countries change and the binding constraints shift. Second, there is still a long way to go in meeting the infrastructure needs of the poorest countries of the world. Third, privatization has not delivered as much investment as expected, and those without access to infrastructure services are the most penalized by this failure. Estache and Fay find that one of the main reasons for a lack of clear-cut answers regarding infrastructure is the lack of objective data on the sector, which leaves it vulnerable to ideological rather than fact-based decision making. Data gaps are highlighted throughout their overview, including on basic issues such as costs and tariffs or the share of public or private resources allocated to expand or maintain the sectors. They argue that to produce substantive answers to core questions without recourse to ideology, it is essential for the international community to take the data agenda much more seriously than in the past. Furthermore, in light of the crisis and falling infrastructure finance, particularly in private sector funding, new ideas on how to move forward in the sector are needed.

William Cline in chapter 9 revisits his 1982 article on the "fallacy of composition," reexamining it in light of the current environment. Cline's original argument questioned the feasibility of generalizing the G-4—Hong Kong, China; Korea; Singapore; and Taiwan, China—model of growth based on the rapid growth of exports, on the grounds that if all developing economies pursued it, their combined manufactured exports would eventually trigger protection in industrial countries. His 1984 book identified a safe speed limit of about 10–15 percent annual growth of developing country exports of manufactures, well below the 25–35 percent rate of Korea and Taiwan, China in the 1960s and 1970s.

Cline's chapter in this volume revisits this question in light of a quarter century of experience. It finds that developing countries' aggregate manufactured exports grew at about 10 percent annually, a robust pace, but within the speed limits previously envisioned. Even so, in key sectors such as apparel, import penetration levels have exceeded thresholds that, according to earlier estimates, would provoke protection, suggesting the importance of increased WTO discipline. The base of manufactured exports from poor countries remains small relative to that of China and the original G-4, so there should be considerable room for export growth from these newcomers. Although he does not explicitly address the postcrisis world, one conclusion to draw from Cline's argument is that the aggregate shift in demand away from exports in large emerging markets may open more export space for poorer developing countries. When combined with the rapid growth in South-South trade, this offers some renewed hope for the model of export-led growth for less developed countries.

In chapter 10, Philippe Aghion, David Hemous, and Enisse Kharroubi evaluate whether the cyclical pattern of fiscal policy can affect growth. This is a particularly important topic in light of the current efforts in developed and large developing economies to stimulate domestic demand through fiscal measures. This chapter, similar to chapter 2, questions long-standing assumptions in the study of short-term and long-term economic performance. According to the authors, macroeconomic textbooks generally impose a strict separation between the analysis of long-run growth and the short-term analysis, which focuses on the effects of macroeconomic policies (fiscal or monetary) aimed at stabilizing the economy following shocks. Yet recently this view that short-run stabilization policies do not matter for long-run growth has been challenged.

This chapter goes further, looking at the effect of countercyclical fiscal policy on industry growth, depending on industry financial constraints. Empirical evidence shows that industries with heavier financial constraints tend to grow faster in countries with more stabilizing fiscal policy. The authors' main empirical finding is that the interaction between financial constraints in an industry and fiscal policy countercyclicality has a positive, significant, and robust impact on industry growth of comparable (or even greater) importance to that of more structural features. Practically speaking, this has far-reaching implications for the conduct of macroeconomic policy over the business cycle, with both ex ante and ex post effects on innovation and productivity. A more countercyclical fiscal policy increases the incentives for innovation ex ante by reducing the risk that innovation will fail in the future due to adverse macroeconomic shocks; ex post it helps to reduce the proportion of firms that will have to reduce productivity-enhancing investments following a major shock.

Part 3 of this volume looks at long-term challenges to growth. In chapters 11 and 12, David Wheeler and Robert Mendelsohn, respectively, address issues of climate change in light of current debates on its regulation and impact on economic growth. Both chapters acknowledge that much uncertainty still exists on the nonscientific aspects as well as the scale, scope, and timing of certain initiatives (World Bank 2009c). While both authors agree that the science is clear that the buildup of greenhouse gases will cause the earth to warm, they have different assessments of the potential economic impacts of warming. They both agree, however, that the challenge is to develop a strategy that supports at the very least moderate measures now in order to retain the potential for more rigorous measures when the economics and politics become feasible. They are also in agreement that developing countries must be full participants because they will be most heavily affected by global warming and because the scale of their emissions is rapidly approaching parity with that of developed countries.

In chapter 11, David Wheeler addresses the implications of climate change for developing countries and public policy, arguing that efficient mitigation of emissions will require carbon pricing via market-based instruments (charges or auctioned tradable permits). To lay the foundations for confronting the global challenge, he advocates two priority actions. The first is to establish an international institution mandated to collect, verify, and publicly disclose information about emissions from all significant global carbon sources. The second is to establish four global consortia charged with (a) the reduction of greenhouse emissions, (b) the accelerated development of clean technologies, (c) the financing of their rapid diffusion in developing countries, and (d) the support for developing country adaptation to the impacts of unavoidable climate change. These consortia should be empowered to set objectives and priorities using the best available scientific, technical, and economic evidence. Their operations should be transparent and independently audited for results.

In chapter 12, Mendelsohn argues that the impact of climate change on the global economy is likely to be quite small over the next 50 years and that severe impacts even by the end of the century are unlikely, despite the grim descriptions of the consequences of climate change for long-term economic growth. In reality, according to Mendelsohn, long-term economic growth is threatened more by excessive near-term mitigation efforts than by climate change. Mendelsohn asserts that because marginal damages rise as greenhouse gases accumulate, the optimal policy is dynamic, growing stricter over time. This balanced economic approach to the problem will address climate change with minimal reductions in economic growth. Partly, this dynamic policy reflects the fact that technical change is going to improve our ability to control greenhouse gases over time. The more aggressive the near-term mitigation program, however, the greater the risk that climate change will slow long-term growth.

Finally, in chapter 13, Bloom, Canning, and Fink examine demographic change, a field that the IMF regards as the major threat to long-term fiscal solvency (IMF, Fiscal Affairs Department 2009). They examine the impact of population aging on the labor force and the implications for long-term economic growth. Although labor force participation rates are projected to decline during the period 2000 to 2040 in most countries, due mainly to changes in their age distribution, the ratio of labor force to population will increase in most countries. This is because low fertility will cause lower youth dependency that will offset the skewing of adults toward the older ages when labor force participation is lower. The increase in labor force to population ratios will be further magnified by increases in age-specific rates of female labor force participation associated with lower fertility. These factors suggest that economic growth will continue apace, notwithstanding the phenomenon of population aging.

For the OECD countries, the declines projected to occur in both labor force participation and the ratio of labor force to population suggest modest declines in the pace of economic growth. But even these effects can be mitigated by behavioral responses to population aging—in the form of higher savings for retirement, greater labor force participation, and increased immigration from labor-surplus to labor-deficit countries. Countries that can facilitate such changes may be able to limit the adverse consequences of population aging. When seen through the lens of several mitigating considerations, there is reason to think that population aging in developed countries may have less effect than some have predicted. In addition, policy responses related to retirement incentives, pension funding methods, investments in health care of the elderly, and immigration can further ameliorate the effect of population aging on economic growth.

To conclude, this volume brings together expertise from around the world on a wide range of subjects that will affect the economic growth of developing countries in the years to come. Part 1 provides detailed analysis of the contributing factors, at both the national and global levels, that led the world economy into the morass in which it currently finds itself and proposes novel ideas for reform. Part 2 explores specific policy ideas relevant to the economic growth of developing nations in a post-crisis world. Part 3 lays out long-term trends and challenges that all countries will have to navigate in their quest for growth, made newly relevant by the pressures of the current environment. At this point in the evolution of the financial and economic crisis, it is clear that they will cast a long shadow over the development process, especially for poor countries. This volume seeks to shed light on the state of the post-crisis world and possible ways forward.

References

Acemoglu, Daron, Philippe Aghion, and Fabrizio Zilibotti. 2002. "Vertical Integration and Distance to Frontier." NBER Working Paper 9191. National Bureau of Economic Research, Cambridge, MA.

Aghion, Philippe, and Peter Howitt. 1992. "A Model of Growth through Creative Destruction." *Econometrica* 60 (March): 323–51.

Aghion, Philippe, Leah Boustan, Caroline Hoxby, and Jerome Vandenbussche. 2009. "The Causal Impact of Education on Economic Growth." Working Paper. Harvard University, Cambridge, MA.

Aghion, Philippe, Yann Algan, Pierre Cahuc, and Andre Shleifer. 2008. "Regulation and Distrust." The National Bureau of Economic Research (NBER) Working Paper. NBER, Cambridge, MA.

Algan, Yann, and Pierre Cahuc. 2006. "Civic Attitudes and the Design of Labor Market Institutions: Which Countries Can Implement the Danish Flexicurity Model?" IZA Discussion Paper 1928 (January). Institute for the Study of Labor, Bonn.

Anderlini, Jamil. 2009. "'Buy China' Policy Set to Raise Tensions." *Financial Times*, June 16.

Barr, Nicholas. 2009. Comments at the Harvard workshop of the Commission on Growth and Development. Transcript. World Bank, Washington, DC.

Barr, Nicholas, and Peter Diamond. 2009. "Reforming Pensions." *International Social Security Review* 62 (2): 5–29.

Barth, James, Gerald Caprio, and Ross Levine. 2006. *Rethinking Bank Regulation: Till Angels Govern.* Cambridge, U.K.: Cambridge University Press.

Bhagwati, Jagdish. 2004. *In Defense of Globalization.* New York: Council on Foreign Relations.

Bhagwati, Jagdish, Arvind Panagariya, and T. N. Srinivasan. 2004. "The Muddles over Outsourcing." *Journal of Economic Perspectives* 18 (4): 93–114.

Blinder, Alan. 2007. "How Many U.S. Jobs Might Be Offshorable." Working Paper 60. Princeton University, Department of Economics, Center for Economic Policy Studies, Princeton, NJ.

———. 2009. "Offshoring: Big Deal or Business as Usual." In *Offshoring of American Jobs: What Response from U.S. Economic Policy?* ed. Jagdish Bhagwati and Alan Blinder. Cambridge, MA: MIT Press.

Bourguignon, François. 2007. "The Challenges of Inclusive Global Development." Presentation to the Development Committee, World Bank, Washington, DC.

Bown, Chad. 2009. *Global Antidumping Database.* Washington, DC: World Bank (July). www.brandeis.edu/~cbown/global_ad/.

Brahmbhatt, Milan. 2008. "Weathering the Storm: Economic Policy Responses to the Financial Crisis." Working Paper. World Bank, Washington, DC.

Bresser-Pereira, Luiz Carlos, and Paulo Gala. 2007. "Why Foreign Savings Fail to Cause Growth." Final version of a paper originally presented at the São Paulo School of Economics, Getúlio Vargas Foundation, São Paulo. May 23, 2005.

Burman, Leonard E. 2009. "A Blueprint for Tax Reform and Health Reform." Research report (April 7). Urban Institute, Washington, DC. www.urban.org/url.cfm?ID=1001262.

Claessens, Stijn, M. Ayhan Kose, and Marco E. Terrones. 2008. "What Happens during Recessions, Crunches, and Busts? CEPR Discussion Paper DP7085. Centre for Economic Policy Research, London.

Collier, Paul. 2007. *The Bottom Billion: Why the Poorest Countries Are Failing and What Can Be Done about It*. New York: Oxford University Press.

Commission of Experts of the President of the General Assembly. 2009. *Recommendations by the Commission of Experts of the President of the General Assembly on Reforms of the International Monetary and Financial Systems*. New York: United Nations.

Commission on Growth and Development. 2008. *The Growth Report: Strategies for Sustained Growth and Inclusive Development*. Washington, DC: World Bank.

———. 2009. *Post-Crisis Growth in Developing Countries*. A Special Report. Washington, DC: Commission on Growth and Development.

Cooper, Richard. 2009. Presentation at the "PREM Knowledge and Learning Forum 2009," Washington, DC. April 28.

Davies, Lizzy. 2009. "Sarkozy and Merkel Tell U.S. That Europe Will Lead Way towards 'Moral' Capitalism." *Guardian*, January 8.

Dell'Ariccia, Giovanni, Enrica Detragiache, and Raghuram Rajan. 2005. "The Real Effect of Banking Crises." IMF Working Paper 05/63. International Monetary Fund, Washington, DC.

Demirgüç-Kunt, Aslı, and Luis Serven. 2009. "Are All the Sacred Cows Dead? Implications of the Financial Crisis for Macro and Financial Policies." Policy Research Working Paper 4807. World Bank, Washington, DC.

Easterly, William, Timothy Irwin, and Luis Serven. 2007. "Walking up the Down Escalator: Public Investment and Fiscal Stability." Policy Research Working Paper 4158. World Bank, Washington, DC.

Economist. 2009. "Decoupling 2.0." *Economist*, May 21.

Eichengreen, Barry. 2009. "Commercialize the SDR Now." *Gulf Times*, May 3.

Eichengreen, Barry, and Yung Chul Park. 2008. "Asia and the Decoupling Myth." Department of Economic and Social Affairs Working Paper 69. University of California, Berkeley.

El-Erian, Mohamed. 2009. "A New Normal." *pimco.com*, May. www.pimco.com/LeftNav/PIMCO+Spotlight/2009/Secular+Outlook+May+2009+El-Erian.htm [accessed July 21, 2009].

Energy Information Administration. 2009. *International Carbon Dioxide Emissions and Carbon Intensity*. Washington, DC: Energy Information Administration (April).

Estache, Antonio, and Danny Leipziger. 2009. *Stuck in the Middle: Is Fiscal Policy Failing the Middle Class?* Washington, DC: Brookings Institution Press.

Exman, Fernando. 2009. "Brazil Injects Cash in State Bank to Boost Lending." *reuters.com,* January 22. www.reuters.com/article/euIpoNews/idUSN2254449520090122 [accessed July 21, 2009].

Financial Times. 2009. "No Free Lunches, Even at G-8, Says IMF Chief." *Financial Times,* July 9.

Freund, Caroline. 2009. "The Trade Response to Global Downturns: Historical Evidence." Policy Research Working Paper 5015. World Bank, Washington, DC.

G-20. 2009. *Declaration on Strengthening the Financial System.* Communiqué. London: G-20.

Gamberoni, Elisa, and Richard Newfarmer. 2009. "Trade Protection: Incipient but Worrisome Trends." Trade Notes. World Bank, International Trade Department, Washington, DC.

Giles, Chris. 2009. "Pension Strains Risk Decades of Social Crisis, Warns OECD." *Financial Times,* June 24, p. 4.

Gill, Indermit, and Homi Kharas. 2007. *An East Asian Renaissance: Ideas for Economic Growth.* Washington, DC: World Bank.

Goldin, Claudia, and Lawrence Katz. 2007. "The Race between Education and Technology: The Evolution of U.S. Educational Wage Differentials, 1890 to 2005." NBER Working Paper W12984. National Bureau of Economic Research, Cambridge, MA.

Gómez-Ibáñez, José. 2008. "Private Infrastructure in Developing Countries: Lessons from Recent Experience." In *Workshop on Global Trends and Challenges.* Cambridge, MA: Commission on Growth and Development.

Gros, Daniel. 2009. "Collapse in Eastern Europe? The Rationale for a European Financial Stability Fund." Commentary. Centre for European Policy Studies, Brussels.

IIF (Institute of International Finance). 2009. *Capital Flows to Emerging Market Economies.* Washington, DC: IIF.

IMF (International Monetary Fund). 2007. *World Economic Outlook: Globalization and Inequality.* Washington, DC: IMF.

———. 2009. *World Economic Outlook.* Washington, DC: IMF.

IMF, Fiscal Affairs Department. 2009. "The State of Public Finances: Outlook and Medium-Term Policies after the 2008 Crisis." IMF, Washington, DC.

IMF, Fiscal Affairs and Research Departments. 2008. "Fiscal Policy for the Crisis." Staff Position Note. IMF, Washington, DC.

Jesuit, David, and Vincent Mahler. 2004. "State Redistribution in Comparative Perspective: A Cross-National Analysis of the Developed Countries." Paper presented at the annual meeting of the American Political Science Association, Chicago, IL. September.

Kashyap, Anil, Raghuram Rajan, and Jeremy Stein. 2008. "Rethinking Capital Regulation." Paper prepared for the Federal Reserve Bank of Kansas City symposium "Maintaining Stability in a Changing Financial System," Jackson Hole, WY. August 21–23.

Kose, Ayhan, Christopher Otrok, and Eswar Prasad. 2008. "Global Business Cycles: Convergence or Decoupling?" IMF Working Paper 08/143. International Monetary Fund, Washington, DC.

Krugman, Paul. 2009. "How Did Economists Get It So Wrong?" *New York Times*, September 6.

Lawrence, Robert Z. 2008. *Blue-Collar Blues: Is Trade to Blame for Rising U.S. Income Inequality?* Washington, DC: Peterson Institute for International Economics.

Le, Tuan Minh, Blanca Moreno-Dodson, and Jeep Rojchaichaninthorn. 2008. "Expanding Taxable Capacity and Reaching Revenue Potential: Cross-Country Analysis." Policy Research Working Paper 4559. World Bank, Washington, DC.

Leipziger, Danny. 2009. "How to Explain Argentina and Where It Is Headed?" Note. Washington, DC.

Leipziger, Danny, and William O'Boyle. 2009. "The New Economic Powers (NEPs): Leadership Opportunities Post Crisis." *World Economics* 19 (3): 43–80.

Leipziger, Danny, and Hyun Ja Shin. 1991. "Demand for Protections: A Look at Antidumping Cases." *Open Economics Review* 2 (1): 27–38.

Leipziger, Danny, and Michael Spence. 2007. "Globalization's Losers Need Support." *Financial Times*, May 15, p. 15. http://dannyleipziger.com/documents/economicviewpoint14.pdf.

Lin, Justin, and Yan Wang. 2008. "China's Integration with the World: Development as a Process of Learning and Industrial Upgrading." Policy Research Working Paper 4799. World Bank, Washington, DC.

Mattoo, Aaditya, and Arvind Subramanian. 2009. "A Crisis Round of Trade Negotiations?" *iie.com*, March 30. www.iie.com/publications/papers/paper.cfm?ResearchID=1173 [accessed April 16, 2009].

Mishkin, Frederic. 2006. *The Next Great Globalization: How Disadvantaged Nations Can Harness Their Financial Systems to Get Rich*. Princeton, NJ: Princeton University Press.

Nordhaus, William D. 2006. "The 'Stern Review' on the Economics of Climate Change." NBER Working Paper 12741. National Bureau of Economic Research, Cambridge, MA.

OECD (Organisation for Economic Co-operation and Development). 2008. "Growing Unequal? Income Distribution and Poverty in OECD Countries." OECD, Paris, October.

———. 2009a. "Crisis Highlights the Need for Sweeping Pension Reforms, Says OECD." *oecd.com*, June 23 (accessed June 29, 2009).

———. 2009b. *OECD Economic Outlook* 85 (June). Paris: OECD.

Pew Global Attitudes Project. 2008. *Some Positive Signs for U.S. Image: Global Economic Gloom; China and India Notable Exceptions*. Washington, DC: Pew Research Center.

Quigley, John M. 2009. "Urbanization, Agglomeration, and Economic Development." Working Paper. World Bank, Washington, DC.

Rajan, Raghuram. 2005. "Has Financial Development Made the World Riskier?" NBER Working Paper 11728. National Bureau of Economic Research, Cambridge, MA.

———. 2009. "Cycle-Proof Regulation." *Economist*, April 9.

Reinhart, Carmen, and Kenneth Rogoff. 2009. "The Aftermath of the Financial Crisis." NBER Working Paper 14656. National Bureau of Economic Research, Cambridge, MA.

Rodrik, Dani. 2009. "The Bumpy Road Ahead." *Korea Times*, June 14.

Rodrik, Dani, and Arvind Subramanian. 2008a. "We Must Curb International Flows of Capital." *Financial Times*, February 25.

———. 2008b. "Why Did Financial Globalization Disappoint?" Working Paper 2008-0143. Harvard University, Weatherhead Center for International Affairs, Cambridge, MA.

Romer, Paul. 1990. "Endogenous Technological Change." *Journal of Political Economy* 98 (5): 71–102.

SAIS (School of Advanced International Studies). 2009. "New Ideas in Development after the Financial Crisis." Transcript. Johns Hopkins University, SAIS, Washington, DC.

Sapir, Andre. 2005. "Globalization and the Reform of European Social Models." Policy Brief. Bruegel, Brussels.

Schelling, Thomas. 2007. "What Development Economists Need to Know about Climate Change." PREM Seminar Series (December 18). World Bank, Washington, DC.

Schumpeter, Joseph. 1942. *Capitalism, Socialism, and Democracy.* New York: Harper.

Spence, Michael, Patricia Clarke Annez, and Robert Buckley, eds. 2009. *Urbanization and Growth.* Washington, DC: World Bank.

Stiglitz, Joseph. 2002. *Globalization and Its Discontents.* New York: Norton.

———. 2006. *Making Globalization Work.* New York: Norton.

———. 2009. "Wall Street's Toxic Message." *Vanity Fair*, July.

Subramanian, Arvind. 2009a. "Coupled Economies, Decoupled Debates." *Business Standard*, April 9.

———. 2009b. "India's Goldilocks Globalization." *Newsweek*, June 6.

United Nations. 2006. *World Economic and Social Survey 2006.* New York: United Nations.

United Nations Population Fund. 2007. *State of the World Population 2007.* New York: United Nations.

U.S. Census Bureau. 2009. *Historical Income Inequality Tables.* Washington, DC: U.S. Census Bureau (August).

Watts, Jonathan. 2009. "South Korea Lights the Way on Carbon Emissions with Its 23 Billion Pound Green Deal." *Guardian*, April 21.

Wolf, Martin. 2009. "This Crisis Is a Moment, but Is It a Defining One?" *Financial Times*, May 19.

World Bank. 2007. *Global Economic Prospects: Managing the Next Wave of Globalization.* Washington, DC: World Bank.

———. 2008a. *International Trade and Climate Change: Economic, Legal, and Institutional Perspectives.* Washington, DC: World Bank.

———. 2008b. *World Development Indicators.* Washington, DC: World Bank.

———. 2009a. *Global Development Finance.* Washington, DC: World Bank.

———. 2009b. *Private Participation in Infrastructure Database.* Washington, DC: World Bank (July).

———. 2009c. *World Development Report 2009: Reshaping Economic Geography.* Washington, DC: World Bank.

WTO (World Trade Organization). 2008. *International Trade Statistics 2008.* Geneva: WTO.

PART 1

The Global Financial Crisis: Causes, Mitigation, and Reform

CHAPTER 2

The Crisis of 2008: Structural Lessons for and from Economics

Daron Acemoglu

We do not yet know whether the global financial and economic crisis of 2008 will go down in history as a momentous or even a uniquely catastrophic event. Unwritten history is full of long-forgotten events that contemporaries thought were epochal. On the other side of the scale, many persons in the early stages of the Great Depression belittled its import. Although it is too soon to tell how the second half of 2008 will feature in history books, there should be no doubt that it signifies a critical opportunity for the discipline of economics. It is an opportunity for us—and here I mean the majority of the economics profession, myself included—to be disabused of certain notions that we should not have accepted so readily in the first place. It is also an opportunity for us to step back and consider what are the most important lessons we have learned from our theoretical and empirical investigations—that remain untarnished by recent events—and to ask whether they can provide us with guidance in current policy debates.

This chapter presents my views on what intellectual errors we have made and what lessons these errors offer us moving forward. My main objective,

This chapter was initially published as a paper in *CEPR Policy Insight*, No. 28 (January 2009). See www.cepr.org/pubs/PolicyInsights/PolicyInsight28.pdf. The author would like to thank David Autor, Ricardo Caballero, Simon Johnson, Bengt Holmstrom, and James Poterba for comments.

however, is not to dwell on the intellectual currents of the past, but to stress that economic theory still has a lot to teach economists and policy makers as we make our way through the crisis. I argue that several economic principles related to the most important aspect of economic performance—the long-run growth potential of nations—are still valid and hold important lessons in our intellectual and practical deliberations on policy. But these principles have played little role in recent academic debates and have been entirely absent in policy debates. As academic economists, we should be reminding policy makers of these principles and the implications of current policies for the growth potential of the global economy.

Lessons from Our Intellectual Complaisance

The crisis is still evolving, and much uncertainty remains about what happened in the financial markets and inside many corporations. We will know more in the years to come. With what we know today, many of the roots of our current problems are already apparent. But most of us did not recognize them before the crisis. Three notions impelled us to ignore these impeding problems and their causes.

The first is that the era of aggregate volatility had come to an end. We believed that through astute policy or new technologies, including better methods of communication and inventory control, we had conquered the business cycles. Our belief in a more benign economy made us optimistic about the stock market and the housing market. If any contraction must be soft and short lived, then it becomes easier to believe that financial intermediaries, firms, and consumers should not worry about large drops in asset values.

Even though the data show a robust, negative relationship between income per capita and economic volatility, and many measures show a marked decline in aggregate volatility since the 1950s, and certainly since the prewar era, these empirical patterns mean neither that the business cycles have disappeared nor that catastrophic economic events are impossible. The same economic and financial changes that have made our economy more diversified and individual firms better insured have also increased the interconnections among them. Since the only way to diversify idiosyncratic risks is to share them among many companies and individuals, better diversification also creates a multitude of counterparty relationships. Such interconnections make the economic system more resilient to small shocks because new financial products successfully diversify a wide range of idiosyncratic risks and reduce business failures. They also make the economy more vulnerable to certain low-probability, tail events precisely because the interconnections that inevitably precipitate the greater diversification create potential domino effects among financial institutions, companies, and households. In this light, perhaps we should not find it surprising that years of economic calm can be followed by tumult and notable volatility.

There is another sense in which the myth of the end of the business cycle is at odds with fundamental properties of the capitalist system. As Schumpeter argued long ago, the workings of the market system and the innovation dynamics that constitute its essence involve a heavy dose of creative destruction, where existing firms, procedures, and products are replaced by new ones. Much of creative destruction takes place at the micro level. But not all of it. Many companies are large, and replacement of their core business by new firms and new products will have aggregate implications. Moreover, many general-purpose technologies are shared by diverse companies in different lines of business, so their failure and potential replacement by new processes will again have aggregate ramifications. Equally important, businesses and individuals make decisions under imperfect information and potentially learn from each other and from past practices. This learning process will introduce additional correlation and co-movement in the behavior of economic agents, which will also extend the realm of creative destruction from the micro to the macro.

The large drops in asset values and the simultaneous insolvencies of many companies should alert us that aggregate volatility is part and parcel of the market system. Understanding that such volatility will be with us should redirect our attention toward models that help us to interpret the various sources of volatility and delineate which components are associated with the efficient working of markets and which result from avoidable market failures. A more in-depth study of aggregate volatility also necessitates conceptual and theoretical investigations of how the increasingly interconnected nature of our economic and financial system affects the allocation of resources and the allocation and sharing of risks of both companies and individuals.

Our second too-quickly-accepted notion is that the capitalist economy functions in an institution-less vacuum, where markets miraculously monitor opportunistic behavior. Forgetting the institutional foundations of markets, we mistakenly equated free markets with unregulated markets. Although we understand that even unfettered competitive markets are based on a set of laws and institutions that secure property rights, ensure enforcement of contracts, and regulate firm behavior and product and service quality, we increasingly abstracted from the role of institutions and regulations in supporting market transactions in our conceptualization of markets. Institutions received more attention over the past 15 years or so than before, but the thinking was that we had to study the role of institutions to understand why poor nations were poor, not to probe the nature of the institutions that ensured continued prosperity in the advanced nations or how they should change in the face of ever-evolving economic relations. In our obliviousness to the importance of market-supporting institutions, we were in sync with policy makers, who were lured by ideological notions derived from Ayn Rand novels rather than economic theory. We let their policies and rhetoric set the agenda for our thinking about the world and worse, perhaps, even for our policy advice. In hindsight, we should not be surprised that unregulated profit-seeking individuals took risks from which they benefited and others lost.

We now know better. Few among us would argue today that market monitoring is sufficient against opportunistic behavior. Many inside and outside academia may view this as a failure of economic theory. I strongly disagree with this conclusion. On the contrary, the recognition that markets live on foundations laid by institutions—that free markets are not the same as unregulated markets—enriches both theory and its practice. We must now start building a theory of market transactions that is more in tune with their institutional and regulatory foundations. We must also turn to the theory of regulation—of both firms and financial institutions—with renewed vigor and additional insights gained from current experience. A deep and important contribution of the discipline of economics is the insight that greed is neither good nor bad in the abstract. When channeled into profit-maximizing, competitive, and innovative behavior under the auspices of sound laws and regulations, greed can act as the engine of innovation and economic growth. But when unchecked by the appropriate institutions and regulations, it will degenerate into rent seeking, corruption, and crime. It is our collective choice to manage the greed that many in our society inevitably possess. Economic theory provides guidance on how to create the right incentive systems and reward structures to contain it and turn it into a force for progress.

The third notion that has been destroyed by recent events is less obvious, but one that I strongly held. Our logic and models suggested that even if we could not trust individuals, particularly when information was imperfect and regulation lackluster, we could trust the long-lived large firms—the Enrons, the Bear Stearns, the Merrill Lynchs, and the Lehman Brothers of this world—to monitor themselves and their own because they had accumulated sufficient reputation capital. Our faith in long-lived large organizations was shaken but still standing after the accounting scandals at Enron and other giants of the early 2000s. It may now have suffered the death blow.

Our trust in the self-monitoring capabilities of organizations ignored two critical difficulties. The first is that, even within firms, monitoring must be done by individuals—the chief executives, the managers, the accountants. And in the same way that we should not have blindly trusted the incentives of stockbrokers willing to take astronomical risks for which they were not the residual claimants, we should not have put our faith in the ability of individuals to monitor others simply because they are part of a large organization. The second is even more troubling for our way of thinking about the world: reputational monitoring requires that failure be punished severely. But the scarcity of specific capital and know-how means that such punishments are often not credible. The intellectual argument for the financial bailout of fall 2008 has been that the organizations clearly responsible for the problems we are in today should nonetheless be saved and propped up because they are the only ones that have the specific capital to get us out of our current predicament. This is a valid argument and not unique to the current situation. Whenever the incentives to compromise integrity, to sacrifice quality, and to take unnecessary risks exist, most companies will do so in tandem. And because the ex post vacuum of specific skills, capital, and knowledge that their punishment will create makes such a course of action too costly for society, all kinds of punishments lose their effectiveness and credibility.

The lessons for our thinking from this chain of reasoning are twofold. First, we need to rethink the role of the reputations of firms in market transactions, taking into account the general equilibrium—the scarcity value of their skills and expertise when the reputations of several of them fail simultaneously. Second, we need to revisit the key questions of the economics of organization so that firm reputations are derived from the behavior—and interactions—of directors, managers, and employees, rather than from that of the hypothetical principal maximizing the net present discounted value of the firm.

When we look at the academic tally, we can always blame ourselves for missing important economic insights and not being more farsighted than policy makers. We can even blame ourselves for being complicit in the intellectual atmosphere leading up to the current disaster. On the bright side, the crisis has increased the vitality of economics and highlighted several challenging, relevant, and exciting issues. These include the ability of the market system to deal with risks, interconnections, and the disruptions brought about by the process of creative destruction, issues related to a better framework for regulation and the relationship between underlying institutions and the functioning of markets and organizations. It should be much less likely in the decade to come for bright young economists to worry about finding new and relevant questions on which to work. .

Lessons from Our Intellectual Endowment

Although various notions we held dear need rethinking, several other principles that are part of our intellectual endowment are useful for understanding how we got here and for forewarning us against the most important policy mistakes in our—and more important in policymakers'—attempts to deal with the crisis. Perhaps not surprising given my own intellectual background, I think these principles are related to economic growth and political economy.

First, it is obvious why we should heed issues of economic growth. Barring a complete meltdown of the global system, even with the ferocious severity of the global crisis, the possible loss of gross domestic product for most countries is in the range of a couple of percentage points, and most of this might have been unavoidable given the economic overexpansion in prior years. In contrast, modest changes in economic growth will accumulate to much larger numbers within one decade or two. Thus from a policy and welfare perspective, it should be self-evident that sacrificing economic growth to deal with the current crisis is a bad option.

Economic growth deserves our attention not only because it has a prominent role in meaningful calculations of welfare, but also because many aspects of growth and its main sources are reasonably well understood. There is broad theoretical and empirical agreement on the roles of physical capital, human capital, and technology in determining output and growth. But equally, we also understand the role that innovation and reallocation play in propagating economic growth, and we recognize the broad outlines of the institutional framework that makes innovation, reallocation, and long-run growth possible.

Recent events have shed no doubt on the importance of innovation. On the contrary, we have enjoyed prosperity over the past two decades because of rapid innovations—quite independent of financial bubbles and troubles. We witnessed a breakneck pace of new innovations in software, hardware, telecommunications, pharmaceuticals, biotechnology, entertainment, and retail and wholesale trade. These innovations are responsible for the bulk of the increases in aggregate productivity we enjoyed over the past two decades. Even the financial innovations, which are somewhat tainted in the recent crisis, are in most cases socially valuable and have contributed to growth. Complex securities were misused to take risks, with the downside being borne by unsuspecting parties. But when properly regulated, they also enable more sophisticated strategies for risk sharing and diversification. They have enabled and ultimately will again enable firms to reduce the cost of capital. Technological ingenuity is the key to the prosperity and success of the capitalist economy. New innovations and their implementation and marketing will play a central role in renewed economic growth in the aftermath of the crisis.

The other pillar of economic growth is reallocation. Because innovation often comes in the form of Schumpeterian creative destruction, it will involve production processes and firms relying on old technologies being replaced by the new. This is only one aspect of capitalist reallocation, however. Volatility that is part of the market economy also exhibits itself by incessantly changing which companies and which services have greater productivity and greater demand. Such volatility, perhaps strengthened now more than ever because of the greater global interconnections, is not a curse against which we should defend ourselves, but, for the most part, an opportunity for the market economy. By reallocating resources to where productivity and demand are, the capitalist system can exploit volatility. The developments of the last two decades again highlight the importance of reallocation, since economic growth, as usual, took place in tandem with output, labor, and capital moving away from many established companies and toward their competitors, often foreign competitors, and away from sectors in which the United States and other advanced countries ceased to have comparative advantage and toward those where their advantages became stronger.

The final principle that I emphasize relates to the political economy of growth. Economic growth will only take place if society creates the institutions and policies that encourage innovation, reallocation, investment, and education. But such institutions should not be taken for granted. Because of the reallocation and creative destruction brought about by economic growth, there will always be parties, often strong parties, opposed to certain aspects of economic growth. In many less-developed economies, the key aspect of the political economy of growth is to ensure that incumbent producers, elites, and politicians do not hijack the political agenda and create an environment inimical to economic progress and growth. Another threat to the institutional foundations of economic growth comes from its ultimate beneficiaries. Creative destruction and reallocation not only harm established businesses but also their workers and suppliers, sometimes even destroying the livelihood of millions of workers and peasants. It is then easy for impoverished populations suffering from adverse shocks and economic crises—particularly in societies where the political economy never generated an effective safety net—to turn against the market system and support populist policies that will create barriers against economic growth. These threats are as important for advanced economies as they are for less developed countries, particularly in the midst of the current economic crisis.

The importance of political economy has been underscored by recent events. It is difficult to tell the story of the failure of regulation of investment banks and the financial industry at-large over the past two decades and of the bailout plan approved without making some reference to political economy. The United States is not Indonesia under Suharto or the Philippines under Marcos. But we do not need to go to such extremes to imagine that when the financial industry contributes millions to the campaigns of members of the U.S. Congress, it will have an acute influence on policies that affect its livelihood or that when investment bankers set up—or fail to set up, as the case may be—the regulations for their former partners and colleagues without oversight, it will likely lead to political economy problems. It is difficult to envisage a scenario in which current and future policies will not be influenced by the backlash against markets that those who have lost their houses and livelihoods feel at the moment.

Absent Lessons

Policies designed to contain and end the global crisis have considered many economic factors. But their impacts on long-run economic growth, innovation, reallocation, and political economy have been conspicuous in their absence in the ensuing debate.

A large stimulus plan that includes bailouts for banks, the financial sector at-large, auto manufacturers, and others will undoubtedly influence innovation and reallocation. This is no reason for not endorsing the stimulus plan, but it is important to consider the full set of implications. Reallocation will clearly suffer as a result of many aspects of the current stimulus plan. In the auto industry, market signals suggest that labor and capital should be reallocated away from the Detroit Big Three and that highly skilled labor should be reallocated away from the financial industry and toward more innovative sectors. The latter reallocation is critically important in view of the fact that Wall Street attracted many of the best (and most ambitious) minds over the past two decades; we now realize that although these bright young minds contributed to financial innovation, they also used their talents to devise new methods of taking large risks, the downside of which they would not bear. Halted reallocation will also mean halted innovation.

Several additional areas of potential innovation may directly suffer as a result of the current crisis and our policy responses to it. Improvements in retail and wholesale trade and service delivery will undoubtedly slow down as consumer demand contracts. A key area of innovation for the next decade and beyond—energy—may also become a casualty. The demand for alternative energy sources was strong before the crisis and promised a platform, similar to what we enjoyed in computing, pharmaceuticals, and biotechnology, with powerful synergies between science and profits. With the decline in oil prices and the odds turning against the much-needed tax on gasoline, some of the momentum is undoubtedly lost. If bailouts are not tied to the appropriate reorganization of the auto companies, then another important aspect of the drive toward new energy-efficient technologies will have been squandered as well.

All of these concerns are not sufficient to make us refrain from a comprehensive stimulus plan. In my view, however, the reason for a stimulus plan is not to soften the blow of the recession but is again related to economic growth. The risk that we face is one of an expectational trap—consumers and policy makers becoming pessimistic about future growth and the promise of markets. We do not understand expectational traps well enough to know exactly how they happen and what economic dynamics they unleash. And yet this does not deny the dangers that they pose. Consumers delaying purchases of durable goods can certainly have major effects, particularly when inventories are high and credit is tight. An expectational trap of this sort would deepen and lengthen the recession and create extensive business failures and liquidations rather than the necessary creative destruction and reallocation.

In my opinion, however, a greater danger from an expectational trap and a deep recession lies elsewhere. We may see consumers and policy makers start to believe that free markets are responsible for the economic ills of today and shift their support away from the market economy. We would then see the pendulum swing too far, taking us to an era of heavy government involvement rather than the needed foundational regulation of free markets. I believe that such a swing and the antimarket policies that it would bring would threaten the future growth prospects of the global economy. Restrictions on trade in goods and services would be a first step. Industrial policy that stymies reallocation and innovation would be a second, equally damaging step. When the talk is of bailing out and protecting selected sectors, more systematic proposals on trade restrictions and industrial policy may be around the corner.

A comprehensive stimulus plan, even with all of its imperfections, is probably the best way of fighting off these dangers, and on balance there are sufficient reasons for academic economists as well as concerned citizens to support current efforts as insurance against the worst outcomes we may face. Nevertheless, the details of the stimulus plan should be designed so as to cause minimal disruption to the process of reallocation and innovation. Sacrificing growth out of our fear of the present would be as severe a mistake as inaction.

The risk that belief in the capitalist system may collapse should not be dismissed. After all, the past two decades were heralded as the triumph of capitalism, so their bitter aftermath must be the failure of the capitalist system. It should be no surprise that I disagree with this conclusion, since I do not think the success of the capitalist system can be found in or was based on unregulated markets. We are experiencing not a failure of capitalism or free markets per se, but a failure of unregulated markets—in particular, of unregulated financial sector and risk management. As such, it should not make us less optimistic about the growth potential of market economies—provided that markets are based on solid institutional foundations. But since the rhetoric of the past two decades equated capitalism with lack of regulation, this nuance will be lost on many who no longer have a house or a job.

A backlash is thus inevitable. The question is how to contain it. The policy responses of the past several months have only made matters worse. It is one thing for the population at-large to think that markets do not work as well as the pundits promised. It is an entirely different level of disillusionment for them to think that markets are just an excuse for the rich and powerful to fill their pockets at the expense of the rest. But how could they think otherwise when the bailouts have been designed by bankers to help bankers and to minimize damage to those responsible for the debacle in the first place?

This is not the place to formulate concrete proposals to improve the stimulus and bailout packages, nor do I have that expertise. Although the economics profession was partly complicit in the buildup of the current crisis, we still have important messages for policy makers. They do not pertain to the details of the bailout plan, on which many pundits are only too keen to express an opinion, but on the long-run perspective. We should instead be vocal in emphasizing the implications of current policy proposals for innovation, reallocation, and the political economy foundations of the capitalist system. Economic growth ought to be a central part of the discussion, not an afterthought.

CHAPTER 3
Financial Innovation, Regulation, and Reform
Charles W. Calomiris

Financial innovations often respond to regulation by sidestepping regulatory restrictions that would otherwise limit activities in which people wish to engage. Securitization of loans (for example, credit card receivables or subprime residential mortgages) is often portrayed, correctly, as having arisen in part as a means of "arbitraging" regulatory capital requirements by booking assets off the balance sheets of regulated banks. Originators of the loans were able to maintain lower equity capital against those loans than they would have needed to maintain if the loans had been placed on their balance sheets.[1]

© 2009 The Cato Institute. Reprinted by permission from *Cato Journal*, Vol. 29, No. 1, Winter 2009, pp. 65–91. The author thanks Richard Herring, Charles Plosser, and Peter Wallison for helpful discussions.

1   Financial innovations involving regulatory arbitrage can be complex. Securitized assets implicitly often remain connected to the balance sheet of the bank that originated them, despite the fact that the liabilities issued by the securitization conduits are not legally protected by the originating bank; lenders not only provide explicit credit enhancements to their off-balance-sheet conduits, but also offer implicit "guarantees" to the market. These implicit guarantees are valued by the market, which expects originators to voluntarily stand behind the securitized debts of their off-balance-sheet conduits, at least under most circumstances. This phenomenon is known as implicit recourse (see Calomiris and Mason 2004).

Capital regulation of securitization invited this form of off-balance-sheet regulatory arbitrage and did so quite consciously. Several of the capital requirement rules for the treatment of securitized assets originated by banks, and for the debts issued by those conduits and held or guaranteed by banks, were specifically and consciously designed to permit banks to allocate less capital against their risks relating to those conduits than they would have had to maintain against similar risks held on their balance sheets (Calomiris 2008b). Critics of these capital regulations have rightly pointed to these capital requirements as having contributed to the subprime crisis by permitting banks to maintain insufficient amounts of equity capital per unit of risk undertaken in their subprime holdings.

Capital regulations that were less strict than those applying to commercial banks permitted investment banks to engage in subprime-related risk with insufficient budgeting of equity capital. Investment banks faced capital regulations under Securities and Exchange Commission guidelines that were similar to the more permissive Basel II rules that apply to commercial banks outside the United States. Because those capital regulations were less strict than capital regulations imposed on U.S. banks, investment banks were able to leverage their positions more than commercial banks. Investment banks' use of overnight repurchase agreements as their primary source of finance also permitted them to "ride the yield curve" when using debt to fund their risky asset positions; in that respect, collateralized repos appeared to offer a substitute for low-interest commercial bank deposits.[2] But as the collateral standing behind those repos declined in value and became risky, "haircuts" associated with repo collateral became less favorable, and investment banks were unable to roll over their repo positions, a liquidity risk that added to their vulnerability and made their equity capital positions even more insufficient as risk buffers.

There is no doubt that the financial innovations associated with securitization and repo finance were motivated at least in part by regulatory arbitrage. Furthermore, there is no doubt that if on-balance-sheet commercial bank capital regulations had determined the amount of equity budgeted by all subprime mortgage originators, then the leverage ratios of the banking system would not have been so large and the liquidity risk from repo funding would have been substantially less, both of which would have reduced the magnitude of the financial crisis.

Yet I do not agree with those who argue that the subprime crisis is mainly a story of government "errors of omission," which allowed banks to avoid regulatory discipline due to the insufficient application of existing regulations for on-balance-sheet commercial bank capital to the risks undertaken by investment banks and off-balance-sheet conduits. The main story of the subprime crisis instead is one of government "errors of commission," which were far more important in generating the huge risks and large losses that brought down the U.S. financial system.

---

2   Repos grew so quickly that they came to exceed in size the total assets of the commercial banking system, as discussed in Gorton (2009).

What Went Wrong and Why?

The subprime crisis reflected first and foremost the willingness of the managers of large financial institutions to take on risks by buying financial instruments that were improperly priced, which made the purchases of these instruments contrary to the interests of the shareholders of the institutions that invested in them. As Calomiris (2008b) shows, on an ex ante basis, risk was substantially underestimated in the market during the subprime boom of 2003–07. Reasonable forward-looking estimates of risk were ignored intentionally by senior management of financial institutions, who structured compensation packages to maximize the incentives for asset managers to undertake these underestimated risks. In the absence of "regulatory arbitrage," budgeting a little more regulatory capital would have reduced the amount of risk undertaken and given the system a larger cushion for managing its losses, but the huge losses from underestimated subprime risk still would have occurred.

The risk-taking mistakes of financial managers were not the result of random mass insanity; rather, they reflected a policy environment that strongly encouraged financial managers to underestimate risk in the subprime mortgage market. Risk taking was driven by government policies; government *actions* were the root problem, not government *inaction*. How do government policy actions account for the disastrous decisions of large financial institutions to take on unprofitable subprime mortgage risk? In what follows, I review each of the major areas of government policy distortions and how they encouraged the conscious undertaking of underestimated risk in the market (see also Calomiris 2008a, 2008b; Calomiris and Wallison 2008; Eisenbeis 2008).

Four categories of government error were instrumental in producing the crisis. First, lax Fed interest rate policy, especially from 2002 through 2005, promoted easy credit and kept interest rates very low for a protracted period. The history of postwar monetary policy has seen only two episodes in which the real Fed funds rate remained negative for several consecutive years; those periods are the high-inflation episode of 1975–78 (which was reversed by the anti-inflationary rate hikes of 1979–82) and the accommodative policy environment of 2002–05. According to the St. Louis Fed, the Federal Reserve deviated sharply from its "Taylor rule" approach to setting interest rates during the 2002–05 period; Fed fund rates remained substantially and persistently below the levels that would have been consistent with the Taylor rule, even if that rule had been targeting 3 or 4 percent long-run inflation.

Not only were short-term real rates held at persistent historic lows, but because of peculiarities in the bond market related to global imbalances and Asian demands for medium- and long-term U.S. treasuries, the treasury yield curve was virtually flat during the 2002–05 period. The combination of low short-term rates and a flat yield curve meant that long-term real interest rates on treasury bonds (which are the most relevant benchmarks for setting rates for mortgages and other long-term fixed-income assets) were especially low relative to their historic norms.

Accommodative monetary policy and a flat yield curve meant that credit was excessively available to support expansion in the housing market at abnormally low interest rates, which encouraged overpricing of houses. There is substantial empirical evidence showing that when monetary policy is accommodative, banks charge less for bearing risk (reviewed in Calomiris 2008b), and this seems to be a pattern common to many countries in the present and the past. According to some industry observers, low interest rates in 2002–05 also encouraged some asset managers (who cared more about their fees than about the interests of their clients) to attract clients by offering to maintain preexisting portfolio yields notwithstanding declines in interest rates; that financial alchemy was only possible because asset managers decided to purchase very risky assets and pretend that they were not very risky.

Second, numerous government policies specifically promoted subprime risk taking by financial institutions. Those policies included (a) political pressures from Congress on the government-sponsored enterprises (GSEs)—Fannie Mae and Freddie Mac—to promote "affordable housing" by investing in high-risk subprime mortgages, (b) lending subsidies policies via the Federal Home Loan bank system to its member institutions that promoted high mortgage leverage and risk, (c) Federal Housing Administration (FHA) subsidization of high mortgage leverage and risk, (d) government and GSE mortgage foreclosure mitigation protocols that were developed in the late 1990s and early 2000s to reduce the costs to borrowers of failing to meet debt service requirements on mortgages, and, almost unbelievably, (e) 2006 legislation that encouraged rating agencies to relax their standards for measuring risk in subprime securitizations.

All of these government policies encouraged the underestimation of subprime risk, but the politicization of Fannie Mae and Freddie Mac and the actions of members of Congress to encourage reckless lending by the GSEs in the name of affordable housing were arguably the most damaging policy actions leading up to the crisis. In order for Fannie and Freddie to maintain their implicit (now explicit) government guarantees on their debts, which contributed substantially to their profitability, they had to cater to the political whims of their masters in the government. In the context of recent times, that meant making risky subprime loans (Calomiris 2008a; Calomiris and Wallison 2008). Fannie and Freddie ended up holding $1.6 trillion in exposure to toxic mortgages, which constitutes half of the total non-FHA outstanding amount of toxic mortgages (Pinto 2009).

A review of e-mail correspondence between risk managers and senior management at the GSEs reveals that those positions were taken despite the objections of risk managers, who viewed them as imprudent and who predicted that the GSEs would lead the rest of the market into huge overpricing of risky mortgages (Calomiris 2008a). Indeed, it is likely that absent the involvement of Fannie and Freddie in aggressive subprime buying beginning in 2004, the total magnitude of toxic mortgages originated would have been less than half the actual amount, since Fannie and Freddie crowded market participation in more than they crowded it out.

What aspects of GSE involvement in the market suggest that, on net, they crowded in, rather than crowded out, private investment in subprime and Alt-A mortgages? First, the timing of GSE involvement was important. Their aggressive ramping up of purchases of these products in 2004 coincided with the acceleration of growth in subprime mortgages. Total subprime and Alt-A originations grew from $395 billion in 2003 to $715 billion in 2004, reaching more than $1 trillion in 2005 (Calomiris 2008b: table 2). Furthermore, the GSEs stayed in these markets long after the mid-2006 flattening of house prices, which signaled to many other lenders the need to exit the subprime market; during the last year of the subprime and Alt-A origination boom, when originations remained near peak levels despite clear evidence of impending problems, the GSEs were crucial in maintaining financing for subprime and Alt-A securities.

The GSEs also were uniquely large and protected players in the mortgage market (due to their GSE status) and thus could set standards and influence pricing in ways that other lenders could not. These unique qualities were noted by Freddie Mac's risk managers when they referred to Freddie's role in "making a market" in no-docs mortgages. After 2004, and continuing long after the subprime market turned down in 2006, originators of subprime and Alt-A mortgages knew that the GSEs stood ready to buy their poorly underwritten instruments, and this GSE legitimization of unsound underwriting practices gave assurance to market participants that there was a ready source of demand for the new product. That assurance had important consequences both for initially accelerating and later maintaining the large flow of subprime and Alt-A mortgage deals and for promoting the overpricing and overleveraging of these instruments. That market-making role of the GSEs had consequences for the expansion of the market and the pricing of subprime and Alt-A mortgages and mortgage-backed securities that exceeded the particular securities purchased or guarantees made by the GSEs.

Third, government regulations limiting who can buy stock in banks made effective corporate governance within large financial institutions virtually impossible, which allowed bank management to pursue investments that were unprofitable for stockholders in the long run, but very profitable for management in the short run, given the short time horizon of managerial compensation systems.

Pensions, mutual funds, insurance companies, and banks are restricted from holding anything but tiny stakes in any particular company, which makes these informed professional investors virtually impotent in promoting any change within badly managed firms. Hostile takeovers, which often provide an alternative means of discipline for mismanaged nonfinancial firms, are not a feasible source of discipline for financial companies; banks are service providers whose franchise consists largely of human capital, and the best parts of that human capital can flee to competitors as soon as nasty takeover battles begin (a poison pill even better than standard takeover defenses). What about the possibility that a hedge fund or private equity investor might intervene to become a major blockholder in a financial firm and try to change it from within? That possibility is obviated by the Bank Holding Company Act, which prevents any entity with a controlling interest in a nonfinancial company from acquiring a controlling interest in a bank holding company (the definition of the size of a controlling interest was relaxed in the wake of the 2008 crisis to encourage more block holding, but that change was too little and too late).

When stockholder discipline is absent, managers are able to set up the management of risk within the firms they manage to benefit themselves at the expense of stockholders. An asset bubble (like the subprime bubble of 2003–07) offers an ideal opportunity; if senior managers establish compensation systems that reward subordinates based on total assets managed or total revenues collected without regard to risk or future potential loss, then subordinates have an incentive to expand portfolios rapidly during the bubble without regard to risk. Senior managers then reward themselves for having overseen that "successful" expansion with large short-term bonuses and make sure to cash out their stock options quickly so that a large portion of their money is safely invested elsewhere by the time the bubble bursts.

Fourth, prudential regulation of commercial banks by the government has proven to be ineffective. That failure reflects (a) problems in measuring bank risk resulting from regulation's ill-considered reliance on credit-rating agencies' assessments and internal bank models to measure risk and (b) the too-big-to-fail problem (Stern and Feldman 2004), which makes it difficult to enforce effective discipline on large, complex banks, even if regulators detect that they have suffered large losses and accumulated imprudently large risks.

With respect to the former, I reiterate that the risk measurement problem is not merely that regulators and their rules regarding securitization permitted the booking of subprime risks off of commercial bank balance sheets; the measurement of subprime risk, and the capital budgeted against that risk, would still have been much too low if all the subprime risk had been booked entirely on commercial bank balance sheets. Regulators utilize different means to assess risk, depending on the size of the bank. Under the simplest version of regulatory measurement of bank risk, subprime mortgages have a low asset risk weight (50 percent that of commercial loans), even though they are much riskier than most bank loans. The more complex measurement of subprime risk (applicable to larger U.S. banks) relies on the opinions of rating agencies or the internal assessments of banks, and it should come as no surprise that neither of those assessments is independent of bank management.

Rating agencies, after all, are supposed to cater to buy-side market participants, but when their ratings are used for regulatory purposes, buy-side participants reward rating agencies for underestimating risk, since that helps the buy-side clients to avoid regulation. Many observers wrongly believe that the problem with rating agencies' grade inflation of securitized debts is that the *sellers* of these debts (sponsors of securitizations) pay for ratings; on the contrary, the problem is that the *buyers* of the debts want inflated ratings because they receive regulatory benefits from those inflated ratings.

The too-big-to-fail problem relates to the lack of credibility of regulatory discipline for large, complex banks. For small banks, the failure to manage risk properly results in "intervention" by regulators, under the Federal Deposit Insurance Corporation Improvement Act (FDICIA) framework established in 1991, which forces the sale or liquidation of insufficiently capitalized banks. But for large, complex banks, the prospect of intervening is so potentially disruptive to the financial system that regulators have an incentive to avoid intervention. The incentives that favor "forbearance" can make it hard for regulators to ensure compliance.

The too-big-to-fail problem magnifies the so-called moral hazard problem of the government safety net; banks that expect to be protected by deposit insurance, Fed lending, and Treasury-Fed bailouts and that believe they are beyond discipline will tend to take on excessive risk, since the taxpayers share the costs of that excessive risk on the downside. And just as important, banks that are protected by the government from the discipline of the marketplace will be too tolerant of bad management, since managerial errors that are normally punished by failure will be hidden under the umbrella of government protection.

The moral hazard of the too-big-to-fail problem was clearly visible in the behavior of the large investment banks in 2008. After Bear Stearns was rescued by a Treasury-Fed bailout in March, Lehman Brothers, Merrill Lynch, Morgan Stanley, and Goldman Sachs sat on their hands for six months awaiting further developments (that is, either an improvement in the market environment or a handout from Uncle Sam). In particular, Lehman did little to raise capital or shore up its position. But when conditions deteriorated and the anticipated bailout failed to materialize for Lehman in September 2008—showing that there were limits to Treasury-Fed generosity—the other major investment banks immediately either were acquired or transformed themselves into commercial bank holding companies to increase their access to government support.

The too-big-to-fail moral hazard problem is not a natural consequence of the existence of large, complex institutions. Like the other policy failures enumerated here, it reflects government decisions. In the case of too-big-to-fail, the government has made two key errors. First, protection has been offered too frequently (for example, the bailout of Continental Bank in 1984 was not justified by plausible "systemic risk" concerns); some of the moral hazard cost associated with too big to fail could be eliminated just by being more selective in applying the doctrine. Second, if the government did more to create a credible intervention and resolution process for large, complex banks that become troubled, then much of the cost of too big to fail could be eliminated. If, for example, the government required that a feasible and credible intervention plan be maintained on an ongoing basis for every large, complex institution, then it would not need to forbear from intervening in such institutions when they become deeply undercapitalized.

To be feasible and credible, an intervention plan would have to ensure the seamless continuing operation and funding of the institution's lending and other important market transactions and would have to define in advance loss-sharing arrangements among the subsidiaries within the organization that deal with one another (and those loss-sharing arrangements would have to be approved in advance by the various countries' regulators in which the subsidiaries are located). One of the most intractable problems of complex, globally diverse banks is defining loss-sharing arrangements across borders in the midst of a financial crisis. Bankruptcy procedures appear to be too cumbersome for dealing with the smooth transfer of control and funding, and the lack of a prearranged agreement among regulators about loss sharing means that bankruptcy (as in the case of Lehman) can entail complex, protracted adjudication of intersubsidiary claims in many different legal venues.

The "bridge bank" structure exists in the United States and a few other countries as a means of transitioning to new control and funding sources, but this structure has not been used during the subprime crisis, perhaps because it is too difficult to define its structure and determine loss-sharing arrangements across subsidiaries after the fact. The primary policy failure relating to too-big-to-fail problems is not the decision to forbear from intervening in the midst of the crisis, but rather the decision not to prepare properly for the eventuality of having to intervene.

In summary, the greatest threats that financial sector policy must confront have to do with the ways in which government policy shapes the rules of the game to promote willfully excessive, value-destroying risks. The pursuit of value-destroying risks arises most easily during moments of accommodative monetary policy, and the low-interest-rate environment of 2002–05 was among the most accommodative in U.S. history. Value-destroying risk taking during the recent subprime mortgage boom and bust was motivated by (1) political pressures to lend unwisely (for example, the pressures that led Fannie and Freddie to pursue the expansion of "affordable housing," despite its costs to taxpayers and unwitting home buyers), (2) bank agency problems (that is, policies that allow bankers to avoid stockholder discipline in pursuit of their own self-interest), and (3) safety net protections (including too-big-to-fail policies) that make value-destroying risks personally beneficial to financiers and their stockholders.

Regulatory Reform for a World Populated by Humans

One response to the litany of woe outlined above is to suggest that the raft of government distortions that produce financial sector disasters should be eliminated. If there were no government safety nets, no government manipulation of credit markets, no leverage subsidies, and no limitations on the market for corporate control, one could reasonably argue against the need for prudential regulation. Indeed, the history of financial crises shows that in times and places where these government interventions were absent, financial crises were relatively rare and not very severe (Calomiris 2007).

That laissez-faire argument, however, neglects two counterarguments. First, substantial negative externalities may be associated with bank risk management. Part of the benefit from one bank's reduction of its risk is shared by other banks (since the failure of one large institution can have repercussions for others), and this implies that if banks are left to their own devices, they will choose levels of risk that are higher than the socially optimal levels.

Second, it is not very helpful to suggest regulatory changes that are far beyond the feasible bounds of the current political environment. It is useful to point to the desirability of many simultaneous fundamental reforms of government policy, but it is also useful to outline a policy reform strategy for a world that is not amenable to the reasoned arguments of libertarian economists. Absent the elimination of government safety nets, government credit subsidies, and government limits on corporate control, government prudential regulation is a must, even for those who are not convinced by the argument regarding risk management externalities. Until and unless these three categories of existing government distortions are eliminated, we must mitigate their harmful effects by establishing effective prudential regulations.

If one is going to design a regulatory system that works in the presence of these various distortions, it will have to be designed on the basis of principles that transcend the mathematics of finance. As Barth, Caprio, and Levine (2006) rightly note, bankers are not angels, and neither are bank regulators or members of Congress or cabinet secretaries. Bank managers often are willing to take advantage of stockholders or game the government safety net. Regulators are corruptible, particularly when they are threatened by superiors who encourage them to follow the path of least political resistance. Politicians will pressure banks to make unprofitable loans and will be too generous in their construction of bank safety nets because constituencies reward them for doing so.

Successful bank regulation takes into account these human failings and devises mechanisms that succeed reasonably well in spite of them. The trick in regulatory reform is to use the public outrage during a moment of crisis as an opportunity to pass robust reforms that will work after the crisis is over and the threats of political influence, safety nets, and managerial agency have returned. That is not easy, but experience and empirical evidence suggest that some solutions to these problems are more successful than others.

In the remainder of this essay, I review several ideas for regulatory reform that are desirable not only because they make sense technically as ways to measure and manage risk, but also because they affect the incentives of bankers and bank regulators; in other words, because they are relatively robust to the government policy problems and human failings at the heart of the subprime crisis. This is not an exhaustive review of financial regulation or even banking regulation. My focus is on the structure and content of bank prudential regulation, with an emphasis on how to structure regulatory mechanisms that would improve the effectiveness of the measurement and management of risk in the banking system.

I review six categories of policy reform that would address weaknesses of the policy environment that gave rise to the subprime crisis, including those reviewed above. These six areas are (1) smarter "micro prudential" regulation of banks, (2) new ideas for "macro prudential" regulation of bank capital and liquidity standards, (3) the creation of detailed, regularly updated, prepackaged "bridge bank" plans for large, complex financial organizations, (4) reforms to eliminate the distortions in housing finance induced by government policies that encourage high risk and leveraging, (5) reforms that would improve stockholder discipline of banks, and (6) initiatives to encourage greater transparency in derivatives transactions.

Making Micro Prudential Capital Regulation Smarter

Prudential capital regulation refers to regulations that try to measure bank risk and budget capital (equity plus other capital accounts) accordingly to protect against potential loss related to that risk. *Micro prudential capital regulation* refers to setting capital based on analysis of the circumstances of the individual institution. Below I also consider *macro prudential regulation*, which refers to the variation over time in the minimum amounts of capital, liquidity, and provisioning for loss required of banks that occurs as a function of the macroeconomic state of the economy.

The two key challenges in micro prudential capital regulation are (1) finding ways to measure accurately the value and riskiness of different assets and (2) ensuring speedy intervention to prevent losses from growing once banks become severely undercapitalized. These are not just technical issues. Banks, supervisors, regulators, and politicians often have incentives to understate losses and risks and to avoid timely intervention. Timely intervention is crucial, however. If subprime risk had been correctly identified in 2005, the run-up in subprime lending in 2006 and 2007 could have been avoided; banks would have had to budget much more capital against those positions, which would have discouraged continuing growth in subprime lending. Furthermore, banks that have experienced large losses often have incentives to increase their risk further, since they have little of their own capital left to lose; that go-for-broke "resurrection" risk taking can only be prevented by regulators if they identify and intervene in severely undercapitalized banks in a timely manner.

How can regulation ensure accurate and timely information about the value and riskiness of assets? The key problem with the current system of measuring asset values and risks is that it depends on bank reporting, supervisors' observations, and rating agencies' opinions. None of those three parties has a strong interest in correct and timely measurement of asset value and risk. Furthermore, even if supervisors were extremely diligent in their effort to measure value and risk accurately, how could they successfully defend low valuations or high estimates of risk that were entirely the result of the application of their models and judgment?

The essence of the solution to this problem is to bring objective information from the market into the regulatory process and to bring outside (market) sources of discipline in debt markets to bear in penalizing bank risk taking. These approaches have been tried with success outside the United States, and they have often worked. With respect to bringing market information to bear in measuring risk, one approach to measuring the risk of a loan is to use the interest rate paid on a loan as an index of its risk. Higher-risk loans tend to pay higher interest. Argentine bank capital standards introduced this approach successfully in the 1990s by setting capital requirements on loans using loan interest rates (Calomiris and Powell 2002). If that had been done with high-interest subprime loans, the capital requirements on those loans would have been much higher.

Another complementary measure would be to require banks to issue some form of credibly uninsured debt. Forcing banks to access uninsured debt markets forces them to meet an external source of market discipline, which means that they have a strong incentive to satisfy market concerns about the value and riskiness of their assets. Furthermore, the interest rates paid on at-risk debts provide valuable information about market perceptions of bank risk (a proverbial canary in the coal mine), which would be immune to manipulation by bankers, supervisors, regulators, or politicians.

Segoviano (2008) shows that the spreads on bank credit default swaps (CDSs) contained very informative market opinions about differences in risk across banks in 2008 and about the mutual dependence among large banks with respect to risk. That experience is not unusual; a large body of evidence supports the efficacy of using market information and discipline to measure and control bank risk. The evidence of the effectiveness of this approach spans many countries and comes from historical as well as current examples.

The Gramm-Leach-Bliley Act of 1999 required the Fed and Treasury to consider that approach in the form of a subordinated debt requirement. A Fed report (Board of Governors 1999) showed that substantial research favored this approach, but lobbying from the big banks to avoid discipline encouraged Treasury Secretary Lawrence Summers and Fed Chairman Alan Greenspan to kill this promising idea. Now is the time to bring this idea back by requiring banks to offer credibly uninsured debt instruments as part of their capital structure. A variety of possible instruments could be required to provide market information about risk and market discipline. The Shadow Financial Regulatory Committee (2000) offered a blueprint of how to structure the rules surrounding a minimum subordinated debt requirement. That proposal, which was written prior to development of the CDS market, could provide a useful alternative to subordinated debt in the form of the market pricing of credit risk insurance. Flannery (2009) discusses the potential advantages of contingent capital certificates (CCCs)—debts that convert to equity when banks suffer sufficient portfolio losses—rather than straight subordinated debt for this purpose; Flannery argues that CCCs might work better than subordinated debt as a source of information about risk and a form of market discipline, given the greater potential for rapid loss on CCCs when losses become large.

Finally, with respect to the use of credit-rating agencies' opinions to measure the riskiness of assets held in bank portfolios, given the low likelihood that regulators will be willing to eliminate entirely the use of ratings in favor of reliance on market opinions, there is a second-best alternative reform. Ratings used for regulatory purposes should be provided in numerical form, not as letter grades. Letter grades as forward-looking opinions have no objective meaning that can be evaluated and penalized for inaccuracy after the fact. But numerical estimates of the probability of default (PD) and loss given default (LGD) do have objective, measurable meanings. Rating agencies that provide ratings used by regulators (the so-called nationally recognized statistical rating organizations, NRSROs) should have to provide specific estimates of the PD and LGD for any rated instrument, not just a letter grade.

Rating agencies already calculate and report such statistics retrospectively on instruments that they rate, and presumably their letter grades are meant to translate into forward-looking predictions of these numbers. But requiring NRSROs to express ratings using numbers would alter their incentives to rate risk either too high or too low. If NRSROs were penalized for underestimating risk (say, with a six-month "sit out" from having their ratings used for regulatory purposes), they would have a strong self-interest in estimating risk correctly, since the reduced demand for their services during the sit out would reduce their fee income. It would be easy to devise an algorithm for such a sit out: if an NRSRO's estimates of either the PD or the LGD are sufficiently low relative to actual experience for a sufficiently long time, they would be punished with a six-month sit out.

Another proposal for making micro prudential regulation smarter would be to raise regulatory requirements for organizations that are large and highly complex. This policy could take the form of a higher capital requirement, a higher provisioning requirement, or a higher liquidity requirement. The argument in favor of such a policy is that, in the presence of the too-big-to-fail problem, large, complex banks are (1) less likely to manage risk properly and (2) more likely to create problems for the financial system if they become undercapitalized. Forcing them to maintain higher capital, greater liquidity, or both would offset some of the social costs associated with their decision to become too big to fail.

These proposed reforms to micro prudential regulation could be extremely helpful, but by themselves they are insufficient. Recent experience has shown that even honest market opinions and bona fide credit ratings vary in quality over time, and regulatory surcharges for large banks probably would not have deterred the credit boom of 2002–07. During the subprime boom, especially given the agency problems in asset management that accompanied the policy-induced bubble, risk was underestimated in the market across-the-board. Micro prudential rules that rely on signals from the market will not work adequately when distortionary policies promote the systemic underestimation of risk in debt markets. Recognizing that limitation to micro prudential regulation is the primary motivation for adopting additional reforms, including a relatively new idea in financial regulation known as macro prudential policy.

Macro Prudential Regulation Triggers

Macro prudential regulation means varying the key parameters of prudential regulation (capital requirements, liquidity requirements, and provisioning policies) according to macroeconomic circumstances. That variation takes two forms: (1) normal cyclical variation in minimum capital requirements as part of countercyclical economic policy and (2) special triggers for increased prudential requirements when asset bubbles seem to be occurring.

The first of these ideas reflects the long-standing recognition that minimum capital requirements that are constant throughout the business cycle are procyclical in their effects: recessions produce bank loan losses, which reduce capital, which forces banks to shrink their lending, which deepens recessions. Repullo and Suárez (2008) simulate bank capital and asset decisions in a model of dynamically optimizing banks under the Basel standards and show that the standards induce substantial procyclicality of credit supply. Adding a simple leverage limit (like the one that already exists as an additional capital requirement in the United States) reduces the procyclicality of credit somewhat, but the best approach is to vary prudential regulation over the business cycle so that capital, reserve, and provisioning standards are loosened a bit at the onset of recessionary shocks. To maintain the adequacy of those requirements during recessions, therefore, one would have to raise minimum capital requirements during boom times, probably substantially above the current minimum capital requirements that apply under either the Basel standards or the U.S. leverage standard.

The second macro prudential idea—increasing capital requirements by more than normal during boom times when the boom also coincides with a high degree of financial vulnerability, as during an asset bubble—has been a topic of debate for the past decade. It reflects the commonly held view that both the pre-2001 Internet bubble and the pre-2007 subprime bubble (and the related phenomena that occurred in parallel outside the United States) could have been avoided if policy makers had leaned against the wind to prevent the bubbles from inflating.

Before embracing that idea, however, advocates of macro prudential regulation must be able to answer three questions: (1) Why should prudential regulation, rather than monetary policy, be the tool used to lean against the wind during bubbles? (2) Is it feasible to identify bubbles in real time and to vary prudential requirements to respond to them? (3) What are the potential costs of implementing such an approach?

In answer to the first question, the Fed and other central banks already have their hands full using one tool (the short-term interest rate controlled by the central bank) to hit two targets (low inflation and full employment). Adding a third target to monetary policy (namely, identifying and deflating asset bubbles) would be undesirable because it would complicate and undermine the ability to use interest rates to meet the key goals of monetary policy. This distraction would also make it harder to hold central banks to account for achieving low inflation and high employment: if we try to incorporate secondary objectives into interest rate policy, we may give central banks an excuse for failing to meet their primary objectives.

Furthermore, prudential regulation is ideally suited to addressing asset market bubbles, since loose credit supply has been so closely identified historically with the growth of asset bubbles. Prudential regulations would clearly succeed in reducing the supply of credit by tightening capital, liquidity, and provisioning requirements, and this is the most direct and promising approach to attacking the problem of a building asset price bubble, assuming that one can be identified.

How good are we at identifying bubbles in real time? Is it realistic to think that policy makers can identify a bubble quickly enough and adjust prudential regulations in a timely manner to mitigate the bubble and increase the resilience of the banking system in dealing with the consequences of its bursting? Recent research and experience are encouraging in this respect. Borio and Drehmann (2008) develop a practical approach to identifying ex ante signals of bubbles that policy makers could use to vary prudential regulations in a timely way in reaction to the beginning of a bubble. They find that moments of high credit growth that coincide with either unusually rapid stock market appreciation or unusually rapid house price appreciation are followed by unusually severe recessions. A signaling model that identifies bubbles in this way (that is, as moments in which both credit growth is rapid and one or both key asset price indicators is rising rapidly) would have allowed policy makers to prevent some of the worst boom-and-bust cycles in the recent experience of developed countries. They find that the signal-to-noise ratio of their model is high; adjusting prudential rules in response to a signal indicating the presence of a bubble would miss few bubbles and only rarely signal a bubble in the absence of one.

Recent experience by policy makers has also been encouraging. Spain (the thought leader in the advocacy of macro prudential regulation) displayed success in leaning against the wind recently by establishing provisioning rules that are linked to aggregate credit growth. Colombia was successful in applying a similar approach in 2007 and 2008 (Uribe 2008). Financial system loans in Colombia grew from a 10 percent annual rate as of December 2005 to a 27 percent rate as of December 26. Core growth of the consumer price index rose from 3.5 percent in April 2006 to 4.8 percent in April 2007, real GDP grew 8 percent in 2007, and the current account deficit doubled as a percentage of GDP from the second half of 2006 to the first half of 2007, rising from 1.8 to 3.6 percent of GDP. That credit boom occurred in spite of attempts by the central bank to use interest rate policy to lean against the wind; interest rates were raised beginning in April 2006 and by mid-2008 had been raised a total of 4 percentage points. In 2008 the central bank and the bank superintendency took a different tack, raising reserve requirements and provisioning requirements on loans and imposing other rules to limit borrowing from abroad. The banking system's risk-weighted capital ratio rose to 13.9 percent, and credit growth fell to 13 percent in 2008. Colombian authorities are now basking in praise for having reduced credit growth and strengthened their banks' capital positions in a manner that will substantially mitigate the backlash suffered by Colombian banks from the global financial collapse.

Macro prudential regulation could use a variety of warning signs as triggers for higher regulatory standards. Rather than simply focusing on credit growth, Borio and Drehmann (2008) suggest that a combination of credit growth and asset price appreciation may be optimal. Brunnermeier and his co-authors (2009) argue for the desirability of including measures of systemic leverage and maturity structure.

What economic costs would be associated with adopting macro prudential triggers to combat asset bubbles? Presumably, the main costs would result from false positives (that is, the social costs associated with credit slowdowns and capital raising by banks during periods identified as bubbles that are in fact not bubbles). These costs, however, are likely to be small. If a bank believes that extraordinary growth is based in fundamentals rather than a bubble, then that bank can raise capital in support of continuing loan expansion (in fact, banks have done so during booms in the past). The cost to banks of raising a bit more capital during expansions is relatively small; those costs consist primarily of adverse-selection costs (reflected in fees to investment banks and underpricing of shares), which tend to be small during asset price booms. Indeed, some researchers argue that "hot" markets tend to produce overpriced equity, meaning that banks might enjoy negative costs (positive benefits) of raising capital during such periods.

Most important, macro prudential triggers would promote procyclical equity ratios for banks, which would mitigate the agency and moral hazard problems that encourage banks to increase leverage during booms. Adrian and Shin (2008) show that, during the subprime boom, commercial banks and (even more so) investment banks substantially raised their leverage (which was permitted because regulatory capital standards underestimated their asset risk).

Prior to the establishment of government safety nets and other policies noted earlier, banks behaved differently. Calomiris and Wilson (2004) show that during the boom era of the 1920s, New York City banks expanded their lending dramatically, and their loan-to-asset ratios also rose as the banks actively promoted the growth in economic activity and stock prices during the 1920s. But the banks also recognized the rising risk of their assets and made adjustments accordingly. Rising asset risk led the banks to substantially raise their equity capital. New York banks went to the equity market frequently in the 1920s and on average increased their market ratio of equity to assets from 14 percent in 1920 to 28 percent in 1928. Virtually no New York City banks failed during the Great Depression. In a sense, the primary goal of macro prudential regulation is to restore the natural procyclical tendency of bank equity ratios, which has been discouraged by government policies that removed market constraints and incentives and thus deterred banks from budgeting higher capital during booms.

Prepackaged "Bridge Bank" Plans for Large, Complex Banks

The too-big-to-fail problem can only be addressed adequately if regulators and bankers alike believe that regulators will be willing and able to intervene and resolve undercapitalized large, complex banks in a timely fashion. The United States established prompt corrective action guidelines in the 1991 FDICIA legislation, which was meant to constrain regulatory discretion about intervention and resolution, avoid regulatory forbearance, and ensure rapid action by regulators. And the United States has established a bridge bank structure that can be applied to speed the resolution of banks that are taken over by regulatory authorities (Herring 2009). Despite these actions, however, none of the large U.S. banks that became undercapitalized during the recent crisis has been resolved through such a structure.

The only way that prompt corrective action can be credibly applied to large, complex banks is if the social costs of intervening in those banks are considered sufficiently low at the time intervention is called for; otherwise, political and economic considerations will prevent intervention. To that end, commercial banks should be required to maintain updated and detailed plans for their own resolution, with specific predefined loss-sharing formulas that can be applied across subsidiaries within an institution operating across national borders. Those loss-sharing formulas must be preapproved by the regulators in the countries where those subsidiaries operate. The existence of such a prepackaged plan would make intervention and resolution credible.

Requiring detailed and credible prepackaged, preapproved resolution plans would have ex ante and ex post benefits for the financial system. Ex ante, it would make large, complex banks more careful in managing their affairs and internalize the costs of the complexity within those organizations. In other words, because complexity and its risks are hard to manage, planning the resolution of large, complex institutions is harder and more costly. If the institutions are forced to plan their resolutions credibly in advance, and if it is very costly for them to do so, then they may appropriately decide to be less complex and smaller. Ex post, changes in the control over distressed banks would occur with minimal disruption to other financial firms, and because financial problems could be resolved more quickly, managerial incompetence would be corrected more speedily, and "resurrection risk taking" would be avoided.

Reforming Housing Finance

The United States has made access to affordable housing a centerpiece of government policy for generations. The philosophy behind this idea is that homeowners have a stake in their community and in their society and thus make better citizens. The argument may have merit, and the costs of promoting access to housing (especially the cost from crowding out of non-housing investments) may be warranted. But highly leveraged homeowners (for example, those borrowing 97 percent of the value of their home using an FHA guarantee) have little stake in their home; indeed, it might be more accurate to refer to them as homeowners in name, but renters in reality.

The key error in U.S. housing policy has been the use of leverage subsidies as the means used by which the government encourages homeownership. Prospective homeowners are helped by the government only if they (or their lending institution) are looking for cheap credit, and the size of the subsidy they receive is proportional to their willingness to borrow. FHA guarantees, Federal Home Loan advances, and government guarantees of GSE debts all operate via leverage.

These subsidies are delivered in an inefficient and distorting manner. Subsidizing the GSEs has been inefficient, since much of the government subsidy has accrued to GSE stockholders; only a portion has been passed on to homeowners in the form of lower interest rates on mortgages. Leverage subsidies also distort bank and borrower decisions by encouraging them to expose themselves and the financial system to too much risk related to movements in interest rates and changes in housing prices. It is remarkable to think that the U.S. financial system was brought to its knees by small declines in average U.S. housing prices, which would have had little effect if housing leverage had been maintained at reasonable levels.[3]

The GSEs, which are now in conservatorship, should be wound down as soon as possible, and the FHA and Federal Home Loan banks should be phased out. In their place, the United States could establish an affordable housing program that assists first-time homeowners with their down payment (for example, offering people with low income a lump-sum subsidy to apply toward their down payment).

Improving Bank Stockholder Discipline

Sweeping changes should be made to the regulation of bank stockholders. As described above, current regulations almost guarantee that large banks will be owned by a fragmented group of shareholders who cannot rein in managers, thus encouraging managers to use the banks to feather their own

---

3 The most popular measure of house prices, the Case-Shiller index, substantially overstates the decline in house prices due to regional bias and selectivity bias in the measurement of price change, as discussed in Calomiris (2008b). Average house prices in the United States, properly measured, declined from their peak by less than 10 percent as of the end of 2008.

nests. That agency problem not only produces significant ongoing waste within banks, but also makes the allocation of capital in the economy inefficient. Banks are supposed to act as the brain of the economy, but they will not do so if their incentives are distorted by managers in pursuit of ends other than maximum value for their shareholders. And, in the presence of circumstances conducive to bubbles, as we have seen recently, incentive problems can translate into systemic crises with deep costs, including interruptions in the normal flow of credit, widespread job losses, and destruction of wealth throughout the economy.

A first-best solution would be outright repeal, or at least a significant relaxation, of the Bank Holding Company Act restrictions on ownership of banks, along with removal of other restrictions that make it hard for stockholders to discipline managers (ceilings on institutional investors' holdings and the Williams Act). These reforms seem unlikely to be enacted at the present time. In the presence of continuing distortions related to corporate governance, bank stockholders, who should be the first line of defense against unwise risk taking by bank management, are unable to exert much of a role. That implies even more of a burden on regulators to implement reforms in micro and macro prudential regulation as well as resolution policies that limit the social costs associated with banking crises.

Transparency in Derivatives Transactions

The growth of over-the-counter (OTC) transactions in recent years has raised new challenges for prudential regulation. OTC transactions are not always cleared through a clearinghouse. Counterparty risk in transactions that do not involve a clearinghouse is borne bilaterally by contracting parties, and the true counterparty risk can be hard to measure, because the aggregate amount of transactions and the net amount of transaction exposure of any one counterparty are not known to the other counterparties. This problem is magnified by the "daisy chain" effect. If A is a counterparty of B, and C is a counterparty of B, then the counterparty risk that A bears in its dealings with B is partly the result of the counterparty risk that B bears in its dealings with C, which is unobservable to A.

The lack of transparency about counterparty risk not only creates risk management problems for banks but also complicates the regulatory process. Regulators are not able to monitor or control individual institution risk (via micro prudential rules) or aggregate risk (via macro prudential rules) if they cannot observe risk accurately. Furthermore, since the counterparty risks in OTC transactions are especially great for large, complex banks, the opacity of those risks aggravates the too-big-to-fail problem. Large, complex banks may even have incentives to undertake more hard-to-observe risk precisely because its complexity and opacity help to insulate them from intervention.

How should prudential regulatory policy respond to this problem? Regulators need to address two separate issues: encouraging clearing and encouraging disclosure. Policy reforms related to clearing mainly address the problem of counterparty risk opacity. Policy reforms related to disclosure mainly address the problem of monitoring and controlling the net risk positions of individual banks and the systemic consequences of those positions.

With respect to clearing, one option for dealing with systemic consequences of opacity in counterparty risk would be to require all derivatives contracts to be cleared through a clearinghouse. This is not the same as requiring all transactions to be *traded* on an exchange. Some OTC derivatives are cleared in clearinghouses even though they are not traded on the exchanges affiliated with those clearinghouses. When clearing through the clearinghouse, counterparty risk is no longer bilateral; rather it is transferred to the clearinghouse, which effectively stands in the middle of all transactions as a counterparty and thereby eliminates the problem of measuring counterparty risk or having to worry about "daisy chain" effects relating to it. Of course, relying on clearinghouses to centralize counterparty risk requires faith in the efficacy of the self-regulatory rules that ensure the stability of the clearinghouse (for example, margin requirements), but the self-regulatory record has been exceptionally good to date.

The problem with requiring all OTC transactions to clear through a clearinghouse is that this may not be practical for the most customized OTC contracts. A better approach would be to attach a regulatory cost to OTC contracts that do not clear through the clearinghouse (in the form of a higher capital or liquidity requirement). This would serve to encourage, but not require, clearing through a clearinghouse. For contracts where the social benefits of customization are high, fees will compensate banks for the higher regulatory costs of bilateral clearing.

With respect to disclosure, one option would be to require all derivatives positions to be publicly disclosed in a timely manner. Such a policy, however, has undesirable consequences. Bankers who trade in derivatives believe that disclosing their derivatives positions could place them at a strategic disadvantage with respect to others in the market and might even reduce aggregate market liquidity. For example, if Bank A had to announce that it had just undertaken a large long position in the dollar-yen contract, other participants might expect that it would be laying off that risk in the future, which could lead to a decline in the supply of long positions in the market and a marked change in the price that would clear the market. A better approach to enhancing disclosure, therefore, would be to require timely disclosure of positions only to the regulator and to require public disclosures of net positions with a lag.

Conclusions

This essay has reviewed the major government policy distortions that gave rise to the subprime turmoil and suggested robust policy reforms to deal with them (that is, reforms that take into account the existence of those distortions and the political economy of regulation and supervision). The proposed reforms would reduce the costs of distortions related to agency problems, too-big-to-fail problems, and government manipulation of housing credit markets.

Proposed reforms fall into six areas: (1) micro prudential regulation, (2) macro prudential regulation, (3) the creation of credible plans for resolving large, complex banks, (4) the reform of housing policy to eliminate leverage subsidies as the means of promoting homeownership, (5) the removal of barriers to stockholder discipline of bank management, and (6) policies that promote improvements in counterparty risk management and transparency in OTC positions.

The following summarizes the 12 policy reforms proposed in this essay:

1. The use of loan interest rates in measuring the risk weights applied to loans for purposes of setting minimum capital requirements on those loans
2. The establishment of a minimum uninsured debt requirement in addition to other capital requirements for large banks; the specific form of this requirement requires further discussion (candidates include a specially designed class of subordinated debt, CDS issues, or contingent capital certificates)
3. The reform of the use of credit-rating agencies' opinions either to eliminate their use or to require that NRSROs offer numerical predictions of PD and LGD, rather than letter grade ratings, and be held accountable for the accuracy of those ratings
4. A regulatory surcharge (which takes the form of higher required capital, higher required liquidity, or more aggressive provisioning) on large, complex banks
5. Macro prudential regulation that raises capital requirements during normal times in order to lower them during recessions
6. Additional macro prudential regulatory triggers that increase regulatory requirements for capital, liquidity, or provisioning as a function of credit growth, asset price growth, and possibly other macroeconomic risk measures
7. Detailed and regularly updated plans for the intervention and resolution of all large, complex banks, prepared by these banks, that specify how control of the bank's operations would be transferred to a prepackaged bridge bank if the bank became severely undercapitalized; these plans would also specify formulas for sharing losses among international subsidiaries of the institution, and the algorithm specifying those loss-sharing arrangements would be preapproved by the relevant regulators in countries where the subsidiaries are located
8. The winding down of Fannie Mae and Freddie Mac, the phasing out of the FHA and Federal Home Loan banks, and the replacement of those leverage subsidies with down payment assistance to low-income, first-time home buyers
9. The elimination of bank holding company restrictions on the accumulation of controlling interests in banks

10. The relaxation of Williams Act requirements that buyers of more than a 5 percent interest in a company must announce that they are acquiring a significant interest in a company and the elimination of regulatory limits on the percentage interest that institutional investors can own in public companies

11. The enactment of regulatory surcharges (via capital, liquidity, or provisioning requirements) that encourage the clearing of OTC transactions through clearinghouses

12. Requirements for timely disclosure of OTC positions to regulators and lagged public disclosure of net positions.

References

Adrian, Tobias, and Hyun Song Shin. 2008. "Financial Intermediaries, Financial Stability, and Monetary Policy." Paper prepared for the economic policy symposium, "Maintaining Stability in a Changing Financial System," Federal Reserve Bank of Kansas City, Jackson Hole, WY. August 21–23.

Barth, James R., Gerard Caprio Jr., and Ross Levine. 2006. *Rethinking Bank Regulation till Angels Govern.* Cambridge, U.K.: Cambridge University Press.

Board of Governors of the Federal Reserve System. 1999. "Using Subordinated Debt as an Instrument of Market Discipline." Staff Study 172 (December). Board of Governors of the Federal Reserve System, Washington, DC.

Borio, Claudio, and Mathias Drehmann. 2008. "Towards an Operational Framework for Financial Stability: 'Fuzzy' Measurement and Its Consequences." BIS Working Paper (November). Bank for International Settlements, Basel.

Brunnermeier, Markus, Andrew Crocket, Charles Goodhart, Avinash D. Persaud, and Hyun Shin. 2009. "The Fundamental Principles of Financial Regulation." Geneva Reports on the World Economy 11 (preliminary conference draft). International Center for Monetary and Banking Studies, Geneva.

Calomiris, Charles W. 2007. "Victorian Perspectives on Modern Banking Crises." Working Paper. Columbia Business School, New York.

———. 2008a. "Statement before the Committee on Oversight and Government Reform, United States House of Representatives." U.S. House of Representatives, Washington, DC. December 9.

———. 2008b. "The Subprime Turmoil: What's Old, What's New, and What's Next." Paper prepared for the economic policy symposium, "Maintaining Stability in a Changing Financial System," Federal Reserve Bank of Kansas City, Jackson Hole, WY. August 21–23.

Calomiris, Charles W., and Joseph R. Mason. 2004. "Credit Card Securitization and Regulatory Arbitrage." *Journal of Financial Services Research* 26 (1): 5–27.

Calomiris, Charles W., and Andrew Powell. 2002. "Can Emerging Market Bank Regulators Establish Credible Discipline? The Case of Argentina, 1992–99." In *Prudential Supervision: What Works and What Doesn't*, ed. Frederic S. Mishkin, 147–96. Chicago: University of Chicago Press.

Calomiris, Charles W., and Peter J. Wallison. 2008. "The Last Trillion-Dollar Commitment: The Destruction of Fannie Mae and Freddie Mac." AEI

Financial Services Outlook (September). American Enterprise Institute, Washington, DC.

Calomiris, Charles W., and Berry Wilson. 2004. "Bank Capital and Portfolio Management: The 1930s' Capital Crunch and Scramble to Shed Risk." *Journal of Business* 77 (3): 421–55.

Eisenbeis, Robert A. 2008. "Financial Turmoil and Central Bank Responses: US, UK, EU, Japan, and Others." Paper presented at the Brookings-Tokyo Club, Wharton conference, "Prudent Lending Restored: Securitization after the 2007 Mortgage Securities Meltdown," Brookings Institution, Washington, DC. October 16.

Flannery, Mark. 2009. "Market Discipline in Bank Supervision." *Oxford Handbook of Banking,* ed. Allen Berger, Phil Molyneux, and John Wilson. Oxford Handbook in Finance. Oxford: Oxford University Press.

Gorton, Gary. 2009. "Information, Liquidity, and the (Ongoing) Panic of 2007." NBER Working Paper 14649 (January). National Bureau of Economic Research, Cambridge, MA.

Herring, Richard. 2009. "Resolution Strategies: Challenges Posed by Systemically Important Financial Institutions." Paper presented at the Financial System Regulatory Summit, Federal Reserve Bank of Philadelphia. January 29.

Pinto, Edward J. 2009. "Statement before the Committee on Oversight and Government Reform, United States House of Representatives." U.S. House of Representatives, Washington, DC. December 9, 2008.

Repullo, Rafael, and Javier Suárez. 2008. "The Procyclical Effects of Basel II." Paper presented at the Ninth Jacques Polak Annual Research Conference, International Monetary Fund, Washington, DC. November.

Segoviano, Miguel. 2008. "Macroeconomic Stress Testing, Systemic Risk, and Banking Stability Measures." IMF Working Paper (November). International Monetary Fund, Washington, DC.

Shadow Financial Regulatory Committee. 2000. *Reforming Bank Capital Regulation: A Proposal by the U.S. Shadow Financial Regulatory Committee.* Washington, DC: American Enterprise Institute Press.

Stern, Gary H., and Ron J. Feldman. 2004. *Too Big to Fail: The Hazards of Bank Bailouts.* Washington, DC: Brookings Institution Press.

Uribe, José Darío. 2008. "Financial Risk Management in Emerging Countries: The Case of Colombia." Paper presented at the twelfth annual conference of the Central Bank of Chile, November.

CHAPTER 4
Financial Crisis and Global Governance: A Network Analysis

Andrew Sheng

This chapter attempts to use network theory, drawn from recent work in sociology, engineering, and biological systems, to suggest that the current crisis should be viewed as a network crisis. Global financial markets act as complex, scale-free, evolving networks that possess key characteristics requiring network management if they are to function with stability.[1]

The current global financial crisis has elicited several excellent studies and reviews at the regulatory and policy levels.[2] While these studies contribute much to analyses of the multiple causes of the crisis, no unifying framework explains the behavioral characteristics of the market and policy makers that led to the crisis.

The widespread use of communication and computer technology in the last 30 years gave rise to increasing awareness that networks play a major

The author is grateful to all workshop participants, especially Michael Spence, for helpful comments and insights. Dr. Cheng Jiuyan and Ms. Wang Ting of Tsinghua University and Ms. Zhang Jingchun of China Banking Regulatory Commission, Beijing, helped with research assistance.

1 *Scale free* means that the connectivity of nodes is not random, but exhibits power law characteristics. The term was coined by Barabási (2003).
2 See Brunnermeier and others (2009); Commission of Experts (2009); de Larosiere (2009); Group of Thirty (2009); Turner (2009).

role in the growth of financial markets. For example, Metcalfe's law was a widely believed hypothesis that the value of networks was proportional to the square of the number of connected users of the system, n (Shapiro and Varian 1999). The law gave competitors in the financial system a profit- and growth-driven rationale to integrate hitherto segmented markets and products, such as banking, insurance, fund management, and capital markets. In the 1990s, the trend accelerated as financial deregulation permitted banks, insurance companies, securities houses, and funds to merge or form holding companies in a drive to become giant "financial Wal-Marts," offering one-stop financial services to the consumer and investor.

In a seminal work, *The Rise of the Network Society,* Manuel Castells characterizes society in the information age as a set of global "networks of capital, management, and information, whose access to technological know-how is at the roots of productivity and competitiveness" (Castells 1996: 471). By the time of the 1997–98 Asian financial crisis, there was increasing awareness of the high degree of contagion among not just banks, but also whole financial systems and the complex interlinkages at the trade and financial levels (Sheng 2009a). By the turn of the twenty-first century, network models have become increasingly accepted as useful analytical tools in computer and information systems, cellular telephone networks, and the Internet.

The collapse of Lehman Brothers on September 15, 2008, signified that the nature of modern financial crisis is unprecedented in its complexity, depth, speed of contagion and transmission, and scale of loss. Early papers have been written on the network nature of the crisis, because without an understanding of the nature of the crisis, regulatory and policy solutions will be flawed (see Sheng 2005, 2009c; Haldane 2009).

There is general agreement that this particular financial crisis was unusual due to its intense complexity (Caballero and Simsek 2009), not just the elaborate interconnectivity of markets and counterparties, but also the almost incomprehensibility of the financial derivatives where almost no one, not even the issuer or major market maker, had a complete picture of the toxicity. Each participant deluded himself that his risks were hedged through various derivative instruments, when in reality the quality of such instruments was highly suspect and in many cases added to risks. When the environment becomes too complex, market participants do not understand the complete picture and unexpected events create confusion, leading to panic and flight to quality.

What we need is a framework to simplify the understanding of such complex markets, in which the interaction between market participants operating under asymmetric information is dynamic, but not always stable. Such a framework needs to deal not only with a systemwide perspective, but also with the vulnerabilities at the detail level (the weakest link). We need to recognize that the network analysis does not have predictive capacity, although it is useful in laying out an organizational framework to decipher current behavior, revealing, it is hoped, our lack of appreciation of the problems of externalities, wrong incentives, weak structures, and flawed processes. Its major insight is that the process of change is nonlinear, interactive, interconnected, and the outcome of experimentation, accident, or manipulation by participants, which include financial institutions, investors, regulators, and policy makers.

The chapter is organized as follows. After this brief introduction, the chapter surveys the concepts of networks, their defining characteristics, applications to financial markets, and the need for supervision and implications for national and global governance; briefly examines the current financial crisis in the light of network analysis; and surveys the recent reforms in financial regulation and architecture. It concludes with an analysis of the policy implications of network analysis.

Understanding Financial Networks

Networks can be a very useful representation of complex financial systems (Allen and Babus 2008). Since networks of relationships come in all shapes, sizes, and forms, there is no single network or framework to encompass all applications.

Generally speaking, a network describes a collection of nodes and the links between them. In a network, the key elements are the nodes or players and links. Nodes involved in networks can be called "vertices," "individuals," "agents," or "players," depending on the setting. In the real world, the nodes can be individual people, financial firms, countries, or other organizations; a node can even be a Web page belonging to a person or an organization. The minute a node connects or links with another node, a network is formed.[3]

Nodes link with each other for a common purpose or use in which mutual benefit is derived. In this simple construction, human society is a network whereby citizens join together for common purpose, such as mutual support, security, and economies of scale. Once networks are formed, some nodes are better connected to others because of their superior benefits to users, and these are generally described as "hubs."

For example, a bank is a hub that connects with its customers in providing payment and credit services. A central bank is a hub of bank hubs, where the commercial banks settle their interbank transactions on a final basis. A stock exchange is a trading, clearing, and settlement hub between stockbrokers (nodes) who are, in turn, linked to their own network of customers. We can see from this simple model of financial systems that the same retail customer can be linked to different banks, brokers, or insurance companies through different products. This means that networks exhibit a high degree of interdependence, with both direct and indirect connections between financial institutions and counterparties.

---

3   A useful survey of work on networks can be found in Jackson (2008). Other recent books include Barabási (2003) and Newman, Barabási, and Watts (2006).

Characteristics of Networks

Like all organizations or social systems, networks have certain characteristics, such as architecture or structure, common purposes or objectives, values, standards, incentives, and processes. However, how different networks link or interact with each other can lead to collective action decisions or outcomes that involve conflict, negotiation, cooperation, payoffs, and different games and strategies that result in totally uncharted situations. The insight to note is that nodes or hubs are always "gaming" with each other across the network and that the global financial market is a network of constantly changing networks.

There are two types of networks: networks of informal human relationships and networks of formal organizational structures and platforms. The web-like structure of networks is the formal framework discussed here, but often it is the human networks that control or drive formal institutions.[4] Networks are almost Darwinian in evolution, but at the same time, it is not clear why some networks survive, some thrive, and some wither and disappear.

First, a network is a set of interconnected nodes that have architecture. It can be a network of individuals, firms, and institutions (market participants) connected in order to exchange information, products, and services or to reduce risks. The goals and purposes could be complex, but common values, rules, processes, codes, or standards generally facilitate interconnectivity and interoperability and therefore bring benefits of collective action, economies of scale, lower transaction costs, and lower risks. Specifically, common standards, such as language, enable more efficient communication and lower transaction or friction costs. The more widely used a common standard, the greater the network.

Network architecture is essentially a tradeoff between efficiency and robustness or stability. There are three basic network topologies: the star or centralized network, the decentralized network, and the distributed network, with the star system being most efficient, as there is only one hub, but the most vulnerable in the event that the central hub fails (see figure 4.1). The widely distributed network, such as the Internet, is much more resilient to viruses and hacker attacks because of multiple hubs, where links can be shut down, bypassed, and repaired without damaging the whole system, even if a collection of important hubs is destroyed. The self-organizing behavior of the Web ensures its own survival, and it has no single architect.

Transaction costs are lowered in a star network because linkage is through one central hub, with that hub enforcing standards and protecting property rights for links. Despite its efficiency, the star topology is fragile in the event that the single hub is destroyed by accident, disaster, or competition. Competition between hubs for links or users actually results in different types of architecture as well as different benefits and costs to users.

---

4   I am grateful to Dr. Venu Reddy for pointing out this difference. The Chinese call informal network relationships "guanxi," or connections.

Figure 4.1. Network Topology: Tradeoff between Efficiency and Robustness

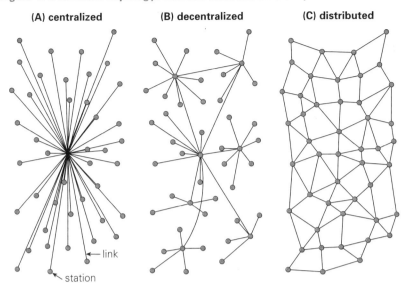

Source: Baran (1964), reproduced in Barabási (2003: 145, fig. 11.1).

Second, nodes do not connect with each other at random. If Metcalfe's law is to be believed, each hub will try to increase the number of connections or users in order to increase its own value. Network scientist Albert-László Barabási has called the competition between nodes for links their fitness. Whether a node decides to link with another node is what Barabási calls preferential attachment, the deciding factor being the cost of communication. The scale-free topology and preferential attachment are the explanatory factors driving the creation of the Internet, whereby Google, Yahoo, and other Web sites compete for more links in order to enhance their own value and the value to their users. In order to attract more nodes, the hub would have to offer more "free goods" than competitors through the principle of "the more you give, the more you receive," or what I call the network altruism principle. This explains the "loss leader" sales attraction in supermarkets and the way Google offers free Web addresses and superior search services in order to gather the most users.

Third, hubs and clusters are efficient, because the shortest route between two distant nodes may be through a hub. In social networks, this is popularly known as the six degrees of separation, as distant contacts can connect usually through at least six well-networked persons. The more the efficient hubs cluster together and share and exchange information, the greater the network externality, as each node benefits from higher efficiency in accessing information and knowledge and can cooperate to produce greater output (Economides 1993). This is known as the cluster effect of knowledge hubs. Economies of scale increase with clusters and critical mass, but mostly because production and distribution processes (including exchange of information and decision making) occur at faster speed, enabling faster decision making and less expensive transactions.

Fourth, preferential attachment and network externalities taken together explain why a "winner takes all" situation is common to networks. The hubs compete with each other until one or several leading hubs emerge to dominate activities. In other words, networks exhibit power law characteristics. Globally, more than two-thirds of financial information is distributed through two major information networks (Reuters and Bloomberg). Similarly, airline bookings are through two major reservation or airline alliances (Star Alliance and One World). More than 80 percent of global credit card business goes through Visa, MasterCard, or American Express.

This "rich get richer" aspect of networks can be seen in the way that markets have become more and more concentrated, with a small number of big players dominating the business and a large number of small players feeling marginalized. For example, there were 100 or so stock exchanges in the United States during the nineteenth century. With the arrival of the telegraph and now the Internet, the global equity market trading is essentially dominated by two dominant exchanges, the New York Stock Exchange/Euronext and Nasdaq/Open Market Exchange. Physicists have also noted that the appearance of power laws often signals a transition from disorder to order (Barabási 2003: 72).

According to this network perspective, the United States is today the super hub of global financial markets, with the U.S. dollar as the dominant currency. The second major hub is the London market, which shares the common-law background and English language advantage, plus London's historical, political, and economic ties with Europe and the rest of the world. Hence, between London and New York, where most of the wholesale banks, investment houses, and asset management funds are operationally located, the two financial centers may account for more than half of global market transactions.

An important study commissioned by the National Research Council (National Academy of Sciences) and the Federal Reserve Bank of New York found that the Fedwire interbank payment network, which transacts $1.2 trillion daily, has 66 banks accounting for 75 percent of daily value, with 25 banks completely connected (Kambhu, Weidman, and Krishnan 2007, quoted in May, Levin, and Sugihara 2008).

Fifth, networks are scale free and not static, because each hub continually seeks to increase its links through its own competition or cooperation strategy. The nodes of a scale-free network are not randomly or evenly connected. Scale-free networks include many "very connected" nodes, hubs of connectivity that shape the way the network operates. The ratio of very connected nodes to the number of nodes in the rest of the network remains constant as the network changes in size. If one hub becomes dominant, the smaller hubs can cooperate or ally with other hubs to compete with the dominant hub. At the local level, some networks can become dominant by imposing control over their links through enforcement of rules or standards. As there is no universal law, there is no single architect for the global network of markets. The world is always evolving through continuous competition between different hubs arising from innovation, technology, and even random events. Just as there are competing standards, there are competing values and competing networks. Networks are therefore path dependent, because they emerge from different social, historical, and political environments.

Sixth, since markets are by their nature competitive, they adapt and evolve around their environment. A body of work by Andrew Lo, professor at the Massachusetts Institute of Technology, and others contends that financial markets are adaptive and evolutionary through competition, adaptation, and natural selection (Lo 2004, 2005). Markets operate through four key types of arbitrage: cost arbitrage, information arbitrage, taxation arbitrage, and regulatory or governance arbitrage. Markets simply shift to areas with the lowest transaction costs. In local markets, if there are obstacles to growth, the market simply moves offshore, which is why we have witnessed the rapid growth of offshore financial centers relative to onshore financial markets. Markets are, by their competitive nature, pluralistic, disciplined, and adaptive, with good feedback mechanisms (Kay 2003).

Once we begin to look at markets as networks through either engineering or sociological perspectives, we move outside classical economics into the realm of political and institutional dynamics. Competitive behavior and the use of common standards and rules often lead to procyclical behavior, particularly since interactions between different market participants with different information and values carry significant leads and lags. Networks therefore have inherent feedback mechanisms that are sometimes stable and sometimes violently destabilizing.

Applying Network Theory to Financial Markets and Institutions

The above insights have powerful implications for the way we look at financial markets and institutions (Sheng 2005). The decision tree of multiple network games fans out into complex areas, some of which may be dead ends and some may open up new avenues of opportunity. Every now and again, the system may experience a crisis.

We can see that financial markets evolve through the innovation of specific products and standards that improve their "preferential attachment," attract more users, and therefore dominate other networks. These networks develop externalities through common standards, processes, and infrastructure that generate positive economies of scale that attract links to other networks.

In other words, domestic markets are networks of different networks, and property rights are cleared in hubs called exchanges and clearinghouses and protected through courts and regulatory agencies. Of course, property rights can also be protected through self-regulatory or collective behavior.

The global market is a network of local networks, in which the weakest link is possibly the weakest node, link, cluster, hub, or local network. We do not know why or where the system is weak until it is subject to stress. Hence, we need to look at global financial stability holistically or throughout the whole network to identify the weakest links.

In sum, the network perspective forces us to look at the issues more forensically, within the total context and a longer time frame. We must stress test not just the nodes and hubs, but also the crucial linkages that could bring about the vulnerabilities. We have to trace the roots of problems to their source.

Network Characteristics of the Current Global Crisis

Globalization has networked together hitherto highly localized financial markets, and a series of historical events and macro trends created the conditions that led to the current crisis.

First, the global imbalance, which led to excessive liquidity that generated excessive credit and leverage, was due to the decline in the U.S. saving rate and U.S. dependence on external resources. Indeed, the U.S. banking system evolved from a traditional retail banking system to a highly leveraged wholesale banking system funded largely through the securitization of assets to facilitate growth of the global imbalance.

In surplus economies, such as Japan, inappropriate policies led to asset bubbles in the 1990s that created post-bubble loose monetary policy to combat the resultant deflation. Low interest rates encouraged growth of the leveraged carry trade and, given disparities in national interest rates and exchange rates, gave rise to large capital flows. The Asian crisis of 1997–98 and the 2000 dot-com bubble were all consequences of excessive leverage, large capital flows, loose monetary policy, and lax financial regulation.

Second, the fall of the Berlin Wall led to the arrival of cheap labor from the former centrally planned economies, which created low inflation and boosted global trade and economic growth.

Third, global trade and finance were encouraged through the massive deregulation in tariffs and capital controls. The age of deregulation, which was intellectually bound in free-market fundamentalist philosophy, allowed the huge regulatory arbitrage in accounting, tax, and regulatory standards that created the rise of "shadow banking." Innovation through financial engineering gave rise to new financial instruments and derivative products, ostensibly to hedge risks, but inadvertently allowed the creation of embedded leverage and huge systemic risks.

Fourth, financial engineering and globalization could not have happened without massive improvements in information and communication technology. The speed and complexity of innovation dazzled policy makers and central bankers, who believed that the growth in prosperity was due to improved productivity, improved risk management, and successful monetary policy skills. In hindsight, prosperity was created largely as a result of leverage.

In short, the four global mega trends of wage, interest rate, knowledge, and regulatory arbitrage gave rise to the four excesses of liquidity, leverage, risk taking, and greed.

Fundamentally, the U.S. economy went into unsustainable deficits, and its subprime mortgage market was the basis for financial leverage and engineering that ultimately financed consumer expenditure in excess of capacity. The reversal of the housing bubble and problems in the subprime mortgage market were the triggers that pricked the U.S. bubble in 2007.

Viewing the global financial market as a network of national networks highlights several significant network features of the present crisis:

- The network architecture played a role in determining its fragility or vulnerability to crises. Network concentration created a number of large, complex financial institutions that dominate global trading and are larger than even national economies. However, they are regulated by an obsolete regulatory structure that is fragmented into national segments and further compartmentalized into department silos, none of which has a systemwide view of the network that allows the identification of systemwide risks.
- Increasing complexity of networks is related to their fragility. Complexity is also positively correlated with the externalities of network behavior, and few regulators understood or were able to measure these externalities.
- The high degree of interconnectivity drove the value as well as the risks of hubs or financial institutions. The failure of one hub, such as Lehman Brothers, revealed interconnections that were not apparent to regulators, such as the impact on American International Group (AIG) and, through AIG, on the solvency of banks and investments.
- Networks have negative and positive feedback mechanisms due to the interactivity between players and between hubs and nodes as they compete. The regulators assumed that only negative feedback was prevalent, so that markets would return to equilibrium. Instead, the markets had positive feedback because of momentum trading and rules or codes that embed procyclicality features.
- There was no lack of information or transparency, but too much information was not understandable.
- Regulators ignored the distorted incentive structures that promoted risk taking, and regulators failed to minimize moral hazard, even though there were clear lessons from earlier financial crises.
- The roles and responsibilities for network governance were not allocated clearly. In the absence of a single global financial regulator, effective enforcement of regulation across a global network requires complex cooperation between different regulators. How do we avoid regulatory competition and a "race to the bottom"?

Systemwide View of Networks

There is now consensus that the primary problem of the current global financial architecture is that it is global in terms of transactions, but national in terms of legislation and supervision. As Bank of England Governor Mervyn King (2009) vividly expressed, "Global banking institutions are global in life, but national in death." This is the inherent problem of a global architecture that is regulated in national silos. Worse, the regulation of financial activities even within a nation can be segmented into so many departments that regulatory arbitrage is a major game for financial institutions. The fact that AIG Financial Products, the subsidiary of AIG most responsible for its losses, was regulated by the Office of Thrift Supervision, which had little comparative advantage in regulating such complex derivatives, is a classic example of regulatory arbitrage.

Financial markets have become highly integrated, but financial regulation remains largely compartmentalized into separate jurisdictions. The result is that no one body is responsible or accountable for the whole system. Each agency—the central bank, the financial regulator (irrespective of whether it is a super regulator or multiple regulators), and the ministry of finance—felt that the root problems and solutions might be outside their own jurisdiction.

Hence, the Group of Thirty (2009: 8) was correct in its Core Recommendation I: "Gaps and weaknesses in the coverage of prudential regulation and supervision must be eliminated. All systemically significant financial institutions, regardless of type, must be subject to an appropriate degree of prudential oversight."

There is also recognition that current regulatory competition engenders a "race to the bottom," as each financial regulator deregulates for fear of business drifting to underregulated or unregulated financial centers.

To avoid this race to the bottom, there should be coherent, appropriate oversight of all financial institutions, markets, and activities, consistent with their risks; gaps and underregulated areas should be avoided. However, to do this, one needs a comprehensive regulatory system that has universal coverage and is, at the same time, effective and legitimate. In other words, we need an effective system of global financial regulation that fairly allocates gains and losses of financial activities.

We are unable to arrive at a global financial regulator for two important reasons. First, there is no fiscal mechanism to allocate or distribute losses arising from uniform monetary and financial policies or to obtain taxation to do so. No sovereign country is willing to cede fiscal and monetary sovereignty to a global financial authority. Second, no independent global judiciary can arbitrate property rights disputes over such loss allocation, particularly in the bankruptcy of global financial institutions.

The only regional body that seems able to move in that direction is the European Union (EU), partly because it is both a political and a monetary union with European laws and an institutional framework for allocating gains and losses. Even in the EU, the allocation of fiscal and bank rescue costs is controversial, and, in the short run, the costs are still paid for largely at the national level.

This inability to arrive at a global financial regulator contrasts with the global trade system, whereby the World Trade Organization (WTO) is able to enforce trade disputes through a system approved by treaty. Perhaps the fundamental reason for this difference is that the benefits of free trade are obvious, as were the mistakes of trade protectionist action during the 1930s. However, since the services trade is historically more protected at the national level and the concentration of financial services skills is predominantly Anglo-Saxon, some countries are reluctant to open up to free trade in financial services. Even WTO members accept the general argument that countries can impose prudential rules in financial services, provided they are not discriminatory to foreign players. It is likely that no global financial regulator will evolve unless the costs of the current crisis or future financial crises are so large as to force national authorities to cede their sovereign powers to a global body.

Complexity

Their scale-free and gaming nature suggests that networks inherently grow more and more complex. What is the motivation behind the growing complexity?

The two core issues of all institutions are the principal-agent problem and information asymmetry. There is inherent inequality in all societies and economies because of an unequal endowment of knowledge and access to information. However, increasing complexity is the tool by which the agent can take advantage of the principal. The greater the information asymmetry or complexity, the greater the ability of the agent to cheat the principal and the weaker is the agent's accountability.

Hence, the current incentive structure within financial institutions (read financial engineers) is to make situations more complex, because the higher the "knowledge premium," the more they profit at the expense of the principal (read investors and regulators). The financial engineers persuaded the investors and the regulators that their models were hedging and managing the risks, whereas in reality, the higher profits from the complex derivatives were derived from higher levels of embedded leverage. Unfortunately, the regulatory system failed to conduct sufficient due diligence on behalf of the principal, the public at-large.

The conclusion from this analysis is that we cannot solve a crisis by adding complexity; instead, we should try to resolve it by identifying and simplifying "coarse" rules and enforcing these rigorously. As hedge fund risk manager Richard Bookstaber (2007) pointed out in his congressional testimony, "If the potential for systemic risk stems from market complexity, adding layers of regulation might actually make matters worse by increasing the overall complexity of the financial system."

Externalities

The Geneva report on the fundamental principles of financial regulation correctly identifies that financial regulation is justified "where there are sufficient externalities that the social, and overall, costs of market failure exceed both the private costs of failure and the extra costs of regulation" (Brunnermeier and others 2009: 2). The report argues that the two risk-spillover externalities are fire-sale externalities and interconnectedness externalities. The fire-sale externality arises since each individual financial institution does not take into account the impact that its own fire sales will have on asset prices in a possible future liquidity crunch. The second negative externality is the fact that financial institutions have become so interconnected that they become not just "too big to fail," but "too interconnected to fail," creating the moral hazard that they will be bailed out in times of crisis.

The reality is that through implicit deposit insurance, the current system subsidizes institutions that cause negative externalities for others. Micro behavior of excessive risk taking has wide systemic risks.

In an important study of complex systems with reference to banking, diverse researchers from oceanography, biology, and zoology bring parallels from the ecological system to the study of banking. May, Levin, and Sugihara (2008) observe that "tipping points," "thresholds," and "breakpoints" describe the flip of a complex dynamic system from one seemingly stable state to an unstable lower-level state. They lament the fact that very little is spent on studying systemic risk as compared with what is spent on managing conventional risk in individual firms, but the costs of a systemic risk event for a national or global economy are huge.

There are three possible reasons why systemic risk was overlooked. The first is sheer ignorance. Private sector participants may simply have had no idea that what they were doing carried huge social costs. The second is that they could have been aware of the social costs, but were not able to measure such externalities and assumed that these would be taken care of by the regulators or the government. This is classic moral hazard behavior. The third is that since financial regulators allowed the financial innovation or financial engineering that created the massive leverage without testing or verifying the possible social costs, they inadvertently permitted the moral hazard to reach crisis levels.

Unfortunately, the inherent nature of externalities is that it is almost impossible for an individual firm to calculate the extent of the spillover externality and even the interconnectedness externalities. This requires information and expectations about the future that are highly subjective and most likely to be wrong. Indeed, this would be a highly contentious area of financial regulation. Until disaster happens, private sector participants would argue vehemently that regulatory costs or restrictions to limit these two externalities are too high in (a) preventing financial innovation and (b) overestimating the costs of failure. Regulatory arbitrage and competition between financial centers would inevitably shift the transactions to another "user-friendly" center until the collective action becomes a race to the bottom.

Indeed, one defense for why financial regulators allowed such financial innovation without detailed due diligence (like the U.S. Food and Drug Administration in approving new drugs) was that the externalities were outside their experience. Until the current crisis, financial engineering appeared to distribute risks outside the banking system, and respected leaders such as Alan Greenspan repeatedly affirmed this untested belief.

Interconnectivity

Interconnectivity between institutions, markets, and systems lies in the spillover or externalities inherent in products, institutions, and activities. Network interconnectivity occurs not simply through mutually exclusive channels, but through highly complex interrelationships that are not always fully understood or observable.

Economic historian Michael Bordo (2001) correctly points out that contagion between two or more nodes should be termed transmission, noting, "In the golden age, financial crises were transmitted across the world through the links of the fixed exchange rate gold standard."

How is loss or fear of loss transmitted and spread throughout the network? German economist Friedrich Sell (2001) was the first to integrate notions of contagion in epidemiology and financial markets. He drew the parallel between the spread of an epidemic to contagion in financial markets (see figure 4.2). In epidemiology, disease is transmitted when the reproductive rate of a virus reaches a critical mass and more and more humans are infected. However, humans also develop immunity until at some stage most humans become immune to the disease. The pandemic process is similar to a decision tree in game theory.

Loss can cascade throughout the (financial market) network like a pandemic, because the failure (or loss) in one node causes losses in other nodes through its links. Loss-avoidance behavior therefore can result in panic as the losses spread throughout the network.

Figure 4.2. Expansion Process of an Epidemic

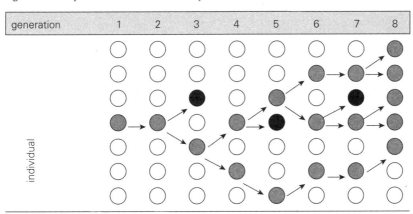

Source: Sell 2001.

This cascading impact of loss-avoidance behavior was noted by a 2007 research study initiated by the National Research Council (National Academy of Sciences) and the Federal Reserve Bank of New York on systemic risk (Kambhu, Weidman, and Krishnan 2007): "Market-based systemic crises are often characterized by a coordination failure: a wide cross section of market participants simultaneously decide to reduce risk taking and effectively refrain from financial activities, such as trading stocks, issuing debt and equity, and lending."

Interconnectivity means that the regulator as well as the financial institution would need to have radically different management information systems (MISs) that can detect connections and risks that are not apparent from current MIS models. For example, most banks do not have very good information on the links of their counterparties, especially whether different counterparties are either affiliated or interconnected in different manners.

Interactivity of Feedback Loops in Networks

Interactivity means the continuous interaction and games being played between different market participants and between the private sector and the regulators and policy makers. The dynamic gaming leads to outcomes that are not always predictable, in the same way that action by regulators may suffer from the law of unintended consequences. A common fallacy among market participants is that the action of a single market player has no consequence for the market as a whole. In practice, this is often not true, as even very small-value transactions in a thinly traded market could have dramatic influence on price volatility.

Interactivity, or the gaming in the network, leads to feedback loops, which in turn explain the inherent procyclicality of financial markets. Feedback mechanisms exist because of information asymmetry, leads and lags in behavior between transactors in a network transaction, and differences in transaction costs. The prevailing efficient-market hypothesis assumes that markets will occasionally diverge, but eventually return to equilibrium, in what engineers recognize as *negative* feedback—volatility recedes back to the mean (Umpleby 2009).

Experienced fund manager George Soros has argued that financial markets also have *positive* feedback, through what he calls reflexivity (Soros 1998). As market activity gathers momentum, information bias and herd behavior occur and drive the market in larger and larger oscillations, causing a wrecking ball effect, with volatility and movements becoming larger and larger until the system crashes.

The real concern of regulators is not whether such procyclicality exists, but whether tools exist to dampen or stop the damage from such procyclicality and *when* the regulator should intervene.

How to deal with procyclicality boils down to three choices. The first and noncontroversial issue is to remove procyclical elements within the existing rules and standards, such as mark-to-market accounting, the Basel Capital Accords, and dynamic loan-provisioning requirements.

The regulatory community has agreed to this action after the horse has bolted out of the stable.

The second is to construct rules that guide regulators on when to act anticyclically. For example, Goodhart and Persaud recommend that capital be increased after assessment of risks using a few simple, transparent rules (Brunnermeier and others 2009). The Bank of Spain uses dynamic provisioning rules as risks escalate. Regulators like to use such rules to avoid taking personal responsibility for making judgments on when and how to take anticyclical action. Hence, rule-based decision making is fine if the markets behave according to the rules, but in the complex, interactive, and interconnected world, the evidence to support such decision-making rules may not be clear cut, and regulators and policy makers must make informed judgments on the balance of risks and whether or not to take anticyclical action.

The third choice is to recognize that the only way to break out of the classic paralysis of collective action is for individual leaders to be willing to take tough action, even though the evidence may not be complete. In essence, to quote former Fed chairman William McChesney Martin, one has to be willing to take personal responsibility for "taking away the punch bowl when the party gets interesting."

Transparency and Information Overload

Transparency refers to a process by which information about existing conditions, decisions, and actions is made accessible, visible, and understandable to market participants. The strange thing about this current crisis is that it happened in full transparency and in front of everyone. The reforms made after the Asian and dot-com crises made more information accessible and visible, with major reforms in accounting and corporate disclosure. Currently, full risk warning and information are disclosed on the Web sites of Lehman's, AIG, the Federal Reserve, the Bank of England, the European Central Bank, and the International Monetary Fund, but the crisis still happened.

Everyone also agrees that the roots of the crisis are so complicated that almost no one understood where to begin to stop it. The problem was not a lack of information, but too much information that was not understandable. The financial derivatives such as collateralized debt obligations (CDOs), credit default swaps (CDSs), and conduits were so complicated that investors, the originating and selling banks, and their financial regulators did not understand their complexity and toxicity. Would more rules on transparency help? I doubt it.

In practice, transparency has become a game of information overload so that the receiver is misled or does not want to admit that he either does not understand or does not know what to do with most of the information. With the legal requirement to have full disclosure, the system was "gamed" by companies and financial institutions supported by their expensive lawyers learning how to disclose so much information and risks that they are responsible for nothing when anything goes wrong. The truth is buried in fine print, but only if you know how to find it. The law was satisfied under "legal transparency," but ultimately society as a whole paid the price.

This is where the governance structure is critical. The onus should be on boards of directors of financial institutions to understand or demand from management the information needed to assess risks, including systemic and concentration risks. If the board is made fully accountable for the identification and disclosure of such risks, then action will be taken to undertake the due diligence needed to understand where the true risks are. Consequently, the board must question thoroughly: if profits are too good to be true, then they are too good to be true.

Hence, one area of reform is that instead of making a complex system more complex, we should try to make it more simple and understandable. Even 2,500 years ago, the Chinese legalist philosophers and bureaucrats understood that laws should be made simple, easy to understand, easy to learn, and easy to implement and enforce.

Incentives

There is consensus that the primary incentive for excessive risk taking in the financial community was a management compensation scheme that rewarded short-term risk taking and ignored future costs or losses. Rewarding bank management and hedge fund managers with hefty bonuses and options based on short-term risk taking pushed the financial sector toward processes and standards that tried to take profits upfront, without measuring the inherent long-term risks.

A slew of market practices mutually reinforced the path to crises. The application of fair-value accounting and use of models to measure the value of financial derivative products resulted in future profits being measured on discounted present-value terms, while ignoring (difficult-to-measure) future costs and disexternalities. The lower the level of interest rates due to loose monetary policy and high liquidity from the global imbalance, the higher the price of these leveraged products. Since these products were marked either to market or to models, unrealized capital gains were taken to profits without considering the sustainability of such high profits or the possibility of a sharp reversal due to crowded trades or market illiquidity. Needless to say, the higher the recorded profits, the higher the bonuses.

Thus leverage was built into the behavior of bankers, without the financial regulators appreciating that the growing derivative trade and valuation were a castle built on sand.

Although it was widely acknowledged in the academic community after the Asian crisis that moral hazard is the most dangerous incentive in a system where the state stands to guarantee (implicitly or explicitly) the financial system, most regulators took little action against moral hazard until it surfaced in the Northern Rock runs in 2007. Why was there little appreciation that the higher the inherent leverage in the financial system, especially in the financial derivative business, the greater the moral hazard?

A possible explanation lies in the failure of financial regulators to appreciate the enormous risks inherent in financial markets in what can be called the Soros asymmetry of risks. Soros's insight, used to explain why credit default swaps are dangerous and should be banned, can be generalized for the asymmetry of risks in all financial products. The first step is to recognize that "there is an asymmetry between long or short in the stock market ... going long has unlimited potential on the upside, but limited exposure on the downside. Being short is the reverse. The asymmetry manifests itself in the following way: Losing on a long position reduces one's exposure, while losing on a short position increases it" (Soros 2009: 166).

In other words, given the high degree of leverage in the system, the systemic risks were nonlinear and exponential. Since the financial regulators could not agree on a simple measure of overall leverage and allowed banks to use internally rated models to measure their own risks and therefore capital needs, the embedded leverage increased sharply. The total leverage of the global financial system (using the notional value of financial derivatives) could be as much as 14 times GDP, compared to current upper limits of traditional leverage (measured as banking asset, stock market capitalization, and debt market value) of roughly five times GDP (Sheng 2009b: 331). Including below-the-line liabilities, the fact that the five U.S. investment banks at the end of 2007 were leveraged 88 times capital meant that the moral hazard was extremely high.

The second step is to recognize that "the CDS market offers a convenient way of shorting bonds. In that market, the risk-reward asymmetry works in opposite ways to stocks. Going short bonds by buying a CDS contract carries limited risk but unlimited profit potential; by contrast, selling CDSs offers limited profits but practically unlimited risks" (Soros 2009: 166). Selling CDSs to the market ultimately was AIG's fatal mistake.

Soros goes one further. "The third step is to take into account reflexivity and recognize that the mispricing of financial instruments can affect the fundamentals that market prices are supposed to reflect. ... This means that bear raids on financial institutions can be self-validating, which is in direct contradiction to the efficient market hypothesis" (Soros 2009: 167).

If I interpret Soros correctly, the combination of Soros asymmetry of risks, moral hazard, and reflexivity created a self-fulfilling situation in which financial institutions became more and more leveraged until their own speculators collapsed the system through bear raids.

During the 1997–98 Asian crisis, several central banks that had insufficient foreign exchange reserves to rescue their domestic banks or corporations that were grossly overextended in foreign exchange and maturity mismatches became vulnerable to bear raids on their currencies. The collapse of the currencies brought the economies to low-level equilibrium situations that took many years to recover from.

We should, therefore, pay more attention to why there were no incentives for regulators and policy makers to act anticyclically more effectively and forcefully.

Recent debate in the United Kingdom suggests that there should be an independent body (a financial policy committee) responsible for macro prudential systemic financial stability, with the central bank being responsible for micro prudential regulation. Presumably, the independent body would strengthen the "trust but validate" function of external supervision, in contrast to the current "comply and explain" approach.

Division of Labor between Home and Host Regulators

The consensus that the scope of regulation should cover the whole perimeter of systemically important financial institutions and activities means that we have to define what is systemic and who should do what. The present crisis has demonstrated that risk concentrations can rapidly emerge from unregulated black holes or underregulated "shadow banking" areas where managers, regulators, and policy makers have little or no information on what is happening. Hence, there is general agreement that regulation should be made more consistent and that supervisory oversight and enforcement should converge toward international standards of best practices. This is more easily said than done.

First, what is not systemic in a mature market can be highly systemic in an emerging market. For example, a hedge fund that is not systemically important in a large, mature home market can indeed be very systemic in an emerging market, especially when it can act in concert with other hedge funds in the unregulated over-the-counter (OTC) market. The issue is not just about systemic size of trading or exposure, but also about misselling, market manipulation, insider dealing, and fraud.

Second, recent experience suggests that what was thought not to be systemic can rapidly evolve to become highly systemic. Indeed, few regulators were aware that the CDS market had such systemic implications for the health of the banking system and the liquidity of the asset-backed securities market. AIG had to be rescued in order to stem the systemic contagion if it failed.

Third, as long as a financial institution or activity is not supervised in its home territory, and in the absence of the cooperation and legal authority of the home authority, it would be impossible for the host authority to obtain the necessary information to assess systemic implications or to undertake investigation and enforcement, when trading activities can involve several markets and also OTC or unregulated markets. Without effective international cooperation, no host regulator can protect host-country investors and counterparties.

Fourth, the present memorandum of understanding between home and host regulators does not have sufficient legal standing or powers of mediation in the event of disagreements between home and host regulators.

Indeed, the questions raised by the de Larosiere report on important supervisory failures within the EU are directly applicable to the international arena (de Larosiere 2009: 39–41), including:

- Too much emphasis on supervision of individual firms and too little on the macro prudential side
- Ineffective early-warning mechanisms, especially no mechanisms to ensure that assessments of risks are translated into action
- Lack of competencies; the failure of oversight points to the need for well-staffed, experienced, and well-trained supervisors in all states
- Failure to challenge supervisory practices on a cross-border basis; there is no mechanism to enable host countries to challenge effectively the decisions of home regulators who failed to recognize risks
- Lack of frankness and cooperation between supervisors; supervisors in different states were not prepared to discuss with appropriate frankness and at an early stage the vulnerabilities of the financial institutions that they supervised
- Lack of consistent supervisory powers between member states; these differences, including differences in insolvency laws, would require changes in law
- No means for supervisors to take common decisions; this inability may be due to lack of legal powers to take decisions or inability to reach coordinated responses within nations and also with cross-border counterparties.

Conclusions and Policy Implications

At the Davos meeting on January 27, 2009, Forum Chairman Klaus Schwab argued, "What we are currently experiencing with the financial crisis and its consequences is the birth of a new era—a wake-up call to overhaul our institutions, our systems, and, above all, our thinking." I conclude by drawing some highly tentative observations on how the network framework can be used to improve financial sector governance.

First, appreciating the dynamics of market behavior suggests that too much stability or overregulation could breed complacency of market participants and, hence, a lack of immunity against market volatility. This calls for greater tolerance of risk and willingness to open markets gradually to stresses on a controlled basis. Gradualism seems preferable to "big bang" in raising system immunity. Opening up, or reforming in modular form or "chunks," seems a sensible and tested way forward.

Second, resilience of networks comes from openness to diversity and new ideas and technology. The resilience of networks is honed through actual market stresses, so that participants learn through their mistakes. In other words, immunity cannot be built up through protection. Taking an open-minded approach to market risk and trusting market participants to learn from their mistakes are more helpful than micro managing the intermediation process. Allowing more competition and diversity of products, institutions, and processes would avoid "monoculture" and therefore greater concentration and fragility.

Third, networks operate not only on interconnectivity and interactivity, but also on interdependence. Policy and outcomes in networks are not the responsibility of one person or institution, but the cooperative effort of multiple stakeholders. Cooperative efforts in network management and governance are a given. How we cooperate or deal with the consequences of lack of cooperation will shape network behavior or outcomes. The current outcome is a global tragedy of the commons, whereby lack of cooperation resulted in a race to the bottom and financial and ecological disasters.

Fourth, network perspectives suggest more caution on regulatory intervention. The self-organizing power of networks suggests that there is a basic instinct for survival and resilience. Banks engaging in derivative activities are engaging in risk diversification. Government intervention to rescue basically failed institutions may have much larger unintended consequences than we can imagine. The dilemma is that bad incentives, particularly moral hazard, are being entrenched, which explains why salaries in many rescued institutions have not declined as much as salaries in the real sector.

If complex networks cannot be disentangled or repaired overnight, not even at the national level, then it is quite realistic to assume that the global financial architecture will not reform so quickly or voluntarily. It will evolve from competition within the system.

The net conclusion is that there is unlikely to be a "big bang" in financial sector reforms, even as the current financial crisis evolves, until there is much better understanding of the causes and characteristics of the change in the ecology of financial markets. This suggests that a research agenda on network analysis could yield many fruitful insights on how to improve financial and global governance.

What are the implications of this brief survey of the network framework for the current global financial architecture and the direction of regulatory change? To recap, the network analysis views the global financial structure as a complex, evolutionary network of local networks, highly concentrated with power law distribution of transactions by value, highly interactive, and currently prone to financial instability due to volatile capital flows arising from structural imbalances and policy errors. Although the balance of economic power is changing from the rich to the emerging large countries such as China and India, the basic rules of the game have not changed. There is still considerable momentum to maintain the status quo, so that the inherent push by vested interests for asset bubbles and higher leverage remains intact.

We have to live with the reality that, unless the social losses are traumatic, the status quo will only change incrementally, not radically. Since the power centers, including large, complex financial institutions and other vested interests, are continually protecting their interests, it is unlikely that those in control will relinquish their powers voluntarily. Indeed, the European presence on the Financial Stability Board increased further with the addition of Spain and the European Commission, so that Europeans now account for six out of 20 members.

How would the network framework assist us in thinking about reforming the current global financial architecture? First, the network topology or structure matters. We need a systemwide view with a good understanding of the weakest links and risk concentrations. Given the inherent existence of power laws in networks, we have to recognize that networks are not equal and that increasing concentration through "too big to fail" or "too interconnected to fail" are real risks. We need to think more about bringing more competition and diversity into the global networks, in order to avoid oligopolistic behavior from preventing innovation and the tendency toward "monoculture." Avinash Persaud and others have pointed out how the use of uniform accounting standards (fair-value accounting) and similar models encouraged markets to move in one direction, thus adding to procyclicality. This is particularly evident when similar trading models, using basically similar information, create large herding effects, perpetuating momentum trading and self-fulfilling expectations.

Second, financial regulators should address the issue of *complexity* using different tools and techniques. I mention only two. As pioneered by J. Doyne Farmer (2001), Andrew Lo (Khandani and Lo 2007), May, Levin, and Sugihara (2008), and others, regulators should use more financial market modeling, looking at financial markets as dynamic, evolving, adaptive ecosystems that experience periods of instability, rather than as mean-reverting, stable systems that return to equilibrium. Systemwide modeling using balance sheets and flows would enable regulators and the market to understand better the stress levels and tolerable limits of leverage.

Regulators should use more forensic techniques, using cross-jurisdictional examinations of product trail on an "end-to-end" basis, looking at how financial products evolve from origination, trading, clearing, and settlement to distribution throughout the system. The audit trail should look at how each investor or intermediary manages its risks. This cross-sectional forensic study would yield much more industrywide information and behavioral patterns than the current emphasis on institution-based stress tests and examinations. Regulators must also have systemwide data on embedded leverage, by insisting that popularly traded products be cleared or registered on central clearing platforms. Financial regulators have to adopt the perspective of public health policy.

As a matter of regulatory philosophy, regulators must try to reduce complexity in the system, so that products, standards, and rules are easily understandable by all parties alike. However difficult the task, all rules and processes should be reduced to key principles and objectives, so that the rules can be interpreted against these fundamental principles. This calls for more judgment by both regulators and regulated alike.

In general, what regulators should appreciate is that mass behavior is influenced more by a few clear and simple rules, firmly enforced, than by multiple complex rules, lightly or underenforced.

Third, on the issue of interconnectivity, network engineers in information technology understand the importance of working in modules. Technological breakthroughs are generally achieved in modular form. Network reforms should divide the systems into modules, with relevant firewalls and risk controls, so that reforms can be achieved on a *modular* basis (Beinhocker 2007: 175). For example, interconnectivity and related leverage can be understood by building key settlement and clearing infrastructure on a modular basis, product-by-product, and by analyzing such data. Regulators spend too few resources mining the information at their command.

On the question of whether large, complex financial institutions are too large and complex because of their interconnectivity, the modular solution suggests that we should create firewalls between their key lines of business, so that the high-risk areas are segmented from the public utility part of banking business.

Fourth, the issue of interactivity or feedback mechanisms should be addressed by removing the procyclical bias in current standards and rules. There is now agreement on this move. However, regulators must be aware that what matters is the reflexive action of market participants to the perceived behavior of regulators themselves. If regulators tolerate risky behavior or do not firmly and decisively act to stop moral hazard behavior, then market participants will behave as if regulators permitted such behavior. In a sense, regulatory discipline through enforcement is the thin red line stopping excessive risk taking by market participants.

My personal opinion is that the attempt to go for clear-cut, transparent rules rather than discretion has gone too far. No rule is applicable for all time, given the interactive gaming of financial markets. The reality is that such rules require information that may not be available for clear decisions to be made. The risk of waiting for definitive evidence may mean that regulatory action is too little, too late. Regulators always have to make judgments based on partial or sometimes unreliable information. The community at-large must support independent regulators to make such informed judgments and accept the fact that sometimes those judgments are made on the risk-aversion side, since the costs of financial crises are unpredictable.

Fifth, on the incentive structure, the U.S. Congress has recently passed legislation to enable regulators to control or ban certain compensation arrangements for finance executives who are perceived to encourage excessive risk taking. There is strong resistance within Wall Street to cut bonuses and salaries on the assumption that financial skills are scarce and that to cut salaries would reduce financial sector performance. This argument is self-serving.

In my view, the level of bonuses and profits is derived not from the skills of these financial executives, but from the scale of leverage they embed in the system. Hence, if the regulation limits the level of leverage, the bonuses will be capped. This raises a fundamental question of whether the financial industry will forever grow faster and more profitable than the real sector. At the heart of the issue are the tolerable limits of leverage in the whole economy, at both the sectoral and the national levels. There is no fixed formula for the limits of leverage, but for each economy, and on a global level, there must be limits, which should be identified and strictly enforced.

In sum, it is hoped that the network framework will open up new avenues of research into the complexities of the financial sector and its links with the real economy.

Bibliography

Allen, Franklin, and Ana Babus. 2008. "Networks in Finance." Working Paper 08-07. Wharton Financial Institutions Center, University of Pennsylvania, Philadelphia.

Barabási, Albert-Laszlo. 2003. *Linked: How Everything Is Connected to Everything Else and What It Means to Business, Science, and Everyday Life*. New York: Plume Books.

Baran, Paul. 1964. *Introduction to Distributed Communications Networks*. RM-3420-PR. Santa Monica, CA: Rand Corporation. www.rand.org/publications/RM/baran.list.html.

Beinhocker, Eric D. 2007. *The Origin of Wealth: Evolution, Complexity, and the Radical Remaking of Economics*. Cambridge, MA: Harvard Business School Press.

Bookstaber, Richard. 2007. Testimony submitted to the House Financial Services Committee on Systemic Risks: Examining Regulators' Ability to Respond to Threats to the Financial System, Washington, DC. October 2.

Bordo, Michael D. 2001. "An Historical Perspective on the East Asian Crisis." In *The Political Economy of the East Asian Crisis: Tigers in Distress*, ed. Arvid Lukauskas and Francisco Rivera-Batiz. Cheltenham, U.K.: Edward Elgar.

Brunnermeier, Markus, Andrew Crockett, Charles Goodhart, Martin Hellwig, Avinash Persaud, and Hyun Shin. 2009. "The Fundamental Principles of Financial Regulation." Geneva Report on the World Economy 11 (January). International Center for Monetary and Banking Studies, Geneva; Centre for Economic Policy Research, London.

Caballero, Ricardo J., and Alp Simsek. 2009. "Complexity and Financial Panics." NBER Working Paper 14997 (May). National Bureau of Economic Research, Cambridge, MA.

Castells, Manuel. 1996. *The Rise of the Network Society, The Information Age: Economy, Society, and Culture*. Vol. 1. Oxford: Blackwell Publishers.

Commission of Experts of the President of the General Assembly. 2009. "Recommendations on Reforms of the International Monetary and Financial System." United Nations, New York. March 19. www.un.org/ga/president/63/letters/recommendationExperts200309.pdf.

de Larosiere, Jacques. 2009. "The High-Level Group on Financial Supervision in the EU." European Commission, Brussels. February 25. http://ec.europe .eu/internal_market/finances/docs/de_larosiere_report_en.pdf.

Economides, Nicholas. 1993. "Network Economics with Application to Finance." *Financial Markets, Institutions, and Instruments* 2 (5, December): 89–97.

Farmer, J. Doyne. 2001. "Toward Agent-Based Models for Investment." In *Benchmarks and Attribution Analysis*, 61–70. Charlottesville, VA: Association for Investment Management and Research.

Group of Thirty. 2009. *Report on Financial Reform.* New York: Group of Thirty (January). www.group30/pubs/reformreport.pdf.

Haldane, Andrew G. 2009. "Rethinking the Financial Network." Speech delivered at the Financial Student Association, Amsterdam. April.

Jackson, Matthew O. 2008. *Social and Economic Networks.* Princeton, NJ: Princeton University Press.

Kambhu, John, Scott Weidman, and Neel Krishnan, eds. 2007. *New Directions for Understanding Systemic Risk.* A Report on a Conference Cosponsored by the Federal Reserve Bank of New York and the National Academy of Sciences. Washington, DC: National Academies Press.

Kay, John. 2003. *The Truth about Markets.* London: Penguin.

Khandani, Amir E., and Andrew W. Lo. 2007. "What Happened to the Quants in August 2007?" *Journal of Investment Management* 5 (4, fourth quarter): 5–45.

King, Mervyn. 2009. Speech to British Bankers' Association, Mansion House, Bank of England, London. June 17.

Lo, Andrew. 2004. "The Adaptive Market Hypothesis: Market Efficiency from an Evolutionary Perspective." *Journal of Portfolio Management* 30 (August 15): 15–29.

———. 2005. "Reconciling Efficient Markets with Behavioral Finance: The Adaptive Market Hypothesis." Massachusetts Institute of Technology, Sloan School; National Bureau of Economic Research, Cambridge, MA.

May, Robert M., Simon A. Levin, and George Sugihara. 2008. "Ecology for Bankers." *Nature* 451 (21, February): 893–95.

Newman, Mark, Albert-László Barabási, and Duncan J. Watts. 2006. *The Structure and Dynamics of Networks.* Princeton, NJ: Princeton University Press.

Sell, Friedrich L. 2001. *Contagion in Financial Markets.* London: Edward Elgar.

Shapiro, Carl, and Hal R. Varian. 1999. *Information Rules: A Strategic Guide to the Network Economy.* Cambridge, MA: Harvard Business School Press.

Sheng, Andrew. 2005. "The Weakest Link: Financial Markets, Contagion, and Networks." Working Paper (December). Bank for International Settlements, Basel.

———. 2009a. "The First Network Crisis of the Twenty First Century: A Regulatory Post-Mortem." *Economic and Political Weekly*, India (special issue on global financial and economic crisis, March): 81–98.

———. 2009b. *From Asian to Global Financial Crisis: An Asian Regulator's View of Unfettered Finance in the 1990s and 2000s.* New York: Cambridge University Press.

———. 2009c. "From Asian to Global Financial Crisis: Third Lall Memorial Lecture." Indian Council for Research in International Economic Relations, New Delhi. February. www.icrier.res.

Soros, George. 1998. *The Crisis of Global Capitalism: Open Society Endangered.* New York: Public Affairs.

———. 2009. *The Crash of 2008 and What It Means: The New Paradigm for Financial Markets.* New York: Public Affairs.

Turner, Lord Adair. 2009. *The Turner Review: A Regulatory Response to the Global Banking Crisis.* London: Financial Services Authority (March). www.fsa.gov.uk/pubs/other/turner_review.pdf.

Umpleby, Stuart. 2009. "From Complexity to Reflexivity: The Next Step in the Systems Sciences." PowerPoint slides, George Washington University, Washington, DC. www.gwu.edu~umpleby.

Underhill, Geoffrey R. D. 2007. "Global Financial Architecture, Legitimacy, and Representation: Voice for Emerging Markets." Garnet Policy Brief (January). University of Amsterdam.

Williams, George M., Jr. 2008. *The Macroprudential Regulator: Modeling the Financial Network.* Research report for Alert, Dewey, & LeBoeuf LLP (September 11).

World Economic Forum. 2009. "The Global Agenda 2009." World Economic Forum, Geneva.

Xafa, Miranda. 2007. "Global Imbalances and Financial Stability." IMF Working Paper WP/07/111 (May). International Monetary Fund, Washington, DC.

CHAPTER 5
Understanding Global Imbalances
Richard N. Cooper

In this chapter, I want to cast doubt on two related propositions that are widely accepted as truths: Americans save too little, and the United States runs a current account deficit—$788 billion in 2006—that is unsustainable and risks precipitating a disorderly adjustment that would damage the world economy in the relatively near (usually unspecified) future. My doubts should not be considered as new truths, but as plausible alternative hypotheses about how the world works these days and how we reached such large global imbalances.

I begin with U.S. savings because it relates to the broader topic of global imbalances through the national accounts identity, which links the current account deficit to the difference between domestic investment and national savings. A current account deficit cannot be reduced without reducing the excess of investment over savings. Few argue that the United States should invest less (except perhaps in housing during the housing boom), which implies that if the U.S. current account deficit, nearly 6 percent of gross domestic product (GDP) in recent years, is to be reduced, national savings— the sum of private and public saving—must be increased. If, as some analysts

This chapter draws on Cooper (2007, 2008).

(for example, Cline 2005) suggest, the deficit should not exceed 3 percent of GDP and if investment is to be protected, savings must increase by 3 percent of GDP—that is, from 13 percent of GDP to 16 percent in terms of 2006 shares. (I use gross savings and investment throughout, as is appropriate in a world of rapid technological change. "Replacement" investment is typically technologically superior to its predecessor, and in any case a well-run firm will evaluate all large investments afresh, moving depreciation allowances into new activities if that is economically appropriate.)

Savings and investment in the national accounts, which were designed more than 60 years ago at the height of the industrial age, are defined largely in terms of structures and equipment (although computer software was recently added). This is hardly appropriate for a so-called knowledge economy. Economists conceive of savings as consumption that is deferred today for the sake of greater consumption at some time in the future, perhaps by oneself, perhaps by future generations. Using this definition of savings, several items should be added to the "saving" as currently recorded in the national accounts. An obvious list would include educational expenditures, expenditures on research and development, purchases of consumer durables, and "intangible" investment by businesses in research, training, and branding (following Carrado, Hulten, and Sichel 2006). Adding these items to savings and investment for 2005 raises those quantities from 13.5 and 20.1 percent of GDP as defined in the national accounts to 39 and 44 percent of augmented GDP (augmented by 15 percent to allow for the expanded concept of investment). These figures do not suggest that Americans are short-changing the future, particularly when allowance is made for the high returns to education and to research and development. Recent poll results notwithstanding, it is extremely improbable that future Americans will be materially worse off than the current generation. So far as I can tell, the pipeline of prospective innovations is full; we would have to have a severe catastrophe for these, and the associated investment, not to mature into higher per capita income, as they have steadily done during the past half century. Our biggest legacy to the next generation is our successful apparatus—both institutions and incentives—for innovation and technological change.

From the perspective of the household, allowance should also be made for capital gains on real and financial assets, which are increasingly mobilizable through innovations in financial markets such as home equity loans and reverse mortgages, and for expected legacies. Unlike new investment, these do not add to social returns in the future (although some part of capital gains on equities may reflect the intangible investments made by corporations), but they are legitimately "savings" from the household's perspective. Household net worth rose by 6.5 percent a year over the period 1990–2005 and by 8 percent in 2005 alone—a year, recall, that recorded headline-grabbing news regarding negative personal savings in the national accounts.

Of course, these are aggregate figures; they do not address the issue of distribution. There are doubtless many families who would be well advised to save more in their own interests. Moreover, household net worth fell in 2008, with the decline in the price of houses and many financial assets. But that is presumably a transitory phenomenon.

What about global imbalances? The revised calculations of savings and investment do not affect the discrepancy between them, since savings and investment are raised by the same amount. They are meant to suggest, rather, that it will be difficult, if not impossible, to raise U.S. national savings further, except through the federal budget. Private saving may rise of its own accord as house prices decline or even stabilize for any length of time, but households are not likely to be receptive to significant reductions in their consumption over the long term.

Can a current account balance in excess of $700 billion a year, more than 5 percent of GDP, be sustained? The answer from a technical economic point of view (as distinguished from psychological or political perspectives, which are not addressed here) is an unambiguous affirmative. Some argue that it is large without precedent and into the "danger range" of developing countries that have in the past run into payments crises. Some argue that it cannot be sustained either because foreigners will cease to be willing to invest enough in the United States or because the United States will run out of assets attractive to foreigners or both. Some concede that it might be sustainable at its current high level, but that the growth trend cannot be sustained. Some judge it to be undesirable, not least on grounds that it permits higher current consumption but bequeaths higher liabilities to future generations. Whether it is desirable or not depends, of course, on the feasible alternatives, not on abstract considerations.

In this section I address quantitatively two issues: whether foreign savings will be adequate to finance a continuing and even rising U.S. deficit and whether U.S. financial claims will be sufficient to satisfy potential foreign demand for them. I also address foreign motivation to invest in the United States.

A U.S. current account deficit (which equals net foreign investment in the United States) of $788 billion in 2006 is certainly unprecedentedly large. But it is smaller than the deficit that would have resulted if world financial markets had been fully globalized. By full globalization of financial markets we mean that savers around the world allocate their savings according to the relative size of national economies, without any bias toward domestic investments. Such a "gravity model" for world financial flows is, of course, a vast simplification, but it is a useful starting point.

The U.S. share of the world economy (calculated at market exchange rates) was 30 percent in 2000, rising slightly in 2001–02 and then declining to 27.5 percent in 2006. With no home bias, the rest of the world would have invested these shares of their savings in the United States. Americans, by the same token, would have invested 70 percent of their savings in the rest of the world in 2000, rising to 72.5 percent in 2006. Applying these percentages to savings (from the national accounts) in the rest of the world and the United States, respectively, would have resulted in net foreign investment of $480 billion in the United States in 2000, compared with an actual flow of $417 billion, rising to $1.2 trillion in 2006, compared with an actual flow of $788 billion. This number can be expected to rise over time, until the slow decline in U.S. share fully offsets the rise in foreign saving or until U.S. saving rises sufficiently sharply to overcome the annual increases in foreign saving.

This calculation takes gross savings as given and ignores actual investment opportunities, including yield, risk, and liquidity. In this respect, it is similar to the gravity models of trade, which focus on economic size and distance and ignore the structure of comparative costs, hence the incentives to trade. I now turn to incentives.

Demography and the Savings-Investment Balance

Current account surpluses imply an excess of national savings over domestic investment. Why do these occur, especially in view of the budget deficits run by many countries that absorb much of the excess private saving? A significant rise in oil prices since 2002 increased government revenue of oil-exporting countries in the first instance, producing budgetary surpluses. Much of this saving will be transitory as revenues enter the income stream, raising private incomes and import demand, or as oil prices fall. However, some oil-exporting countries have now emulated Kuwait and Norway in setting aside a portion of their large oil earnings and investing them in the rest of the world for the sake of future generations, so significant savings from these countries may endure for many years.

There are many reasons for high saving, related inter alia to uncertainty and even insecurity about the future, imperfect arrangements for consumer credit for large purchases, management incentives for retaining rather than distributing corporate earnings, memories of past periods of adversity, and so on. But one factor that has received too little attention, or indeed even misleading attention, is the dramatic demographic transformation that many countries are experiencing. Much has been written about the aging of societies, with appropriate focus on unfunded pension and medical care commitments by governments. Aging, however, is occurring for two quite different and mostly unrelated reasons: increasing longevity, which has risen, on average, 8.2 years in the United States over the past half century and an extraordinary 30 years in Japan, and declining natality.

The increasing longevity, without a corresponding increase in working age, may be expected to increase household savings for retirement, but also precautionary savings, since lives are not only longer, but also uncertain in their length. The standard model of life-cycle saving behavior, in which dissaving occurs in older years, typically assumes a known or a known expected time of death. In reality, there is much uncertainty and, thanks to steadily advancing medical technology, perhaps even increasing uncertainty about the time of death. Ceteris paribus, this should increase saving, even beyond retirement, especially in a context of growing uncertainty about the financial viability of many public pension schemes. Americans have been made aware of the future problems of U.S. Social Security, but public pension schemes in many other countries are in much worse shape.

Aging of society through lower natality has perhaps an even greater influence on the national saving-investment balance, however, by reducing investment. Low natality implies, over time, declining numbers of young adults, hence fewer new households, hence lower demand for schools and housing and all the appurtenances associated with housing, such as appliances and furniture. Less new capital is also required to equip new members of the labor force with the average stock of productive capital. In addition, young adults these days are, on average, the most highly educated and the most flexible members of the labor force, geographically and occupationally. A decline in their numbers will thus have a negative impact, ceteris paribus, on productivity growth in an era of continuous advances in technology and changes in the composition of demand.

Saving rates have dropped in Japan, although less than life-cycle devotees expected, but investment has dropped even more. Private saving in Germany has risen, mostly absorbed by a 4 percentage point increase in the public deficit between 2000 and 2005, but investment has fallen sharply. A roughly similar pattern has occurred in the newly rich Asian economies. In contrast, investment has risen in developing Asia, exceeding 37 percent of GDP by 2005, but saving has risen even more in these rapidly growing economies.

The projections for population in these countries, and others, are striking. Most rich countries, along with China, now have a net reproduction ratio below unity—that is, populations are not reproducing themselves. The average number of children per woman of child-bearing age is 1.4 in Germany and Japan; 1.0 in Hong Kong, China; and 1.0 in Singapore (a ratio of 2.1 children is required to sustain a population in the long run). The total populations of Germany and Japan have already peaked, despite increasing longevity. The number of young adults has been declining for some time, and this trend will continue.

Among the rich countries, the United States stands out as a strong exception: while birth rates have declined, they remain above 2, and the U.S. population is augmented by more than a million immigrants a year, who in general are young and well integrated over time into the U.S. labor force. The U.S. Census Bureau makes projections for the number of young adults (ages 15–29) in the world's largest economies plus four newly rich Asian economies: together, in 2006 their current account surpluses (when Germany is augmented by its two close economic neighbors, the Netherlands and Switzerland) equaled 90 percent of the U.S. deficit. (The surpluses of oil exporters equaled an additional 46 percent of the U.S. deficit. The U.S. deficit, in turn, equaled 70 percent of total world deficits.) Young adults decline by roughly 1 percent a year in China, Germany, Japan, and the four newly rich Asian economies. In sharp contrast, the number of young adults in the United States is expected to rise 7 percent over the next two decades, and the actual increase will probably be even greater because of conservative assumptions regarding immigration.

China, of course, is in different circumstances from Germany, Japan, and other rich countries. The rural population, while down 20 percentage points of total population over the past two decades, remains large, so much more rural-urban migration can be expected. The rapid growth of the urban labor force can be expected to continue, and along with it demand for housing, schools, and productive capital stock. Moreover, the incomes of Chinese have grown rapidly and can be expected to continue rising, with a related housing boom, as people not only change location but also upgrade the amount and quality of their living space. China's investment rates are high. But with per capita incomes growing at more than 7 percent a year, in the presence of desires for lumpy expenditures and a poor capital market, Chinese saving rates have increased, even while consumption has grown rapidly. Moreover, many Chinese state-owned enterprises have been modernized and downsized, improving their earnings, while others enjoy quasi-monopoly profits. Until 2008 state-owned enterprises in China did not have to pay dividends to their government owners, so as earnings have increased, so have recorded corporate savings.

Why Invest in the United States?

Given that some of the largest and richest countries have excess savings, as do some poor countries such as China, why do excess savings go heavily to the United States? After all, under simple neoclassical economic assumptions, excess national savings should flow to regions of the world where return to capital is highest, and those in turn are assumed to be regions with a low ratio of capital to other factors of production, most notably labor but also arable land and specific natural resources.

This widely accepted proposition is at a high level of generalization. Discerning investors do not invest on the basis of the high levels of generalization that economists are comfortable with and indeed seem to prefer. Details are all important, and some details are increasingly being recognized. It is more and more common to see references to "risk-adjusted" yield differentials rather than merely to yield differentials, an all-important qualification. Security of investment is important, often trumping high yields for many investors, especially those investing for retirement. Recent experience in Argentina, Bolivia, Russian Federation, and República Bolivariana de Venezuela has reminded everyone that private investment is not always secure, especially if it is foreign private investment. Also, in the most capital-poor countries, yield is often low, due to strong complementarities between invested capital and the institutional setting, interpreted broadly as including, but not limited to, public infrastructure and an educated, or at least a disciplined and functionally literate, labor force.

Despite these qualifications, much private foreign capital has entered developing countries in recent years, over $500 billion (net) in 2005, mostly East Asia and Central Europe, over $700 billion in 2006, and over $900 billion in 2007. But this compares with $1 trillion in foreign private funds invested in the United States in 2005, nearly $1.6 trillion in 2006, and nearly $1.6 trillion in 2007.

There are several reasons for foreign funds to seek the capital-rich United States as a locus for investment. First is simply the size of the U.S. economy. Property rights are secure in the United States, and dispute settlement is relatively speedy and impartial. The United States continues to be a dynamic economy, despite its wealth, partly because it has favorable demographic trends, but also because it is highly innovative and relatively more flexible than other mature economies (and many immature ones). Its financial markets are even larger relative to the rest of the world than its GDP, accounting for more than 40 percent of the world's securities (stocks and bonds) and probably more than half of marketable securities if allowance is made for the nonavailability of many shares of companies in other countries (for example, because they are in government hands).

Because of its size and institutional arrangements, many marketable securities are much more liquid in the U.S. market than in other financial markets, increasing their attractiveness to passive investors, and the market offers a wide diversity of financial assets in terms of their risk characteristics. Finally, in recent times, yields on U.S. debt instruments have been higher than those in many other rich countries, notably Japan and continental Europe. (Yields have been even higher in the United Kingdom and Australia, which share some of the characteristics of the United States. It is perhaps not a coincidence that net foreign investment in those countries has also been high; that is, they have run substantial current account deficits relative to GDP. Canada, which might be thought to be in a similar situation, has run current account surpluses; perhaps its trade is so heavily concentrated on the United States that running a trade deficit would be very demanding, and yields on Canadian bonds, unusually, have been lower than those on U.S. bonds.)

Foreign investment in the United States is overwhelmingly denominated in U.S. dollars; indeed, it simply represents purchases of U.S. domestic instruments by people or institutions who happen to reside abroad. Most of them therefore run an exchange risk measured in their home currency. Does this risk overwhelm the yield differentials? Apparently not. One possible reason is that foreign investors may not be conscious of the exchange risk they are running. This seems extremely unlikely, given that most of the investors are sophisticated financial institutions, and some economists have been unsparing in pointing out the exchange risks, with more than adequate publicity.

Foreign investors must find the characteristics of their investments sufficiently attractive to overcome the exchange risks. Or they may discount the exchange risk. One possible reason is that they believe there is little reason to expect movements in exchange rates to be large enough to overcome the yield differentials, because they implicitly accept the structural reasons developed here for believing that large current account deficits are, in fact, sustainable or some other set of explanations. Or they may believe that large currency appreciations would be sufficiently damaging to other economies to elicit countervailing actions by monetary authorities, so that exchange rate movements among major currencies will be limited by future central bank action.

Much has been made of the fact that some of the financing of the U.S. deficit has come from central bank purchases of dollar-denominated assets. In some of these cases, central banks are simply acting as financial intermediaries on behalf of their aging publics, who either choose not to or are not permitted to invest directly abroad. Suffice it to say here that the inflow of funds to the United States is overwhelmingly private in origin (if not always in beneficial ownership), and was four-fifths of the totals for 2005 through 2007.

How Long Can the United States Provide Assets for Purchase?

What about investment possibilities in the United States? Will foreigners soon acquire so many U.S. assets that their availability will be exhausted? Not anytime soon. It is useful first to examine some simple debt dynamics and then to look at the relationship of U.S. external indebtedness to the availability of U.S. assets.

The accumulation of current account deficits affects a country's net international investment position (NIIP). If we let D represent NIIP, Y = GDP, r = net return on D, and B = the deficit in trade in goods and services (excluding investment income) and unilateral transfers, then $dD = B + rD$. Stabilizing D relative to GDP implies that dD/D equals the growth in nominal GDP. If we suppose that the growth in nominal U.S. GDP in the coming years will be 5 percent, then a stable D/Y would require that $B/D + r = 0.05$.

At the end of 2005, the NIIP of the United States was negative $2.3 trillion, 17 percent of U.S. GDP during 2006. The current account deficit was around 6 percent of GDP. What implications can we draw from this starting point for the future of the U.S. international position?

Several points need to be made about the imprecise fit between the simple debt dynamic and U.S. circumstances. First, the U.S. NIIP reflects the difference between much larger foreign claims on the United States and U.S. claims on the rest of the world. The average yield on U.S. claims significantly exceeds the average yield on foreign claims. While the NIIP turned negative in 1987, U.S. net earnings on foreign investment were still positive in 2007, 20 years later. Thus r in the equation above as applied to the United States has been negative for many years, recently between 1 and 2 percent.

Second, to move from accumulated current account positions to the net international investment position requires adjustment for changes in non-transactional valuations both for foreign claims on the United States and for U.S. claims on the rest of the world. These have strongly favored the United States. Thus over the period 1990–2005, the cumulative U.S. current account deficit was $4.40 trillion, while the increase in the net debtor position of the United States was $2.04 trillion, less than half. The main reason for this difference is the rise in market value of existing claims. In other words, the "total return" on U.S. investments abroad, and on foreign investments in the United States, exceeds the earnings on those investments recorded in the balance of payments. Average annual total return on U.S. overseas investments since 1990 (including exchange rate effects, discussed below) was 10.0 percent, compared with a total return of 6.2 percent on foreign investments in the United States. Thus if total returns are counted, the United States on average runs an even larger surplus on investment earnings than that reported in the balance of payments accounts, despite a significantly negative NIIP. The main reason for this is that equity investment, both direct investment and portfolio equity, makes up a substantially larger share of U.S. claims on the rest of the world (61 percent) than is true for foreign investments in the United States (35 percent). Americans act as risk-taking intermediaries in the world economy, selling fixed-interest claims and investing in equity; they thus earn an equity premium in the world economy.

In addition, changes in exchange rates affect valuations when converted into U.S. dollars, in which the U.S. NIIP is reckoned. Most U.S. assets abroad are denominated in other currencies, whereas most foreign claims on the United States are denominated in dollars. When the dollar depreciates against other currencies, the value of U.S. claims rises relative to foreign claims, and the reverse occurs when the dollar appreciates. These combined valuation effects can be substantial. Thus in 2005 the U.S. current account deficit was $729 billion, but the NIIP actually increased by $200 billion, a reversal that also occurred in 1999. Remarkably, the ratio of NIIP to GDP declined from more than 23 percent in 2001 to less than 17 percent in 2006, despite large and growing current account deficits during this period.

Third, the ratio of NIIP to GDP is far below where it would be in a "no home bias" world, where foreigners would hold nearly 30 percent of their assets in the United States, two and a half times the ratio they currently hold. On these grounds, it could still rise significantly.

How much of the United States do foreigners own? Here it is necessary to look at gross foreign investment in the United States, before netting it against American investment abroad. Total foreign claims (net claims for banks) on the United States at the end of 2005 were $11.1 trillion, 89 percent of GDP during that year and roughly the same percentage of the private nonresidential stock of fixed capital. The share of foreign ownership has increased steadily for the past two decades. But foreigners do not generally buy the capital stock, and their share is not rising nearly as rapidly as one might suppose based on the dollar values alone. remarkable feature of the

U.S. economy is that the total value of financial assets has risen significantly more rapidly than the underlying economy. The Federal Reserve estimates total financial assets in the U.S. economy at the end of 2006 to have been $129 trillion (this figure is, of course, sensitive to the system of classification used in the flow of funds accounts and does not include derivatives), 9.7 times 2006 GDP. Total financial assets were only 4.8 times GDP 40 years earlier, in 1965. Put another way, while nominal GDP grew 7.4 percent a year in 1965–2006, total financial assets grew 9.2 percent a year.

This phenomenon reflects, among other things, innovations by the financial sector, devising financial instruments to appeal to a wider variety of circumstances and tastes. This articulation of financial assets—not all of which prove to be of high quality, as the subprime mortgage debacle demonstrated—appeals to many foreigners as well as Americans, and foreigners invest in a wide array of financial instruments. So while gross foreign investment in the United States equaled GDP in magnitude, it amounted to only 11 percent of total financial assets in the United States. The share has risen from 3 percent in the mid-1980s, but the rise has been slow.

Total financial assets include claims by one sector on another. We can say that fundamentally the U.S. economy is "owned" by households in the United States plus nonprofit organizations (churches, foundations, universities, and so forth) plus foreigners. The share of foreign ownership grew from 7 percent in 1980, to 17 percent in 2000, and to 23 percent in 2006. This ownership represents claims on future output of the U.S. economy. It remains well below the level of foreign ownership that would obtain in a "no home bias" world. It also remains well below the levels of foreign ownership (relative to GDP) that have been reached in many other countries, including Australia, France, Germany, Italy, Spain, and the United Kingdom. So while the foreign-owned share of U.S. financial assets cannot grow without limit, it can grow for many years before straining the American capacity to provide financial assets.

Evaluation

Viewed in the context of globalization and demographic change in other rich countries, the large U.S. current account deficit is both comprehensible and welfare enhancing from a global point of view, so long as Americans invest the funds productively. Prospective retirees around the world are making investments that they believe are profitable and secure. If this is so, strong government efforts to reduce the deficit significantly may be deeply misguided at best and run a serious risk of precipitating a financial crisis and economic recession that its proponents hope to forestall, as fiscal contraction in the United States fails to be matched by fiscal expansion elsewhere and as speculative capital moves heavily into currencies expected to be revalued against the U.S. dollar.

Not so long ago it was argued that as a rich country, the United States should be running a current account surplus, not a deficit. More recently, it has been suggested that for sustainability the deficit needs to be reduced to no more than around 3 percent of GDP. This reduction would require that U.S. expenditure drop, relative to output, by 3 percentage points of U.S. GDP, roughly 1 percent of GDP in the rest of the world. Foreign surpluses, taken together, would have to decline by 3 percent of U.S. GDP, implying a rise in demand relative to output elsewhere in the world.

It is often said that to bring about the required substitutions in product demand, the U.S. dollar must depreciate, probably significantly, perhaps by 30 percent on a trade-weighted basis. So the additional demand in the rest of the world must be domestic demand. For export-oriented economies such as China, Germany, and Japan, currency appreciation is likely to discourage, not encourage, productive investment. So the additional demand must come from domestic consumers or governments. Many governments have been concerned about excessive government deficits in recent years and are engaged in "fiscal consolidation," that is, reducing their deficits. This is especially true for Germany and Japan, two countries with large current account surpluses. What will induce aging consumers to spend more? Easier monetary policy, which in Euroland is outside the control of national governments, would in a world of high capital mobility tend to weaken currencies, not strengthen them. The prescription must include more stimulative fiscal policy combined with tighter monetary policy and currency appreciation. Europe's midterm policy, reflected in the Lisbon agenda of 2000, has focused on fiscal consolidation plus measures to improve productivity and output, resulting (as explicitly desired) in greater international competitiveness, not greater domestic demand.

China, which controls its exchange rate, could decide to revalue its currency, as many have urged. But even if China were to eliminate its current account surplus, only a fraction would accrue to the United States, as U.S. imports from China would switch to other low-income countries. That would still leave a current account deficit in excess of the targeted level. Moreover, what would an appreciation large enough to eliminate China's surplus do to China's economy, where exports have led China's growth? Exports have not been China's only source of growth in demand. Public and private construction has boomed, and Chinese consumption has grown in excess of 8 percent a year during 1989–2005, the highest growth in the world. But exports have been the driving sector.

The argument developed here suggests that the U.S. deficit can continue for some years and even rise above its current level. Of course, a significant depreciation of the dollar might nevertheless occur. Financial markets are driven by psychological as well as by economic factors. If enough people decide to sell dollars, the dollar will depreciate. If foreigners collectively decide to invest less in the United States than the current account deficit (plus U.S. capital outflow), then the dollar will depreciate.

A large drop in the dollar would have grave economic consequences, reducing exports and depressing investment in other rich countries. For this reason, their monetary authorities are likely at some point to intervene in foreign exchange markets to limit the resulting economic downturn, in effect substituting official for private capital investment in the United States and thereby putting effective limits on any depreciation of the dollar.

Of course, the current account deficit cannot rise indefinitely relative to GDP; neither can foreign-owned assets rise indefinitely as a share of total U.S. assets. Sooner or later the process of financial globalization will slow, and eventually stop, probably well before the hypothetical state of "no home bias" is reached. Moreover, aging societies will eventually reach the point at which they cease acquiring new foreign assets and begin to liquidate their outstanding claims. Then the U.S. deficit must decline, perhaps significantly. The trade deficit will need to decline even earlier, as foreigners begin to consume the earnings on their U.S. investments. But that point may not be reached for many years, especially if people work longer and continue to save past conventional retirement age, as many do.

As Asians and Europeans begin to consume their overseas earnings and their assets, total expenditures in their countries will rise relative to output, and surpluses will decline and eventually disappear. This process alone will help to reduce the U.S. deficit, without any depreciation of the dollar against their currencies. To what extent the dollar needs to depreciate will depend on the emerging consumption patterns in the aging societies, in particular on the mix between tradable and nontradable goods and services, keeping in mind that these categories are themselves constantly changing, as more nontradables join the category of tradables, with increased possibilities for offshoring. Even nontradables can enter the international accounts insofar as they are provided by temporary migrant workers who remit earnings to their home countries. Elder care is likely to involve both processes—diagnoses of measured symptoms from remote locations and in situ help by migrant workers, as the children and grandchildren and great-grandchildren of the elderly choose to stay in the labor force.

Another possibility involves retirement of Asians and Europeans in the United States, just as some Canadians do now. Their assets would then cease to be foreign claims on the United States.

The adjustment process involves the classic transfer problem in a more complex setting. How much, if at all, the dollar needs eventually to depreciate will depend on all of these factors and certainly cannot be foretold years in advance of the required adjustment.

The United States has a vibrant, innovative economy. Its demographics differ markedly from those of other rich countries, in that birth rates have not fallen nearly so far and immigration, concentrated in young adults, can be expected to continue on a significant scale. In these respects, the United States, although rich and politically mature, can be said to be a young and even a developing country. It has an especially innovative financial sector, which continually produces new products to cater to diverse portfolio tastes. The United States has a comparative advantage, in a globalized market, in producing marketable securities and exchanging low-risk debt for higher-risk equity. It is not surprising that savers around the world want to put a growing portion of their savings into the U.S. economy. The U.S. current account deficit and the corresponding surpluses elsewhere, described as imbalances, involve intertemporal trade and do not necessarily signal economic disequilibria in a globalized world economy. They may well remain large for years to come.

Postscript

This paper was first presented in September 2007, updated with revised data through 2007. It did not anticipate a freezing up of parts of the financial system, especially beginning in September 2008, both induced by and contributing to a fall in U.S. housing prices and the prices of many financial assets. Although the financial crisis originated in the United States, it quickly became global in scope, albeit with unequal incidence. It led to a deep recession as banks and other financial institutions became extremely risk averse and deleveraged their balance sheets, making credit everywhere difficult to get, despite dramatic moves by central banks to lower short-term interest rates and to increase liquidity in financial markets.

Many cross-border claims—assets and liabilities, debt as well as equity—will be reduced by the end of 2008, and the impact on the net international investment position of the United States is uncertain at this time. The U.S. current account deficit dropped to $700 billion in 2008 due to the slowdown of the U.S. economy and may even drop to $400 billion in 2009 due to the U.S. recession and to a drop in the price of imported oil.

These are dramatic developments. But I see no reason to alter the basic reasoning of the paper, which was long term in its emphasis on globalization of financial markets and on differential demographic change in many countries.

Alarmed by the large global imbalances, some analysts predicted a financial crisis. A financial crisis arrived. But it was not due, as forecast, to a flight from the dollar followed by a sharp rise in U.S. interest rates. Ironically, while many U.S. securities (especially mortgage-backed securities and the collateralized debt obligations based on them) came to be shunned and illiquid, the dramatic increase in risk aversion and the flight to safety and to liquidity enhanced the attractiveness of U.S. treasuries and led to a significant decline in their interest rates, as well as to an appreciation of the U.S. dollar in the second half of 2008.

Financial crises can have many origins. Large global imbalances were not among the origins of the crisis of 2008, except insofar as American access to excess foreign savings contributed to low mortgage rates in the United States and thus facilitated a boom in residential construction and in mortgage lending, a development that also occurred in several other countries. But low long-term interest rates were a facilitating factor, not the main cause of the crisis. Rather, it resided in a mood of euphoria in financial markets, combined with and reinforced by financial incentives for participants based largely on short-term performance and insufficiently on longer-term risks.

References

Carrado, Carol, Charles R. Hulten, and Daniel E. Sichel. 2006. "Intangible Capital and Economic Growth." NBER Working Paper 11948 (January). National Bureau of Economic Research, Cambridge, MA.

Cline, William R. 2005. "The United States as a Debtor Nation." Peterson Institute for International Economics, Washington, DC.

Cooper, Richard N. 2007. "Living with Global Imbalances." *Brookings Papers on Economic Activity* 2: 91–107.

———. 2008. "Global Imbalances: Globalization, Demography, and Sustainability." *Journal of Economic Perspectives* 22 (3): 93–112.

CHAPTER 6
Macro Crises and Targeting Transfers to the Poor

Ravi Kanbur

The discourse on the current global macro crisis, as happens during all such crises, has highlighted the plight of the poor in coping with the consequences.[1] Of particular significance is the use of existing policy instruments, and possibly the design and implementation of new ones, to protect the poor during the crisis and to maintain their capacity to benefit from the rebound when it comes. There is, of course, a large literature on redistribution to and targeting the poor. The objective of this chapter is to relate this general literature to issues that arise during macro crises and to ask whether the same principles can be used to illuminate the tradeoffs faced by policy makers as they address the consequences of the crisis on the poor. In particular, the central issue considered is whether tighter targeting of transfer programs toward the poor is warranted during a crisis.

Macro crises come in many varieties. A common feature is that during the crisis average purchasing power falls dramatically (otherwise they

This chapter was written for the Commission on Growth and Development. It was first published in the *Journal of Globalization and Development* (vol. 1, issue 1, January 2010). © 2010 The Berkeley Electronic Press. Reprinted with permission.

1   For an excellent overview of the discourse, which also touches on some of the points covered in this chapter, see Ravallion (2008).

would not be macro crises). The distribution around the average, however, could move in different ways, and individual movements around the distribution could have many different patterns. Each of these factors will affect the design of poverty-targeted programs, and this chapter uses the literature on targeting as a base from which to analyze pro-poor programs during macro crises.

Even in "normal times," the tradeoffs inherent in balancing efficiency and distribution are involved and intricate. The literature has considered this balance primarily in the context where redistribution has efficiency costs in a second-best world with limited policy instruments. A more recent literature has, quite rightly, highlighted the efficiency gains from redistributive policies in this very same second-best world.[2] However, to the extent that these are net gains—the difference between gross efficiency gains and gross costs of redistribution—the design of policy to minimize the efficiency costs of redistribution still has relevance.

A particular class of policy instruments where these issues come to the fore are programs and interventions that explicitly target the poor as an objective (at least partially). These include subsidies on a range of commodities including food, fuel, energy, and water. The subsidies can be generalized in nature, applying to rich and poor alike, with the targeting relying on consumption differences between rich and poor across commodities. Or they can be targeted only to those who satisfy criteria that identify poverty. Another class of programs, which has been present for a long time in some developing countries, but whose use has exploded in the last two decades, consists of conditional cash transfers.[3] These provide cash benefits in response to some action from the beneficiary—like working on a public works site for employment schemes, keeping children in school, or attending health clinics. Sometimes, combinations of conditions are used. These programs can be further restricted to those who satisfy a poverty criterion.

The general education and health system can also be viewed as a redistributive mechanism. In fact, it has often been argued that these expenditures by the state are poorly targeted to the poor. However, reform of these systems is an issue for the long term. The general tax system can also be viewed as a redistributive instrument. Even if it is viewed only as a source of revenue for the targeted programs described above, the targeting of the tax system itself—its progressivity—will affect the targeting of government financial transfers as a whole. But again, these reforms are of a long-term nature. This chapter does not focus on education and health policy or on general tax policy. The focus, rather, is on instruments for getting purchasing power into the hands of the poor from the expenditure side of government policy.

The chapter proceeds as follows. First, it reviews the theory of targeting, highlighting the tradeoffs between fine targeting of programs toward the poor versus broader coverage. Second, it treats the macro shock as permanent and examines how the nature of the tradeoff changes, deriving

---

2   This literature has been reviewed in World Bank (2005).
3   For a recent review, see Fiszbein and Schady (2009).

guidelines for the use of alternative policy instruments and design of new ones. Third, it extends the insights to the case where the shock is temporary: how should this change the deployment of existing instruments during a crisis and the design of new instruments for a world of temporary, but sharp, downturns? A final section concludes.

Tradeoffs in Targeting

The modern literature on targeting goes back at least as far as Akerlof's (1978) formalization of the use of a limited number of policy instruments to pursue a poverty minimization strategy, taking into account information and incentive constraints, broadening and enriching the Mirrlees (1971) and Diamond and Mirrlees (1971) optimal taxation framework. Besley and Kanbur (1988, 1993) provide an account of the key conceptual elements in the theory of targeting in the context of developing countries. This section lays the groundwork for the discussion of targeting during crises by examining the basic principles of targeting and identifying some of the key tradeoffs involved.[4]

Consider a government that has a given budget for poverty reduction, poverty being identified as the shortfall of consumption from an agreed poverty line. Suppose initially that there are no informational or administrative problems; the government can costlessly identify each person's consumption relative to the poverty line. Suppose further that there are no behavioral responses and hence no incentive effects of alternative government interventions. In such a situation, how best should the government use its budget to alleviate poverty?

The answer depends on the precise nature of the government's poverty objective (Bourguignon and Fields 1990). If, on the one hand, the objective is to minimize the "headcount ratio"—the fraction of units below the poverty line—then the answer is to start with units closest to the poverty line and to go down from there, lifting units to the poverty line until the budget runs out. If, on the other hand, the objective is to minimize the aggregate poverty gap—the sum of all the shortfalls of consumption from the poverty line—then at the margin, it does not matter who among the poor is given the transfer, since the aggregate poverty gap would be reduced by the same amount. Finally, consider a poverty objective where greater weight is given to the poorest of the poor, as in the aggregate squared poverty gap. Now the strategy is the following. Start with the poorest unit. Give this unit transfers until it reaches the level of the next poorest unit. Then give these units transfers until they are raised to the level of the next unit. And so on until the budget is exhausted. This would be the strategy to follow for all poverty measures in the Foster, Greer, and Thorbecke (1984) family of poverty measures, where the degree of poverty aversion (the "FGT alpha") is

---

4   For a comprehensive review of principles and experience, see Grosh and others (2008).

greater than one (for the squared poverty gap measure, the degree of poverty aversion is two).

This analysis is useful as a benchmark of "perfect targeting," which means giving the poor just enough to bring them up to the poverty line and avoiding leakages to the nonpoor. The total resource required for this is simply the sum of all the poverty gaps. If this amount is not available, poverty cannot be eliminated by redistribution. But even if this amount were available, it is highly unlikely that poverty could be eliminated, because perfect targeting is, of course, an ideal that is unlikely to be met in practice. As Besley and Kanbur (1993) argue, three central issues arise: information, incentives, and political economy.

The informational problem is quite simply that it is not costless to identify who is poor and who is not and to measure the precise poverty gap for each poor person. Put another way, the policy instruments available are far coarser than perfect targeting requires. At the other extreme, it may not be possible to distinguish individuals from each other at all, forcing us to make the same transfer to all. This "demo-grant" instrument is not very well targeted, but it is least costly in terms of informational requirements. In practice two types of instruments are available to policy makers that can bridge the gap between perfect targeting and "perfectly imperfect" targeting: indicator targeting and self-targeting.

Indicator targeting uses (more) easily observable characteristics of individuals to condition transfers, relying on the correlation between the (relatively more easily) observable attributes and (more difficult to observe, verify, and monitor) income-consumption-purchasing power. Each individual with the same value of the indicator variable (for example, area of residence, color of skin, gender, age) is treated identically, so there will be some "leakage" since some individuals in the category will be above the poverty line. But if the policy maker knows the statistical properties of the bivariate distribution between the indicator variable and consumption, say, through a representative household survey, for example, transfers to different values of the indicator variable can be modulated to achieve greater poverty reduction than could be achieved with an equal transfer to everybody. The theory of such transfers, inspired by Akerlof (1978), is worked out in Kanbur (1987) and Besley and Kanbur (1988). Essentially, the differential in transfers to different values of the indicator variable should increase as the poverty differential between them increases.

Self-targeting, in contrast, uses differences between the behavior of richer and poorer individuals—induced, in turn, by differences in preferences or in opportunity costs of time, for example. Using a poverty alleviation budget to subsidize the consumption of commodities differentially relies on differences in consumption patterns. As shown by Besley and Kanbur (1988), the key targeting indicator is the fraction of total consumption of a commodity that is accounted for by those below the poverty line. Differences in this value between two commodities govern the differential rate of subsidy between them. The opportunity cost of time can be used to self-target if the transfer is proportional, say, to time expended in getting the transfer. The most obvious example of this is a public works scheme with a given wage. Clearly, only those for whom the opportunity cost of time (earnings in alternative activity) is less than the wage will turn up to work on the site. If this is, in turn, negatively associated with poverty status, lowering the wage will tighten the poverty targeting of the transfer effected through the public works scheme.[5]

All of the above supposes no incentive effects of the transfer scheme itself. To see the consequences of these effects, take the case where there are no informational constraints and consider the perfect targeting scheme where every poor person is given just the transfer to get them up to the poverty line and no more. What this means is that as the nonprogram resources of a poor person increase, program transfers are reduced one for one. In other words, the effective marginal tax rate is 100 percent. This removes all incentives for the poor to increase their resources (incomes, say) through their own efforts. Indeed, it removes incentives even to maintain their incomes at the levels they were before the program. In the extreme, no one in poverty would earn any income, and the costs of poverty elimination would increase, perhaps dramatically.

Perfect targeting implies and requires 100 percent effective marginal tax rates. This leads to a tradeoff with incentives to earn income (generate nonprogram resources). At the other extreme, the demo-grant has a 0 percent effective marginal tax rate, but it is very poorly targeted. Kanbur, Keen, and Tuomala (1994) show that if the objective is to minimize poverty, then neither extreme is appropriate; in fact, the optimal transfer withdrawal rates on the poor—in other words, the effective marginal tax rates—are on the order of 60–70 percent. This should give a quantitative feel for how far incentive effects can pull us from the perfect targeting benchmark.

The third issue with perfect targeting of a given budget for poverty reduction arises when considering the source of the budget. To the extent that this budget comes from the operation of political economy forces within the country in question, the fact that those above the poverty line get nothing at all from perfect targeting (indeed this "zero leakage" is part of the definition of perfect targeting) may determine how much budget becomes available for this program. As proposed by Besley and Kanbur (1993) and formalized by Gelbach and Pritchett (2000), one of the costs of fine targeting may be that the total budget for poverty reduction may become smaller.[6] Coarser targeting involves leakages to the nonpoor, but precisely for this reason it may help to build a political coalition between the poor and the near-poor to increase the budget for the program. Hence, in Gelbach and Pritchett's telling phrase, "leakier can be better" for poverty reduction. These arguments are, of course,

---

5   The targeting properties of public works schemes have been analyzed extensively by Ravallion (1999, 2006).

6   Anand and Kanbur (1991) argue that these forces were present in the aftermath of targeting of generalized rice subsidies in Sri Lanka during the crisis of the late 1970s.

well rehearsed in the debates on "universalism" versus "means testing" for welfare states in rich countries. But they have particular resonance for targeting the poor in poor countries.

The above sets the frame for how the large literature on targeting, only touched on here, approaches the tradeoffs in ensuring that transfers intended for poverty reduction reach the poor. How are these tradeoffs altered when the economy undergoes a massive negative shock that reduces average incomes and purchasing power and possibly alters the income distribution in significant ways? The next section takes up the case where the shock is permanent.

Tradeoffs after a Permanent Shock

This section considers the case where the macro crisis permanently alters the distribution of income. As noted earlier, the mean of the distribution must fall, and dramatically so, for any crisis worth that label. This by itself will increase poverty if the shape of the distribution remains unchanged. But what happens to the shape of the distribution? This can be quite complex and depends on the detail of the nature of the crisis and the structure of the economy. A financial crisis may well affect upper incomes more drastically, thereby reducing overall inequality. However, if, for example, the direct effect (through export contraction) is on employment, inequality may well increase. Thus it is necessary to consider both cases—where the crisis, although reducing the mean for sure, either decreases or increases overall inequality.

Beyond the ambiguity in the change in overall inequality, the composition of the distribution can also change in intricate ways, with certain occupations, regions, and socioeconomic groupings losing more than others—perhaps some even winning as others lose heavily. If these are the groupings that are being used to target, then the macro shock, through its impact on the detailed composition of the distribution, could affect targeting tradeoffs as well. But the changes in the distribution will affect targeting tradeoffs in other ways as well. Moreover, it is expected that the crisis will, in the first instance, reduce the resources available for poverty reduction, and this will also affect the tradeoffs. Specifically, will the shock shift the balance in favor of finer targeting or away from it? This is a central policy question, since arguments are heard in both directions, and intuition and instinct pull us first one way and then the other.

Let us consider in turn the three issues highlighted in the previous section—information, incentives, and political economy. Starting with the informational constraints to perfect targeting, it can be argued that it is now worth spending more resources to identify the poor and how poor they are, so as to better deploy the reduced resources toward the goal of poverty reduction. There is indeed a literature on the administrative costs of targeting, which shows that fine targeting does not come cheap. The tradeoff is now between using some more of the diminished resources to reduce "leakage" to the nonpoor and leaving less for the actual transfer. The final answer is ambiguous, depending on the precise nature of how targeting improves with greater administrative outlays and how much the needs of the poor for transfers increase with the crisis.

Turning to the use of indicator targeting as a response to informational constraints, consider the proposition that differential per capita transfers to different groups should follow the differential in poverty between those groups. A reduction in the overall budget for poverty reduction would not change this conclusion. If anything, it would strengthen it, in the sense that when resources are tight, deviation from the rule would lead to even bigger losses in the objective of minimizing poverty. What about changes in the underlying income distribution? The answer would depend very much on how poverty incidence was changed across the policy-relevant groups. If the increase in poverty was uniform, then the allocation, at least its direction, would not be affected. However, if at the other extreme the relative poverty ranking of the two groups reversed as a result of the crisis (even as poverty went up in both groups), the allocation rule would dictate a shift in priorities. Detail matters, therefore, and thus information on the impact of the crisis on poverty by salient socioeconomic groups is crucial in determining an optimal response.

For self-targeting through differential subsidy of commodity groups, the key ratio is total consumption of a commodity by the poor divided by total consumption of the commodity in the economy as a whole. A generalized reduction in incomes may change this ratio depending on the precise nature of the Engle curve for each commodity, but it is unlikely to reverse rankings across commodities. However, since poverty will have increased, poverty minimization will require that more of the available resources go to subsidize commodities where the key ratio is highest. The same will hold true if total resources available for transfer are reduced. In this sense, therefore, the crisis will require a tightening of targeting to the poor. Self-targeting through choice of wages in public works schemes will require lower wages as the total resources available fall, especially if the crisis also lowers returns to other activities and hence the opportunity cost of working at the public works site. In this sense, again, the crisis requires a tightening of the targeting regime.

Let us turn now to the tradeoffs around the incentive effects from fine targeting. As noted in the previous section, Kanbur, Keen, and Tuomala (1994) argue that the optimal, poverty-minimizing, income tax schedule implies effective marginal tax rates on the poor on the order of 60–70 percent. This is done in the Mirrlees (1971) optimal income taxation framework. It is also shown that as the mean of the income distribution falls, the optimal marginal tax rate on the poor increases. The intuition behind this is that since the poor are now poorer, there is a greater pull to provide support to the poorest of the poor. The budget constraint, however, requires that this be "clawed back" faster as incomes increase—hence the higher marginal tax rates even on the poor themselves. A similar intuition holds for the case where, holding mean constant, overall inequality of the underlying income distribution increases.[7] The poor are now poorer and require greater support, necessitating higher marginal tax rates to meet the budget constraints. These higher marginal tax rates will, of course, have incentive effects on the poor, but this is traded off against the need for finer targeting to support the very poorest, since the crisis has made them even poorer. The argument runs in reverse if inequality falls during the crisis. However, for a crisis that increases inequality as well as lowers the mean, the theory of targeting with incentive effects also suggests a tightening of the targeting toward the poorest of the poor.

Consider now the political economy dimensions of targeting. As noted earlier, fine targeting, which by definition excludes the near poor and the nonpoor, makes the best use of available resources for poverty minimization, but reduces political support for the transfer program and hence the total resources available for the program. The informational arguments tilt the balance in favor of fine targeting in a crisis, and it can also be shown that incentive effects of fine targeting do not overturn this conclusion. But fine targeting tends to reduce the total available resources for the transfer program, exactly at the time that resources have been reduced as a result of the crisis. Indeed, on this reasoning, there is the danger of a downward spiral as fewer resources lead to finer targeting, leading to fewer resources, further tightening of targeting, and so on. When overall resources fall, and needs increase as the result of a tightening, the political economy arguments thus favor a loosening, not a tightening, of targeting if the objective is to maximize transfers to the poorest in a time of heightened constraints. These arguments thus align with popular calls that the well off should share the burden of the crisis and that "we are all in this together."

What, then, does the theory of targeting have to say about targeting transfers to the poor at a time of macro crisis? The answer depends very much on whether the targeting regime or the resources are exogenous. If the resources are independent of the targeting regime, the case for finer targeting is strong (although not unequivocal), even when incentive effects are taken into account. However, if the targeting regime can be picked by the technocrats, say, and the resources are then decided by the domestic political economy, finer targeting is not necessarily the answer—in fact, a case may be made for looser targeting. In either case, the argument for additional external resources is strong, not only to replenish reduced domestic resources for poverty reduction, but also to prevent a downward spiral of finer and finer targeting with fewer and fewer resources.

---

7   A formal analysis is provided in Kanbur and Tuomala (1995).

Temporary Shocks

The previous discussion treats the macro shock as permanent, so that the existing theory of targeting "in comparative static manner" is simply applied to the new situation with a different distribution of income and reduced resources for poverty reduction. But what if the macro shock is, as one would hope, temporary? This leads to several considerations that are not present in the permanent shock scenario.

The literature on poverty has highlighted the risk and vulnerability associated with poverty, the costs of this for the poor, and the central role of safety nets in addressing these problems. The focus of this large literature is on idiosyncratic shocks, and risk sharing (or lack thereof) among the poor.[8] Macro crises, however, are not idiosyncratic; they are systemic shocks that affect everybody. There may be some scope for risk sharing if the impact of the crisis is to benefit some poor, while hurting others, but this is not the scenario uppermost in policy makers' minds when they think of macro shocks. In the present context, the shocks considered here are systemic, not idiosyncratic, ones.

If the macro shock were truly temporary, in the sense that an equal and opposite shock (in the appropriate sense) will eventually restore the economy to a long-run average path, then there is, in principle, no need to change transfers policy at all. The same amount of resources, and the same targeting regime, that applies to the long-run average state of the economy could apply in good times and in bad times, using appropriate saving and borrowing by the government for smoothing.

But there are (at least) two arguments in the literature questioning whether a temporary shock is in fact all that temporary. First, temporary shortfalls in consumption for the poor translate into long-run consequences for economic and human development, so long-run economic and social well-being of the poor tracks the negative shock; it is not counteracted to an equal and opposite extent by an equal and opposite positive shock. Second, government actions to address the temporary shock cannot be reversed when the shock is reversed, leaving an inappropriate redistributive structure in place for the long run. The first suggests moving aggressively to address the temporary shock—essentially as though it were a permanent shock. The second suggests caution and moving only on reversible policy changes, even if this means some of the temporary shock is not addressed and has long-term consequences.

With this background, let us think through the case for finer targeting with a temporary (but severe) negative macro shock. The above structure of argument allows us to assess a common piece of advice to policy makers: "In a macro crisis do not expand programs, like generalized subsidies, that are not well targeted to the poor. These are not an efficient way of reaching the poor, and when the crisis passes you will be stuck with a targeting

---

8   For a representative selection of papers in this literature, see Dercon (2004).

regime that will be inefficient in terms of poverty alleviation." It should be clear that the validity of this advice depends on the detailed specification of and interaction between the purely technical aspects of targeting and its political economy dimensions.

With the shock (temporary but with long-term consequences for the poor), suppose finer targeting is indeed suggested by the non–political economy analysis, as discussed in the previous section: with reduced resources and greater needs, greater support for the poorest in difficult times requires the support to be clawed back rapidly. In this view there is certainly not a case for loosening the targeting. And, it is further argued, loosening of the targeting will be difficult to reverse when the economy returns to its long-term path because of political economy pressures. But this second part of the argument reveals a conceptual problem in the whole sequence, because the political economy dimension has a logic of its own, into which irreversibility plays in a nuanced way.

If changes in the targeting regime are indeed irreversible (or at least difficult to reverse), and the political economy of resource mobilization for poverty alleviation transfers plays out conditional on the targeting regime, then the "leakier is better" analysis suggests that poverty reduction has nothing to fear from a move toward looser targeting in the wake of a crisis. Looser targeting should help to increase resources for poverty alleviation. If anything, moving toward finer targeting is problematic. Finer targeting, if irreversible, will lead to lower overall resources for antipoverty transfers in the future and perhaps even in the near term. Less fine targeting with fixed resources will be less efficient for poverty reduction, but, if irreversible, it will lead to more resources used for the antipoverty transfers in the future and perhaps even immediately. Thus the policy advice to move to finer targeting to weather temporary but severe negative shocks is not necessarily valid if the political economy dimensions of irreversibility of the targeting regime are taken into account.

. However, one type of policy move can be unequivocally supported in the face of temporary shocks: this is to invest in removing the irreversibilities that led to the dilemmas in the first place. Thus improving income and consumption-smoothing instruments for the poor, so that negative shocks do not have long-term effects on them, is an obvious answer. There is a large literature on this, and it is not discussed further here (see Dercon 2004). Rather, the focus is on improving flexibility through the operation of various income transfer programs. There are both technocratic and political economy dimensions to this.

To illustrate the issues involved, consider a type of program often used to help the poor in crises: public works schemes. Specifically, consider India's National Rural Employment Guarantee Act, which aims to guarantee 100 days of employment a year to rural households (at the local minimum wage).[9] When rural employment falls, this program is meant to kick in to

---

9   An introduction to this is provided in Basu, Chau, and Kanbur (2007).

shore up incomes. It is flexible in design in the sense that employment is offered at the wage to all those who show up; thus the program can be scaled up or scaled down as employment conditions improve. But there are two key questions. First, what is being done with the labor employed? Second, where will the resources come from to finance an expansion of the program?

Assessments of public works schemes show that the value of assets created is a key component of the benefit of these schemes—indeed it is argued that, in many cases, it is this value that tips the cost-benefit into supporting the program as public expenditure.[10] It is also recognized that a central design feature determining whether valuable assets are created is the presence or otherwise of a "shelf of projects" ready to go when demand for employment increases as the result of a crisis. Without these, the workers are indeed "digging holes to fill them up again." While still useful as a form of targeting of transfers (recall the opportunity cost arguments made in the previous section), clearly much more could be achieved. But this requires planning before the crisis and expending resources to prepare and update projects, which will only be activated as necessary. This investment in flexibility is well worth making, but it is one that standard assessment systems—for example, those of donors—do not seem to appreciate and finance. To expend resources to prepare projects that may not be implemented immediately is not something that donor systems are designed to incorporate. This is also a problem for community-driven participatory project design. It is not easy to explain to local communities why the projects that they have spent so much time helping to design, and for which there is immediate need, are to be held off until there is an employment crisis. But these are hurdles, at the local, national, and international levels, that will have to be overcome to increase flexibility of public works schemes and thus to improve their role in targeting transfers during crises.

The above supposes that the resources available (wage costs of increased employment and complementary nonlabor costs of the projects) will increase as the employment needs increase in the wake of a crisis. If the resources do not increase, employment will be rationed, with no improvement in poverty and perhaps even a worsening if rationed employment is allocated to favor the better off. But how can an increase in resources be assured? In the Indian case, the device used is that of a justiciable guarantee. In effect, the polity makes the central government and the state governments liable in law to provide the employment. If they do not, they can be taken to court. It is hoped that the costs to government of this action by public interest litigation will be sufficiently high to ensure that government makes sufficient resources available. In other words, the political economy is guided toward providing the resources by raising the costs to key actors of not doing so.

---

10 Ravallion (1999). Murgai and Ravallion (2005) argue that the poverty impact of the National Rural Employment Guarantee Act depends crucially on the value of assets created.

At least two questions can be raised regarding this method of achieving flexibility and ensuring that resources do flow to the poor in a crisis. First, it is difficult to monitor the guarantee. Ground-level officials have myriad ways of discouraging employment applicants (for example, by holding the public works projects far from villages.). While some of these can be accounted for in law (for example, requiring that the public works be no farther than a certain distance from the village of the applicant), there is residual discretion that simply cannot be addressed.[11] Second, it relies on the fact that being taken to court is costly for officials and that they and the public will abide by court judgments. Increased and continued use of courts in this way may well reduce the effectiveness of this device over time.

A similar exercise can be conducted for each transfer program, asking how its technical design can be made more flexible so that, with a given degree of targeting, it can be expanded or contracted easily, the flexibility being both a technical issue and one of political economy. With this background for individual programs, the overall set of programs as a whole can be seen as the instrument for helping the poor during a crisis, with reallocation of resources across programs as well as changes in individual programs as the needs of the crisis become apparent.[12]

Finally, as has been noted at several points in this and the previous sections, external resources can help to ease the many painful tradeoffs that policy makers face during crises. Over the long term, they can help in putting in place more flexible transfer programs that can move quickly to adjust as crises erupt. In the short term, they can reduce the need for looser targeting, or the use of court-backed guarantees, to generate greater resources domestically. The looser targeting made possible by greater external resources can help to reduce the informational and incentive costs of fine targeting.[13]

Conclusions

A central question for policy makers concerned to help the poor through a macro crisis is how to target scarcer resources at a time of greater need. Technical arguments suggest that finer targeting, through tightening individual programs or reallocating resources toward more tightly targeted programs, uses resources more efficiently for poverty reduction. These arguments survive even when the greater informational costs and the incentive effects of finer targeting are taken into account. But political economy arguments suggest that finer targeting will end up with fewer resources allocated to that program and that looser targeting, because it knits together the interests of the poor and the near-poor, may generate greater resources

---

11 Basu, Chau, and Kanbur (2009) present a theory of employment guarantees where credibility of the guarantee is center stage.
12 The argument for treating the collectivity of transfer programs as a system is made in Kanbur (2009).
13 Implications for donors like the World Bank are developed further in Kanbur (2009).

and hence be more effective for poverty reduction despite being "leakier." Overall, the policy advice to avoid more loosely targeted programs during crises needs to be given with considerable caution. However, the advice to design transfer systems with greater flexibility, in the technical and the political economy senses, is strengthened by the arguments presented here. The case for external assistance—to design flexible transfer systems ex ante and to relieve the painful tradeoffs in targeting during a crisis—is also shown to be strong.

References

Akerlof, George. 1978. "The Economics of 'Tagging' as Applied to the Optimal Income Tax, Welfare Programs, and Manpower Planning." *American Economic Review* 68 (1): 8–19.

Anand, Sudhir, and Ravi Kanbur. 1991. "Public Policy and Basic Needs Provision in Sri Lanka." In *The Political Economy of Hunger*. Vol. 3: *Endemic Hunger*, ed. Jean Drèze and Amartya Sen, 59–92. Oxford: Clarendon Press.

Basu, Arnab, Nancy Chau, and Ravi Kanbur. 2007. "The National Rural Employment Guarantee Act of India, 2005." In *The Oxford Companion to Economics in India*, ed. Kaushik Basu. New York: Oxford University Press.

———. 2009. "A Theory of Employment Guarantees: Contestability, Credibility, and Distributional Concerns." *Journal of Public Economics* 93 (3-4, April): 482–97.

Besley, Timothy, and Ravi Kanbur. 1988. "Food Subsidies and Poverty Alleviation." *Economic Journal* 98 (392, September): 701–19.

———. 1993. "The Principles of Targeting." In *Including the Poor*, ed. Michael Lipton and Jacques van der Gaag, 67–90. Washington, DC: World Bank.

Bourguignon, François, and Gary Fields. 1990. "Poverty Measures and Anti-Poverty Policy." *Recherches Economique de Louvain* 56 (3-4): 409–28.

Dercon, Stefan, ed. 2004. *Insurance against Poverty*. New York: Oxford University Press.

Diamond, Peter, and James Mirrlees. 1971. "Optimal Taxation and Public Production II: Tax Rules." *American Economic Review* 61 (3, pt. 1, June): 261–78.

Fiszbein, Ariel, and Norbert Schady. 2009. *Conditional Cash Transfers for Attacking Present and Future Poverty*. Policy Research Report. Washington, DC: World Bank, Development Research Group.

Foster, James, Joel Greer, and Erik Thorbecke. 1984. "A Class of Decomposable Poverty Measures." *Econometrica* 52 (3, May): 761–66.

Gelbach, Jonah, and Lant Pritchett. 2000. "Indicator Targeting in a Political Economy: Leakier Can Be Better." *Journal of Policy Reform* 4 (2): 113–45.

Grosh, Margaret, Carlo del Ninno, Emil Tesliuc, and Azedine Ouerghi. 2008. *For Protection and Promotion: The Design and Implementation of Effective Safety Nets*. Washington, DC: World Bank.

Kanbur, Ravi. 1987. "Measurement and Alleviation of Poverty: With an Application to the Impact of Macroeconomic Adjustment." *IMF Staff Papers* 34 (March): 60–85.

———. 2009. "Systemic Crises and the Social Protection System: Three Proposals for World Bank Action." Working Paper 235. Cornell Food and Nutrition Program, Cornell University, Ithaca, NY. www.kanbur.aem.cornell.edu/papers/SystemicCrisesAndTheSocialProtectionSystem.pdf.

Kanbur, Ravi, Michael Keen, and Matti Tuomala. 1994. "Labor Supply and Targeting in Poverty Alleviation Programs." *World Bank Economic Review* 8 (2): 191–211.

Kanbur, Ravi, and Matti Tuomala. 1995. "Inherent Inequality and the Optimal Graduation of Marginal Tax Rates." *Scandinavian Journal of Economics* 96 (2): 275–82.

Mirrlees, James A. 1971. "An Exploration in the Theory of Optimum Income Taxation." *Review of Economic Studies* 38 (114): 175–208.

Murgai, Rinku, and Martin Ravallion. 2005. "Employment Guarantee in Rural India: What Would It Cost and How Much Would It Reduce Poverty?" *Economic and Political Weekly*, July 30, pp. 3450–55.

Ravallion, Martin. 1999. "Appraising Workfare." *World Bank Research Observer* 14 (1): 31–48.

———. 2006. "Transfers and Safety Nets in Poor Countries: Revisiting the Tradeoffs and Policy Options." In *Understanding Poverty*, ed. Abhijit Banerjee, Roland Benabou, and Dilip Mookerjee. Oxford: Oxford University Press.

———. 2008. "Bailing out the World's Poorest." Policy Research Working Paper 4763. World Bank, Washington, DC.

World Bank. 2005. *World Development Report 2006: Equity and Development*. New York: Oxford University Press.

PART 2
How to Foster Real Growth

CHAPTER 7
Growth after the Crisis

Dani Rodrik

The last 50 years were a remarkable period in world economic history. Not only did we experience unprecedented rates of technological advance and economic growth, but an increasing number of hitherto poor countries—those in the periphery of the North Atlantic economic core—were able to participate in this progress. The current crisis presages a new era, one that may be significantly less hospitable to the growth of poor countries. It is too early to know how long it will take for financial stability to be restored in the advanced countries and recovery to set in. But even with the worst of the crisis over, it is likely that we will enter a period in which world trade will grow at a slower pace, there will be less external finance, and the appetite of the United States and other rich nations to run large current account balances will be significantly diminished.

This chapter focuses on the implications of this scenario for the growth prospects of developing nations. In particular, it asks whether we can reconcile two apparently conflicting demands on the world economic system. On the one hand, global macroeconomic stability requires that we avoid

The author thanks Roberto Zagha for persuading him to write this chapter and Mario Blejer, Robert Lawrence, and Arvind Subramanian for comments.

large current account imbalances of the type that the world economy experienced in the run-up to the crisis. Epitomized by the U.S.-China bilateral trade relationship, these imbalances played at the very least an important supporting role in bringing on the financial crisis. In the next stage of the world economy, there will be much greater pressure on countries with large deficits or surpluses to reduce these imbalances through adjustments in their currency and macroeconomic policies.

On the other hand, a return to high growth in the developing countries requires that these countries resume their push into tradable goods and services. As I argue below, countries that grew rapidly in the postwar period were those that were able to capture a growing share of the world market for manufactures and other nonprimary products. Prior to the crisis of 2008, this push was accommodated by the willingness of the United States and a few other developed nations to run large trade deficits. This is no longer a feasible strategy for large or middle-income developing nations.

Are the requirements of global macro stability and economic convergence at odds with each other? Will the developing nations' need to generate large increases in the supply of tradables inevitably clash with the world's intolerance of trade imbalances?

Not necessarily. There is, in fact, no inherent conflict, once we understand that what matters for growth in developing nations is not the size of their trade surplus or even the volume of their exports. As I show in this chapter, what matters for growth is their *output* of nontraditional tradables, which can expand without limit as long as domestic demand expands at the same time. Maintaining an undervalued currency has the upside that it subsidizes the production of tradables, but it also has the downside that it taxes the domestic consumption of tradables, which is why it generates a trade surplus. It is possible to have the upside without the downside, by directly encouraging the production of tradables. A large part of this chapter is devoted to making this rather simple, important, and overlooked point.

There are many ways in which the profitability of tradables can be enhanced, including reducing the cost of nontraded inputs and services through appropriately targeted investments in infrastructure. But it is reasonable to expect that industrial policies will be part of the arsenal. So the external policy environment will have to be more tolerant of such policies, including explicit subsidies on tradables (as long as the effects on the trade balance are neutralized through appropriate adjustments in the real exchange rate). Permissiveness on industrial policies is the "price" to be paid for greater discipline on real exchange rates and external imbalances.

The bottom line is that the growth potential of developing nations need not be severely affected as long as the implications of this new world for domestic and international policies are well understood.

To trace the likely effect of the crisis on growth, we need to have a good fix on the drivers of growth. So I begin the chapter by providing an interpretation of growth performance in the world economy since the end of the Second World War. I argue that the engine of growth has been rapid structural change in the developing nations—from traditional, primary products to nontraditional, mostly industrial products. This structural transformation was facilitated by what I call productivist policies in successful countries. I then ask how the contours of the world economy post-crisis are likely to affect this process. Slow growth in the developed world and reduced appetite for international lending do not directly threaten growth prospects in developing nations. The threat is that lower demand for (or acceptance of) imports from developing countries will make it harder for these countries to engage in rapid structural change. This threat can be averted by developing nations employing more balanced growth strategies that allow the consumption of tradables to expand alongside production. I present the simple analytics of subsidies on tradables to show how it is possible to engineer structural change in the direction of tradables without generating trade surpluses along the way. I also provide some illustrations of the kind of policies that can be used.

The Miracle Years

The period since 1950 has been unique in terms of economic growth. As figure 7.1 reveals, what is truly remarkable about this era is not that the *overall* rate of economic growth has been high by historical standards. Taken as a whole, the post-1950 period did not greatly outperform the gold standard era of 1870–1913. What stands out after 1950 are the stupendously high rates of growth achieved by the *best-performing* countries. Japan, the Republic of Korea, and China were the growth champions during the three subperiods 1950–73, 1973–90, and 1990–2005, respectively, with annual per capita growth rates between 6 and 8 percent. These rates are historically unprecedented and greatly exceed those experienced by the growth champions of earlier eras. For example, the most rapidly growing country under the classical gold standard, Norway, registered a per capita annual growth rate barely above 2 percent.

So something happened in the world economy after about 1950 that allowed it to support much more rapid economic convergence in the lower-income countries. What was this change? Commodity price–led booms and capital-inflow cycles can explain short-term changes in economic performance, and these clearly had something to do with the high growth that occurred throughout the developing world in the decade prior to the crash of 2008. But the longer-term nature of the expansion of the growth frontier suggests that something more fundamental, and much more secular in nature, changed as well.

Conventional accounts, heavily influenced by the Chinese miracle of the last quarter century, emphasize the enabling role of globalization. This too provides a poor explanation. The international integration of markets in goods and assets gathered speed slowly and reached its apogee only after the 1990s, whereas economic convergence on the part of successful countries

Figure 7.1. Growth of GDP per Capita in Select Regions and Time Periods

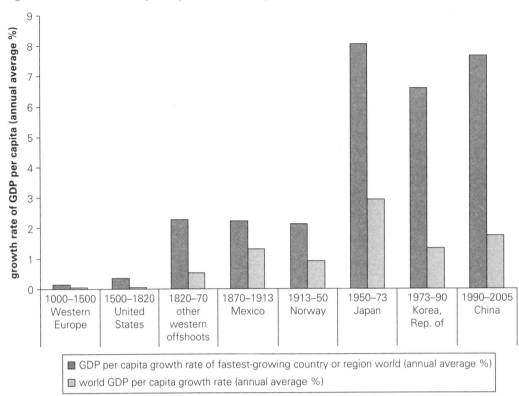

Source: Maddison 2001; World Bank, various years.

was as rapid in the couple of decades after 1950 as it has been more recently. China was preceded by Korea, which was, in turn, preceded by Japan. If anything, a greater number of developing countries in Asia, Latin America, and Africa experienced rapid convergence in the initial decades after the Second World War than in more recent decades (Rodrik 2007b: ch. 1).

What is common about Japan, Korea, and China is that they based their growth strategies on developing industrial capabilities, rather than on specializing according to their (static) comparative advantages. They each became manufacturing superpowers in short order—and much more rapidly than one would have expected based on their resource endowments. China's export bundle was built up using strategic industrial policies that forced foreign companies to transfer technology and, as a result, resembles one for a country that is three or four times as rich (Rodrik 2006). Korea started out with very little manufacturing capability and quickly moved from simple manufactures (in the 1960s) to more complex products (in the 1970s). Japan, unlike the other two countries, had developed an industrial base (prior to the Second World War), but this base was totally destroyed in the war and was restored thanks to trade and industrial policies that protected domestic producers.

The general lesson to be drawn from the experience of these postwar growth champions is this: high-growth countries are those that undertake rapid structural transformation from low-productivity ("traditional") to high-productivity ("modern") activities. These modern activities are largely tradable products, and, within tradables, they are mostly industrial ones (although tradable services are clearly becoming important as well).[1] In other words, poor countries become rich by producing what rich countries produce.

This experience is quite different from the nineteenth-century pattern of growth, where success in the periphery was based on specialization in commodities and primary products. It explains why high performers in the postwar period have been able to grow so much faster than the growth champions of earlier eras (for example, Mexico in 1870–1913 or Norway in 1913–50; figure 7.1).

The close association between movement into industry and high growth is evident in the postwar data. This is shown in figures 7.2 and 7.3 for two measures of industrial activity, the share of industrial value added in gross domestic product (GDP) and the share of industrial employment in total employment, respectively. I have regressed five-year averages for economic growth on corresponding averages for industrial activity, controlling for initial income levels as well as fixed effects for countries and time periods. The economically relevant distinction here is between modern and traditional, not between industry and the rest of the economy. There are modern, tradable activities in agriculture (for example, horticulture) and services (for example, call centers) as well. But in the absence of data for a large enough sample of countries, I use "industry" as my proxy for nontraditional activities.

The scatter plots show what happens to growth when the shares of industrial output or employment change over time within a country. (Note that country fixed effects absorb time-invariant factors specific to individual economies.) In each case, the message is loud and clear. An expansion of industrial activity is closely associated with faster economic growth. Moreover, unlike what a simple comparative advantage story would suggest, this relationship is not any weaker in lower-income countries. The slope coefficient changes very little over different income ranges.

Why is transition into modern industrial activities an engine of economic growth? As I discuss in Rodrik (2008) and in line with a long tradition of dual-economy models, the answer seems to be that significant gaps exist between the social marginal productivities in traditional and modern parts of developing economies. Even very poor economies have economic activities—horticulture in Ethiopia, auto assembly in India, consumer electronics in China—where productivity levels are not too far off from

---

[1] See Felipe and others (2007) for a recent analysis of the patterns of structural change in Asia, which emphasizes that many services have become important contributors to economywide total factor productivity growth alongside industry.

Figure 7.2. Relationship between Industrial Share in GDP and Economic Growth

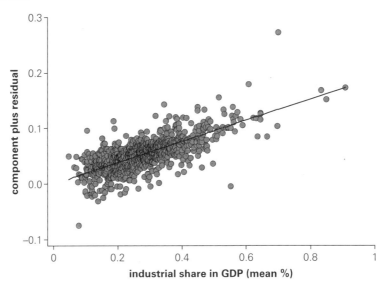

Source: Author's calculations using data from World Bank, various years; Center for International Comparisons, various years.

Figure 7.3. Relationship between Share of Industrial Employment in Total Employment and Economic Growth

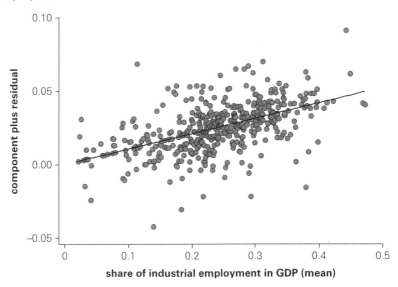

Source: Author's calculations using data from World Bank, various years; Center for International Comparisons, various years.
Note: Each point in the figure corresponds to a five-year subperiod during 1960–2004 for a specific country. The growth rates control for initial income levels and country and period fixed effects.

what we observe in the advanced economies.[2] As resources move from traditional activities toward modern activities, economywide productivity increases. These gaps can be due to a wide range of features that are specific to underdevelopment. I discuss two broad categories in Rodrik (2008). One has to do with institutional weaknesses, such as poor protection of property rights and weak contract enforcement, which make themselves felt more intensively in tradable activities. The second are various market failures and externalities—for example, learning spillovers and coordination failures—associated with modern activities. In both cases, industrial activity and investment are underprovided in market equilibrium. Anything that speeds up structural transformation in the requisite direction will speed up the rate of economic growth.

What is the secret for achieving this structural transformation? Even though actual policies have differed significantly across successful countries, one can still identify some important common elements. First, it is clear that sound "fundamentals" have played a role, as long as we interpret the term quite broadly and do not associate it with any specific laundry list of policies (such as the Washington Consensus or the governance reforms that are currently in fashion). Thus all successful countries have had governments that have prioritized economic growth, followed market-friendly policies, and maintained macroeconomic stability. These appear to be the sine qua non of economic growth. But the ways in which these principles can be put into practice are so numerous and context specific that enunciating them hardly provides a guide to action (Rodrik 2007b).

Second, all successful countries have followed what one might call productivist policies. These are activist policies aimed at enhancing the profitability of modern industrial activities and accelerating the movement of resources toward modern industrial activities. They go considerably beyond the conventional recommendation to reduce red tape, corruption, and the cost of doing business. In addition (or sometimes instead), they entail the following:

- Explicit *industrial policies* in support of new economic activities (trade protection, subsidies, tax and credit incentives, special government attention)
- Undervalued currencies to promote tradables
- A certain degree of *repression of finance*, to enable subsidized credit, development banking, and currency undervaluation.

---

2 What is also striking is that significant heterogeneity exists in productivity within modern activities as well. This is documented in detailed McKinsey productivity studies (McKinsey Global Institute 2001, 2003) as well as recent academic work (Bartelsman, Haltiwanger, and Scarpetta 2006; Hsieh and Klenow 2007). One way to interpret these findings is to recognize that segments of what we normally think of as modern are really more akin to traditional activities. The structural transformation that is called for is also *within* these sectors.

It is true that industrial policies have often failed. But it is also true that it is virtually impossible to identify countries, whether in Asia (Korea; Taiwan, China) or in Latin America (Chile), that have done well without them. Just as it is the case with fiscal policy, say, or education policy, what distinguishes good performers from bad performers is not the presence or absence of the policy, but the skill with which it is implemented.

The reason that undervaluation of the currency works as a powerful force for economic growth is that it acts as a kind of industrial policy. By raising the domestic relative price of tradable economic activities, it increases the profitability of such activities and spurs capacity and employment generation in the modern industrial sectors that are key to growth. Table 7.1, adapted from Rodrik (2008), shows the mechanism at work. Columns 1 and 2 are fixed-effects panel regressions, which establish that high levels of the real exchange rates (undervalued currencies) are associated with larger industrial sectors, measured by either output or employment. Columns 3 and 4 are the second stage of two-stage least squares (TSLS) regressions, which show that undervalued currencies result in higher growth *through* their effects on the size of industry. As discussed in detail in Rodrik (2008), this association between undervalued currencies and high growth is a robust feature of the postwar data, particularly for lower-income countries.

Undervaluation has the practical advantage, compared to explicit industrial policies, of being an across-the-board policy not requiring selectivity and therefore entailing fewer agency problems (rent seeking and corruption). Perhaps this accounts for its widespread success in promoting development, as just documented. But it also has several disadvantages. First, it requires that the macroeconomic policy framework be sufficiently flexible and adaptable to the needs of undervaluation: a real exchange rate depreciation is possible only if the economy can generate an increase in saving relative to investment, which has obvious implications for fiscal and other policies (Rodrik 2008). Second, undervaluation does an imperfect job of targeting modern economic activities: traditional primary products receive a boost in profits alongside new industrial activities. And third, undervaluation is not just a subsidy on the production of tradables; it also acts as a domestic tax on their consumption (it raises the relative price of imported goods). That is why it produces an excess supply of tradables—a trade surplus. The last point is of special relevance to the subject of this chapter, and I return to it below.

Finally, an important *external* element enabled the postwar growth miracles to take place. The advanced nations of the world, and the United States in particular, essentially had an attitude of benign neglect toward the policies in the developing world that made the industrial transformation possible. The General Agreement on Tariffs and Trade (GATT) system placed very few restrictions on developing countries. The disciplines were few and far between on trade policies and nonexistent on subsidies and other industrial policies. The International Monetary Fund (IMF) could be tough when it came to conditionality on monetary and fiscal policies, but only in instances where countries faced external deficits (and had *over*valued

Table 7.1. Impact of Undervaluation on Industrial Activity: Panel of Five-Year Subperiods, 1960–2004

Independent variable	Industry share in GDP		Growth (TSLS)	
	(1)	(2)	(3)	(4)
ln current income	0.079** (9.99)	0.025 (1.51)		
ln initial income			−0.134** (−8.33)	−0.071** (−4.39)
ln undervaluation	0.024** (3.62)	0.042** (4.87)		
Share of industry in GDP			1.716** (7.59)	
Share of industry in employment				1.076** (6.15)
Time dummies	Yes	Yes	Yes	Yes
Country dummies	Yes	Yes	Yes	Yes
Number of observations	985	469	938	459

Source: Author's calculations.
Note: Industry and agriculture shares in GDP are in constant local-currency units. In columns 3 and 4, industry shares are regressed on undervaluation, income, and lagged income in the first stage.
** Significant at the 1 percent level.

currencies). There was no presumption in favor of financial liberalization or capital-account opening, since many of the advanced economies themselves retained financial controls well into the 1970s. Consumers in the United States were happy to absorb the excess supply of tradables on the world market, even at the cost of rising borrowing from abroad.

The global environment became less permissive over time. Unlike its predecessor, the World Trade Organization (WTO) placed severe restrictions on the conduct of industrial policies in middle-income developing countries. Financial liberalization and capital mobility became the norm, with developing countries expected to converge toward "best practice" in these areas (although it became recognized, in the aftermath of the Asian financial crisis, that too rapid liberalization may be undesirable). Finally, the U.S. trade deficit with China and the undervaluation of the renminbi became serious issues, with the IMF charged to carry out surveillance over "currency manipulation" (although in practice the effort led nowhere).

Despite these changes, until the present crisis the global context remained largely benign with respect to developing countries' need to diversify into industrial products in order to accelerate their growth. It is much less clear that we will be able to say the same about the environment going forward.

What Will Be Different after the Crisis?

It is a safe bet that financial stability in the United States and other advanced countries will eventually be restored in one way or another. Given the magnitude of the crisis, however, its residue is likely to linger for quite a while. In particular, developed countries may not recover quickly, and their growth may remain low or nonexistent for some years to come. Japan's stagnation following its crisis in the early 1990s—after a period of very high growth—provides one worrisome antecedent. It is difficult to know whether the United States and Europe will replicate this experience, but it is certainly impossible to rule out the possibility.

While slower growth in the advanced countries would be bad news, its implications for the developing world would be largely indirect. When rich nations grow more slowly (or not at all), the stock of knowledge and technology that is available to firms in poor countries is not reduced. The potential for productivity enhancement and catch-up remains fully in place. From an economic standpoint, the rate of growth of developing countries depends not on the speed at which rich countries grow, but on the difference between their and rich nations' income *levels*—that is, the convergence gap. The former does affect the latter, but only slowly and over time.

The indirect effects operate through the channels of international trade and finance. Three likely developments are of potential concern: (a) reduced appetite for cross-border lending, (b) slower growth in world trade, and (c) less tolerance for large external trade imbalances. I discuss each in turn.

Reduction in Cross-Border Lending

Weaknesses in the financial markets of developing nations had little to do with the emergence of the financial crisis of 2008. Nevertheless, since it will take some time for the trend toward deleveraging and flight to safety to reverse itself, it is reasonable to expect that there will be some predictable, negative effects on capital flows to developing countries.

Whether one thinks that this is a big deal or not depends on one's views about the growth process in developing nations. If we believe that the binding constraint to growth lies on the saving side, then we would conclude that a reduction in net inflows comes with a significant growth penalty. This would be the conventional inference drawn from the neoclassical growth model and the presumption that private returns to investment are higher in poor nations than in rich nations. But the experience of the last few decades gives us ample reason to take this view with a heavy grain of salt. The presumption that the saving constraint binds in most poor nations is contradicted by one important stylized fact: high growth and net capital inflows are negatively (rather than positively) correlated across developing countries. This was demonstrated in an important paper by Prasad, Rajan, and Subramanian (2007), whose central finding is shown in figure 7.4. China, of course, is the best-known case of a high-growth country with a trade surplus, but as the evidence of Prasad, Rajan, and Subramanian shows, China's experience is not an anomaly. Rapidly growing countries are more likely to be net exporters of capital than net importers (and this is true even when aid flows, which tend to go disproportionately to the worse-off countries, are taken out).

Figure 7.4. Net Capital Outflows and Growth in Various Countries, Pre-1990 and Post-1990

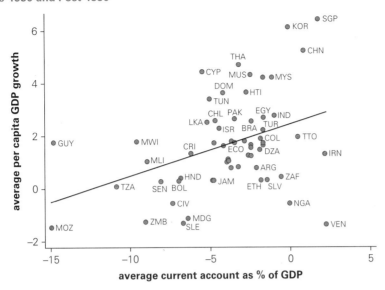

Source: Prasad, Rajan, and Subramanian 2007.
Note: Each point in the figure corresponds to a five-year subperiod during 1960–2004 for a specific country. The growth rates control for initial income levels and country and period fixed effects.

This should not be a surprise in light of the growth story laid out in the previous section. The binding constraint in that interpretation is not the supply of loanable funds, but investment demand in tradables. What limits growth is not access to finance, but the low (private) profitability of modern tradables. Accordingly, the key to growth is not more finance, but enhanced private profitability in tradables. Moreover, in typical second-best fashion, more finance can result in lower growth if it aggravates the more significant constraint. How? Through the effect of capital inflows on the real exchange rate. As shown in Prasad, Rajan, and Subramanian (2007) and Rodrik (2008), countries with larger net capital inflows and more open capital accounts tend to have more overvalued currencies. This mechanism goes a long way to explain why financial globalization has proved so disappointing for the vast majority of developing nations (Rodrik and Subramanian 2009).

No doubt there are some countries for which low domestic saving is indeed a binding constraint. This constraint can be relaxed, in principle at least, through access to foreign finance. Brazil, for example, has built a diversified agricultural and industrial base (thanks in large part to industrial policies in earlier decades), but all indications are that investment levels in modern economic activities are constrained primarily by the high cost of capital driven by low domestic saving (Hausmann 2008). Turkey represents a similar case. Growth and investment in Brazil and Turkey go up and down with net capital inflows. However, since capital flows are highly volatile and subject to "sudden stops," neither Brazil nor Turkey has been able to generate consistently high growth since the end of the 1980s. So even in saving-constrained cases such as these, the appropriate remedy lies not in resuscitating financial globalization, but in focusing on domestic policies (such as, in this instance, reductions in fiscal deficits and encouragement of private saving).

Neither is there much cause to be concerned about a reduction in global risk sharing. In principle, higher levels of gross (two-way) flows allow countries to insure themselves against idiosyncratic risks. But here, too, the evidence cuts the other way. Kose, Prasad, and Terrones (2007) find that consumption risk sharing has actually declined in the developing world since the 1990s (while it has improved in the rich countries). One reason, of course, is the greater prevalence of financial crises in a financially globalized world.

The bottom line is that developing nations should not shed too many tears if the world economy experiences some financial deglobalization. Countries that have been recipients of large capital inflows may even end up seeing their growth prospects improved, since they will now experience less pressure for real exchange rate appreciation. And experiencing fewer financial crises is nothing to get upset about.

Less Buoyant World Trade

Lower growth in the advanced countries also implies a lower rate of expansion of their demand for imports, which has implications for both prices and quantities in world trade.

On the price side, two relative prices matter to developing nations—the terms of trade and the relative price of industrial goods—and they are likely to move in opposite directions. Consider first the terms of trade. The developed and developing worlds share the same terms of trade, which are the inverse of each other. As long as domestic demand is slower to pick up in the developed world than in the developing world, which is my baseline assumption here, the terms of trade are likely to move in the rich countries' favor. This will constitute a net loss of real income to the developing countries, but it is unlikely to have much of a perceptible effect on their growth *rates*. To the extent that developing countries are able to continue to diversify into new products (of the type produced in the rich countries), they can avoid large terms-of-trade declines, as rapidly growing countries have, to date, managed to do.

The second relative price of consequence is the price of industrial goods relative to primary goods on world markets. This is of independent interest to the developing countries, because it affects the relative profitability of their modern tradable sectors and hence the speed with which structural change and economic growth take place through the mechanisms I have already discussed. This relative price is not exactly the inverse of the rich countries' terms of trade, but it is likely to be negatively correlated with it (since developed countries are net industrial exporters and net commodity importers). Consequently, this particular channel presents some good news for the growth prospects of developing countries. Slower growth in the North reduces the prospects of a Dutch disease in the South.

What about the quantity effects? We normally associate a slower pace in export volumes with lower economic growth, but on closer look the causal effect from the former to the latter is not at all clear. In the very short run, there may be positive Keynesian effects from export demand. But it is hard to believe that exports can act as an engine of growth for Keynesian, excess-capacity reasons over the medium to longer run. And if they could, developing nations could simply substitute fiscal stimulus and get growth that way!

For export quantities to matter for economic growth over the longer run, one must believe either in learning or other spillovers from exports, which have been hard to document, or in the story I laid out above, in which tradables are special because that is where the higher-productivity activities are. The two accounts differ on the importance they attach to the act of exporting per se. The "spillovers-from-exporting" story relies on the technological or marketing externalities that are created when a tradable good crosses an international boundary. The "tradables-are-special" story is indifferent to whether international trade actually takes place or not.

In table 7.2, I report the results of regressions where the two hypotheses are allowed to compete against each other. Each column is a regression estimated with fixed effects for countries and time periods, using a panel of five-year subperiods. The regressors, in addition to the fixed effects, are lagged income (to account for convergence), the share of industrial value added in GDP, and the share of exports in GDP. In order to allow comparison of the estimated coefficients on the industry and export shares, I have standardized these indicators. So the coefficient tells us the estimated effect of a single standard-deviation change in the relevant variable.

Table 7.2. Exports and Industrial Output as Determinants of Growth in GDP per Capita: Panel of Five-Year Subperiods, 1960–2004

Independent variable	Full sample (1)	Post-1990 sample (2)	Post-1990 sample, export outliers removed (3)	Developing-country sample (4)
ln initial income	−0.043** (−7.98)	−0.125** (−8.56)	−0.125** (−8.32)	−0.045** (−5.57)
Share of industry in GDP	0.016** (4.54)	0.028** (3.57)	0.028** (3.53)	0.021** (4.06)
Share of exports in GDP	0.007** (2.67)	0.006 (1.69)	0.006 (1.49)	−0.001 (−0.34)
Time dummies	Yes	Yes	Yes	Yes
Country dummies	Yes	Yes	Yes	Yes
Number of observations	850	417	410	527

Source: Author's calculations.

Note: Industry and export shares are standardized variables. Column 3 excludes observations where export shares exceed 100 percent. Column 4 excludes observations where per capita GDP is greater than $6,000.

** Significant at 1 percent level.

The first column runs the regression on the entire post-1960 sample for which there are data. Industry and export shares are both statistically significant, but the estimated impact of industrial activity is more than twice as powerful: a one-standard-deviation increase in industrial shares is estimated to increase growth by 1.6 percentage points, while the corresponding increase in export shares boosts growth only by 0.7 percentage point. Moreover, the result with export shares is not robust. When the sample is restricted to post-1990 data (column 2), the estimated coefficient on exports becomes insignificant. And the difference in the magnitude of the effects rises to a factor of between 4 and 5 (0.028 versus 0.006). When a few observations corresponding to countries with very high export shares (for example, Luxemburg and Hong Kong, China) are excluded, the significance of the export variable is reduced further (column 3). Perhaps most important, when we restrict the sample to developing countries, the coefficient on the export share turns slightly negative (and is statistically insignificant), while the coefficient on the industry share rises (to 0.021) and remains strongly significant (column 4). The horse race between industrial activity and export orientation has a clear winner.

As long as what matters is industrial (and other nontraditional) output, an increase in world trade can even be a mixed blessing for many developing countries. Leaving aside the presence of large trade imbalances, to which I turn in the next section, growth in exports implies growth in imports. If the former add to demand for domestically produced tradables, the latter subtract from it. A *balanced* increase in international trade creates no additional net demand for domestic tradables. If imports are dominated by industrial products, as is the case in many developing nations, a large expansion of trade can even be bad for domestic industrial output.

The experiences of various groups of developing countries have differed in this respect. For countries like China and many other low-cost suppliers of manufactures, which were rapidly diversifying into industrial products and became large importers of primary commodities, the expansion of global trade was an unambiguous benefit for their industrial sector. But many other countries found their industrial sectors coming under severe competition from precisely these low-cost sources. Countries ranging from Ethiopia to Mexico found their manufacturing firms getting squeezed by imports.

Whether the depressed returns to import substitution were more than offset by the higher returns to exporting (and thus whether the net effect of trade on industrial activity was positive) depended very much on the nature of other economic policies in place. The evidence seems to indicate that the large-scale entry of China and other low-cost producers in world markets affected middle-income countries particularly adversely. This is shown in figure 7.5, which displays the relationship between income levels and industrial activity in the periods before and after 1990. This relationship is quite (log)linear in the earlier period, but becomes visibly concave after 1990. What the picture makes clear is that countries at low income levels

Figure 7.5. Income Gradient of Industrial Shares in GDP

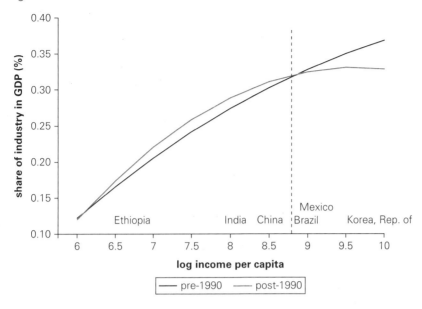

Source: Author's calculations.
Note: Relationship is based on a quadratic fit.

were able to support much higher levels of industrial activity after 1990 compared to earlier periods, while the opposite was true for countries at medium- and higher-level incomes. What was an enabling environment for China and India was not nearly as hospitable for Mexico or Brazil.

The bottom line is that reduced buoyancy in world trade is of smaller consequence for the growth of developing nations than is usually imagined. What matters for growth is the ability to expand industrial economic activities, not trade per se. Industrial activity can increase without increasing trade, if domestic demand rises alongside. The kind of policy changes needed to achieve this outcome are discussed below.

Smaller Current Account Imbalances

Finally, industrial nations are likely to tolerate smaller current account imbalances, both as a consequence of lower growth and because of the lesson from the crash of 2008 that indicate large imbalances portend trouble down the road. So countries with large trade surpluses—anything close to or higher than 5 percent of GDP—are likely to come under pressure to adjust their currency and macroeconomic policies, especially if these countries are large and systemically important.

As a matter of accounting, a trade surplus is a source of net demand for a country's tradables. So we do expect trade surpluses and growth to go together, especially in countries that are diversifying into "modern" tradables such as industrial products. This is an important reason behind the negative, rather than the positive, association between net capital inflows

(current account deficits) and growth, noted above. Might the lower tolerance of current account surpluses from larger developing countries act as
a serious constraint on their growth potential in years ahead?

Once again, we need to remember that the key to growth is the domestic
output of modern tradables, not the excess supply thereof. Systematic evidence on this is provided in table 7.3, which presents the results of another
horse race, this time between industry shares and trade surpluses. The main
result is that once industry shares in GDP are controlled for, trade surpluses exert no additional positive effect on economic growth. This is true
for the full sample (column 1), for post-1990 data (column 2), for samples
in which large trade deficits or surpluses have been removed (column 3),
and for samples restricted to developing countries (column 4). In each one
of these runs, the industry variable is highly significant, while the trade
surplus is not.

The implication for developing nations that have gotten hooked on
trade surpluses as their "engine of growth" should be clear: there is no
need to sacrifice growth as long as domestic demand for tradables increases
alongside domestic supply. Undervaluation of the currency may be out.
But there are other policy options, as I discuss in the next section, that can
spur both the consumption and the production of tradables.

Promoting Industrialization without Trade Surpluses

Let us return to the interpretation underlying the growth dynamics sketched
out above. In this model, poor countries are poor because too few of their
resources are in modern, high-productivity activities. Fast growth happens
when there is rapid structural transformation from low-productivity traditional sectors to high-productivity modern activities. The reason that this

Table 7.3. Trade Surpluses and Industrial Output as Determinants of Growth in GDP per Capita: Panel of Five-Year Subperiods, 1960–2004

Independent variable	Full sample (1)	Post-1990 sample (2)	Post-1990 sample, trade surplus outliers removed (3)	Developing-country sample (4)
In initial income	−0.041** (−7.89)	−0.126** (−8.90)	−0.122** (−8.32)	−0.045** (−5.58)
Share of industry in GDP	0.018** (4.79)	0.029** (3.75)	0.041** (4.39)	0.021** (3.97)
Trade surplus as percent of GDP	−0.002 (−1.25)	0.003 (1.02)	−0.007 (−1.19)	−0.002 (−1.17)
Time dummies	Yes	Yes	Yes	Yes
Country dummies	Yes	Yes	Yes	Yes
Number of observations	850	417	359	527

Source: Author's calculations.
Note: Industry share and trade surplus are standardized variables. Column 3 excludes observations where the absolute value of the trade surplus exceeds 20 percent of GDP. Column 4 excludes observations where per capita GDP is greater than $6,000.
** Significant at 1 percent level.

transformation is not an automatic, market-led process is that there are severe market or institutional failures whose costs are borne disproportionately by the modern sectors. Sometimes transformation is blocked because of low domestic saving and high cost of capital, which keep investment and structural change sluggish. But more typically the problem is a large wedge between private and social returns in modern sectors. These sectors are subject both to learning spillovers and coordination failures and to high costs imposed by weaknesses in legal and regulatory institutions. These weaknesses are hard to remove in short order, and the experience of advanced economies is that they are addressed only through the long course of decades, if not centuries.[3]

So while it would be desirable to address these shortcomings directly, by removing market failures and fixing institutions, as a practical matter such an agenda is too broad and ambitious and hence too unrealistic. As noted previously, successful countries have pursued growth strategies that alleviate these constraints indirectly, by raising the relative profitability of modern activities through other means. What all of these strategies have in common is that they act as *subsidies* on tradables.

Once we strip these strategies to their essence, it becomes easier to understand what is central and what is incidental to their working. In particular, we can see that a strategy of subsidizing tradables need not be associated with undervalued exchange rates and trade surpluses.

The point can be made with the help of figure 7.6, which shows the equilibrium in the market for tradables. The supply of tradables is increasing in the relative price of tradables (R, the real exchange rate), while the demand is decreasing. Start from an initial equilibrium (R^0, Q^0) where there is no excess supply of tradables and therefore the trade balance is zero (panel A). Now suppose the government imposes a production subsidy on tradables. This shifts the supply schedule for tradables out, since, for any level of R, producers of tradables are now willing to supply a larger amount (panel B). Where will the new equilibrium be? If we assume that the real exchange rate remains at R^0, the subsidy would produce not only an increase in the output of tradables, but also a trade surplus (an excess supply of tradables).

But as is shown in panel C of figure 7.6, this is not necessarily the final equilibrium. Unless the government adopts additional macroeconomic policies to maintain the real exchange rate unchanged, there will be an endogenous appreciation of the real exchange rate to R^2, which spurs domestic consumption of tradables and brings the trade balance back to zero. In this final equilibrium, the output of tradables is still higher, even though the real exchange rate has appreciated and the trade balance has been reestablished. That is because the real exchange rate appreciation needed to bring the trade balance back to zero is (proportionately) less than the magnitude of the initial subsidy, since, unlike the subsidy,

---

3   This need not always be the case, of course. Some government-imposed constraints (for example, red tape) are easier to fix than others (for example, inefficient courts).

Figure 7.6. Equilibrium in the Market for Tradables

a. Initial equilibrium

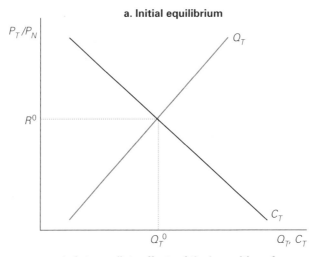

b. Intermediate effects of the imposition of a production subsidy on tradables

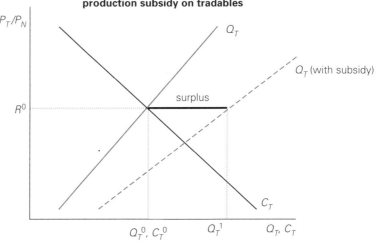

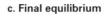

c. Final equilibrium

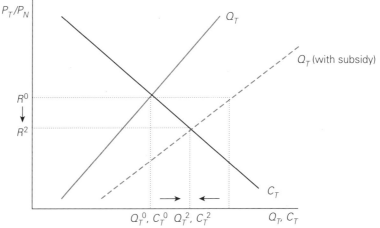

Source: Author.

it affects both the consumption and production margins. Therefore, it does not fully undo the effect of the subsidy on the supply side. The full details are worked out in an explicitly general-equilibrium framework in the appendix to this chapter.

As this analysis demonstrates, it is possible to enhance production incentives for tradables, and to do so by as wide a margin as is necessary, without creating spillovers to the rest of the world in terms of trade imbalances. Unlike currency undervaluation (which taxes domestic consumption of tradables), a policy of explicitly subsidizing tradables (combined with macroeconomic policies that maintain external balance) boosts the domestic consumption of tradables.

What form should this subsidy take in practice? In the rest of this section, I discuss three approaches for increasing the effective producer price of tradables: (a) industrial policies, (b) lower input costs for tradables, and (c) incomes policies. All of these pose practical policies in implementation, so the appropriate mix will depend on the circumstances of each country.

Industrial Policy

In principle, industrial policy is ideally suited to the problem at hand. What needs to be done is to enhance the relative profitability of nontraditional products that face large information externalities or coordination failures or that suffer particularly strongly from the poor institutional environment. That is what good industrial policy attempts to do. Tax exemptions, directed credit, payroll subsidies, investment subsidies, and export-processing zones are some of the forms in which industrial policy gets implemented. What is distinctive about these policies is that they target specific firms or sectors and therefore privilege some at the expense of others. That is what makes industrial policy controversial, of course. But as long as the targeting is done broadly and well—as long as it focuses on new activities at the outer margins of a country's underlying competence—the potential upside is large. The advantage of industrial policy relative to currency undervaluation is precisely that it allows greater fine-tuning and discrimination: traditional tradables (such as primary products and industrial products in which a country has already established itself) need not be subsidized, and the consumption of tradables need not be taxed (as explained previously).

There is still a sense in which subsidies on modern tradables can spill across borders. Even if the net supply of tradables does not increase *in aggregate*, the net supply of those that are targeted for promotion will. Other developing countries will be on the receiving end of this, and if they remain passive, their own industrialization incentives will be blunted. But the right way of expressing this problem is to say that the use of "optimal" industrial policies in some countries increases the costs of not using such policies in others. As some countries alleviate their market imperfections, the costs of not dealing with these imperfections get exacerbated elsewhere. So as long as all countries follow industrial policies that are optimal from their perspective, there are no spillovers to contend with. The spillovers in question can be effectively neutralized as long as other developing countries are following appropriate industrial policies as well.

The two chief arguments against industrial policy are that governments can never do the requisite targeting properly since they lack sufficient information and that even if they could, the process would become rife with rent seeking and corruption. There are good counterarguments to both objections (Rodrik 2007a; 2007b: ch. 4). First, it makes little sense to hold the conduct of industrial policy to the unrealistic standard that governments must always be able to pick the winners. In view of the uncertainties involved, mistakes are not only unavoidable, but part and parcel of optimal program design: if the government never makes any mistakes, it is probably not being ambitious enough. The much more meaningful and desirable requirement is that governments be able to recognize their mistakes and change course when needed. That is obviously a much weaker desideratum than omniscience. And it can be achieved through appropriate institutional design (see Rodrik 2007b: ch. 4).

With respect to corruption, that is a real danger, of course. But industrial policy is hardly the only area of government policy that is susceptible to corruption. Education policy and tax policy, to name just a couple of other areas, are equally at risk. Yet we never advise governments that they should give up on collecting taxes or that they should not finance education and build schools. Instead, we try to think of ways in which these systems can be rendered less susceptible to corruption and rent seeking. There is no reason why industrial policy should be any different. Once again, appropriate institutional design holds the key to better implementation.

The main external obstacle to the wider use of industrial policies by the larger developing countries is the WTO's Agreement on Subsidies. This agreement prohibits the use of subsidies that take the form of fiscal expenditures conditioned on export performance. More seriously, it also renders "actionable" the use of subsidies that have the effect of increasing exports, even if they are not directly conditioned on exports. (Least developed countries are exempt from these rules.) A literal application of this standard would rule many kinds of industrial policies, the objective of which is precisely to increase the domestic supply of tradables. Only subsidies that encourage import substitution would remain exempt.

In practice, of course, there are many loopholes, and one can debate the extent to which this and other WTO agreements actually restrict the space for industrial policies (Rodrik 2007b: ch.4). But it is also the case that the restrictiveness of the Agreement on Subsidies has not been put to a real test. As long as countries were free to use currency policies to encourage industrialization, the WTO constraint did not bind all that much. So China could hugely subsidize its tradables through an undervalued remninbi, while abiding (barely) by WTO rules on subsidies or local content.

In a world where economic growth requires the encouragement of modern economic activities in developing nations, the Agreement on Subsidies makes little economic sense.[4] It rules out a desirable second-best policy for promoting economic diversification and structural change. It has the unintended consequence of inducing governments to favor an inferior policy (in view of its spillovers into trade imbalances), namely undervalued currencies. Worse still, it may encourage trade protection as a defensive measure against industrial imports. If we want greater international oversight on currency practices, as I think we should, we need to substantially relax discipline over industrial subsidies.[5]

Reducing Input Costs for Tradables

A second type of government policy that can shift relative incentives in favor of tradables is to reduce the costs of inputs that are used intensively by modern economic activities. Certain types of specialized industrial or professional skills (such as machinists or call center operators) fit the bill well. Government investment in training in such areas will have the effect of incentivizing modern tradables (and do so in most cases without threatening conflict with the WTO). While straightforward in theory, however, this approach also faces some practical obstacles. The difficulty is that many of the most obvious strategies produce asymmetric effects across different groups of tradables.

Consider, for example, what is perhaps the most immediate policy that comes to mind: reducing trade costs in the form of transport and logistics costs. Such costs can be a significant deterrent to trade, which is why many governments are so keen to invest in trade infrastructure (modernization of ports and improvement of transport). But the effects of this on industrial incentives are ambiguous, for the same reason that trade liberalization yields uncertain dynamic gains. A reduction in trade costs helps export activities, but it also hurts import substitution activities, because it takes some "natural protection" away from them. The net result depends on whether more new, dynamic activities are crowded in than are crowded out. It cannot be determined a priori without some careful prospective analysis.

Or consider reducing tariffs on intermediate inputs. This is good for all final goods producers, but not so good for competing intermediate-goods producers at home. The net effect is once again indeterminate.

---

4   There is a good case to be made that the prohibition on subsidies has little economic rationale, independent from the developmental argument I am making here. After all, subsidies are trade creating (unlike import barriers), and a country that subsidizes its tradables gives the rest of the world an economic "gift" to the extent that the subsidy results in greater supply and lower world prices. The WTO's approach to subsidies is mercantilist and overly influenced by the interests of competing producers.

5   Oversight of currency practices is usually thought of as being the province of the IMF. But Mattoo and Subramanian (2008) have argued that the WTO is a much more suitable organization for this purpose since what is at stake are imbalances in trade flows, and the WTO has the capacity to make its rulings stick. The discussion here suggests that any move in this direction should have as a direct quid pro quo the weakening of the discipline on subsidies.

Wage Restraint

The single most important nontraded input in the modern sector is labor. Developing countries typically have segmented labor markets, where formal sector wages may differ significantly from wages in informal activities and the rural sector. In such settings, the institutional and regulatory setting exerts a large influence on determination of the wages most relevant to modern sector firms. Consequently, changes in these arrangements can have a correspondingly significant effect on the relative profitability of modern tradable activities.

In societies where a habit of cooperation exists among social partners, it may be possible to negotiate wage restraint in the formal parts of the economy in return for the expectation of continued job creation. Unions that are able to think long term and to internalize the interests of their future as well as present membership may be persuaded to moderate wage demands.

Unfortunately, such social pacts are more common in advanced economies with centralized wage bargaining (such as Sweden, Austria, or Ireland) than in developing ones (for example, Mauritius). When they are set up, it is typically as a temporary arrangement to deal with a severe macroeconomic crisis (for example, Mexico in 1987, Korea in 1997). Institutions of conflict management are weak in developing countries, along with all other institutions. For the vast majority of developing nations, therefore, this is no easy alternative to explicit industrial policy.

Concluding Remarks

How hospitable will the global environment be for economic growth in the developing world as we emerge from the present financial crisis? The answer depends, I have argued, on how well we manage the following tension. On the one hand, global macro stability requires that we prevent external imbalances from getting too large. On the other hand, growth in poor nations requires that the world economy be able to absorb a rapid increase in the supply of tradables produced in the developing world.

For many small developing countries, undervaluation of their currencies remains a viable industrialization strategy, although it is not even second best for reasons I have discussed above. Given their small footprint in world trade, it is unlikely that they will make a large appearance on the radar screen of surveillance over "currency manipulation practices." But middle-income and large developing nations have to transition into alternative strategies. They will have to contemplate—and the rest of the world will have to allow—the use of various explicit industrial promotion measures for nontraditional tradables, including subsidies. Combined with real exchange rate appreciation, such subsidies would boost the supply of nontraditional goods, but be neutral with respect to the trade balance. In effect, industrial policy can be assigned to the structural transformation target, while the exchange rate is assigned to the external balance.

Removing the real exchange rate as a tool for development does represent a cost to the larger developing countries. But failure to realize that alternative approaches exist and can be used as substitutes would greatly magnify the adverse effects on growth.

If the need for such a strategy is not recognized and trade rules on subsidies are enforced blindly, we are likely to find ourselves in a period of great tension in international economic relations. This tension will exhibit itself not only as a North-South divide, but also as a cleavage within the developing world. As the relative size of advanced economies and their markets shrink, manufactured exports from low-cost suppliers will spill over into the markets of middle-income countries with greater force. If the latter do not have their own industrial promotion and diversification strategies, they will come under strong pressure from domestic industry to react in a defensive manner, by erecting protectionist barriers against imports from other developing countries. Restricting the policy space on industrial policies will have the unintended consequence of fostering trade protection.

So there is room for guarded optimism with regard to the prospects for developing nations. The good news is that developing countries can continue to grow rapidly, even with some slowdown in world trade and reduced appetite for capital flows and trade imbalances. The bad news is that the favorable outcome will not happen on its own, as a result of the magic of market forces. As we reform global rules and redesign domestic strategies, we need to ensure that the environment will be as conducive to structural transformation in the developing world as it has been for the last 50 years.

References

Bartelsman, Eric, John Haltiwanger, and Stefano Scarpetta. 2006. "Cross-Country Differences in Productivity: The Role of Allocative Efficiency." Draft report. December. http://econweb.umd.edu/~haltiwan/alloc_eff_july3108.pdf.

Center for International Comparisons. Various years. Penn World Tables. Philadelphia: University of Pennsylvania, Center for International Comparisons of Production, Income, and Prices.

Felipe, Jesus, Miguel Leon-Ledesma, Matteo Lanzafame, and Gemma Estrada. 2007. "Sectoral Engines of Growth in Developing Asia: Stylized Facts and Implications." ERD Working Paper 107 (November). Asian Development Bank, Tokyo.

Hausmann, Ricardo. 2008. "In Search of the Chains That Hold Brazil Back." Harvard University, Kennedy School, Center for International Development, Cambridge, MA. August.

Hsieh, Chang-Tai, and Peter J. Klenow. 2007. "Misallocation and Manufacturing TFP in China and India." NBER Working Paper 13290 (August). National Bureau of Economic Research, Cambridge, MA.

Kose, M. Ayhan, Eswar S. Prasad, and Marco E. Terrones. 2007. "How Does Financial Globalization Affect Risk Sharing? Patterns and Channels." IMF Working Paper 07/238. International Monetary Fund, Washington, DC.

Maddison, Angus. 2001. *The World Economy: A Millennial Perspective.* Paris: OECD.

Mattoo, Aaditya, and Arvind Subramanian. 2008. "Currency Undervaluation and Sovereign Wealth Funds: A New Role for the World Trade Organization." Working Paper (January). Peterson Institute for International Economics, Washington, DC.

McKinsey Global Institute. 2001. *India: The Growth Imperative.* San Francisco: McKinsey.

———. 2003. *Turkey: Making the Growth and Productivity Breakthrough.* Istanbul: McKinsey.

Prasad, Eswar, Raghuram G. Rajan, and Arvind Subramanian. 2007. "Foreign Capital and Economic Growth." *Brookings Papers on Economic Activity* 1: 153–209.

Rodrik, Dani. 2006. "What's So Special about China's Exports?" *China and World Economy* 14 (5, September-October): 1–19.

———. 2007a. "Normalizing Industrial Policy." Paper prepared for the Commission on Growth and Development, Washington, DC (August).

———. 2007b. *One Economics, Many Recipes.* Princeton, NJ: Princeton University Press.

———. 2008. "The Real Exchange Rate and Economic Growth." *Brookings Papers on Economic Activity* (Fall): 365–413.

Rodrik, Dani, and Arvind Subramanian. 2009. "Why Did Financial Globalization Disappoint?" *IMF Staff Papers* 56 (1, Spring): 112–38.

World Bank. Various years. World Development Indicators. Washington, DC: World Bank.

Appendix: Production Subsidies on Tradables in General Equilibrium

This appendix divides the economy into two sectors, producing tradable and nontradable goods, respectively. Let us take the price of nontraded goods to be the numeraire and fix it to 1. The demand side of the economy is represented with the expenditure function $E(R, 1, u)$, where u stands for aggregate utility and R is the (relative) price of tradables and the real exchange rate. The supply side of the economy is represented by a GDP or revenue function given by $G(R, 1)$, in which the factor endowments of the economy are repressed since they are taken to be in fixed supply throughout.

Of interest are the effects of a production subsidy on tradables, s. The direct effect of such a subsidy is to increase the supply price of tradables, so the GDP function is rewritten as $G(R + s, 1)$, while the expenditure function remains unchanged.

Equilibrium in this economy can be expressed using three equations. Note first that the partial derivative of $G(.)$ with respect to the price of tradables, expressed as $G_1(R + s, 1)$, gives the supply of tradables, Q_T.

$$Q_T = G_1(R + s, 1). \tag{7.1}$$

The second relationship is an expenditure-equals-income identity:

$$E(R, 1, u) = G(R + s, 1) - s\, G_1(R + s, 1). \tag{7.2}$$

The subsidy is assumed to be financed through lump-sum taxes, so the income available for private sector consumption is GDP minus the tax revenue needed to finance the subsidy. The last term in equation 7.2 is the corresponding tax revenue. Finally, we express equilibrium in the market for tradable goods:

$$E_1(R, 1, u) = G_1(R + s, 1), \tag{7.3}$$

where $E_1(.)$ is the (Hicksian) demand for the tradable good. By Walras's Law, equations 7.2 and 7.3 guarantee that the market equilibrium for nontraded goods holds as well. These three equations determine the three endogenous variables in the system, Q_T, R, and u.

From equation 7.1, it is evident that the output of the tradable good depends exclusively on what happens to its supply price, $R + s$. If this price increases in response to an increase in the subsidy, the supply response will be positive.

Performing the comparative statics of the system yields the following result:

$$\frac{d(R + s)}{ds} = \left[\frac{E_{11}(.)}{E_{11}(.) - R_{11}(.)} \right] \left[1 - sR_{11}(.) \frac{E_{1u}(.)}{E_u(.)} \right]^{-1}.$$

To interpret this expression, focus first on the case where the subsidy is "small"; the expression is evaluated at $s = 0$. Since $E_{11}(.) < 0$ and $R_{11}(.) > 0$ from the properties of expenditure and revenue functions, $d(R + s)/ds$ is unambiguously positive in this case, which is to say that the appreciation of the real exchange rate does not fully undo the incentive effects of the subsidy.

In the case where s is not zero or very small to begin with, income effects come into play, as captured by the last term in the expression. Since $R_{11}(.)\left(E_{1u}(.)/E_{u}(.)\right)$ is positive, the second bracketed term cannot be signed in general. But it is conventional to assume, as part of a stability requirement, that this term is not larger than 1, so that $d(R + s)/ds$ remains positive.

CHAPTER 8
Current Debates on Infrastructure Policy

Antonio Estache and Marianne Fay

Economic historians will credit the exceptional global financial crisis of the first decade of the twenty-first century for many major changes in global economic policy priorities. One of them is bringing infrastructure back to the forefront of the policy agenda around the world, as has been the case in developing countries for some time now. Indeed, while infrastructure investment is generally a recurring item on the agenda of developing countries, since the early 1980s it has often enjoyed only "lip service" among developed countries. This changed with the major recovery packages that followed the crisis starting in 2008. Significant scaling up of investment in infrastructure may indeed be one of the most recognizable characteristics of the recovery packages because most developed-country governments have bet on the large multiplier effect of infrastructure-based stimuli, even if there are disagreements about how large these effects are and hence how large the infrastructure stimulus should be. No matter the actual effectiveness of these multipliers, these stimuli will at least address some of the congestion, service rationing, lost jobs, and lost income that are the consequences of gaps in the quantity and quality of infrastructure.

Infrastructure investment has become a priority in both developed and developing countries and will be for some time.[1]

History will also judge the extent to which large infrastructure investments will boil down to macroeconomic financial efforts without much concern for the microeconomic incentive problems of the sector. For instance, the new generation of infrastructure policy packages recognizes a role for the public sector in using tax money to pay for needed investment, hoping to recover much of this investment through user fees. But these packages tend to ignore the crucial details associated with the maintenance, affordability, and financing of investments and the sustainable distribution of tasks between the public and the private sector. They also ignore the governance problems of a sector known for its white elephants, cost overruns, and overly optimist forecasts of demand. They finally omit the role of concerns for short-term political gains in the selection of project payoffs in spite of the risks of long-term fiscal costs to society.

In that context, as the world jumps on the infrastructure bandwagon, it may be useful to take stock of what we have learned over the last 25 years from the evolution of the appropriate organization, management, and operation of the electricity, telecommunications, transport, and water and sanitation sectors. The sum of commitments to increase expenditures in these sectors ranges from 4 percent to more than 10 percent of gross domestic product (GDP) in some cases. For these new infrastructure projects to deliver on their promises at a fair cost to users and taxpayers, it will be crucial to minimize costly policy mistakes. Summarizing the lessons from past policy mistakes and omissions is the main purpose of this chapter.[2]

The chapter is organized as follows. It summarizes the importance of the context for identifying the current policy issues in infrastructure, offers an overview of the current state of the sector, and summarizes the intensive academic debate on the interactions between growth and infrastructure. It then looks at the thorny question of how much infrastructure is needed to sustain growth levels consistent with poverty reduction objectives and the efficiency-equity tradeoffs that may be associated with the decision of where these investments should be made. This is followed by a discussion of the poverty-related dimensions of the problems of access to infrastructure and a debate of the relative role of the private and public sector in infrastructure, focusing on the main institutional changes observed in the last 10–15 years and on their implications for the effectiveness of service delivery. A final section concludes.

---

1 The pressure to invest in the sector is reinforced and will be strongly sustained by the need to address the important contribution of transport and energy to greenhouse gas emissions.

2 While the chapter is aimed at policy audiences in developing and emerging economies, many of the lessons drawn should be useful to the policy makers of developed economies who place their hopes on infrastructure as a key ingredient of socially sustainable economic growth.

The Relevance of the Context

The perception of politicians, users, operators, investors, and academics on what is good and what is not good for infrastructure has evolved significantly since the end of the reconstruction period that followed World War II. Until the late 1980s, with a few high-profile exceptions in the developed Anglo-Saxon world starting in the 1970s, these sectors were clearly seen as a public sector responsibility, and governments were looking inward for means to improve their quality and volume. But during the 1990s, as the concern for fiscal discipline started to prevail globally and unhappiness with underperforming public providers grew, reductions in the size of the public sector became a must. Received wisdom was then that the private sector was going to take over infrastructure services, leaving only a residual role for governments (deregulation, restructuring, and the regulation of residual monopolies). The time had come for the private sector to show what it could do after a long frustrating experience with an underperforming public sector.

The initial vision did not play out as expected. Almost 20 years after privatization began to be touted as the solution to infrastructure woes, the role of the large-scale private sector in the delivery of infrastructure services in energy, water, or transport is far from being as widespread as many had hoped for, at least in developing countries. This is why many governments have stopped betting on an acceleration of private investment in the sector for the years to come. Local micro or small-scale private providers have jumped in to compensate for the failures of the model envisaged by the promoters of large-scale privatizations as well as for the failures of the remaining public monopolies. But given the fact that scale economies are defining characteristics of most infrastructure services, this could mean higher than needed costs for residential users.

The costs of the failure to get the vision to materialize are not minor. There is a strong and widespread sense among policy makers that some of the differences in growth rates between East Asia and other parts of the world can be attributed to the failure to invest sufficiently in infrastructure. Users' frustration with the switch from tax financing of these services to user financing only worsened the unhappiness with the new vision. The related rejection of the privatization experience has now become an effective political campaign issue around the world.

It is in this specific context that the infrastructure component of recovery programs is being implemented in developed and emerging countries and that the strategy to close the infrastructure gap is taking place in less developed countries. On the one hand, the large commitments made to invest in infrastructure are so popular and so easy to endorse politically around the world precisely because many governments are struggling to compensate for the collective failure in the 1990s to improve the quantity or the quality of infrastructure. On the other hand, there are strong views on the need to reconsider much more carefully than during the 1990s the appropriate form in which the private sector and the public sector will collaborate on the scaling up of infrastructure.

The emerging vision is that there is a need for significant improvements in the management and operation of infrastructure, but that the choice is no longer simplistically dichotomous between public and private, and the interests of users and taxpayers will have to be much better protected from the risks of residual monopolies in the sector. Pragmatism dominates this new vision. The public sector is expected to retain a much more important role in financing than admitted during much of the last 25 years, while the private sector will help in meeting the significant needs associated with infrastructure construction, operation, and to some extent financing. The role of the private sector in financing will most likely be limited to sectors such as telecommunications, energy generation, and transport services in which commercial and political risks are lower.

The State of the Infrastructure Sectors

Many of the issues to be discussed in this chapter are anchored in a basic problem: the insufficient stock of infrastructure and hence the insufficient flow of associated services. To give a sense of this gap, table 8.1 provides a quantitative snapshot of the sector based on the latest data available on the service coverage provided to populations in each sector for country group-ings reflecting income levels. The main conclusions are obvious: (a) access remains shockingly low in poor countries, despite the donor-funded efforts of the last decades, and (b) we are remarkably ignorant of how well or badly the sector is doing.

The Big Picture

First, the level of access to infrastructure services is, as expected, strongly correlated with a country's average income (for a fuller discussion of the evidence on access, quality, and prices in infrastructure, see Estache and Goicoechea 2005). By and large, the residents of developed countries all have access to a minimum level of services. Among developing coun-tries, upper-middle-income countries have the highest access rates (in the

Table 8.1. Access to Utilities Services, by Sector and Country Income Level

Income level	Percentage of population with access to networked electricity (2000)	Number of fixed and mobile telephone subscribers per 1,000 people (2005)	Percentage of population with access to improved water sources (2005)	Percentage of population with access to sanitation (2005)
Low	31	114	75	61
Lower-middle	82	511	82	77
Upper-middle	87	901	94	91
Developing	58	523	83	80

Source: World Bank 2007b.

developing world) and are very close to meeting the infrastructure needs of all but 10 percent of their population. The lowest-income countries are far from meeting those needs, in particular in terms of electricity.

Second, progress in achieving full coverage varies significantly across sectors. It has been reasonably good in water and in telecommunications (driven, in the case of telecommunications, by the technological revolution that has lowered costs and made service possible even in relatively low-density areas). Sanitation continues to be a problem, but it is attracting increasing attention as a result of growing interest in environmental problems. Somewhat surprising, the biggest problem is the energy sector. The absence of a widely available meaningful indicator precludes transport from being included in this comparison.

If one considers table 8.1 as a baseline from which progress from reform could be measured, the challenge is not a modest one. While the international community has been increasingly concerned with the importance of infrastructure needed to produce the investment that will generate growth—as illustrated by the results of investment climate surveys—this table suggests that it would be a major mistake to ignore household needs. Indeed, the political sustainability of infrastructure reforms depends on household needs being taken into account, as the experience of Latin America demonstrates (see Fay and Morrison 2006 for a discussion).

The challenge is not a minor one for the international donor community, but it is one that is increasingly being recognized. Commitments to improve access rates to water and, to some extent, telecommunications have been formalized through the Millennium Development Goals (MDGs). The commitments to electrification have been added as part of the Johannesburg Declaration, but much less progress is being made on that front. No similar collective commitment exists for the transport sector. Overall, progress is being made, but implementation is slow, so that, in many countries, the goals are not being met.[3]

The Big Holes in the Big Picture

Table 8.1 summarizes most of the information available to policy makers. The remaining data on these sectors tend to focus on technical dimensions. Some is relevant to policy (for example, power generation capacity), but much is too specific to technical issues. Compared to the information available on health or education, for instance, the information gap in the infrastructure sector is huge and shows no sign of narrowing.[4]

On transport, for instance, very little information is available on what could serve as a reasonable baseline to assess the economic or social performance of the sector. We know, for instance, that road density in the poorest

---

3   For a discussion of the countries and sectors for which the MDGs are unlikely to be met, see World Bank (2005a).

4   Living Standard Measurement Surveys, Demographic and Health Surveys, and household consumption surveys do not provide the required data to address the issue well. First, the sector is generally not well covered in these surveys. Second, there are significant differences in the quality of the data available for urban and rural areas.

developing countries is about a third what it is in the richest developing countries and about a sixth what it is in developed countries. However, these data do not capture the quality or even dimension of the infrastructure and give the same weight to a one-lane rural road and a 12-lane ring road. The heterogeneity in what the stock data measure may well be the worst for roads.

Similarly, on energy, most of the information available on access rates is based on extrapolations from a small sample of representative countries. The last worldwide diagnostic of access rates in the sector was conducted in 2000 by the International Energy Agency on behalf of the international community. Household surveys provide additional information, but there are major compatibility issues. Anyone interested in information on prices or quality in the sector will have to work with heroic assumptions to try to generate some credible comparable cross-country data sets.

The data on access to water are somewhat better to the extent that the United Nations–anchored Joint Monitoring Program has managed to generate some degree of continuity and consistency in the monitoring of progress, although these data sets also rely on some controversial assumptions and extrapolations.

Only for the telecommunications sector can a reasonably good picture be generated, thanks in large part to the efforts of the International Telecommunications Union. This sector has attracted the most interest among academics. Research goes where data are, not necessarily where problems are!

The problems with the monitoring of access rates may surprise many. Even more surprising is the failure to monitor progress on the affordability and quality of these services—dimensions that should be part of the baseline needed to track progress, particularly as regards poverty. This information is not available in most developing countries. Most of the related information published is anecdotal, and cross-country comparisons are often not meaningful, because quality standards and service pricing practices vary significantly across countries.

An ideal baseline would also include information on the cost of the sector. This is particularly important in view of the size of the projects and the associated financial transactions. Comparable cost data in infrastructure are largely unknown in developing countries. As such, the frequent message urging policy makers to improve cost recovery because the provision of infrastructure costs too much for the taxpayers is seldom based on an accurate estimate of the cost-recovery tariff or its affordability for poor households. Moreover, the cost to taxpayers is seldom known. Recent work on quasi-fiscal deficits represents a rather heroic attempt to come to grips with this issue (Ebinger 2006).

Data on public spending on infrastructure are largely nonexistent, as very few countries estimate how much they spend on infrastructure (one exception is India) and the International Monetary Fund's Government Financial

Statistics do not collect this information. A worldwide database exists that compiles information on investments funded through projects that involve a public-private partnership, but this database has its limitations (see http://ppi.worldbank.org/).

The Upshot

There is a long way to go in meeting the infrastructure needs of the poorest countries of the world. The MDGs help by motivating efforts to address some of them or at least prompting the international community to monitor progress. This is not the case for energy and transport, since they are not part of the core MDGs. As a result, the commitments to monitor progress are more subdued and certainly not consistent with the importance of these sectors to growth. On the other hand, the critical importance of both energy and transport to the climate change agenda might provide a welcome impetus to collect better information and monitor progress. The accountability of governments, operators, and donors requires a lot more information than is currently available. To get things done, measurement is needed. This starts with a good baseline; for now, this only exists in the telecommunications sector.

How Much Do We Know about the Infrastructure-Growth Nexus?

Common sense suggests that modern economies cannot function without infrastructure and that infrastructure is a critical part of any economy's production function.[5] But common sense is not equivalent to evidence when it comes to assessing differences in countries' or regions' growth paths. Even if infrastructure is necessary for modern economies to function, more infrastructure may not cause more growth at all stages of development or at any stage, for that matter. The binding constraints may lie elsewhere—in poor incentives or missing markets, for example. What follows reviews some of the reasons why considerable disagreement remains as to whether infrastructure accumulation can explain countries' differing growth paths.

A Slow Convergence of Views

Infrastructure may affect growth through many channels (see Agénor and Moreno-Dodson 2006 for an overview). In addition to the conventional

---

5   Absent or unreliable transport, electricity, or telecommunications services imply additional costs for firms or prevent them from adopting new technologies. Better transportation increases the effective size of labor markets, and various micro studies suggest an impact on human capital of access to water and sanitation (via health) and electricity and transport (that facilitate access to schools and the ability to study); see Brenneman (2002). Finally, relative infrastructure endowments will affect a region's comparative advantage, hence its development (Estache and Fay 1997).

productivity effect, infrastructure is likely to affect the costs of investment adjustment, the durability of private capital, and both demand for and supply of health and education services. Many of these channels have been tested empirically. This is reflected in the wide variety of findings in the abundant empirical literature on infrastructure and growth or productivity. Indeed, exhaustive reviews of the literature (Briceño, Estache, and Shafik 2004; Gramlich 1994; Romp and de Haan 2005; Straub and Vellutini 2006) show that while some authors find negative or zero returns, others find a high impact of infrastructure on growth.

However, a more careful analysis of the literature shows growing consensus around the notion that infrastructure generally matters for growth and production costs, although its impact seems higher at lower levels of income. Romp and de Haan (2005) note that 32 of 39 studies of Organisation for Economic Co-operation and Development (OECD) countries find a positive effect of infrastructure on some combination of output, efficiency, productivity, private investment, and employment. (Of the rest, three have inconclusive results, and four find a negligible or negative impact of infrastructure.) Romp and de Haan also review 12 studies that include developing countries. Of these, nine find a significant positive impact. The three that find no impact rely on public spending data, which, as discussed below, is a notoriously imprecise measure, especially for cross-country analysis. Other meta-analyses report a dominance of studies that show a generally significant impact of infrastructure, particularly in developing countries. Cesar Calderon and Luis Serven report that 16 out of 17 studies of developing countries find a positive impact, as do 21 of 29 studies of high-income countries.[6] Briceño, Estache, and Shafik (2004) carry out a similar review of about 102 papers and reach similar conclusions.

Nevertheless, there remains tremendous variety in the findings, particularly as to the magnitude of the effect, with studies reporting widely varying returns and elasticities. In other words, the literature supports the notion that infrastructure matters, but it cannot serve to unequivocally argue in favor of more or less infrastructure investments.

The variety of findings is, in fact, not surprising. There is no reason to expect the effect of infrastructure to be constant (or systematically positive), either over time or across regions or countries. Furthermore, estimating the impact of infrastructure on growth is a complicated endeavor, and papers vary in how carefully they navigate the empirical and econometric pitfalls posed by network effects, endogeneity, heterogeneity, and very poor-quality data.

The More, the Merrier (Network Effects)

Infrastructure services are mostly provided through networks, a fact that implies a nonlinear relation with output. Telecommunications exhibit "pure" network externalities, whereby returns to users increase with the number of

---

6 Personal communication relating to work in progress.

users.[7] But roads, rail, and electricity are also networked services, so the impact of new investments on growth, output, or firm costs will depend on the overall state and extent of the network (see Romp and de Haan 2005 for a discussion). In other words, the marginal and average productivity of investments is likely to differ significantly, and the hypothesis of a constant or linear elasticity of output with respect to infrastructure is clearly incorrect.

A few authors have explicitly modeled the nonlinearity of infrastructure impact on output, growth, or production costs. Thus Röller and Waverman (2001) find that the impact of telecommunications infrastructure on output is substantially higher in countries where penetration approaches universal coverage. In the case of roads in the United States, Fernald (1999) finds that returns to investments were very high up to the point when the basic interstate network was completed. He argues that the completion of that network provided a one-time boost in U.S. productivity.

Threshold effects in infrastructure can be modeled in a variety of ways— through a measure of completeness of coverage, as discussed above, or more simply through some measure of income, as in Canning and Bennathan (2000). Hurlin (2006) develops a threshold model whereby the level of available infrastructure is the threshold variable, but the number and value of the thresholds are endogenously determined. Applying this to the multiple-country panel data set of Canning and Bennathan (2000), he finds strong evidence of nonlinearity and concludes that the highest marginal productivity of investments is found when a network is sufficiently developed, but not completely achieved.

The effect of infrastructure may also vary over time as other changes in the economy influence firms' ability to take advantage of it. Thus, in Chile Albala-Bertrand and Mamatzakis (2004) find that infrastructure's productive impact became much more pronounced after 1973, when the Chilean economy liberalized.

In sum, appropriate modeling of infrastructure's effect on growth must include nonlinear effects. If network externalities are not properly captured, the payoffs to infrastructure investments will be underestimated or overestimated. Variables likely to affect this include (a) the stage of development of the network, (b) institutional variables such as the degree of liberalization of the markets, and (c) competition across subsectors that will affect the quality of the overall network.

Does Infrastructure Drive Growth or Vice Versa? (Endogeneity)

Many authors have highlighted the fact that causality may run both ways between income and infrastructure. Indeed, most infrastructure services are both consumption and intermediate goods, and many studies have

---

7   The same can probably be said of water and sanitation networks where the public health value of safe water and sanitation systems is likely to increase the more individuals are served, in a kind of herd-immunity effect.

documented that electricity consumption and demand for telephones and cars increase along with disposable income (Chen, Kuo, and Chen 2007; Ingram and Liu 1999; Röller and Waverman 2001).[8] Similarly, countries tend to increase their investments in environmental amenities as they become wealthier. Even studies that rely on constructed total factor productivity (TFP) estimates (whereby the dependent variable, TFP growth, is by construction orthogonal to capital) may suffer from reverse causation if growth then influences decisions to invest in infrastructure (see Straub and Vellutini 2006 for a discussion).

It may also be the case that a common factor causes both higher income and higher infrastructure endowment. Most of the critique of Aschauer's 1989 work, which launched the infrastructure and growth debate with its findings of implausibly high rates of return, centers on a failure to correct appropriately for the possibility that an omitted variable is driving the results. Later papers (see Gramlich 1994 for an overview of this literature) corrected for this by introducing country (or region) fixed effects and found much lower rates of return. However, the fixed-effect approach precludes looking at the impact of other slow-moving variables, which is why some authors prefer not to use it (for example, Estache, Speciale, and Veredas 2006).

An alternative approach is to try to isolate the impact of changes in infrastructure on long-term growth, typically by using first differences. This approach generates its own set of problems. Indeed, first differences ignore the long-term relationship that exists in the data if infrastructure and growth are co-integrated (which Canning and Pedroni 2004 find to be the case).

One exception is Calderon and Serven (2004), who take pains to deal with the endogeneity of the explanatory variables through the use of generalized method of moments techniques, which look at the impact of the level of infrastructure (not its change) on subsequent growth. They find that an increase of one standard deviation in their index of infrastructure stock would raise the median country's growth rate by 2.9 percentage points, whereas an analogous increase in their infrastructure quality index would raise the growth rate by 0.7 percentage point. They do point out, however, that such increases in the quantity and quality of infrastructure would be extremely costly and would take decades to implement. To give an example, the growth payoff for Argentina and Mexico of catching up to the level and quality of infrastructure of the Republic of Korea would be 2.4 and 2.6 percent, respectively, but would require these countries to invest upward of 7 percent a year for more than 20 years (World Bank 2005b, 2007a).

---

8   The extent of reverse causation may vary across types and measures of infrastructure. For example, road networks that are long lived and slow to change are perhaps less likely to respond to changes in income (particularly in countries that already have a large network and where changes to cope with congestion—such as more lanes, better traffic management, and ring roads—will not substantially affect aggregate measures such as kilometers of roads per capita). This is not the case with telephones or electricity-generating capacity (which responds to energy demand whose income elasticity has been around 0.5 since 1990, according to International Energy Agency 2006).

It may well be that, as discussed later in this section, the fiscal distortion associated with such an effort—and the tradeoffs it would entail with other needed investments—would substantially reduce the net growth effect.

Some studies also devise estimation methods that make clear which way the causality runs (see Romp and de Haan 2005 for a discussion). For example, Fernald (1999) uses industry-level productivity growth in the United States to measure the impact of road investments, while Canning and Pedroni (2004) find robust evidence that causality runs both ways but in the vast majority of cases infrastructure does induce long-run growth effects. (However, they do find a great deal of variation across individual countries, as discussed below.)

Finally, various authors rely on simultaneous equations systems that look at the determinants of supply of (or demand for) infrastructure as well as its impact on output or growth. Röller and Waverman (2001) and Esfahani and Ramirez (2003) are good examples of careful attempts in this direction. Esfahani and Ramirez's paper, one of the few that use first differences, models both income growth per capita and infrastructure accumulation.

In sum, infrastructure causes growth, and growth causes greater demand for (and usually supply of) infrastructure. While disentangling the two is complex, new econometric approaches increasingly allow us to isolate the direction of interest and thereby reduce the overestimation issues that plagued early estimates of infrastructure's impact on growth.

Is Every Infrastructure Project Special? (Heterogeneity)

In the case of noninfrastructure capital, private entrepreneurs arbitrage between different types of investments to maximize overall return. Not so with infrastructure, which generally is not faced with a real market test. As such, we cannot assume that the right capital is built at the right time or place, and we should therefore expect differences in rates of return across different projects. In addition, public infrastructure spending may be affected by public sector spending inefficiency. As a result, although financial estimates of investment in private capital may be a good proxy for the increases in private physical capital and may serve as the basis for constructing a stock figure through a perpetual inventory method, this is much less likely with infrastructure.

There is also a need to better understand how decisions are made to invest in infrastructure, as this is likely to affect the rate of return or the efficiency of a particular investment. (It may also help to identify ways of improving the efficiency of infrastructure expenditure.) Politically motivated projects are likely to exhibit low (or lower) rates of return as their objectives are to bring in the votes rather than to maximize growth. This is certainly not limited to developing countries, as evidenced by the controversies around Alaska's "bridge to nowhere" in the United States.[9] Similarly,

---

9 Alaska's famous $280 million "bridge to nowhere" was one of the 6,371 special projects included in the 2005 U.S. Transportation Equity Act (a six-year $286 billion bill). See http://dir.salon.com/story/news/feature/2005/08/09/bridges/index_np.html for a discussion.

a recent careful attempt to model how investment decisions are made in France concludes, "Roads and railways are not built to reduce traffic jams; they are built essentially to get politicians elected" (Cadot, Röller, and Stephan 2006: 1151).[10]

While some degree of pork-barrel politics is likely to exist everywhere, its extent and impact may vary. De la Fuente and Vives (1995) find little trace of political influence in Spanish infrastructure decisions, while Cadot, Röller, and Stephan (2006) find political influence in France. However, Cadot and his co-authors conclude that in France the resulting distortions are small, possibly because this is a relatively new phenomenon (linked to administrative reforms in the early 1980s) that has mostly affected investments that are small relative to the existing network.

A further complication in the modeling—and one that argues against a constant expected rate of return—is the fact that there may be lags in infrastructure's impact on growth. Most infrastructure is long lived, and its full impact may be slow in coming, as firms adjust slowly to the new opportunities offered. Duggal, Saltzman, and Klein (2007) find the productivity impact of increased information technology infrastructure and associated private capital to have an approximate four- to five-year lag in the United States.

Overall, even if not pork, public infrastructure investment may well have a noneconomic objective such as the physical or social integration of a country or concerns about public health or safety. As such, the investment may not aim to maximize growth. At any rate, careful modeling of the relation between infrastructure and growth should include an analysis of the determinants of infrastructure investments to avoid overestimating the growth- or productivity-related investment needs.

The Upshot

The literature on infrastructure and growth teaches us that infrastructure is important, but its importance varies. It varies across countries and over time, as countries change and the binding constraints shift. It also varies within countries and sectors. Can infrastructure explain differences in growth rates between countries? It certainly contributes, but this literature is unlikely to provide a single answer. Where do we go from here?

How Much Infrastructure Is Needed?

The key infrastructure question for policy makers is often whether an optimal level of infrastructure can be identified. Such an optimum could then serve to derive the investment commitments needed, for which funding must be identified. More prosaically, the concern boils down to a simple question: can we estimate a country's infrastructure investment needs?

---

10 Other papers on the political economy guiding infrastructure investment decisions include Alesina, Baqir, and Easterly (1999); Rauch (1995); Robinson and Torvik (2005).

A Very Brief Introduction to Investment Needs Assessments

Given that neither the market nor the state is likely to provide the optimal level of infrastructure automatically, a key issue for economists working on the topic is how to measure this optimal level of infrastructure. One approach looks at the rate of return on infrastructure. Thus studies that find the rate of return to infrastructure to be negative, zero, or positive often use these findings to conclude that countries are investing too much, the right amount, or not enough in infrastructure.[11] For example, Bougheas, Demetriades, and Mamuneas (2000) find an inverted U-shape relation between infrastructure and the rate of economic growth, with most countries on the upward-sloping part of the curve. This would imply that they are underinvesting in infrastructure. Esfahani and Ramirez (2003) also conclude that a tendency exists toward underprovision. Canning and Bennathan (2000) find variation across countries, but a general tendency for middle-income countries to exhibit shortages in electricity-generating capacity and paved roads. However, while these papers are broadly indicative of whether countries are underinvesting or overinvesting in infrastructure, they cannot identify actual investment needs.

One approach that has been extensively used (and misused) estimates how much investment may be needed to satisfy firm and consumer demand triggered by predicted GDP growth (Briceño, Estache, and Shafik 2004; Fay and Yepes 2003). The model assumes no optimality.[12] The relationship between income level and demand for infrastructure services is established on the basis of past observed behavior in a sample of countries and extrapolated to the future using predicted income growth. However, as Lall and Wang (2006) point out, if past demand was rationed, it may not be a good predictor of unrationed demand. They argue for an approach that incorporates fiscal constraints and supply-side bottlenecks and models the gap between current and optimal level of provisions.

Whatever its limitations (and they are severe), the approach developed by Fay and Yepes forms the basis for many of the current estimates of multicountry investment needs. The most recent estimates generated from an update of the original model are presented in table 8.2. They suggest that the needs are large, particularly within low-income countries, where they have been estimated at around 4 percent of GDP, with an additional 4 percent required for maintenance.

The inclusion of maintenance needs calculated as a fixed proportion of the accumulated capital stock is essential from a practical point of view. The importance of maintenance and the need to budget for it have long been known, but they have only recently been documented in the academic literature. Rioja (2003) and Kalaitzidakis and Kalyvitis (2004) highlight

---

11 In empirical studies that include both infrastructure and overall capital, infrastructure is essentially entered twice, in which case an elasticity estimate no different from zero should be interpreted as infrastructure having the same rate of return as private capital.

12 The model identifies potential demand given expected growth, not the level of infrastructure that would maximize growth or some other social goal.

Table 8.2. Investment and Maintenance Expenditure Needs as a Percentage of GDP, by Country Income Level, Average 2005–15

Income level	Investment	Maintenance	Total
Low	4.2	3.3	7.5
Lower-middle	3.8	2.5	6.3
Upper-middle	1.7	1.4	3.1
Developing	3.2	2.3	6.5

Source: Courtesy of Tito Yepes, based on Fay and Yepes 2003.

the fact that countries tend to underspend on maintenance, a fact that substantially reduces the useful life of infrastructure assets and hence their rate of return. Maintenance expenditure standards are well known and result in predictable annual expenditure outlays when averaged over an entire network. Appropriate, but by no means generous, standards are approximately 2 percent of the replacement cost of capital for electricity, roads, and rail; 3 percent for water and sanitation; and about 8 percent for mobile and fixed lines.

The estimates provided in table 8.2 serve as a rough benchmark for different types of countries. But they assume standardized unit costs and ignore many country and regional specificities. When looking at a particular country, these macro estimates should be complemented with other approaches to allow for some "triangulation."[13] However, these will require the definition of a set of goals, which may be motivated by economic, engineering, social, environmental, or public health concerns. Societies may also differ on the level of services that is deemed appropriate.[14] Table 8.3 illustrates the various ways in which the goals may be set using the example of Mexico, where this exercise was undertaken in the context of a public expenditure review focused on infrastructure.

The gold-plate analysis of country-specific "investment needs" relies on sectoral micro studies. The approaches and methodologies vary depending on the sectors. In the case of electricity, sophisticated economic-engineering

---

13 The process of estimating investment needs is so fraught with assumptions, uncertain data, and so forth that it is common sense to rely on various approaches to generate a series of estimates. To the extent that the estimates appear to converge, there can be more confidence in the resulting recommendations.

14 An interesting example is given by countries in case of the Eastern and Southern Europe now joining the European Union (EU). These countries are required by the accession agreements to pursue a quality of water and sanitation services that was reached in the city of Brussels only in the last few years. However, given that these countries have income per capita much below the EU average, such a high level of service quality represents a huge financial burden (estimated at around €9 billion for Romania, equivalent to 16 percent of its 2004 GDP) and is therefore being subsidized by the EU. Questions remain however, as in other EU accession countries, about the affordability of maintaining these sophisticated systems.

Table 8.3. Different Approaches to Estimating Expenditure Needs in Infrastructure: The Example of Mexico

Benchmarking	Setting targets
Stock target: What would it cost to get Mexico's infrastructure (per capita; per unit of GDP; per square kilometer) to the level of the leader in Latin America and the Caribbean or to the level of the East Asia median?	*Costing exercise:* What would it cost for Mexico to achieve universal service coverage in water and sanitation, electricity, and access to year-round roads?
Flow target: How do Mexico's expenditures on infrastructure compare to those of its peers?	*Engineering-economic models:* Targets are defined as a particular level of coverage and quality.
Econometric growth model: What level of infrastructure coverage is needed to achieve x percent of growth and reduce inequality by z percent. No such model is available yet.	*Power sector:* A well-defined international methodology, applied by CFE, Mexico's largest state power company, is used to estimate the investment needed to maintain the integrity of the network and satisfy predicted expansion in demand.
Econometric demand model: What level of infrastructure coverage will be demanded by firms and consumers for given growth projections? This approach is followed in Fay and Yepes (2003).	*Water and sanitation:* A financial model estimates investment needed to attain the coverage goals set in National Hydraulic Plan.
	Roads: A well-defined methodology is used to estimate rehabilitation and maintenance expenditures; it is combined with road sector expert opinion on the definition of major corridors and investment needed for their completion.

Source: World Bank 2005b.

models can be used to estimate the investments required to maintain the integrity of a network experiencing expanding demand.[15]

These models allow sector specialists to provide various sets of estimates depending on whether the goal is basic reliability or high quality and reliability. In the transport sector, the approach is usually more ad hoc and relies on a combination of sector specialists' estimates and detailed studies (particularly on the need for upgrades or expansions). In the case of water and sanitation, the connection cost of universal coverage is easy to estimate, based on standard prices. However, the cost of associated works is much harder to establish, and there is usually no simple way of estimating the need for rehabilitation.

But even sophisticated sectoral studies can turn into unrealistic wish lists. It is useful, therefore, to do some simple benchmarking. This can entail comparing a country to its peers (as defined, say, by income levels) or to a country that offers a promising example (say, a newly industrial country such as the Republic of Korea) and asking how much it would cost to achieve the service coverage or quality of the comparator country. The comparison can be done on the basis of coverage or quality or expenditure flows.

---

15 Mexico uses the Wien automatic system planning package (WASP IV), a widely used model that analyzes options for generating system expansion, primarily to determine the least costly expansion path that will adequately meet the demand for electric power, subject to user-defined constraints. Similar models are SUPER/OLADE/BID and MPODE, which are used by Colombia and Ecuador, for example.

There usually is a need to include additional provisions for social objectives as well as maintenance. Social objectives may be the ones defined in the MDGs or universal coverage.[16] For middle-income countries, this is usually a small proportion of the overall tab, at least for bare-bones coverage that may not include grid connection. For low-income countries, where both coverage and income are low, the costs can be very high.

What If Budget Constraints Affect the Optimal Level of Infrastructure?

The problem with the approaches described above is that the optimal level of infrastructure provision cannot be divorced from how it is financed. In addition, there may be a tradeoff between increased infrastructure and increased taxes. Aschauer (2000) finds that the level of public *capital* in most U.S. states was below the growth-maximizing level in the 1970s and 1980s, although public *expenditure* was too high (leaving open the question of what is the optimal balance between the two).[17] Kamps (2005), who applies the same model to EU countries, argues that the distortion associated with taxation discourages private investment.

How much should countries spend on infrastructure given competing needs for public spending, fiscal constraints, and limited ability to charge users? One approach is to develop a general-equilibrium model that explicitly incorporates public investment costs and to solve it for infrastructure. Rioja (2001) does this for Brazil, Mexico, and Peru and identifies an optimal (defined as growth-maximizing) level of infrastructure, health, and education spending. However, this study, like others of its kind (for example, Cavalcanti Ferreira and Gonçalves do Nascimento 2005; Estache and Muñoz 2007), relies on parameters of elasticity of growth with respect to infrastructure estimated in other studies, which may or may not be accurate.

Theoretically, Aschauer's (2000) model could be used to calculate the growth or welfare-maximizing level of infrastructure spending. However, it also requires an estimate of the elasticity of output with respect to public capital (which he sets to 0.3 for the United States). Kamps (2005) calculates this elasticity for EU countries, but then constrains it to be constant and equal across countries (in his case at 0.2). One option could then be to apply the Aschauer or Kamps methodology to estimate growth-maximizing stocks of infrastructure (this would require calculating country- or infrastructure-specific elasticities, something the preceding discussion showed to be nontrivial). The cost of reaching or maintaining the optimal level of stock could then be estimated using either country-specific or international prices for these stocks.

---

16 The one original MDG pertaining directly to infrastructure is to "halve by 2015 the proportion of people without sustainable access to safe drinking water and basic sanitation." Electrification has now been included.

17 Rioja (2001) develops a general-equilibrium model that explicitly models public investment's resource cost and uses it to show the optimal level of infrastructure for three countries: Brazil, Peru, and Mexico.

So which way should we go with this literature? Lall and Wang (2006) offer a promising way forward, although their model has not yet been empirically estimated and requires a more complete modeling of infrastructure supply decisions. It also remains a partial-equilibrium analysis. Similarly, the Aschauer (2000) or Kamps (2005) models may well offer the basis for an interesting alternative. However, good data on the cost of infrastructure provision is required to translate these models into figures for investment needs and put them in the perspective of the available fiscal space.

The Upshot

Deciding how much should be spent on infrastructure is clearly not an easy exercise, but it needs to be done and can create basic benchmarks. The literature offers some guidance, although there is a long way to go before the various approaches will generate lower and upper bounds that converge toward a robust assessment of needs—one that accounts for the fact that infrastructure competes with other sectors for scarce resources.

Where Should Infrastructure Investments Be Made?

With the reemergence of economic geography, infrastructure needs are being examined with a spatial twist: the question is no longer simply "how much," but also "where." The answer to that second question is even more problematic than the first for two reasons. First, the most promising research is for now mostly theoretical. Second, spatial development policy debates are often politically charged, with advocacy often prevailing over rationality (witness the older urban-bias debate).

An Introduction to the Relevance of the New Economic Geography to Infrastructure

The "where" question is being addressed in an emerging strand of literature that has little empirical evidence to draw on, at least for developing countries. The new economic geography literature (see Baldwin and others 2003 for an overview) suggests that infrastructure interacts with physical characteristics to affect the comparative advantage of a region, hence its growth and a country's settlement patterns. Puga (2002) offers a nice overview of the arguments and the evidence, particularly as they pertain to transport, which we summarize below.

Infrastructure, particularly transport, is seen by most policy makers as critical in efforts to help disadvantaged regions become more attractive to investors: improved connectivity is usually seen as a key to allowing peripheral regions to better integrate the domestic or international economy.

The impact of improved transport on a backward region is ambiguous, however, as it may remove a natural trade barrier that was protecting local industries and thus contribute to further concentration of employment in the advanced region. This is particularly likely within a country where wage differences are unlikely to be significant. Indeed, in France improved transport links have led to the concentration, rather than the dispersion, of employment (Combes and Lafourcade 2001). In Italy Faini (1983) has argued that the reduction in transport costs between the north and the south led to the deindustrialization of the south.

However, deconcentration within metropolitan areas from the core to the periphery does happen with improved transport. For example, Henderson and Kuncoro (1996) show that many firms moved out of Jakarta to the peripheral areas of the Greater Jakarta metropolitan region in the mid-1980s. These moves were facilitated by the construction of toll ring roads around the city, retaining some agglomeration benefits of the region, but reducing congestion costs (for example, land rents and transport costs), enabling firms to benefit from lower land and labor costs in the periphery. These benefits exceeded the increased costs of transport serving the same market.

Similarly, in Brazil the deconcentration of industry from Greater São Paulo to lower-wage populated hinterland cities followed the transport corridors first through São Paulo State and then into Minas Gerais, the interior state with the main iron ore and other mineral reserves (Henderson, Shalizi, and Venables 2001). But even though the improved interregional transport network in Brazil had significant impacts on productivity and greatly contributed to the prosperity of states and towns at the periphery of the traditional economic core, it did not lead to industrialization in more remote, lagging areas (Lall, Funderburg, and Yepes 2003).

Location theory suggests that the nature and structure of a transport project will affect its impact on the local economy. Thus improving local—as opposed to interregional—infrastructure is much less likely to harm the local economy. Similarly hub-and-spoke networks encourage the concentration of activity in the hubs, as firms located there face lower transport costs than firms in the spokes (Puga 2002).

Interregional networks will, of course, bring benefits to peripheral regions. However, the gap in relative accessibility will widen between central and peripheral regions, even if the biggest absolute gains occur in the remote areas. This point is well illustrated in Europe for high-speed trains (Vickerman, Spiekermann, and Wegener 1999 in Puga 2002). It also explains the lack of impact of the national highway network on Brazil's northeast region, discussed earlier (Lall, Funderburg, and Yepes 2003).

Transport infrastructure simply is not a silver bullet for regional development. Nevertheless, the empirical work quoted above—and much anecdotal evidence—suggests that infrastructure investments are likely to be necessary, if not sufficient, for regional growth. Access to all-weather roads, reliable telephony (for example, through cell phones), and electricity is a prerequisite to allow rural areas to produce higher-value processed goods. Regions cannot export if their transport network results in excessively high costs (Iimi and Smith 2007). However, what will matter is the interaction between these investments and other factors that determine a region's comparative advantage and its ability to market it.

Project selection may also follow a goal of balanced regional development. In that case the result may not be a (national) growth-maximizing investment (although it may well be welfare maximizing). Targeting investments toward poorer regions may, therefore, entail equity-efficiency tradeoffs. This is documented in Spain by de la Fuente (2002a, 2002b), who finds that substantial investments in poorer regions did result in convergence in income, but at the cost of overall national growth.

Investing in Rural or in Urban Areas?

In most countries, much of output and growth is generated in cities, and today about half the world population lives in cities. Moreover, poor people urbanize faster than the population as a whole (see Cohen 2004; Ravallion 2002 for a discussion of population trends). But are these stylized facts sufficient to argue that infrastructure should go mostly to cities?

In most countries the story is much more subtle than urban-rural dichotomies allow. First, the contrast is typically more between leading and lagging regions. Rural population in leading regions, close to booming urban centers with strong demand for their goods and the roads and buses to take their goods to market, will tend to be more prosperous (and have much better infrastructure access) than rural or urban dwellers in lagging regions. This brings us back to the earlier debate on balanced regional development. Second, in some regions (Africa, South Asia) the population remains mostly rural and will remain so for some time. Indeed, while the poor urbanize faster than the rich, a majority of poor people will still live in rural areas long after most people in the developing world live in urban areas (Ravallion 2002).[18]

Ultimately, the choice of the priority is really a policy choice that economists can only serve to inform. In particular, economic work can help in identifying some of the equity-efficiency tradeoffs as well as the channels through which investments may affect local prosperity and well-being. In particular, there is wide agreement that infrastructure in rural areas can improve agricultural productivity and reduce rural poverty.[19] Similarly, there is substantial evidence to show that infrastructure can reduce urban poverty (Henderson 2002).

General-equilibrium modeling can help to identify the distributional impact of infrastructure reform, notably their differing consequences for urban and rural populations. Reforms tend to unbundle the urban and rural responsibilities of operators, ending historical cross-subsidies and forcing choices for more targeted subsidies to system expansions.

---

18 This debate is not new. Almost 30 years ago, Lipton (1977) and Mellor (1976) were concerned with the opposite question: was the urban bias of the international community rational?

19 See Gibson and Rozelle (2002); Jacoby (2000); Lanjouw (1999); Lokshin and Yemtsov (2005); Reardon (2001); Renkow, Hallstrom, and Karanja (2004); van de Walle (2002); van de Walle and Nead (1995).

Boccanfuso, Estache, and Savard (2006), for instance, show that water reforms in Senegal have had a very different initial impact in the capital city, secondary cities, and rural areas. They also show that unless interregional cross-subsidies are an option, most common cost-recovery financing policies will have different consequences for the poor in regions that have different types of providers (that is, large public, large private, or small private).

A particularly interesting analysis of the differing impact of infrastructure investments between rural and urban poor comes from Adam and Bevan (2004). They show that infrastructure investments in Uganda that support tradables have different impacts on the distribution of poverty between rural and urban areas as well as on the real exchange rate and other macroeconomic variables. When infrastructure investment favors tradables (for example, telecommunications or energy, which tend to enjoy a much stronger demand from manufacturing and services than transport), the real exchange appreciation is strongest. When it is biased toward nontradables (for example, rural and urban roads), there is hardly any change in the real exchange rate. The main difference between the two scenarios is distributional. Support to tradables helps all income classes; support to nontradables helps the urban poor and, somewhat counterintuitively, hurts the rural poor, if population migration is ignored. The rural poor gain from more access to food, but they lose from the lower income they receive from food production. This loss is greater the more the infrastructure aid is biased toward nontradable goods.

The Upshot

Deciding where to invest is as hard as or harder than deciding how much to invest. Reduced transport and communication costs will favor additional trade, additional mobility, and possibly additional demand for skilled workers in many of the developing countries. But to get there, some tough decisions need to be made on the location of investments. The tradeoffs are much more complex than often recognized, although recent work such as Adam and Bevan (2004) can help us to understand them. However, we have little understanding of the dynamic impact of infrastructure investments on rural or urban economies or their integration. Continued empirical work on the topic will help the new economic geography literature to become increasingly relevant for policy making.

Are the Infrastructure Needs of the Poor Being Met?

Infrastructure policy failures are typically hardest on the poor. First is the failure to provide for universal access, which has, of course, hurt the poor most. Second is the failure to design tariffs consistent with the poor's cash flows and ability to pay. The MDGs have helped somewhat in putting the access problem on the agenda. The strong voices of discontent with the

Table 8.4. Access to Infrastructure Services by Richest and Poorest 20 Percent of the Population, by Sector and Country Income Level

% of population receiving services

Income level	Electricity		Water		Sanitation		Telephone	
	Poorest 20%	Richest 20%	Poorest 20%	Richest 20%	Poorest 20%	Richest 20%	Poorest 20%	Richest 20%
Low	9.7	68.7	41.1	78.5	27.2	68.8	3.2	24.5
Lower-middle	79.5	99.3	64.5	86.6	48.2	78.7	21.2	66.1
Upper-middle	81.4	99.5	76.7	95	73.4	96.4	32	73.1

Source: Briceño and Klytchnikova 2006.
Note: Data are the most recent available for 2000–04.

privatization experiences, in particular, in Africa, Latin America, and to a lesser extent Eastern Europe, have highlighted the affordability problems. The fact that the infrastructure sector is one of those committed to increase the transparency of the assessment of aid effectiveness is good news and is already providing many useful insights (for a recent overview, see Estache 2009). But many issues can already be discussed with the experience accumulated so far.

How Bad Is the Access Problem for the Poorest?

Table 8.1, presented earlier and summarizing the average access rates per country groups, hides the extent of hardship endured by the poorest population.[20] Table 8.4 (generated from Briceño and Klytchnikova 2006) is based on information collected from household surveys rather than from some extrapolation, as the countrywide average indicators tend to be in energy and water and sanitation. Household survey data have their own limitations, but the snapshot they offer provides useful additional information for policy. In particular, they provide a much better sense of the uneven distribution of the access gaps across income groups at various stages of development. The table shows that gaps between the poorest and richest 20 percent are systematically largest in poorer countries.

How Bad Is the Affordability Problem?

The access gap is only part of the problem. There is also an affordability issue. Infrastructure practitioners rely on rules of thumb to get a sense of the affordability problem in any sector. One such rule of thumb (developed by the World Health Organization) is that households should not need to spend more than 5 percent of their income for water and sanitation—3.5 percent for water alone. In the case of electricity, there is no such formal rule of thumb, but many assume that 4–6 percent is a maximum to spend on energy. The general informal rule suggests that

---

20 In the Demographic and Health Survey data, the poorer and richer are defined based on an asset index used as a proxy of welfare level. In the Living Standard Measurement Survey data, households are ranked by total per capita expenditure.

poor households should not have to spend more than 15 percent of their income for infrastructure services.

Armed with these rules of thumbs, it should be easy to get a sense of the extent of the affordability problem across the world, but it remains impossible, because there is no systematic formal monitoring of this crucial issue. However, several recent books have documented quite carefully the problem within Africa, Eastern Europe, and Latin America—within the limits allowed by significant data constraints.[21] The main lesson to emerge from that research is that even though the share of household expenditure devoted to infrastructure services, including utilities, is only slightly higher in Sub-Saharan Africa than in other regions, the fact that households are so much poorer in Africa than elsewhere makes it more difficult for the population to deal with the current costs of service. This is especially the case among those who are not connected to existing networks, because they tend to pay more for their services than connected households. The cost advantage for connected households is due in part to subsidies (services are often billed at prices below full cost-recovery levels), which are very badly targeted, again simply because access rates to modern services are so low among the poor.

What Can Be Done to Deal with Access and Affordability Problems?

Affordability and access issues were well known when the reforms of the 1990s where implemented. But efficiency concerns prevailed over equity or affordability ones. Recent research does suggest that the reforms generally increased efficiency, although not equally across sectors and across regions. However, these efficiency gains were not always shared with users, particularly the poor. Some of the reasons the poor did not always benefit include the following:

- Tariff rebalancing and restructuring became more efficient, but also often more regressive or at least less progressive.
- Increased bill collections de facto increased tariffs.
- Increased quality and reliability usually were accompanied by higher tariffs to recover higher service costs.
- Cream-skimming by new operators eliminated cross-regional subsidies, slowing investment programs in the poorest regions when governments could not compensate by increasing subsidies.
- Failures to offer payment facilities made it more difficult for the poor to afford new connections.

All this implies that poverty was not addressed carefully in the regulatory and other reform packages implemented during the 1990s. Sadly, addressing

---

21 Estache, Foster, and Wodon (2002) on Latin America for the World Bank; Foster and Yepes (2006) on Latin America; Alam and others (2005) on Eastern Europe; Estache and Wodon 2007 on Africa; Ugaz and Waddams-Price (2003) and Nellis and Birdsall (2005) on the international experience.

the needs of the poorest is not that complex. For access, there are three basic types of instruments: (a) instruments requiring operators to provide access (a service obligation to avoid unilateral exclusion by the provider);[22] (b) instruments reducing connection costs (through cross-subsidies or direct subsidies built into the tariff design or through credit or discriminatory payment plans in favor of the poor); and (c) instruments increasing the range of suppliers (to give users choice, including the option of reducing costs by choosing lower-quality service providers).

For affordability, broadly speaking, all instruments work in at least one of three ways (Estache, Foster, and Wodon 2002): (a) by reducing bills for poor households (through lifelines or means-tested subsidies based on socioeconomic characteristics or the characteristics of the connection, financed through cross-subsidies or direct subsidies built into the tariff design); (b) by reducing the cost of services (by avoiding granting a monopoly when it is not necessary or by providing an incentive for operators to reduce costs and pass on the cost reductions to users); and (c) by facilitating the payment of bills (by allowing discriminatory administrative arrangements in favor of the permanently or temporarily poor).

While these recipes may seem obvious, they are not without controversy. Subsidies, particularly cross-subsidies, continue, to be seen as undesirable policy instruments in many circles, and that bad reputation has tended to spill over in infrastructure for the last 20 years or so. Yet, in spite of their bad reputation, most practitioners will argue that (a) subsidies (direct or not) are needed in most countries, and (b) they are not always as ineffective or distortionary as has been argued.[23] These results seem to hold for both temporary and chronic poverty.[24]

The anecdotal and econometric evidence confirms that subsidies are hard to avoid. According to Foster and Yepes (2006), in the poorest part of Latin America (Bolivia, Honduras, Nicaragua, or Paraguay), more than 50 percent of the households would have to pay more than 5 percent of their income for water or electricity services if tariffs were set at cost-recovery levels. In India and Africa, around 70 percent of the households would have that problem and could be expected to have difficulty paying full cost-recovery tariffs. In these regions, tariffs would likely have to increase by a factor of 10 to reach cost-recovery levels, making it unlikely that poor households could afford them.

And in many countries, cross-subsidies are the only realistic option given fiscal stress and the limited ability to fund subsidies through general taxes. In most instances, tariffs are designed to ensure that usage (after a minimum vital level) is priced at full cost, while amortization of the investment benefits from a subsidy or a cross-subsidy.

---

22 This issue is not addressed here; see Chisari, Estache, and Waddams-Price (2003); Clarke and Wallsten (2002); Cremer and others (2001); Gasmi and others (2002); Laffont (2005).

23 For a recent overview of the literature on subsidies of relevance to infrastructure, see Komives and others (2005).

24 For a useful review of the debate and survey of the empirical evidence, see Ravallion (2003).

When general redistribution is not working, redistribution within the sector can be effective. These instruments are clearly not safe bets, since well-intended targeting mechanisms have also been regressive as a result of the failure to target access, consumption, or both.[25] But bad designs are not equivalent to bad instruments.

The Upshot

The sheer number and geographic dispersion of the poor without access to infrastructure services in many parts of the world are two of the main challenges that reformers must address. It is unlikely that the poor will be able to afford the cost of reasonable levels of safe consumption of infrastructure services without some fiscal support. When general redistribution is not working, redistribution within the sector can be effective. These instruments are clearly not safe bets, since well-intended targeting mechanisms have also been regressive as a result of failures to target access, consumption, or both. But bad designs are not equivalent to bad instruments. Moreover, considering that the users who are connected today most probably benefited from subsidies paid out of general tax revenue during the many years when the utilities (typically public) were running a deficit, cross-subsidies between users are likely to be fair from the viewpoint of intergenerational equity.

How Large a Role for the Private Sector?

Privatization remains a controversial topic among policy makers. During most of the 1990s, following the lead of Prime Minister Margaret Thatcher in the United Kingdom and President Carlos Menem in Argentina, getting the private sector to take charge of most infrastructure investment decisions was one of the most popular ideas among economic advisers. The approach seemed particularly attractive to the many governments faced with fiscal constraints or unable to cope with multiple demands on a shrinking budget or to get public enterprises to deliver quality services cost-effectively.

How Strong Is the Presence of the Private Sector in Infrastructure?

A recent survey (Estache and Goicoechea 2005) documents the presence or absence of large-scale private operators in infrastructure in developing countries. The information is summarized in table 8.5, and three facts emerge.

The first is that telecommunications are most effective in attracting the private sector. The second is that the involvement of the private sector is greater in richer countries. The third is that even in high-income countries, the presence of the private sector is much less widespread than sometimes thought. Only about a third of developing countries can count on private

---

25 Estache, Foster, and Wodon (2002) show how common this is in Latin America.

Table 8.5. Percentage of Countries with Significant Large-Scale Private Investment in Infrastructure, by Sector and Country Income Level, 2004

Income level	Electricity generation	Electricity distribution	Water and sanitation	Railways[a]	Fixed-line telecommunications
Low	41	29	18	34	50
Lower-middle	48	37	50	26	62
Upper-middle	58	48	47	60	72
Developing	47	36	35	36	59

Source: Estache and Goicoechea 2005.
a. 2002.

sector operators for the delivery of electricity, water, or railway services. The largest private sector presence is in the fixed-line telecommunications sector, where about 60 percent of countries rely on private operators. The private sector is estimated to have provided only about 20–25 percent of the investment realized in developing countries, on average, over the past 15 years or so.[26] In Africa it has contributed to less than 10 percent of the needs, and most of this contribution has gone to a handful of countries (Côte d'Ivoire, Kenya, Senegal, South Africa, Tanzania, and Uganda).

This is not to deny the presence of the smaller-scale private sector. In fact, where the state and the large private sector have failed to deliver services, the small-scale, generally local, private sector has filled the gap. The evidence on the private sector's role and details of its costs is mostly anecdotal, however. In a recent survey, Kariuki and Schwartz (2005) identify 23 African countries where small-scale providers are supplying different kinds of services. For about half of these countries, these small-scale providers account for a very large share of water services. Similar information is available for parts of Asia and Latin America. In many countries, small providers are taking the lead in serving low-income households and dispersed populations in rural and periurban areas where large-scale providers are unwilling to go.

Moreover, increasingly, large-scale operators from OECD countries are being replaced by developing-country investors who have emerged as a major source of investment finance for infrastructure projects with private participation. The increasing presence of China and India in Africa or Latin America continues to make the headlines in those parts of the world. Schur and others (2006) argue that in 1998–2004 these investors accounted for more of this finance in transport across developing

---

26 This number has been arrived at by researchers working independently at the U.K. Department for International Development and the World Bank (World Bank 2005a). Very roughly, it has been worked out as follows. The overall investment is estimated using changes in a country's physical capital stocks valued at international prices, while the private sector share is estimated based on total commitments made during the same period by the private sector according to the World Bank Private Participation in Infrastructure (PPI) Project Database. This is likely to be an overestimate, because commitments are not necessarily disbursed (and because these transactions include public funds).

regions—and for more in South Asia and Sub-Saharan Africa—than did investors from developed countries. They show that during 1998–2004, developing-country investors contributed more than half the private investment in concessions (54 percent), slightly less than half in greenfield projects (44 percent), and a smaller share in divestitures (30 percent). The large majority (29 percent) came from local companies investing in projects in their own country ("developing local" investors); of the rest (13 percent), almost all came from investors from nearby countries.

How Much Private Money Is Actually Flowing to Developing Countries?

There is no information on actual disbursements by private investors in infrastructure. There is, however, an international database developed and maintained by the World Bank that includes investments associated with management, concession, greenfield, and divestiture contracts that have reached financial closure (http://ppi.worldbank.org/).

According to these data, between 1990 and 2005, private investors committed $961 billion through more than 3,200 projects. That is an average of $64 billion a year. Figure 8.1 shows that Private Participation in Infrastructure (PPI) projects in developing countries peaked in 1996.

The Asian crisis launched a broadly declining trend for several years afterward. However, in 2004 and 2005 investment recovered. Throughout the period, more than 75 percent of the investment went to the telecommunications and energy sectors. Most investment went to Latin America and East Asia, although in the last two to three years Eastern Europe enjoyed the highest levels of commitment. In fact, Eastern Europe has driven most of the recovery on commitments to private infrastructure projects. Africa and South Asia continue to be only modest beneficiaries of these types of investments.

To put things in perspective, in the 2000–05 period, these investments amounted to 0.85 percent of GDP for lower- and upper-middle-income

Figure 8.1. Infrastructure Projects with Private Participation in Developing Countries, by Sector, 1990–2005

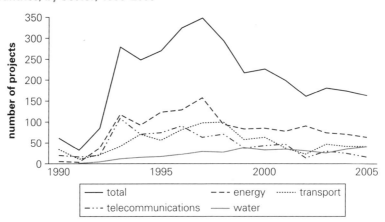

Source: World Bank and Public-Private Infrastructure Advisory Facility, PPI Project Database.

countries and about 0.69 percent for the least-developed countries. This is not minor, but considering the range of investment needs discussed earlier, PPI represents only 10 percent of those needs for the poorest countries and about 25 percent for the richer developing countries. In other words, if the 25 percent is viewed as a benchmark, improvements in the investment climate for infrastructure investors and operators could generate more than a doubling of the private investment currently seen in the poorest countries. To sustain the growth rates needed to reduce poverty, it is essential to ensure that private investment does not crowd out public investment, as often happens. During the 1990s in Latin America and Africa, many governments (and donors) slowed down their investment in infrastructure on the assumption that the private sector would more than compensate. It turns out that the net effect on investment in the sector was negative.

In all sectors, with the exception perhaps of the water sector, there has been a difference in efficiency between public and private operators.[27] In general, private operators have been more efficient, which implies that the users and the taxpayers can potentially benefit more from the private operation of the services. However, the level of efficiency and the distribution of the gains achieved from these more efficient levels have been driven by the quality of the regulatory environment. Experience on that front has not been very good, as discussed later in the chapter.

What Drives the Participation of the Private Sector?

The participation of the private sector depends on many dimensions. Exchange rate risks, commercial or demand risks, regulatory risks, and political instability can all be very damaging. These risks are typically accounted for in estimates of the minimum rate of return that private operators want from a deal in a given country. Ignoring for now the strategic motivations that may lead an operator to enter a country, even if the returns on a specific transaction are not high, most Anglo-Saxon and Nordic analysts, and increasingly analysts anchored in other traditions, believe that the estimated cost of capital associated with a transaction can be a good approximation of the expected minimum return.[28]

Several recent articles estimate the cost of capital for the various subsectors.[29] These estimates suggest that the returns required to start a project have to be at least 2–3 percentage points higher in lower-income countries than in richer developing countries and more than twice what is generally expected in developed countries in infrastructure activities.[30]

---

27 For a recent overview, see Gassner, Popov, and Pushak (2007).

28 There is less of a tradition of relying on this yardstick among Francophone operators—at least in their assessment of potential markets—because they proceed like everybody else and report the cost (and the return) on equity, one of the components of the cost of capital.

29 See Estache and Pinglo (2005) for all developing countries and Sirtaine and others (2005) for Latin America.

30 Sirtaine and others (2005) provide a detailed analysis of the evolution of the cost of capital in Latin America and compare it to the rate of return that can be estimated from the balance sheet of the main infrastructure operators in the region.

The average ex post rates of return for the large OECD operators who have led many of the privatizations of the last 15 years often have been below this cost of capital, particularly in Eastern Europe and in Latin America.

These results explain fairly clearly why the large-scale western private sector is increasing in regions where, increasingly, the operation of utilities is being renationalized. Even when these private operators continue to operate, they rely significantly more on high-cost debt than on equity to finance the investments. These numbers imply that all nonfinancial conditions being equal, the average tariff necessary to generate the minimum required rate of return in the poorest developing countries has to be higher than elsewhere and is increasing, because it needs to cover a higher and increasing cost of capital. This is politically a very difficult position to hold, and fewer and fewer private operators are willing to do so, in particular, in politically sensitive sectors such as water and passenger transport.

What Have We Learned from the "Infrastructure Privatization" Experience So Far?

The experience of the past 15 years has shown that the international community does not yet know how to address risk effectively. East Asia may have been the most effective in revealing that foreign exchange risk matters to infrastructure financing.[31] The first generation of public-private partnerships in East Asia was hit hard by the 1997 crisis. Almost 10 years later, these partnerships have not yet fully recovered, except in China. Experience in Eastern Europe and Africa has shown that there is still a long way to go to understand how institutional reforms work in this sector. Reforms may have to be introduced slowly. Better documentation is needed of just how counterproductive it can be to try to force brutal institutional changes without taking the time to build the institutional capacity consistent with the desired reforms. The difficulties of implementing concession contracts (which are derived from an Anglo-Saxon legal tradition) in Francophone Africa, where lawyers are much more familiar with *affermage* contracts (more typical of the French legal tradition), illustrate the potential for problems. The importance of this risk in Africa has been less well studied than the intensity and the drivers of renegotiation in general and in Latin America in particular (see Guasch 2004 for an overview of the issues in Latin America).

Latin America's recent experience has shown the need to study the social and political risks better, because they matter to the effectiveness of reforms and hence their sustainability. Reforming by decree without an effort to build up support is no longer an option. In this region, the poor have clearly voiced their opinion on what kind of infrastructure services

---

31 Investors in Argentina would probably argue that the pesification of the economy implemented in January 2002 is the best evidence so far of what that risk means.

they want.[32] Very often this implies that policy makers have to understand how to better balance the concern for equity with the need for incentives to invest, which has dominated the past 15 years of reforms. The experience also shows that it is worth looking more carefully into options to ensure that government and operators are committed to increased accountability to users and taxpayers. This can be achieved by adopting regulatory models that allow transparent documentation of efficiency, equity, and fiscal considerations.[33]

The experience also shows that politics matter. Anecdotes from Asia, Eastern Europe, and Latin America show that politicians are unlikely to give up control of a sector that buys votes in democratic societies. Moreover, in societies in which corruption is rampant, they will not give up control of a sector involving large amounts of money and in which contract award processes often provide opportunities for unchecked transactions.

The Upshot

The debate on the role of the public sector in infrastructure continues to be one of the hottest in the academic literature and in political circles. Ideology continues to taint the facts and their interpretation. This debate is possible simply because the facts reveal a complex and sometimes inconsistent picture. The privatization wave has delivered on some of its promises, but not all of them. Efficiency generally has improved, but many argue that most of the improvement should be credited to increased competition and, in the case of telecommunications, to a simultaneous technological revolution. Privatization has not delivered as much investment as expected, and those who lack access to begin with are the most penalized by this failure.

Looking ahead, investors, operators, and governments seem to be internalizing the main lessons of the 1990s and are increasingly effective at mitigating risk. Investors are working more in sectors that are safe bets (such as telecommunications). They are also more effective at picking the cherries. The number of large-scale concessions covering all the operations of a sector is shrinking. Sectorwide responsibilities are increasingly being covered by management or lease contracts that require no private investment. Where investment is taking place, it is done through various types of greenfield projects for specific investments (for example, bulk facilities such as power plants and water treatment plants).

---

32 The rejection of the infrastructure reforms of the 1990s, in particular the increased role of the private sector in the delivery of services, did not play a minor role in the wave of political change in Argentina, Bolivia, Brazil, Uruguay, or República Bolivariana de Venezuela.

33 Indeed, reforms often have fiscal costs, frequently generated as part of renegotiations that could have been anticipated if a consistent framework had been adopted more widely for documenting the sources of costs and incomes of the regulatory operators and accounting for reasonable forecasts of demand. A crucial fact is that the gap between the rate of return of the business and the costs of capital will be paid by taxpayers or by users, and the taxpayer has been called on much more often than is recognized. See Campos and others (2003) on the actual fiscal cost of the sector after 10 years of reform in Latin America.

On the design of financing, many of these projects face increasing costs of capital. To lower this hurdle, many contracts now include off-take agreements that increase the share of risk taken on by the government upfront (rather than reassigning it through ex post renegotiations). This has opened the door to many new operators from developing countries, led by China and India. However, many local country or region-specific actors are more familiar with the specificities of the local market and often more effective at dealing with local political sensitivities. Some challenges are likely to continue. Unless these firms are not depending on any imports or foreign financing, they are likely to be subject to foreign exchange risks similar to those faced by the first generation of private investors and operators in the sector.

The market for government-sponsored guarantees against these risks is unlikely to shrink any time soon. The real question is whether the international financial community, private and public, is willing to scale up its support to private operators working in an environment in which many risks are known, but many more seem to spring up on a regular basis. In the meantime, as long as the private sector does not take the lead or is unable to do so for a variety of economic and political reasons, it seems reasonable to expect that governments somehow will have to take on the responsibility for delivering the services.

How Is the Role of the State in Infrastructure Evolving?

There are three basic debates on the role of the state in infrastructure. The first is the debate about the extent to which the public sector should be the main provider of these services. The second is the debate about how the government should deliver its regulatory responsibility in a sector that is characterized both by market failures and by an extreme sensitivity to political pressure. The final debate is about the optimal allocation across government levels for these two main responsibilities.

What Share of the Services Is the Public Sector Delivering?

The answer to this question is not as obvious as it seems. The answer requires an unbundling of infrastructure services and physical infrastructure. In most developing countries—as well as in many developed countries—the physical infrastructure is to a large extent public. Railway tracks, roads, ports, water pipes, most basic infrastructure associated with fixed telephony, electricity transmission, and distribution or transport of gas are owned and generally operated by the public sector. Many projects are an exception to that rule, but the basic fact is that states finance much of the physical infrastructure necessary to produce the basic infrastructure services.

Table 8.6 reproduces the data from table 8.5 from the viewpoint of countries without a major private actor in infrastructure. In about two-thirds of

Table 8.6. Percentage of Countries without Significant Large-Scale Private Investment in Infrastructure, by Sector and Country Income Level, 2004

Income level	Electricity generation	Electricity distribution	Water and sanitation	Railways[a]	Fixed-line telecommunications
Low	59	71	82	66	50
Lower-middle	52	63	50	74	38
Upper-middle	42	52	63	40	28
Developing	53	64	65	64	41

Source: Estache and Goicoechea 2005.
a. 2002.

the developing countries, the state is the main actor in electricity distribution, water distribution, and railway services. In more than 50 percent of the countries, the state also is the main actor in electricity generation. Only in fixed telecommunications services are there more countries in which the private sector dominates.

In terms of investment, it is useful in this context to revisit information in the previous section from the public sector angle. About 80 percent of infrastructure investments in the last 15 years were public. This figure likely is a lower band, because many of the deals signed during the 1990s in water and transport were renegotiated, and many of those renegotiations resulted in demand for investment and operational subsidies from the state (Campos and others 2003).

From a pragmatic viewpoint, the main problem is that depending on the country group, public sector investment is still 50 to 120 percent lower than what is claimed to be needed to support high growth rates. The lower the income level, the higher the investment gap. The existence of such a gap is, in fact, what initially prompted many governments to enact reform.

Most countries did not think the state was doing a good job at delivering services. We know now that the private sector is unlikely to intervene at the scale needed for the poorest countries to get out of poverty and for middle-income countries to get the critical mass they need to make the last jump to high-income status.

This has two implications that need to be addressed by the international community. First, it is essential for donors to help to scale up investment in infrastructure as well as in health and education. Second, it is essential for countries to learn how to deliver public services better. The foreign private sector may take on the management or operation of many services and over time pass on the knowledge to those countries that need it the most. But in many countries, the scale of the problems is so large that management contracts or leases will not be possible. Structural reforms are needed in the way public enterprises are run. Unfortunately, it looks as if we collectively stopped learning anything about this in the last 20 years (Gómez-Ibáñez 2006). A lot of work is needed in this field, and the debates on how to proceed are likely to be as ideological as the debates on privatization have been for quite some time. The leading advice for now seems to be to systematically corporatize public operators in the sector and possibly to name private managers to run the operations.[34] But this requires a non-trivial political commitment to avoid other forms of interference with the management of public services.

How Should the Government Regulate Its Public Services?

Lack of self-regulation by the state or by public enterprises was a major criticism of the way the infrastructure sector was operated until the 1990s. The recognition that conflicts of interest and excessive political interference could eventually hurt users led to promotion of the idea that regulators should be independent from the political powers. This implied the creation of autonomous regulatory agencies that would be run by an individual or a board of directors. The individual or board would be recruited for skills and for a specific term independent of the political cycles and would enjoy independent sources of revenue. To many, this was also a way of increasing the transparency of transactions in the sector and hence reducing corruption.[35] The creation of this sort of agency also would signal the markets that governments were willing to cut the regulatory risks.

Recent evidence by Andres, Guasch, and Straub (2007) suggests that the creation of regulators across sectors in Latin America that were established under law, funded by a regulatory fee, and given a fixed-term regulatory commission screened by legislators more effectively aligned the cost of capital with the rate of return. Gasmi and others (2002) find equivalent results in the telecommunications sector for a worldwide sample.

Table 8.7 provides a snapshot of the position of countries with respect to this dimension of the role of government. Clearly, the idea of independent regulation has been mainstreamed in the telecommunications sector and to some extent in the energy sector. It is much less popular in the water and transport sectors. Also, as with private sector participation in infrastructure, it is an approach more likely to be adopted by richer countries. This is somewhat to be expected, since the poorest countries face a significantly larger constraint in terms of human capital. In many countries, there is a sense that the opportunity costs of earmarking the capable people to specialized agencies may be too high.

In addition to the capacity issues, two broad concerns are emerging in the countries that have adopted the idea of an independent regulator. The first is a widespread sense among specialists that economic regulation and regulatory processes need to be taken much more seriously. They are essential for reducing opportunities for corruption and ensuring fair distribution of the rents generated by the remaining public and private monopolies in the

---

34 Corporatization has complex implications for project selection. There is a risk that public enterprises will favor financial criteria over economic criteria for project selection unless there is a clear prohibition. With the increased concerns for major externalities, this issue probably is not getting the attention it deserves in policy circles and has long been out of fashion in academic circles.

35 For recent surveys of infrastructure and corruption, see Kenny (2006, 2007).

Table 8.7. Percentage of Countries with Independent Regulatory Agencies, by Sector and Country Income Level, 2004

Income level	Electricity	Water and sanitation	Railways[a]	Fixed-line telecommunications
Low	38	13	2	69
Lower-middle	63	32	8	60
Upper-middle	63	28	19	71
Developing	51	22	8	66

Source: Estache and Goicoechea 2005.
a. 2002.

sector. Accounting rules, contracts, regulatory processes and consultations, tariff or investment review procedures and methodologies, and timetables tend to lack the transparency needed for the accountability of these independent actors. This is not a minor problem. For instance, Bertolini (2006) in a survey of regulators in 2005 finds that less than 30 percent of regulators currently publish contracts and licenses.

But the experience suggests that implementation of the idea is not obvious and may not be appropriate at all stages of development. Eberhard (2007), for instance, shows why a poor independent regulator may be worse than no regulator in some circumstances. There are alternative models for the effective regulation of public and private operators that reduce the risks to the users, taxpayers, and operators. For instance, independent auditors recruited on a retainer basis and with the obligation to conduct regularly scheduled audits and to be available for extraordinary audits have long been considered. The regulation of various African railways concessions and some Eastern European water concessions offers a variation of this model. In all cases, external auditors are supported by local units within ministries or even as independent agencies.

Debate on the need for an independent regulator seems to be progressing slowly toward a more pragmatic approach that recognizes local specificities. One size does not fit all and never did. Progress is being made, but still has some way to go.

Does Decentralization Improve the Performance of the Sector?

Decentralization is the third main topic in discussions of the changes needed in the public sector. Since the 1970s, many countries, particularly developing countries, have shifted responsibilities for expenditure and financing decisions to subnational governments. Responsibility for most urban services (urban buses and railways, water, and even some road constructions) is often municipal. In view of the fast urbanization of most countries of the world, the relative importance of these mandates is likely to increase. It is also resulting in tense discussions between the various levels of government on the appropriate match between the allocation of responsibilities for expenditures and revenue across infrastructure services.

This core policy agenda has generated a lot of interesting academic work on the design of decentralization, but very little directly relevant to infrastructure. Bardhan and Mookherjee (2000, 2003) offer some of the most influential recent theoretical findings on infrastructure, highlighting the role of local corruption on the effectiveness of public service decentralization. They show that under fairly mild assumptions, decentralization, financed by user fees rather than local taxes or intergovernmental grants, generates more efficient outcomes, no matter how poorly local democracy works. The problem is when some of the assumptions are released to account for relatively common real-life situations. First, if user fees are not used—and cost recovery is only very partial for many services—the superiority of decentralized over centralized service provision is no longer as clear-cut. Second, when ability to pay is constrained and user charges cannot be used to finance antipoverty programs, the optimal degree of decentralization depends on the degree of corruption in local and central governments. Most of the academic work on infrastructure decentralization is, however, theoretical. For now, there are relatively reliable empirical tests (see Shah, Thompson, and Zhou 2004 for a general survey and Bardhan and Mookherjee 2006 for a study more focused on infrastructure).

The literature provides a few robust insights. First, decentralization tends to increase total and subnational spending on infrastructure, even more so in developing than in industrial countries (Estache and Sinha 1995; Fisman and Gatti 2002; Faguet 2004). This can have two explanations: (a) centralized regimes tend to ration demand for infrastructure services or (b) decentralization, by reducing the scale of service delivery, increases the unit costs. Second, the interaction between infrastructure, corruption, and any form of decentralization is not a simple one. Fisman and Gatti (2002) conclude that there is a negative correlation between corruption and decentralization, but Faguet (2004) does not find a strong relation either way. Olken (2005) finds that good centralized audits outperform decentralization in reducing the effects of corruption, at least for road maintenance. Finally, fiscal decentralization significantly affects the level and frequency of private participation, but administrative and political decentralization does not. Fiscal decentralization tends to increase private sector participation in infrastructure (Ghosh Banerjee 2006).

The literature and the policy advice on participatory approaches to service delivery can also be seen as an extension of the work on decentralization and points to additional insights of direct relevance to the debate on the pros and cons of decentralization. Mansuri and Rao (2004) and Cornwall (2003) observe that projects claiming "full participation" and "empowerment" have been driven by particular interests or elites, leaving the least powerful with no voice and little choice. The poverty reduction effectiveness of these programs needs to be measured more systematically as well. The one quantitative study of an infrastructure activity is by Olken (2005), who finds that increasing grassroots participation had little impact on reducing the corruption associated with road expenditure in Indonesia.

He shows that top-down monitoring may be a better solution, even in a highly corrupt environment. In other words, traditional regulatory instruments have been more effective than participatory instruments in Indonesia's road program.

But beyond its impact on governance and responsiveness to local needs, there are concerns that decentralization may be associated with a decrease in resources available for infrastructure. The concern stems from the fact that subnational governments tend to have substantially less access to private capital or international donors. Most face such severe credit constraints that their ability to finance infrastructure investments is limited in the absence of support from the central government. The central issue in setting up mechanisms to channel private savings to local bodies for the financing of infrastructure is the assurance to lenders that they will be repaid. But this is often not enough. Indeed, a major impediment to the development of subnational credit markets is the moral hazard of explicit or implicit guarantees of a federal government bailout of subnational debt. For this reason, the development of subnational credit markets requires, inter alia, a strict no-bailout policy for subnational governments in trouble. This approach has been adopted in Mexico, where the capital risk weighting of bank loans to local governments is linked to local credit ratings.

The natural question that emerges is the extent to which the expected payoffs of decentralization might be offset in the case of infrastructure by the loss of economies of scale and the reduced access to sources of financing, which are already generally difficult to obtain for sectors with high-cost lumpy investments and slow cash flows very sensitive to politics. One obvious solution is to pool the credit risks of subnational governments, which, however, involves recentralizing some of the dimensions of infrastructure service delivery. The fact that this market is not very advanced in developing countries—despite strong political pressures in many middle-income countries—indicates the wide range of viewpoints about the desirability and limits of infrastructure decentralization.

The Upshot

The role of governments in infrastructure likely will be a source of ideological debates for the foreseeable future. We know that governments will continue to play a key role as providers and financiers of the sector. Furthermore, governments will continue to have a regulatory role in a sector in which the residual monopolies are likely to be strong. However, we also know that implementation of the mandate to deliver is plagued by potential sources of political interference.

The corporatization of public enterprises does not have a great track record in developing countries, with a few exceptions in Asia. In most other countries, politics have tended to creep back into the agenda of the public and private managers of service providers within three to five years of their corporatization. Similarly, regulators have a poor record of sustainable, fair, and efficient arbitration of the joint interests of users, taxpayers, and operators. Independent regulators have been reasonably effective in the most advanced countries in telecommunications and energy. However, they have encountered many problems in water and transport. In most cases, when a crisis has hit the sector, politicians have taken over regulation. Finally, because decentralization is generally a political decision with economic and administrative consequences, the decentralized management of infrastructure services has been the victim of political disagreements across government levels, which have hurt otherwise rational decisions.

Overall, a review of the experience of the last 15 years is sobering. In spite of the long history of analysis of the potential roles of the state in infrastructure, most of the progress in learning how to get things done has come from the theoretical research. Policy makers have few yardsticks or rules of thumb they can use to set up reforms to get the public to deliver on its assignments—operation, finance, or management. Anecdotes and examples of best practice abound, but credible specific guidelines are scarce.

Concluding Comments

The heterogeneity of the infrastructure business is such that it is difficult to draw specific conclusions for any given subsector or country from a broad-brush overview such as this one. However, some general conclusions can be drawn.

The basic debates have not changed much over the last 25 years or so, and they center on two core questions:

- *Who should be in charge of the sector:* the government or the private sector, the central government or the subnational governments, independent regulators or politicians?
- *Who should pay for the services:* the users, the taxpayers, or, in some cases, the donors?

There are plenty of variations and refinements around these two questions, driven by the relative importance assigned to the concern for efficiency, equity, financial viability, and accountability. Although a lot of learning has taken place on how to address these questions, some of the basic answers are still lacking. And yet they are crucial to the success and the sustainability of many of the current efforts to allow the poorest countries to develop faster and to get the richest country out of the first global financial crisis of the twenty-first century.

One of the main reasons for this lack of clear-cut answers is the lack of objective data on the sector. Data gaps have been highlighted throughout this overview, including on basic issues such as costs and tariffs or the share of public or private resources allocated to expand or maintain the sectors.

In recent years, more subjective data have become available based on questionnaires covering a wide range of topics such as the investment climate, corruption perception indicators, or the sources of happiness for people. There have also been refinements of household consumption and expenditure surveys to generate comparable data on problems in the sector for residential users. But these multiple sources generate information rarely comparable across sources and continue to leave major gaps. Ultimately, these data gaps are what allow ideological debates to dominate substantive debates in this sector. To produce substantive answers to core questions and settle the debates summarized here without recourse to ideology, it is essential for the international community to take the data agenda much more seriously than in the past. Some progress is being made through the MDGs, but there is still a long way to go.

References

Adam, Christopher, and David Bevan. 2004. "Aid and the Supply Side: Public Investment, Export Performance, and Dutch Disease in Low-Income Countries." Working Paper 201. Oxford University, Department of Economics.

Agénor, Pierre-Richard, and Blanca Moreno-Dodson. 2006. "Public Infrastructure and Growth: New Channels and Policy Implications." Policy Research Working Paper 4064. World Bank, Washington, DC.

Alam, Asad, Mamta Murthi, Ruslan Yemtsov, Edmundo Murrugarra, Nora Dudwick, Ellen Hamilton, and Erwin Tiongson. 2005. *Growth, Poverty, and Inequality: Eastern Europe and the Former Soviet Union.* Washington, DC: World Bank.

Albala-Bertrand, José, and Emmanuel Mamatzakis. 2004. "The Impact of Public Infrastructure on the Productivity of the Chilean Economy." *Review of Development Economics* 8 (2): 266–78.

Alesina, Alberto, Reza Baqir, and William Easterly. 1999. "Public Goods and Ethnic Divisions." *Quarterly Journal of Economics* 114 (4): 1243–84.

Andres, Luis, José Luis Guasch, and Stéphane Straub. 2007. "Does Regulation and Institutional Design Matter for Infrastructure Sector Performance?" World Bank, Washington, DC.

Aschauer, David. 1989. "Is Public Expenditure Productive?" *Journal of Monetary Economics* 23 (2): 177–200.

———. 2000. "Do States Optimize? Public Capital and Economic Growth." *Annals of Regional Science* 34 (3): 343–63.

Baldwin, Richard, Rikard Forslid, Philippe Martin, Gianmarco Ottaviano, and Frederic Robert-Nicoud. 2003. *Economic Geography and Public Policy.* Princeton, NJ: Princeton University Press.

Bardhan, Pranab, and Dilip Mookherjee. 2000. "Corruption and Decentralization of Infrastructure in Developing Countries." *Economic Journal* 116 (508): 101–27.

———. 2003. "Decentralization and Accountability in Infrastructure in Developing Countries." Boston University, Boston, MA.

———. 2006. "Decentralization, Corruption, and Government Accountability: An Overview." In *International Handbook on the Economics of Corruption,* ed. Susan Rose-Ackerman. Cheltenham, U.K.: Edward Elgar.

Bertolini, Lorenzo. 2006. "How to Improve Regulatory Transparency." *Gridlines Note* 11 (June). www.ppiaf.org/.

Boccanfuso, Dorothee, Antonio Estache, and Luc Savard. 2006. "Water Sector Reform in Senegal: An Interpersonal and Interregional Distributional Impact Analysis." World Bank, Washington, DC.

Bougheas, Spiros, Panicos Demetriades, and Theofanis Mamuneas. 2000. "Infrastructure, Specialization, and Economic Growth." *Canadian Journal of Economics* 33 (2): 506–22.

Brenneman, Adam. 2002. "Infrastructure and Poverty Linkages: A Literature Review." World Bank, Washington, DC.

Briceño, Cecilia, Antonio Estache, and Nemat Shafik. 2004. "Infrastructure Services in Developing Countries: Access, Quality, Costs, and Policy Reform." World Bank, Washington, DC.

Briceño, Cecilia, and Irina Klytchnikova. 2006. "Infrastructure and Poverty: What Data Are Available for Impact Evaluation?" World Bank, Washington, DC.

Cadot, Olivier, Lars-Hendrik Röller, and Andreas Stephan. 2006. "Contribution to Productivity or Pork Barrel? The Two Faces of Infrastructure Investment." *Journal of Public Economics* 90 (6-7): 1133–53.

Calderon, César, and Luis Serven. 2004. "The Effects of Infrastructure Development on Growth and Income Distribution." Policy Research Working Paper 3400. World Bank, Washington, DC.

Campos, Javier, Antonio Estache, Noelia Martin, and Lourdes Trujillo. 2003. "Macroeconomic Effects of Private Sector Participation in Infrastructure." In *The Limits of Stabilization,* ed. William Easterly and Luis Serven. Palo Alto, CA: Stanford University Press.

Canning, David, and Esra Bennathan. 2000. "The Social Rate of Return on Infrastructure Investment." Policy Research Working Paper 2390 (July). World Bank, Washington, DC.

Canning, David, and Peter Pedroni. 2004. "The Effect of Infrastructure on Long-Run Economic Growth." World Bank, Washington, DC.

Cavalcanti Ferreira, Pedro, and Leandro Gonçalves do Nascimento. 2005. "Welfare and Growth Effects of Alternative Fiscal Rules for Infrastructure Investments in Brazil." World Bank, Washington, DC.

Chen, Sheng-Tung, Hsiao-I Kuo, and Chi-Chung Chen. 2007. "The Relationship between GDP and Electricity Consumption in 10 Asian Countries." *Energy Policy* 35 (44): 2611–21.

Chisari, Omar, Antonio Estache, and Catherine Waddams-Price. 2003. "Access by the Poor in Latin America's Utility Reform: Subsidies and Service Obligations." In *Utility Privatization and Regulation: A Fair Deal for Consumers?* ed. Cecilia Ugaz and Catherine Waddams-Price. Northampton, MA: Edward Elgar.

Clarke, George, and Scott Wallsten. 2002. "Universal(ly Bad) Service: Providing Infrastructure Services to Rural and Poor Urban Consumers." Policy Research Working Paper 2868. World Bank, Washington, DC.

Cohen, Barney. 2004. "Urban Growth in Developing Countries: A Review of Current Trends and a Caution Regarding Existing Forecasts." *World Development* 32 (1): 23–51.

Combes, Pierre Philippe, and Miren Lafourcade. 2001. "Transportation Costs Decline and Regional Inequalities: Evidence from France, 1978–1993." CEPR Discussion Paper 2894. Centre for Economic Policy Research, London, U.K.

Cornwall, Andrea. 2003. "Whose Voices? Whose Choices? Reflection on Gender and Participatory Development." *World Development* 31 (8): 1325–42.

Cremer, Helmuth, Farid Gasmi, André Grimaud, and Jean-Jacques Laffont. 2001. "Universal Service: An Economic Perspective Overview." *Annals of Public and Cooperative Economics* 72 (1): 4–43.

de la Fuente, Angel. 2002a. "The Effect of Structural Fund Spending on the Spanish Regions: An Assessment of the 1994–99 Objective 1 CSF." CEPR Discussion Paper 3673. Centre for Economic Policy Research, London, U.K.

———. 2002b. "Is the Allocation of Public Capital across the Spanish Regions Too Redistributive?" CEPR Discussion Paper 3138. Centre for Economic Policy Research, London, U.K.

de la Fuente, Angel, and Xavier Vives. 1995. "Infrastructure and Education as Instruments of Economic Policy: Evidence from Spain." *Economic Policy* 20 (April): 11–54.

Duggal, Vijaya, Cynthia Saltzman, and Lawrence Klein. 2007. "Infrastructure and Productivity: An Extension to Private Infrastructure and IT Productivity." *Journal of Econometrics* 140 (2): 485–502.

Eberhard, Antone. 2007. "Matching Regulatory Design to Country Circumstances." *Gridlines Note* 23 (May). Public-Private Infrastructure Advisory Facility (PPIAF), Washington, DC.

Ebinger, Jane. 2006. "Measuring Financial Performance in Infrastructure: An Application to Europe and Central Asia." Working Paper 3992. World Bank, Washington, DC.

Esfahani, Hadi Salehi, and Maria Teresa Ramirez. 2003. "Institutions, Infrastructure, and Economic Growth." *Journal of Development Economics* 70 (2): 443–77.

Estache, Antonio. 2009. "Lessons from Impact Evaluations of Infrastructure Projects, Programs, and Policies." European Center for Advanced Research in Economics and Statistics, Université Libre de Bruxelles, Brussels.

Estache, Antonio, and Marianne Fay. 1997. "Ensuring Regional Growth Convergence in Argentina and Brazil: How Can Governments Help?" World Bank, Washington, DC.

Estache, Antonio, Vivien Foster, and Quentin Wodon. 2002. *Accounting for Poverty in Infrastructure Reform: Learning from Latin America's Experience.* WBI Development Series. Washington, DC: World Bank.

Estache, Antonio, and Ana Goicoechea. 2005. "How Widespread Were Infrastructure Reforms during the 1990s?" Research Working Paper 3595. World Bank, Washington, DC.

Estache, Antonio, and Rafael Muñoz. 2007. "Building Sector Concerns into Macroeconomic Financial Programming: Lessons from Senegal and Uganda." World Bank, Washington, DC.

Estache, Antonio, and Maria Elena Pinglo. 2005. "Are Returns to Public-Private Infrastructure Partnerships in Developing Countries Consistent with Risks since the Asian Crisis?" *Journal of Network Industries* 6 (1): 47–71.

Estache, Antonio, and Sarbijit Sinha. 1995. "Does Decentralization Increase Spending on Infrastructure?" Policy Research Working Paper 1995. World Bank, Washington, DC.

Estache, Antonio, Biagio Speciale, and David Veredas. 2006. "How Much Does Infrastructure Matter to Growth in Sub-Saharan Africa?" World Bank, Washington, DC.

Estache, Antonio, and Quentin Wodon. 2007. *Infrastructure and Poverty in Africa*. Directions in Development. Washington, DC: World Bank.

Faguet, Jean Paul. 2004. "Does Decentralization Increase Government Responsiveness to Local Needs: Evidence from Bolivia." *Journal of Public Economics* 88 (3-4): 867–93.

Faini, Riccardo. 1983. "Cumulative Process of Deindustrialization in an Open Region: The Case of Southern Italy, 1951–1973." *Journal of Development Economics* 12 (3): 277–301.

Fay, Marianne, and Mary Morrison. 2006. *Infrastructure in Latin America and the Caribbean: Recent Development and Key Challenges*. Washington, DC: World Bank.

Fay, Marianne, and Tito Yepes. 2003. "Investing in Infrastructure: What Is Needed from 2000–2010." Policy Research Working Paper 3102. World Bank, Washington, DC.

Fernald, John. 1999. "Roads to Prosperity? Assessing the Link between Public Capital and Productivity." *American Economic Review* 89 (3): 619–38.

Fisman, Raymond, and Roberta Gatti. 2002. "Decentralization and Corruption: Evidence across Countries." *Journal of Public Economics* 83 (3): 325–45.

Foster, Vivien, and Tito Yepes. 2006. "Is Cost Recovery a Feasible Objective for Water and Electricity? The Latin American Experience." Policy Research Working Paper 3943. World Bank, Washington, DC.

Gasmi, Farid, D. Mark Kennet, Jean-Jacques Laffont, and William W. Sharkey. 2002. *Cost Proxy Models and Telecommunications Policy*. Cambridge, MA: MIT Press.

Gassner, Katherina, Alexander Popov, and Nataliya Pushak. 2007. "An Empirical Assessment of Private Participation in Electricity and Water Distribution in Developing and Transition Economies." World Bank, Washington, DC.

Gibson, John, and Scott Rozelle. 2002. "Poverty and Access to Infrastructure in Papua New Guinea." Working Paper 1000. University of California, Davis, Department of Agricultural and Resource Economics.

Ghosh Banerjee, Sudeshna. 2006. "Decentralization's Impact on Private Sector Participation in Infrastructure Investment in Developing Countries." World Bank, Washington, DC.

Gómez-Ibáñez, José A. 2006. "Alternatives to Privatization Revisited: The Options for Infrastructure." World Bank, Infrastructure Vice Presidency, Washington, DC.

Gramlich, Edward M. 1994. "Infrastructure Investment: A Review Essay." *Journal of Economic Literature* 32 (3): 1176–96.

Guasch, José Luis. 2004. *Granting and Renegotiating Infrastructure Concessions: Doing It Right*. WBI Development Studies. Washington, DC: World Bank.

Henderson, J. Vernon. 2002. "Urbanization in Developing Countries." *World Bank Research Observer* 17 (1): 89–112.

Henderson, J. Vernon, and Ari Kuncoro. 1996. "Industrial Centralization in Indonesia." *World Bank Economic Review* 10 (3): 513–40.

Henderson, J. Vernon, Zmarak Shalizi, and Anthony Venables. 2001. "Geography and Development." *Journal of Economic Geography* 1 (1): 81–105.

Hurlin, Christophe. 2006. "Network Effects of the Productivity of Infrastructure in Developing Countries." Policy Research Working Paper 3808. World Bank, Washington, DC.

Iimi, Atsushi, and James Wilson Smith. 2007. "What Is Missing between Agricultural Growth and Infrastructure Development? Cases of Coffee and Dairy in Africa." World Bank, Washington, DC.

Ingram, Gregory, and Zhi Liu. 1999. "Determinants of Motorization and Road Provision." Policy Research Working Paper 2042. World Bank, Washington, DC.

International Energy Agency. 2006. *World Energy Outlook*. Paris: International Energy Agency.

Jacoby, Hanan G. 2000. "Access to Markets and the Benefits of Rural Roads." *Economic Journal* 100 (465): 717–37.

Kalaitzidakis, Pantelis, and Sarantis Kalyvitis. 2004. "On the Macroeconomic Implications of Maintenance in Public Capital." *Journal of Public Economics* 88 (3–4): 695–712.

Kamps, Christophe. 2005. "Is There a Lack of Public Capital in the European Union?" *European Investment Bank Papers* 10 (1): 73–93.

Kariuki, Mukami, and Jordan Schwartz. 2005. "Small-Scale Private Service Providers of Water Supply and Electricity: A Review of Incidence, Structure, Pricing, and Operating Characteristics." Policy Research Working Paper 3727. World Bank, Washington, DC.

Kenny, Charles. 2006. "Measuring and Reducing the Impact of Corruption in Infrastructure." Policy Research Working Paper 4099. World Bank, Washington, DC.

———. 2007. "Infrastructure Governance and Corruption: Where Next?" Policy Research Working Paper 4331. World Bank, Washington, DC.

Komives, Kristin, Vivien Foster, Jonathan Halpern, and Quentin Wodon. 2005. "Water, Electricity, and the Poor: Who Benefits from Utility Subsidies?" World Bank, Washington, DC.

Laffont, Jean-Jacques. 2005. *Regulation and Development*. Cambridge, U.K.: Cambridge University Press.

Lall, Somik V., Richard Funderburg, and Tito Yepes. 2003. "Location, Concentration, and Performance of Economic Activity in Brazil." Policy Research Working Paper 3268. World Bank, Washington, DC.

Lall, Somik, and H. G. Wang. 2006. "Improving the Development Impact of Infrastructure, Proposal for a Research Program Grant on Infrastructure." World Bank, Washington, DC.

Lanjouw, Peter. 1999. "Policy Options for Employment in the Rural Non-Farm Sector." Rural Development Note 4. World Bank, Washington, DC.

Lipton, Michael. 1977. *Why Poor People Stay Poor: Urban Bias in World Development.* Cambridge, MA: Harvard University Press.

Lokshin, Michael, and Ruslan Yemtsov. 2005. "Who Bears the Cost of Russia's Military Draft?" Policy Research Working Paper 3547. World Bank, Washington, DC.

Mansuri, Ghazala, and Vijayendra Rao. 2004. "Community-Based and -Driven Development: A Critical Review." *World Bank Research Observer* 19 (1): 1–39.

Mellor, John. 1976. *The New Economics of Growth.* Ithaca, NY: Cornell University Press.

Nellis, John, and Nancy Birdsall, eds. 2005. *Reality Check: The Distributional Impact of Privatization in Developing Countries.* Washington, DC: Center for Global Development.

Olken, Benjamin A. 2005. "Monitoring Corruption: Evidence from a Field Experiment in Indonesia." NBER Working Paper 11753. National Bureau of Economic Research, Cambridge, MA.

Puga, Diego. 2002. "European Regional Policies in Light of Recent Location Theories." *Journal of Economic Geography* 2 (4): 373–406.

Rauch, James. 1995. "Bureaucracy, Infrastructure, and Economic Growth: Evidence from U.S. Cities during the Progressive Era." *American Economic Review* 85 (4): 968–79.

Ravallion, Martin. 2002. "On the Urbanization of Poverty." *Journal of Development Economics* 68 (2): 435–42.

———. 2003. "The Debate on Globalization, Poverty, and Inequality: Why Measurement Matters." Working Paper 3038. World Bank, Development Research Group, Washington, DC.

Reardon, Thomas. 2001. "Rural Non-Farm Income in Developing Countries." Report to the United Nations Food and Agriculture Organization, Rome.

Renkow, Mitch, Daniel G. Hallstrom, and Daniel D. Karanja. 2004. "Rural Infrastructure, Transaction Costs, and Market Participation." *Journal of Development Economics* 73 (1): 349–67.

Rioja, Felix K. 2001. "Growth, Welfare, and Public Infrastructure: A General-Equilibrium Analysis of Latin American Economies." *Journal of Economic Development* 26 (2): 119–30.

———. 2003. "Filling Potholes: Macroeconomic Effects of Maintenance vs. New Investments in Public Infrastructure." *Journal of Public Economics* 87 (9–10): 2281–304.

Robinson, James, and Ragnar Torvik. 2005. "White Elephants." *Journal of Public Economics* 89 (2-3): 197–210.

Röller, Lars-Hendrik, and Leonard Waverman. 2001. "Telecommunications Infrastructure and Economic Development: A Simultaneous Approach." *American Economic Review* 91 (4): 909–23.

Romp, Ward, and Jakob de Haan. 2005. "Public Capital and Economic Growth: A Critical Survey." EIB Papers 2/2005. European Investment Bank, Luxemburg. www.eib.org/infocentre/publications/eib-papers-volume-10 .-n12005.htm.

Schur, Michael, Stephan von Klaudy, Georgina Dellacha, Apurva Sanghi, and Nataliya Pushak. 2006. "The Role of Developing-Country Firms in Infrastructure: A New Class of Investors Emerges." *Gridlines Note* 2 (May). www.ppiaf .org/Gridlines/ 3global.pdf.

Shah, Anwar, Theresa Thompson, and Heng-Fu Zhou. 2004. "The Impact of Decentralization on Service Delivery, Corruption, Fiscal Management, and Growth in Developing- and Emerging-Market Economies: A Synthesis of Empirical Evidence." *CESifo DICE Report* 1: 10–14.

Sirtaine, Sophie, Maria Elena Pinglo, Vivien Foster, and J. Luis Guasch. 2005. "How Profitable Are Private Infrastructure Concessions in Latin America? Empirical Evidence and Regulatory Implications." *Quarterly Review of Economics and Finance* 45 (2-3): 380–402.

Straub, Stéphane, and Charles Vellutini. 2006. "Assessment of the Effect of Infrastructure on Economic Growth in the East Asia and Pacific Region." World Bank, Washington, DC.

Ugaz, Cecilia, and Catherine Waddams-Price. 2003. *Utility Privatization and Regulation: A Fair Deal for Consumers?* Cheltenham, U.K.: Edward Elgar.

van de Walle, Dominique. 2002. "Choosing Rural Road Investments to Reduce Poverty." *World Development* 30 (4): 575–89.

van de Walle, Dominique, and Kimberly Nead. 1995. *Public Spending and the Poor: Theory and Evidence.* Baltimore, MD: Johns Hopkins University Press.

Vickerman, Roger, Klaus Spiekermann, and Michael Wegener. 1999. "Accessibility and Economic Development in Europe." *Regional Studies* 33 (1): 1–15.

World Bank. 2005a. *Global Monitoring Report 2005: Millennium Development Goals; From Consensus to Momentum.* Washington, DC: World Bank. www.worldbank.org/reference/.

———. 2005b. "Mexico: Infrastructure Public Expenditure Review." Report 33483-MX. World Bank, Washington, DC. www.worldbank.org/reference/.

———. 2007a. "Argentina: Infrastructure for Growth and Poverty Alleviation." World Bank, Washington, DC.

———. 2007b. World Development Indicators. Washington, DC: World Bank.

CHAPTER 9

Exports of Manufactures and Economic Growth: The Fallacy of Composition Revisited

William R. Cline

In the early 1980s, development economists debated whether the remarkable growth of the group of four (G-4) East Asian tigers—Hong Kong, China; Republic of Korea; Singapore; and Taiwan, China—which was based on the rapid growth of exports of manufactures, could be generalized to other developing countries. The central question was whether what worked for a few economies of moderate size could work for a large number of economies including some far larger. In particular, the question was whether a generalization of this strategy would so swamp the markets of industrial countries with imports of manufactures that the response would be a wave of protection, frustrating the attempts at rapid export growth by developing countries. This became known as the fallacy of composition (FC) problem: what seemed logical for one country in isolation was logically inconsistent when generalized.

Cline (1982) presented calculations suggesting that FC problems could indeed pose limits on the pace and breadth of generalizing the East Asian growth model. Further calculations in Cline (1984) suggested, nonetheless, that relatively robust rates of growth of manufactured exports from developing countries could be pursued without triggering protection, so long as they observed "speed limits" that were substantially slower than the pace that had so far characterized the East Asian model of growth.

The purpose of this chapter is threefold. First, it examines whether my earlier studies turned out to be consistent with what happened subsequently. This is done both at the global aggregate level, to see whether manufactured exports from developing countries did grow within the speed limits anticipated, and at the sectoral level, to consider whether the import penetration levels that the analysis anticipated would trigger protection were, in fact, reached. Second, this study considers whether developing countries that have not yet achieved substantial export growth in manufactures are well or ill advised to do so, given present-day global patterns of trade and production. Third, it asks whether there is a new macroeconomic variant of the FC problem, additive to or more important than the earlier microeconomic FC concern.

In broad terms, I find the following. First, the expansion of manufactured exports from developing countries over the past quarter century has been robust and a vital source of growth for many countries, but nonetheless has stayed within the speed limits I had postulated in aggregate terms. Second, at the sectoral level, there do seem to have been significant instances of high levels of import penetration that would have triggered protection according to my statistical models of protection but that did not do so, in part because of growing discipline exerted by the General Agreement on Tariffs and Trade (GATT) and then the World Trade Organization (WTO). Third, looking forward, many poor countries could still benefit from pursuing export growth in manufactures, despite the enormous presence of China, the original G-4, and other developing countries in global markets for manufactured goods. This potential reflects the fact that even taken together, the poorer countries constitute only a modest portion of potentially increased manufactured exports relative to the existing developing-country base. Moreover, there is a "product ladder" phenomenon in which exports of simple labor-intensive manufactures seem likely to be passed off from the G-4 (as has already happened), China, and others to the poorer countries. Finally, this essay suggests that there is indeed a new macroeconomic FC problem centered on the conflict between ever-rising trade surpluses in China and elsewhere in Asia and the need for the United States, in particular, to avoid an ever-widening trade deficit and increasingly unsustainable external debt.

The first section of this study briefly recapitulates the analysis in my two 1980s studies and reviews the subsequent FC literature. The second section examines aggregate performance of developing countries in exports of manufactures. The third section examines more detailed sectoral trends in trade and import penetration. The fourth section turns to implications for today's poorer countries. The fifth section addresses the macroeconomic FC problem and the need for real exchange rate adjustment in China and several other key developing countries. A final section concludes.

Early Studies and Subsequent Literature

My early paper on the fallacy of composition (Cline 1982) was written at a time when the G-4 experience was frequently cited as an object lesson on the merits of export-led growth and when inefficient import-substituting industrialization behind protective barriers was rampant in Latin America and other major developing-country regions. Although I recognized the strong emerging evidence on the importance of export growth for economic growth (see, for example, Balassa 1978), I suggested that some caution was warranted because of rising protection in the 1970s in sensitive sectors such as textiles and apparel, footwear, and television sets.

As an "acid test" of the potential for new protection in industrial countries to thwart models of developing-country growth based on rapid expansion of manufactured exports, I calculated what would happen to import penetration ratios if all developing countries were to reach the G-4 export benchmarks. I first normalized for the influence of size of the economy and per capita income on the ratio of exports to gross domestic product (GDP), based on cross-country regressions by Chenery and Syrquin (1975). I found that for the base year 1976, the G-4 had manufactured exports 4.4 times as high as would be predicted by the cross-country patterns. I then estimated that if other developing countries reached the G-4 levels, manufactured exports from developing countries to industrial-country markets would multiply by a factor of 7.5. I then set an arbitrary threshold of 15 percent import penetration (ratio of imports to domestic apparent consumption) for imports from developing countries as a plausible range at which protective response might be triggered. When this screen was applied to detailed sectoral data in a simulated world with G-4 manufacturing export intensity, the result was that this import penetration threshold would have been exceeded in sectors accounting for about 80 percent of industrial-country manufactured imports from developing countries. I concluded, "Generalization of the East Asian model of export-led development across all developing countries would result in untenable market penetration into industrial countries" (Cline 1982: 88).

In my first article, I also briefly mentioned two themes that would be taken up in the later literature. The first was that increased imports of manufactures from developing countries would induce higher exports by industrial countries, which might alleviate protectionist pressures. However, I noted that North-South trade was mainly interindustry rather than intraindustry, so the new export jobs would tend to be in sectors different from those competing with increased imports from developing countries. Any alleviation of protectionist pressure would thus likely be limited. The second theme was that adverse market price effects could moderate the rise in manufactured exports from developing countries well before protectionist responses occurred, because the outward shift of supply from countries following the export-oriented strategy would tend to cause relative prices for these exports to decline. I emphasized, however, that this terms-of-trade effect merely reinforced the policy conclusion that developing countries as a group could not expect to replicate G-4 export results (Cline 1982: 88).

Although the G-4 acid test suggested prudence, it by no means meant that manufactured exports should be ignored. I revisited the issue in a subsequent analysis (Cline 1984). In that study, I estimated a logit model of industrial-country protection by major nontariff barriers as a function of the size of sectoral employment, the import penetration level, and other variables. Application of the model to alternative projected levels of sectoral imports of manufactures from developing countries by 1990 found no generalized predicted rise in protection, although the projections did predict a significant rise in the incidence of U.S. nontrade barriers (from 40 to 47 percent market coverage). The projections were based on simple extrapolation of growth rates in the 1970s, which yielded average real expansion by 14 percent annually, and alternatively on a set of World Bank projections averaging 10 percent. My second study pointed out that phasing in the G-4 benchmark levels by 1990 would translate into growth rates of manufactured exports averaging about 30 percent annually during 1983–90. Similarly, the actual real growth rate of Korea's manufactured exports from the early 1960s to 1980 was around 30 percent annually. The second study (Cline 1984: 129–30) thus concluded,

> There is a speed limit on the expansion of manufactured exports that developing countries would do well to observe … [They] can probably expand their manufactured exports at real rates of 10 to 15 percent annually without provoking a strong protectionist response, … but expansion at rates of 30 percent or higher would be much more likely to provoke problems of market absorption and protection.

Ranis (1985) criticized my 1982 article on three grounds. First, he argued that it overstated the prospective growth of manufactured exports from developing countries by not recognizing different timing among different countries or the likelihood of lesser manufacturing intensity of countries with large endowments of land and other natural resources. Second, he considered its 15 percent threshold for protective response to be arbitrary and suggested that it could be too low. Third, he emphasized that my calculations failed to take account of a likely rise in the share of manufactured exports going from the South to the South rather than from the South to the North. My reply (Cline 1985) emphasized that, on my most important point, Ranis and I were in agreement: "Planners … cannot necessarily expect the benefits of trade liberalization to their countries to be as great as those achieved by the G-4 countries" (Ranis 1985: 545). On the first critique, I responded that my article actually reinforced this main point. On the second, I noted that the 15 percent level for developing-country supply was consistent with my subsequent estimates (Cline 1984) of statistical protection functions at least for large sectors, once supply from industrial countries was taken into account. On the third, as discussed below, we now have a historical record that shows only a modest rise in the share of manufactured exports of developing countries going to other developing countries. My reply did emphasize that I agreed with Ranis on the importance of export growth in developing countries, especially to help countries adjust to the debt crisis. At the same time, I emphasized the speed limit finding of my 1984 study.

Mayer (2003: 2–3) has surveyed the subsequent literature on the fallacy of composition. He identifies four versions of the FC:

> (i) An early version pioneered by Cline (1982) who emphasizes protectionist tendencies in developed countries ... (ii) a more recent version used by Faini, Clavijo, and Senhadji-Semlali (1992) who focus on the partial-equilibrium ... [fact that] the elasticity of export demand for a group of countries is smaller in absolute value than the corresponding elasticity for an individual country ... (iii) a version identified by Havrylyshn (1990) and first tested by Martin (1993) that highlights the general-equilibrium nature of the fallacy of composition ... [And] a further version (iv) [focusing on] whether manufactured exports ... from developing countries have been falling in price compared to those of developed countries.

Although Mayer judges that Martin's reformulation of the issue in general-equilibrium terms was an important advance, he notes the study's "important shortcomings," including "very broad product classification, ... high and constant elasticities of substitution, ... and lack of taking account of adjustment costs in developed countries" (Mayer 2003: 6). He also suggests that despite improvements in several subsequent general-equilibrium model studies, such studies typically continue to suffer from excessively broad sectoral aggregations.

On the fourth issue, Mayer surveys numerous studies and synthesizes the following predominant findings. First, any apparent fall in terms of trade for manufactures from developing countries during the 1960s and 1970s tends to disappear after excluding nonferrous metals, for which there was a large price decline in the early 1970s.[1] Second, for the period from 1970 through the late 1980s, there may have been a small downward trend in barter terms of trade for developing countries in manufactures (price of exports relative to price of imports), on the order of 1 percent annually according to one study. However, this was far overshadowed by rising export volumes, so that the income terms of trade (a measure that incorporates export quantity and hence is a measure of the real import capacity of export earnings) rose briskly, on the order of 10 percent annually, according to the same study. Third, during the 1980s and early 1990s, there was a differential pattern among developing countries. The East and South Asian economies experienced a slight negative trend in barter terms of trade for manufactures, but the least developed countries experienced a strongly negative trend at about 5 percent a year, and the Latin American countries experienced an intermediate outcome. Fourth, countries such as Korea have shifted to higher priced and technologically more sophisticated manufactured exports. More broadly, Mayer suggests

---

1   This was also my finding in Cline (1984: 165).

that it is mainly countries concentrating on exports of labor-intensive manufactures that have experienced falling terms of trade.

The study of Martin (1993: 171) warrants further consideration because of its claim that a general-equilibrium approach "may completely overturn the conventional view of the fallacy of composition." His model uses only three product sectors: manufactures, other goods and services, and nontraded goods. This is obviously too small to say anything meaningful about protection. For example, when apparel and aircraft are lumped together in a single sector, it is impossible to analyze protectionist pressures that might arise in apparel from a surge in imports regardless of a boost in aircraft exports. Instead, such pressures are assumed away. However, Martin does not explicitly test for protection, although some may incorrectly have inferred that his study speaks to this issue; his conclusion that the FC thesis has been turned on its head is curious, given that he does not test one of its main propositions. Instead, his analysis pertains only to the terms-of-trade variant of the FC.

His most relevant test of this variant postulates a 10 percent productivity shock in output of manufactures for developing countries. He then considers the difference between this occurrence in a single region in isolation (for example, East Asia) and in all developing regions. He finds that exports of manufactures rise by a virtually uniform 16 percent for any given developing-country region, in both the individual- and joint-shock cases, with welfare gains that are small in both cases, but systematically higher in the joint-shock exercise because of the availability of cheaper manufactured imports. It should be emphasized, however, that early Korea-style annual growth rates of manufactured exports on the order of 30 percent over several years (greatly exceeding my speed limit) would generate increases on the order of some several hundred percent, not 16 percent, in the space of considerably less than a decade. So his comparative static general-equilibrium test with a 16 percent increase in manufactured exports is something of a straw man when billed as a test of the FC hypothesis. Moreover, because his model does not even consider induced protection in industrial countries (fortunately so, because his sectoral aggregation precludes it), it is at best a test of the manufacturing terms-of-trade variant of the FC, but one using what amounts to a minimal shock compared to actual decadal trends and thus one that not surprisingly finds minimal impacts.

Aggregate Evidence on Performance of Manufactured Exports

Table 9.1 shows estimates of real exports of manufactures by developing countries for benchmark years for the past four decades. The underlying data are in nominal dollar values and refer to exports of Standard Industrial Trade Classification (SITC) categories 5 through 8 less category

Table 9.1. Manufactured Exports from Developing Countries, 1962–2004

Economy	Level (US$ millions at 2000 prices)					Percent of total exports					Real annual growth (%)		
	1962	1980	1990	2000	2004	1962	1980	1990	2000	2004	1962–80	1980–90	1990–2004
Latin America													
Argentina	164	2,740	4,129	8,538	8,991	3.2	23.1	29.3	32.3	29.0	15.7	4.1	5.6
Bolivia	17	49	50	395	274	7.8	3.2	4.7	27.1	13.4	6.0	0.1	12.2
Brazil	164	11,484	18,595	31,878	45,865	3.2	38.6	51.8	57.7	53.3	23.6	4.8	6.4
Chile	84	1,120	952	2,800	3,602	3.8	16.1	9.8	15.4	12.9	14.4	-1.6	9.5
Colombia	67	1,146	1,940	4,270	5,607	3.5	19.6	25.1	32.5	37.0	15.8	5.3	7.6
Costa Rica	38	523	446	3,595	3,544	9.7	35.3	26.8	65.5	62.2	14.6	-1.6	14.8
Ecuador	8	110	72	414	502	1.4	3.0	2.3	8.6	7.3	14.3	-4.2	13.9
Mexico	512	5,009	13,031	138,651	139,318	13.1	18.8	43.3	83.4	81.4	12.7	9.6	16.9
Peru	21	817	695	1,162	1,799	0.9	16.7	18.4	16.9	16.0	20.3	-1.6	6.8
Venezuela, R. B. de	662	488	2,096	2,724	3,881	6.7	1.7	10.2	8.8	11.3	-1.7	14.6	4.4
Subtotal (10)	1,736	23,486	42,006	194,427	213,384	5.5	19.4	32.9	59.1	54.5	14.5	5.8	11.6
Asia													
Bangladesh	138	740	1,377	4,588	4,702	26.0	67.6	77.5	91.1	89.6	9.3	6.2	8.8
China	4,025	12,046	50,594	219,886	490,917	50.2	45.0	71.4	88.2	91.4	6.1	14.4	16.2
Hong Kong, China	2,692	26,539	86,373	192,479	226,293	83.6	91.1	91.8	95.0	94.2	12.7	11.8	6.9
Taiwan, China	537	30,344	70,856	141,061	145,676	57.9	103.9	92.6	95.1	92.8	22.4	8.5	5.1
India	2,642	6,526	14,299	34,591	54,625	44.9	58.6	69.8	76.4	84.1	5.0	7.8	9.6
Indonesia	8	737	10,323	35,241	32,415	0.3	2.3	35.2	56.7	55.5	24.9	26.4	8.2
Korea, Rep. of	42	24,059	69,190	154,892	209,079	17.9	89.9	93.2	89.9	91.0	35.3	10.6	7.9
Malaysia	243	3,600	18,110	78,930	86,365	5.4	18.8	53.9	80.4	75.4	15.0	16.2	11.2
Pakistan	407	1,899	5,016	7,801	10,314	28.5	49.1	78.8	84.8	85.2	8.6	9.7	5.1
Philippines	109	1,804	3,533	34,775	32,245	5.1	21.1	37.8	91.3	89.8	15.6	6.7	15.8
Singapore	1,375	12,333	42,797	117,654	134,406	29.4	43.1	71.1	85.4	83.4	12.2	12.4	8.2

Table 9.1. Continued

Economy	Level (US$ millions at 2000 prices)					Percent of total exports					Real annual growth (%)		
	1962	1980	1990	2000	2004	1962	1980	1990	2000	2004	1962–80	1980–90	1990–2004
Sri Lanka	25	252	1,161	3,463	3,668	1.6	16.2	53.2	63.8	73.9	12.8	15.3	8.2
Thailand	88	2,405	16,645	51,776	65,180	4.6	25.0	63.2	75.3	74.8	18.4	19.3	9.8
Subtotal (13)	12,331	123,284	390,276	1,077,135	1,495,885	32.6	54.1	77.2	86.7	87.6	12.8	11.5	9.6
G-4	4,646	93,275	269,216	606,085	715,454	51.3	82.0	88.3	91.7	90.8	16.7	10.6	7.0
Europe													
Czech Republic	—	—	8,383	25,681	53,747	—	—	84.9	88.4	90.3	—	—	13.3
Hungary	—	8,438	7,568	24,192	43,734	—	65.8	69.1	86.1	88.0	—	-1.1	12.5
Poland	—	15,247	8,371	25,345	53,863	—	67.3	58.2	80.2	80.7	—	-6.0	13.3
Slovak Republic	—	1,156	10,021	22,525	48,429	1.0	26.9	67.7	82.0	84.8	23.5	21.6	11.3
Turkey	17	—	38,325	107,684	221,101	—	—	71.3	84.0	85.7	—	—	12.5
Subtotal (5)	—	—	—	—	—	—	—	—	—	—	—	—	—
Middle East and North Africa	—	71	332	319	355	16.1	0.3	2.6	1.4	1.2	-3.4	15.4	0.5
Algeria	130	492	1,250	974	2,026	16.5	10.9	42.4	21.0	29.7	3.2	9.3	3.5
Egypt, Arab Rep. of	277	6,726	11,914	29,571	33,006	2.5	82.2	86.6	94.2	94.4	30.2	5.7	7.3
Israel	29	297	677	954	2,496	29.4	35.0	55.8	73.8	70.9	14.7	8.2	9.3
Jordan	21	835	2,525	4,761	5,988	8.6	23.5	52.3	64.1	67.9	10.5	11.1	6.2
Morocco	126	204	1,716	360	551	10.2	6.6	35.7	7.8	11.3	5.8	21.3	-8.1
Syrian Arab Republic	71	1,179	2,760	4,505	6,795	8.6	35.7	69.1	77.0	77.5	18.5	8.5	6.4
Tunisia	42	9,805	21,174	41,443	51,217	10.9	21.0	48.0	53.6	52.9	14.7	7.7	6.3
Subtotal (7)	696	—	—	—	—	—	—	—	—	—	—	—	—
Africa	—	364	3	1,101	1,048	0.9	12.9	0.1	14.3	8.9	7.9	-48.9	42.5
Angola	88	73	202	78	118	3.2	3.8	8.5	4.3	5.2	8.2	10.1	-3.9
Cameroon	17	313	473	521	994	1.0	6.8	13.5	14.4	18.8	20.1	4.1	5.3

Côte d'Ivoire	8	1	17	44	72	2.5	0.2	5.0	9.2	11.8	-9.6	24.5	10.3
Ethiopia	8	1	46	156	181	3.7	0.1	4.9	9.3	25.8	-19.6	34.3	9.8
Ghana	50	309	348	325	511	8.7	15.1	29.7	20.7	21.0	10.6	1.2	2.7
Kenya	46	36	48	476	87	5.3	6.3	14.4	58.2	22.5	3.0	2.9	4.2
Madagascar	21	184	917	1,203	1,235	29.7	28.9	65.8	80.8	70.9	4.6	16.1	2.1
Mauritius	80	202	97	56	706	7.3	0.5	0.6	0.2	2.5	1.9	-7.4	14.2
Nigeria	143	106	201	187	460	4.0	15.1	22.5	26.9	38.5	9.0	6.4	5.9
Senegal	21	6,842	8,018	14,045	20,563	14.3	18.1	29.8	53.9	56.5	9.1	1.6	6.7
South Africa	1,329	123	71	106	172	11.0	16.2	18.7	16.2	12.9	3.4	-5.5	6.3
Tanzania	67	52	28	59	165	5.9	10.6	9.1	30.8	47.3	14.0	-6.3	12.7
Togo	4	638	518	539	491	8.1	56.9	30.8	28.0	28.2	8.8	-2.1	-0.4
Zimbabwe	130	9,246	10,986	18,897	26,802	7.2	9.8	18.2	24.9	28.4	8.5	1.7	6.4
Subtotal (14)	2,013	—	—	—	—	—	—	—	—	—	—	—	—
Developing countries	—	165,821	464,442	1,331,903	1,787,287	16.2	33.9	63.0	77.2	78.0	12.7	10.3	9.6
44 countries excluding Europe (5)	16,776	—	502,767	1,439,587	2,008,387	—	—	63.5	77.7	78.8	—	—	9.9
49 countries including Europe (5)	—	—	—	—	—	—	—	—	—	—	—	—	—

Source: See text.
— = Not available.

68 (nonferrous metals, mainly copper). These data are compiled by UNCTAD (2005).[2] The nominal data are deflated to constant dollars of 2000 using the U.S. producer price index (IMF 2006a) to obtain the real estimates in the table.

For purposes of examining the FC hypothesis, the most important estimate in table 9.1 is for the growth of aggregate exports of manufactures from developing countries in the period after 1980. For 44 economies excluding the five European countries, this aggregate grew in real terms at 10.3 percent in 1980–90 and at almost the same pace, 9.6 percent, in 1990–2004. This means that the aggregate growth rate was within the 12 percent or so ceiling suggested in Cline (1982) for the whole quarter century. Adding the five European countries for the period 1990–2004, the aggregate growth rate of manufactured exports was 9.9 percent. Even for Asia, aggregate real manufactured export growth was within the 12 percent speed limit, at an average of 11.5 percent in 1980–90 and 9.6 percent in 1990–2004.

The corresponding absolute amounts rose dramatically, of course, given the power of compound interest. For the 44 non-European countries in the table, real manufactured exports mushroomed from $16.8 billion in 1962 (at 2000 prices) to $165.8 billion in 1980, $464.4 billion in 1990, $1.33 trillion in 2000, and $1.79 trillion in 2004.

China is an important outlier in this experience. After relatively moderate growth of 6.1 percent from 1962 to 1980, China's real manufactured exports grew 14.4 percent annually in 1980–90. In 1990–2004 this pace increased to 16.2 percent annually. Moreover, the rate has accelerated further recently. Thus the annual pace was 14.7 percent in 1990–2000, but surged to 20.1 percent for 2000–04.

Other key patterns in table 9.1 include the following. There was a marked deceleration in the growth rate of manufactured exports of the original G-4 by the 1990s. Whereas the annual rate was 16.7 percent from 1962 to 1980 for the group as a whole (but 35 percent for Korea), the pace eased to 10.6 percent in 1980–90 and to a surprisingly modest 7 percent from 1990 to 2004. With decelerating G-4 growth of manufactured exports and accelerating growth of those from China to much higher levels, the G-4 went from having aggregate manufactured exports about five times those of China in 1980 to only about 1.5 times in 2004.

Several other countries besides China achieved an impressive acceleration even as the original G-4 decelerated. In 1990–2004, more than a dozen developing countries had real growth of manufactured exports averaging

2   The UNCTAD online data are from table 4.1, Trade Structure by Commodity Group, 1980–2004. For 1962, the underlying data are from World Bank (1983). For specific country-years not available in UNCTAD (2005), estimates are based on World Bank (2006) and IMF (2006a). In particular, for countries with data available in UNCTAD (2005) for 2003 but not 2004, the ratio of total exports in 2004 to that in 2003 (from IMF 2006a) is applied to obtain 2004 manufactured exports. Estimates for the Czech Republic and the Slovak Republic for 1990 are based on the total for Czechoslovakia in 1988 apportioned by relative shares of the two successor states in 1994. Estimates for Bangladesh and Pakistan in 1962 are based on the total for Pakistan in that year apportioned by relative shares of the two states after partition in 1972.

more than 12 percent annually: Bolivia, Costa Rica, Ecuador, Mexico, the Philippines, four of the five European countries, Angola, Nigeria, and Togo. Special factors help to explain several of these outcomes. These include Eastern European integration with the European Union (EU) market in 1990–2004, the integration of Mexico with the North American market under the North American Free Trade Agreement, and the decision of Intel to locate a large semiconductor plant in Costa Rica for sourcing world markets.

Although for six countries (Ecuador, Hungary, Poland, Angola, Nigeria, and Togo) the high rates in 1990–2004 may be misleading because they followed negative rates in the 1980s, the basic pattern is one of impressive success of a sizable number of countries in achieving high real growth rates for manufactured products. Whereas the average real growth rate for manufactured exports in 1990–2004 for the 49 countries was 9.9 percent, the median rate was 9.2 percent, showing that the growth was not monopolized by China and a few other countries. India increasingly moved toward the group with rapid growth in manufactured exports, with average rates that rose from 5 percent in the 1960s and 1970s to 7.8 percent in the 1980s and to 9.6 percent in 1990–2004.

Another pattern evident in table 9.1 is that although there has been relatively persistent rapid growth in manufactured exports, growth has tended to decelerate over time. For the 44 countries with data available through the full period, aggregate real manufactured exports decelerated from annual growth of 12.7 percent in 1962–80 to 10.3 percent in 1980–90 and to 9.6 percent in 1990–2004. This easing in the growth rate was to be expected given that in the 1960s and 1970s, growth was from extremely low base levels.

In addition to examining realized real growth rates for manufactured exports, it is possible to test the outcome of the G-4 fallacy of composition argument by seeing whether the ratio of manufactured exports to GDP for developing countries today has reached the 1980 level for the G-4. This test is more lenient than that set forth in my 1984 book, which considered achievement of G-4 ratios by 1990, not 2004. Table 9.2 reports the ratio of manufactured exports to GDP for the 17 developing countries with the largest manufactured exports in 2004.[3] They account for 90.5 percent of total 2004 manufactured exports for the 49 economies shown in table 9.1.

In 1980 the simple average ratio of manufactured exports to GDP for the G-4 was 52.2 percent. If we apply this threshold, then only four of the 17 economies reached G-4 levels by 2004. Three of these were in the original G-4 (Hong Kong, China; Taiwan, China; and Singapore); the fourth is a newcomer, Malaysia.

Korea has still not reached the original G-4 average. Of course, two of the G-4 economies are city-states (Hong Kong, China; and Singapore).

---

3   Excluding Poland and the Czech Republic, for which GDP data in 1980 are not available.

Table 9.2. Exports of Manufactures, 1980 and 2004

Economy	Current U.S. dollars (millions)		% of GDP	
	1980	2004	1980	2004
China	8,150	542,463	4.3	28.1
Hong Kong, China	17,956	250,054	62.8	153.4
Korea, Rep. of	16,279	231,032	25.5	34.0
Taiwan, China	20,531	160,972	49.6	52.6
Mexico	3,389	153,946	1.7	22.8
Singapore	8,344	148,519	71.2	139.0
Malaysia	2,435	95,433	9.8	80.7
Thailand	1,627	72,024	5.0	44.5
India	4,415	60,361	2.4	8.7
Turkey	782	53,514	1.1	17.7
Brazil	7,770	50,681	3.3	8.4
Hungary	5,709	48,326	25.8	48.0
Israel	4,551	36,471	20.9	31.2
Indonesia	499	35,819	0.6	13.9
Philippines	1,221	35,631	3.8	42.1
South Africa	4,629	22,722	5.7	10.7
Pakistan	1,285	11,397	5.4	11.9

Source: China, DGBAS 2005; UNCTAD 2005; World Bank 2006.

Their manufactured exports include entrepôt goods and incorporate large imported inputs. Indeed, today their manufactured exports substantially exceed GDP, averaging 146 percent of GDP. Suppose, then, that the G-4 benchmark is set at the average for just Korea and Taiwan, China in 1980, or 37.6 percent of GDP. This criterion adds Thailand, Hungary, and the Philippines to the list of countries that reached G-4 status (ironically, Korea still does not make the cut). If the test is set at an even weaker benchmark, the 1980 ratio of manufactured exports to GDP for just Korea (25.5 percent), then the list of economies passing this test by 2004 grows further, adding China, Korea itself, and Israel. These three successively easier tests encompass 33, 40, and 81 percent, respectively, of total manufactured exports for the group of 17 economies in the table.

In sum, if the share of manufactured exports in G-4 GDP is used as the test, then strictly speaking the G-4 model was not replicated in the large by even the main manufacturing developing countries over the past quarter century. Even so, they came much closer than many might have expected. It seems highly unlikely that most development economists in the early 1980s would have anticipated that China would reach Korea's (then) level of about one-fourth of GDP in manufactured exports. There would have been a sense, first, that domestic economic policies would not lead to this result (as the reforms were very recent) and, second, that if China tried to replicate Korea's success, it would likely swamp world markets.

Both table 9.1 and figure 9.1 show the shift in developing-country exports from domination by raw materials in the early 1960s to domination by manufactured goods today. For the 44 non-European countries, manufactures rose from only 16 percent of total exports in 1962 to 78 percent in 2004. In 1962, only three economies had more than half of their exports in manufactures: China; Hong Kong, China; and Taiwan, China. By 2004, 23 non-European countries had more than half of exports in manufactures, slightly more than half of the total number of these countries. If each economy is weighted by its share in total 2004 population, then the weighted average share of manufactured goods in total exports rose from 31.5 percent in 1962 to 72.7 percent in 2004. So whether based on trade values or population, over the past four decades the developing world as a whole has swung from being dependent on nonmanufactures for about three-fourths of export earnings (on a population basis or even more—over four-fifths—on a value basis) to being about three-fourths dependent on manufactures for export earnings (both criteria).

There has, however, been a sharp divergence among regions in the shift to manufactured exports. Today every one of the Asian and European developing countries in table 9.1 obtains more than half of its export earnings from manufactures. In contrast, only three of 10 Latin American countries, only four of seven Middle East and North African countries, and only two of 14 African countries in the table do so. The average share of manufactures in exports is only 28 percent for the African countries. For the Latin American countries as a group, the share is 54 percent, reflecting the relatively high shares of manufacturing for the two largest economies

Figure 9.1. Manufactures as Percent of Total Exports, 1962–2004

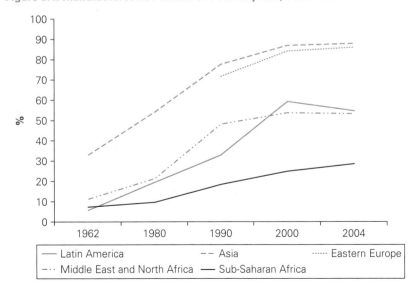

Source: See text and table 9.1.

(especially Mexico) in contrast to much lower shares for most of the smaller economies (again with the remarkable exception of Costa Rica).

Figure 9.1 shows three tiers of intensity for the share of manufactures in exports. Asia and the Eastern European countries are in the top tier, Latin America and the Middle East and North Africa are in the middle tier, and Sub-Saharan Africa is in the bottom tier. This pattern reflects two underlying influences: endowment of natural resources and stage of development.

A simple statistical cross-section regression for 2004 shows these influences on the share of manufactures in exports. The estimating equation is as follows:

$$Z = -89.1 - 10.34 \ln(A) + 10.68 \ln y - 35.64 \, D_O + 5.70 \ln N, (9.1)$$

$$(-4.3) \quad (-4.7) \qquad (4.4) \qquad (-3.8) \qquad (2.1)$$

Adjusted $R^2 = 0.667$; t-statistics are in parentheses, where Z = manufactures as a percentage of total exports, A = land surface per capita (square kilometers per person), y = per capita gross national income at market prices (not purchasing power parity), $D_O = 1$ if the country is a major oil exporter and 0 otherwise, and N is population in millions (data are from World Bank 2005).

As expected, higher per capita income is associated with a higher share of manufactures in exports, reflecting a greater underlying scope for achieving industrial standards of quality sufficient for world competition. Having a larger economy as measured by population also boosts the share of manufactures in exports, reflecting economies of scale. A country with major oil resources and exports has, on average, a share of manufactures in exports that is about 36 percentage points below what otherwise would be predicted. A country with a larger endowment of land per capita (A) also has a lower share. For example, going from Argentina's land density per capita (13 persons per square kilometer, or $A = 0.077$) to that of India (358 persons per square kilometer, or $A = 0.0028$) would be expected to increase the share of manufactures in exports by 34.3 percentage points, other things being equal.

Among the economies in table 9.1, the median population density is 21 persons per square kilometer in Latin America, 53 in Africa, 65 in Middle East and North Africa, 110 in Europe, and 298 in Asia. So greater availability of land per capita would be expected to cause the typical share of exports in manufactures to be lower in Latin America than in Asia, by 27.4 percentage points, and in Africa than in Asia, by 17.9 percentage points.

These estimates suggest that there will be some tapering off of the share of manufactures in exports for Africa, Latin America, and the Middle East and North Africa below the ranges found in Asia and Europe even as per capita income rises. Such a tapering off seems already apparent in figure 9.1. Nonetheless, the lower base also suggests that relatively high growth rates of manufactured exports could continue for some time even in the three regions with high land endowments.

At the same time, the trends in figure 9.1 also reflect the simple fact that manufacturing output has grown much more rapidly in Asia than in Latin America and the Middle East and North Africa. Thus the World Bank (2005: fig. 4.3a) estimates that from 1990 to 2003 real value added in manufacturing rose by about 270 percent for developing East Asia and the Pacific and about 100 percent for South Asia, but only about 75 percent for Middle East and North Africa and 25 percent for Latin America and Sub-Saharan Africa. With all of the regions facing broadly the same international market, domestic factors rather than trade strategy arguably accounted for most of the differential performance in manufacturing output, which in turn largely drove differential performance in manufactured exports. Overall economic growth was much higher in East Asia and the Pacific (about 8 percent from 1980 to 2000) than in Latin America and the Middle East and North Africa (averaging about 2.5 percent). A major reason is that investment was much higher, at about 32 percent of GDP in 1990 and 39 percent in 2003 in East Asia and the Pacific, compared to about 17 and 18 percent, respectively, in Latin America (World Bank 2005: figs. 4b, 4.10a). In short, more rapidly rising manufactured exports in East Asia than in most other developing regions seem likely to be as much a consequence as a cause of higher investment and more rapid growth.

Finally, it is useful to examine one of the key arguments of the 1980s regarding why imports of manufactures from developing countries need not pose a burden for industrial-country markets: namely, that increasingly the developing countries would export manufactures to each other rather than to the industrial countries. An important recent variant on this argument is that the East Asian G-4 countries have eased pressure on industrial-country markets even as China has stepped up this pressure, because they have shifted part of their production to industrial components used by China for exports to industrial-country markets. In this way, some of the rise in industrial-country imports from China essentially represents redirection of imports that in the past would have come from the G-4 newly industrialized countries.

Table 9.3 examines the first of these hypotheses by considering the top 20 developing countries ranked by absolute size of manufactured exports in 2004. These economies accounted for $1.95 trillion in manufactured exports in 2004, or 97 percent of the total for the 49 countries examined in table 9.1.[4] Of the 20 countries, all but three had manufactured exports amounting to 75 percent or more of total exports (and for 11, the ratio was 85 percent or more). Because of their large scale, three economies also had manufactured exports within the top 20, even though their share of manufactures in exports was considerably lower: Brazil (53.3 percent),

---

4 The data are from table 9.1 and are deflated to 2000 prices using the U.S. producer price index.

Table 9.3. Top 20 Developing Countries Ranked by Absolute Size of Manufactured Exports in 2004

Economy	Manufactured exports in 2004 (US$ billions at 2000 prices)	Share of exports to industrial countries in total exports (%)	
		1980	2003
China	491	46.4	54.6
Hong Kong, China	226	62.9	40.6
Korea, Rep. of	209	67.2	43.7
Taiwan, China	146	68.0	43.5
Mexico	139	87.2	94.1
Singapore	134	41.1	38.9
Malaysia	86	59.8	46.0
Thailand	65	58.0	51.5
India	55	49.6	46.7
Poland	54	38.0	74.8
Czech Republic	54[a]	24.2	90.4
Turkey	48	58.1	64.9
Brazil	46	59.7	54.3
Hungary	44	32.6	79.3
Israel	33	81.8	74.6
Indonesia	32	77.7	51.6
Philippines	32	75.4	54.5
Slovak Republic	21[a]	24.2	69.1
South Africa	21	66.8	64.4
Pakistan	10	37.0	55.6
Total	1,947	58.7	54.9

Source: IMF 2006a, 2006c; UNCTAD 2005.
a. 1980.

Indonesia (55.5 percent), and South Africa (56.5 percent). For practical purposes, however, these 20 economies are sufficiently oriented toward manufactures in their export structure that the geographic trends in their total exports can be taken as indicative of the geographic trends in their manufactured exports.

As indicated in table 9.3, for the majority of the economies (12), there was indeed a downward trend in the share of total exports going to industrial-country markets from 1980 to 2004. There were sharp declines for three of the G-4 economies (Korea; Hong Kong, China; and Taiwan, China), all from about two-thirds of exports in 1980 to only about two-fifths in 2004 (although the decline for Singapore was much smaller and from a lower base).

However, there were important movements in the other direction, by amounts that were large in the aggregate, even though the number of countries was smaller. The Eastern European economies sharply increased

Table 9.4. Exports of the East Asian G-4 to China, 1980 and 2003

Economy	1980		2003	
	US$ millions	% of total	US$ millions	% of total
Korea, Rep of.	0	0.0	35,110	18.2
Hong Kong, China	1,249	6.4	95,477	42.7
Singapore	307	1.6	10,134	7.0
Taiwan, China	0	0.0	32,377	22.5
G-4	1,556	2.1	173,098	24.6

Source: IMF 2006a; UNCTAD 2005.

the share of their exports going to industrial-country markets, reflecting the dissolution of the cold war trading arrangements and the move toward integration with the European Union. Mexico further increased its dependence on the North American market. And China, the largest manufactured exporter by 2004, increased the share of its exports going to industrial-country markets, in part because it moved toward direct exports and away from exports through Hong Kong, China.[5]

Overall, the weighted average share of total exports going to industrial-country markets fell for these top 20 manufactured exporters, but only modestly—from about 59 percent to about 55 percent. So although the hypothesis proved accurate that developing countries would increasingly shift the market destination of their manufactured exports from industrial countries to other developing countries, the magnitude of this effect was small, and its role in alleviating pressure on industrial-country markets was modest at best. Thus if the share of these developing countries' exports of manufactures going to industrial-country markets had remained unchanged, the increase in the share at the end of the period would have been only about 4 percentage points above the actual outcome, which in turn would have raised the absolute level of industrial countries' imports of manufactures from these countries by only about 7 percent.

A rising share of the U.S. market in exports for several of these countries was one force behind this outcome. The share of China's exports going to the United States rose sharply, from 5.6 percent in 1980 to 21.2 percent in 2004. The share of the U.S. market in Mexico's exports also rose substantially, from 66.0 to 87.6 percent.

The subhypothesis that manufactured exports from China would partially replace rather than add to those from the East Asian G-4 receives more support from the data. Table 9.4 shows a sharp rise in G-4 exports to China, from only about 2 percent of total exports in 1980 to about 25 percent in 2004. For Korea and Taiwan, China, the 1980 amounts were approximately zero because of cold war closure of markets.

---

5   The Hong Kong, China market accounted for 24 percent of China's total exports in 1980, but only 17.4 percent in 2003 (IMF 2006b).

There was a corresponding reduction of the U.S. market share in the exports of the G-4 from 1980 to 2004: from about 27 to 18 percent for Korea, from 26 to 19 percent for Hong Kong, China, and from 37 to 17 percent for Taiwan, China.[6]

Evidence on Sectoral Import Penetration

Relatively rapid growth of manufactured exports from developing countries, within the speed limits noted above, might nonetheless have triggered protection under the initial FC hypothesis if it were excessively concentrated in a few sectors and resulted in extremely high import penetration ratios in these sectors.

The United Nations Industrial Development Organization (UNIDO 2006) has compiled estimates of trade, production, and apparent consumption (domestic output minus exports plus imports) at detailed sectoral levels that can be used to examine trends in sectoral import penetration levels. Selected results using these data are reported for the period 1981–95 in tables 9.5 and 9.6 and for the period 1995–2003 in tables 9.7 and 9.8.[7] The industrial countries included in the import trends are the United States, Japan, Germany (the Federal Republic of Germany in the first period), France, and Canada. The top sectors ranked by total manufactured imports from developed countries into the U.S. market are included in the analysis, accounting for 94 percent in the U.S. market and an average of 78 percent in the other five industrial-country markets in the first period and 90 percent and an average of about 87 percent, respectively, in the second period.

In terms of the relative importance of the various sectors, by 1995 the traditionally most important sector, apparel, had already lost first place. U.S. imports of apparel by then amounted to about 11 percent of total U.S. manufactured imports from developing countries, but had been passed by radio, television, and consumer electronics at 19 percent and by office and computing machinery at 14 percent (table 9.5). These three leading sectors broadly persisted through 2002 (see table 9.7).

The key trends for testing the protection version of the FC hypothesis are found in import penetration ratios. By 1995 these had risen to quite high levels for a number of sectors, in comparison with levels two decades earlier. Import penetration from developing countries for apparel amounted to about 34 percent for the United States and about 25 percent for the other major industrial countries in 1995 (table 9.5). This represented a sharp increase from 1981, when the corresponding ratios were both about 12. There were similar large increases in office machinery

---

6   The estimates for Taiwan, China include Canada with the United States (UNCTAD 2005).

7   It is necessary to separate the two periods because the data for the former period are from International Standard Industrial Classification (ISIC), Revision 2, which has fewer sectors and differing allocations than the data for the latter period, which are from ISIC, Revision 3.

Table 9.5. Principal Manufactured Imports by Industrial Countries from Developing Countries, 1995
US$ millions

ISIC2	Import	United States	Japan[a]	Germany[b]	France	United Kingdom[c]	Canada[d]
3113	Canning fruits, vegetables	946	688	2,258	1,480	1,435	618
3115	Vegetable, animal oils, fats	865	491	619	342	745	205
3211	Textiles spinning, weaving, finishing	3,609	2,261	1,395	2,615	1,171	522
3212	Textile goods, except apparel	1,694	589	1,009	—	387	138
3220	Apparel, except footwear	27,723	7,588	7,086	4,432	3,065	1,342
3240	Footwear, except rubber, plastic	2,335	359	3,069	1,423	1,159	257
3311	Sawmills	1,635	3,685	426	494	592	67
3319	Wood, cork products not elsewhere classified	974	423	195	—	131	—
3320	Furniture except metal	3,742	479	2,992	1,963	1,226	1,311
3411	Pulp, paper, paperboard	1,043	301	227	345	194	33
3420	Printing	2,369	583	1,258	1,733	1,565	2,029
3511	Basic industry chemicals	4,578	1,934	583	1,310	293	317
3513	Plastics, synthetic fibers	1,598	438	214	—	119	80
3529	Other chemical products	2,735	789	—	1,303	1,172	578
3530	Petroleum refineries	6,910	4,821	617	731	692	213
3551	Tires and tubes	961	95	248	277	135	154
3560	Plastic products not elsewhere classified	2,813	500	3,108	2,788	2,308	1,109
3610	Pottery, china	1,278	65	203	174	124	117
3620	Glass products	863	189	197	100	119	88
3710	Iron, steel	4,743	3,037	594	234	120	265
3720	Nonferrous metals	2,750	2,890	1,371	1,067	481	166
3811	Cutlery, tools, hardware	2,245	206	346	1,481	275	244
3812	Metal furniture	773	108	1,003	—	473	304
3819	Metal products except machinery, equipment	4,015	583	807	—	573	415
3823	Metal and woodworking machinery	1,792	442	522	—	297	211
3824	Other industrial machinery	891	138	62	—	110	71
3825	Office, computing, accounting machines	34,490	2,486	2,138	—	1,970	1,724
3829	Machinery except electrical not elsewhere classified	7,728	1,705	—	—	1,343	—
3831	Electrical industrial machinery	6,526	1,506	494	5,654	363	296
3832	Radio, TV, consumer electronics	47,112	4,453	5,091	—	4,339	2,857
3833	Electrical appliances	1,724	164	104	—	128	119
3839	Other electrical apparatus	7,852	810	622	—	265	423
3841	Ship building	794	72	215	394	71	79

Table 9.5. Continued

ISIC2	Import	United States	Japan[a]	Germany[b]	France	United Kingdom[c]	Canada[d]
3843	Motor vehicles	15,134	327	399	922	396	1,686
3844	Motorcycles, bicycles	997	—	168	208	213	—
3851	Scientific equipment	5,982	2,696	3,412	6,361	2,980	2,809
3852	Photographic, optical goods	7,323	801	2,915	—	1,973	1,180
3853	Watches, clocks	1,770	689	636	—	372	96
3901	Jewelry, related	3,495	1,179	757	1,979	—	142
3903	Sporting goods	884	800	245	—	182	449
3909	Manufacturing not elsewhere classified	2,676	449	1,294	—	1,358	712
	Subtotal	230,365	51,818	48,899	39,811	34,909	23,426
	Other four-digit	14,431	11,902	17,292	14,355	9,513	5,288
	Total	244,796	63,720	66,191	54,166	44,422	28,714

Source: UNIDO 2006.
Note: Categories are principal four-digit ISIC, Rev. 2.
— = Not available.
a. 1993.
b. 1990 (West).
c. 1992.
d. 1994.

(in the United States up from only 2 percent in 1981 to 31 percent by 1995); radio, television, and electronics (up by about 10 percentage points for an approximate doubling in the United States, the United Kingdom, and Canada, but not in Japan or Germany); a similar increase in the same three markets in pottery and china; and a surge from near zero to about 20 percent in motorcycles and bicycles in the United States and Canada (table 9.5).

It would have been heroic in 1981 to predict that import penetration could more than double in apparel over the next 14 years without precipitating stiffer protection. Yet the trend continued forcefully, and by 2003 the penetration of apparel imports from developing countries had reached about 53 percent in the United States and about 49 percent in the other major industrial countries (see table 9.8). Even higher ratios could be found in other sectors: for the United States, 79 percent in footwear, 69 percent in luggage and handbags, 68 percent in games and toys, and 63 percent in knitted and crocheted fabrics. Office machinery and computers were on a par with apparel in the U.S. market, at 53 percent of apparent consumption. For the United States, 20 of the 21 top sectors had import penetration ratios above the 15 percent threshold originally used in Cline (1982). Moreover, several of the penetration ratios were so high by 2003 that they would have triggered the logit-model protection functions estimated in Cline (1984).

Clearly, markets remained more resilient against protection than might have been feared in the face of these dynamic increases in import

Table 9.6. Ratio of Imports from Developing Countries to Apparent Consumption in 1995 and Change from 1981
percent

		1995						Change from 1981					
ISIC2	Import	United States	Japan[a]	Germany[b]	France	United Kingdom[c]	Canada[d]	United States	Japan[a]	Germany[b]	France	United Kingdom[c]	Canada[d]
3113	Fruits, vegetables	2.7	6.4	28.1	—	35.6	17.7	1.5	0.9	−5.2	—	—	3.0
3115	Fats, oils	4.3	6.2	14.5	—	19.0	19.1	1.5	1.3	−4.2	—	—	3.8
3211	Textiles	7.9	7.2	10.8	11.5	12.8	15.0	4.0	0.3	4.3	4.6	—	9.0
3212	Textile goods, except apparel	6.4	4.6	31.1	—	16.5	4.0	4.7	2.4	−12.1	—	—	0.9
3220	Apparel	33.8	20.8	29.7	28.0	25.8	22.7	21.7	11.2	10.6	21.2	9.9	12.1
3240	Footwear	17.7	6.5	46.4	34.9	30.8	22.3	5.9	2.3	11.1	11.2	5.4	8.3
3311	Sawmills	2.4	7.6	3.5	3.7	11.9	0.9	−0.2	5.0	−0.6	0.3	—	−0.6
3319	Wood, cork	14.3	10.0	7.2	—	3.2	—	8.6	5.1	3.1	—	—	—
3320	Furniture	7.5	2.0	18.4	17.6	12.5	37.3	3.9	0.9	—	4.4	1.9	29.6
3411	Paper products	1.3	1.0	—	1.3	2.0	0.8	1.0	0.2	—	0.7	0.9	0.7
3420	Printing	1.3	0.5	6.7	4.5	4.6	17.0	0.5	0.0	1.3	−0.4	0.8	4.1
3511	Industrial chemicals	4.6	4.1	—	3.9	1.2	4.1	3.1	1.0	—	1.5	0.0	2.2
3513	Plastics, synthetic fibers	2.9	1.1	—	—	1.3	1.6	2.5	0.1	—	—	0.9	1.0
3529	Other chemicals	7.1	3.8	—	—	24.5	13.8	2.2	−2.2	—	—	5.4	5.4

Table 9.6. Continued

ISIC2	Import	1995						Change from 1981					
		United States	Japan[a]	Germany[b]	France	United Kingdom[c]	Canada[d]	United States	Japan[a]	Germany[b]	France	United Kingdom[c]	Canada[d]
3530	Petroleum, refinery products	4.9	7.0	1.0	1.8	2.3	1.4	1.1	-2.8	-1.0	-1.1	-0.8	0.3
3551	Tires, tubes	6.2	1.5	2.2	4.4	4.9	2.8	4.4	0.9	0.4	3.0	—	1.7
3560	Plastics	2.3	0.5	9.5	12.1	11.6	14.6	0.2	0.1	1.3	1.1	1.8	2.3
3610	Pottery	23.4	1.1	9.4	—	6.8	34.7	14.5	0.6	1.6	—	3.5	17.9
3620	Glass products	4.0	1.3	2.6	1.6	2.9	5.3	3.1	0.5	1.1	0.7	1.6	3.6
3710	Iron, steel	4.7	2.4	1.6	0.9	0.7	2.7	3.2	0.9	1.0	-0.3	0.2	1.4
3720	Nonferrous metals	3.5	6.7	6.1	5.8	4.5	4.8	-1.2	-1.5	0.4	-0.7	-1.9	3.2
3811	Hardware	10.9	2.9	3.3	3.1	—	13.2	7.0	1.9	1.2	1.3	—	9.5
3812	Metal furniture	4.5	1.7	19.8	—	26.2	46.8	3.6	0.7	0.6	—	—	21.0
3819	Other metal	4.3	0.8	2.3	—	3.4	5.3	3.1	0.5	0.7	—	—	4.2
3823	Metal machinery	5.0	1.8	4.5	—	4.3	—	3.9	1.5	3.2	—	3.3	—
3824	Other industrial machinery	1.6	0.3	0.2	—	1.1	1.5	1.2	0.2	0.1	—	0.6	1.3
3825	Office machinery	31.3	3.0	13.1	—	10.9	—	29.1	2.1	12.1	—	9.2	—
3829	Other machinery	5.3	1.5	—	—	5.4	—	3.6	0.5	—	—	1.8	—

ISIC	Category												
3831	Elect. machinery	13.4	2.2	1.0	8.6	2.8	6.4	10.6	0.8	0.5	5.0	2.0	5.6
3832	Radio, TV, consumer electronics	21.3	2.4	9.9	—	16.9	19.3	11.5	1.6	3.4	—	10.4	7.0
3833	Appliances	16.1	0.4	1.0	—	3.7	17.0	12.6	0.4	0.8	—	2.6	14.0
3839	Other electrical apparatus	14.5	1.5	—	—	3.7	8.2	11.4	1.2	—	—	2.5	7.7
3841	Ship building	5.4	0.6	10.1	17.8	1.9	—	3.9	-0.3	8.0	16.3	1.5	—
3843	Motor vehicles	3.6	0.1	0.4	1.2	0.8	2.9	3.2	0.1	0.1	1.1	0.6	2.8
3844	Motorcycles	23.2	—	8.1	—	28.1	—	19.4	—	—	—	22.1	—
3851	Scientific equipment	6.5	23.1	—	61.6	—	—	3.1	7.1	—	14.5	—	—
3852	Photographic	22.3	—	48.9	—	—	—	12.8	—	-9.5	—	—	—
3853	Clocks	56.2	9.3	—	—	—	—	26.9	5.8	—	—	—	—
3901	Jewelry	31.1	19.6	—	17.7	—	24.7	12.3	2.4	—	1.1	—	3.6
3903	Sporting goods	8.0	16.7	41.1	—	22.9	34.2	1.4	9.3	-4.6	—	—	17.4
3909	Manufacturing not elsewhere classified	7.9	1.5	50.9	—	28.9	26.8	4.5	0.1	—	—	—	11.0

Source: UNIDO 2006.
Note: Categories are principal four-digit ISIC, Rev. 2.
a. 1993.
b. 1990 (West).
c. 1992.
d. 1994.
— = Not available.

Table 9.7. Principal Manufactured Imports by Industrial Countries from Developing Countries, 2003
US$ millions

ISIC3	Import	United States[a]	Japan[a]	Germany	France	United Kingdom	Canada[a]
1512	Fish products	6,747	8,036	730	1,263	843	533
1513	Processed fruits, vegetables	2,249	1,958	1,288	548	395	277
1711	Textile weaving	2,729	1,227	719	531	851	419
1721	Textile products except apparel	5,997	2,118	1,288	814	1,146	352
1730	Knitted, crocheted fabrics	15,550	4,142	3,932	2,258	3,044	688
1810	Apparel except furniture	43,549	11,265	9,153	6,562	8,182	2,482
1912	Luggage, handbags	4,469	1,530	869	777	907	317
1920	Footwear	14,023	2,464	1,865	1,759	1,854	781
2320	Refined petroleum prods.	11,134	9,358	350	1,586	1,866	235
2411	Basic chemicals	5,679	2,781	1,419	1,893	2,247	340
2423	Pharmaceuticals	2,211	618	702	379	693	168
2429	Other chemical products	2,829	1,523	676	311	354	158
2520	Plastic products	7,599	2,485	1,043	744	1,368	630
2710	Iron, steel	6,327	1,795	597	285	467	888
2720	Nonferrous metals	4,824	2,358	1,229	1,186	637	579
2893	Cutlery, tools, hardware	3,291	430	673	321	537	348
2899	Other metal products	9,044	1,626	1,507	645	1,262	761
2912	Pumps, compressors	4,675	653	501	185	361	358
2919	Other general machinery	4,219	1,395	497	341	353	314
2922	Machine tools	2,718	352	687	249	386	300
2930	Domestic appliances	8,544	1,826	1,356	760	1,629	546
3000	Office, computing machines	61,352	16,938	12,876	5,142	6,197	3,837
3110	Electric motors, generators	7,679	2,775	1,272	516	515	588
3120	Electricity distribution apparatuses	5,288	1,334	992	480	462	378
3130	Insulated wire	2,397	833	310	307	315	127
3150	Lighting equipment	5,343	383	865	324	638	397
3190	Other electrical equipment	9,739	2,394	2,310	742	870	662
3210	Electronic valves, tubes	21,965	11,474	6,171	2,431	2,852	1,124
3220	TV, radio transmitters	21,043	1,939	2,707	1,223	2,284	1,431
3230	TV, radio receivers	27,942	7,429	4,952	2,380	2,873	1,936
3311	Medical equipment	4,358	733	566	297	259	127
3312	Measuring appliances	4,931	487	846	252	462	303
3320	Optical, photographic equipment	3,011	1,957	593	488	447	267
3410	Motor vehicles	30,299	387	2,182	1,403	1,556	2,778
3430	Auto parts	9,909	1,121	1,356	713	493	971
3530	Aircraft	2,741	21	543	146	771	36
3610	Furniture	15,065	2,269	1,393	977	1,668	1,094
3691	Jewelry	7,455	923	503	280	924	121

Table 9.7. Continued

ISIC3	Import	United States[a]	Japan[a]	Germany	France	United Kingdom	Canada[a]
3693	Sports goods	3,480	934	458	365	409	300
3694	Games, toys	13,011	1,617	1,909	987	1,842	871
3699	Other manufacturing	7,210	988	919	598	1,028	533
	Subtotal	432,626	116,875	74,804	43,449	56,249	29,356
	Other categories	46,503	19,234	11,133	6,996	9,428	3,601
	Total	479,129	136,109	85,938	50,445	65,677	32,957

Source: UNIDO 2006.
Note: Categories are four-digit ISIC, Rev. 3.
a. 2002.

penetration. The series of multilateral trade negotiations in the GATT and then the WTO no doubt helped to achieve this result. Indeed, the Uruguay Round obtained the commitment by industrial countries to phase out textile and apparel quota restrictions under the Multi-Fibre Agreement by 2005, and this has now been accomplished (albeit with some recent temporary safeguard protection). These results could mean that the first variant of FC, the concern about protective response, has largely been overcome (despite the breakdown in the current Doha Round of WTO negotiations in July 2006).

At the same time, these trends may raise another question: could there be a potential market saturation problem? For example, in footwear the U.S. market share for developing countries is already 79 percent (table 9.7). This means that the pace of future expansion of footwear exports to the United States cannot exceed 1.25 times the growth rate of U.S. domestic consumption of footwear without requiring an absolute decline in U.S. apparel imports from industrial countries. Similarly, with apparel imports from developing countries at about half of apparent consumption for the main industrial countries, the developing countries could expect the growth rate of their exports to equal no more than twice the growth rate of industrial-country consumption of apparel, unless the absolute level of apparel imports from industrial countries were to fall.

Consider the implications for U.S. imports of apparel from developing countries. The income elasticity of U.S. apparel consumption is perhaps about 0.62.[8] If U.S. real per capita income continues to grow at about 2 percent and the population grows at about 1 percent, then apparel consumption will grow at about 2.25 percent (1 percent for population plus 0.62 × 2 percent for rising per capita income). With import penetration already at about 50 percent, these imports could only grow at

---

8   Based on simple comparison of the 2 percent average for growth in real GDP per capita from the three-year base 1983–85 to 1993–95 with real growth in apparent consumption of apparel of 1.25 percent annually over the same period (calculated from UNIDO 2006; deflating apparent consumption with the consumer price index for apparel from BLS 2006; IMF 2006a).

Table 9.8. Ratio of Imports from Developing Countries to Apparent Consumption in 2003 and Change from 1995

percent

ISIC3	Imports	2003						Change from 1995					
		United States[a]	Japan[a]	Germany	France	United Kingdom	Canada[a]	United States[b]	Japan[a]	Germany	France[c]	United Kingdom	Canada[a]
1512	Fish	43.8	20.2	23.1	23.7	19.3	29.8	0.7	4.2	8.0	-1.7	5.5	12.9
1513	Fruits, vegetables	5.4	20.0	11.4	6.5	4.4	5.9	0.0	5.1	1.6	-1.9	1.5	0.7
1711	Textiles	12.2	20.7	—	12.2	—	19.7	3.9	9.9	—	2.7	—	-0.2
1721	Textile products except apparel	26.7	26.2	34.8	25.2	27.9	23.7	13.1	12.8	13.0	10.0	13.8	8.9
1730	Fabrics	62.7	38.0	—	47.3	—	48.1	21.8	21.4	—	21.9	—	24.8
1810	Apparel	52.6	51.6	49.4	—	52.7	40.9	14.2	23.7	14.0	—	22.2	14.9
1912	Luggage	69.1	34.9	58.6	—	—	56.1	16.1	10.4	11.5	—	—	-0.2
1920	Footwear	79.3	41.9	37.8	37.5	—	65.0	11.2	19.9	20.3	15.2	—	24.1
2320	Petroleum products	5.1	11.6	—	2.8	5.1	1.4	-0.6	0.9	—	—	3.8	0.0
2411	Chemicals	4.9	6.4	—	7.3	12.9	3.7	1.3	1.2	—	3.7	—	0.3
2423	Pharmaceuticals	1.5	1.1	2.5	0.9	—	1.6	0.2	0.4	0.9	0.4	—	-0.5
2429	Other chemicals	9.4	—	—	4.0	—	2.9	3.9	—	—	1.7	—	0.8
2520	Plastic products	5.2	3.3	2.8	2.5	5.1	6.2	1.6	2.0	1.2	0.6	2.2	2.2
2710	Iron, steel	8.7	2.9	1.9	1.7	4.1	8.6	2.8	-0.9	-0.6	0.2	2.3	5.2
2720	Nonferrous metals	7.9	7.8	5.8	11.6	8.2	11.2	2.1	-2.5	1.0	1.1	2.8	—
2893	Hardware	9.3	6.8	4.4	6.8	13.7	11.2	3.7	4.6	0.1	2.9	7.2	2.3
2899	Other metals	13.1	6.4	9.1	6.4	12.2	11.8	4.3	3.9	4.0	2.9	7.0	3.5
2912	Pumps	11.3	5.2	3.8	2.7	6.1	—	4.8	3.7	1.8	1.6	3.6	—
2919	Other machinery	8.4	4.9	2.3	3.5	3.7	—	4.0	3.2	1.1	1.7	2.2	—
2922	Machine tools	14.8	2.6	5.0	6.9	—	9.4	7.1	1.7	2.7	4.3	—	5.0
2930	Domestic appliances	27.8	5.9	13.8	14.5	22.2	14.6	9.5	4.5	9.0	7.5	14.6	5.5
3000	Office machinery	52.9	28.4	—	25.8	—	37.2	18.7	19.0	—	8.0	—	—

Code	Product												
3110	Electric motors	35.5	23.9	12.3	13.1	14.0	—	6.6	14.5	5.1	2.1	14.0	—
3120	Electricity distribution apparatus	18.0	6.8	2.3	4.5	8.1	12.7	5.5	4.9	1.2	2.7	8.1	7.0
3130	Wire	20.1	7.6	8.4	11.3	15.1	9.4	8.4	5.1	4.4	6.9	15.1	6.3
3150	Lighting	30.5	4.6	22.7	—	21.1	18.5	10.6	2.5	14.9	—	21.1	8.6
3190	Other electrical equipment	19.8	11.1	14.9	10.4	14.8	18.0	2.7	9.0	-2.9	4.2	14.8	5.9
3210	Electrical valves	24.5	19.9	33.9	22.9	—	20.2	3.5	12.7	—	-1.1	—	0.1
3220	TV, radio transmitters	27.9	6.3	—	8.4	—	32.3	19.0	4.1	—	6.1	—	26.5
3230	TV, radio receivers	—	9.4	—	32.3	32.0	—	—	4.7	—	9.0	32.0	—
3311	Medical equipment	6.2	5.3	4.4	4.1	5.4	4.4	2.1	3.1	2.3	2.9	5.4	2.8
3312	Measurement appliances	7.7	2.9	8.8	2.2	4.9	6.0	3.4	1.9	5.4	1.5	4.9	4.2
3320	Photography	25.2	—	18.3	19.1	17.8	—	11.1	—	6.3	6.4	17.8	—
3410	Motor vehicles	7.5	0.4	1.7	0.8	2.9	—	2.7	0.4	0.9	-0.4	2.9	—
3430	Auto parts	8.0	0.9	2.7	3.5	2.3	4.5	2.9	0.6	1.2	1.8	2.3	2.0
3530	Aircraft	2.9	0.2	—	0.5	4.3	0.4	1.7	0.1	—	0.3	4.3	0.0
3610	Furniture	13.9	13.3	5.7	6.1	9.1	10.5	6.4	8.0	3.6	3.4	9.1	5.2
3691	Jewelry	37.7	24.2	39.3	15.9	—	13.3	8.3	1.6	—	4.6	—	6.8
3693	Sports goods	24.1	27.4	24.4	24.4	34.8	23.3	2.4	12.1	—	0.7	34.8	6.4
3694	Games, toys	68.4	24.4	46.4	58.7	23.3	—	7.8	12.4	—	8.7	58.7	—
3699	Other manufacturing	17.7	5.7	31.5	19.2	18.2	25.3	3.1	2.0	10.3	5.9	18.2	4.2

Source: UNIDO 2006.
— = Not available.
a. 2002.
b. Change from 1997 to 2002.
c. 1996.

4.5 percent annually in real terms if they captured the entire annual increase in U.S. apparel consumption. Suppose instead that they were to grow at 10 percent, the average for all manufactured exports of developing countries in 1990–2004 (table 9.1). This would mean that it would only take nine years for the entirety of U.S. consumption of apparel to come from imports from developing countries, with zero domestic production and zero imports from elsewhere.[9] So after a decade, developing-country exports to the United States could grow no faster than 2.25 percent annually because of complete market saturation combined with slow growth in demand, even with no protection whatsoever. Of course, additional demand might be prompted by price reductions, but then there would be terms-of-trade FC problems.

In short, it is fair to ask whether a new FC challenge is facing developing-country manufactured exports: are they already so high in many sectors that their growth rates will be increasingly constrained to those of underlying sectoral consumption in the markets in question, which are much lower than the growth rates of trade have been?

Implications for Poor Countries

The broad thrust of the aggregative and sectoral evidence is that closure of markets in industrial countries in the face of rising imports from the south has not been a serious constraint on export-led growth. This openness has held up even under the pressure of remarkable import growth from the new manufacturing giant, China (which, despite enormous growth, remains below the G-4 today as a source of manufactured exports).

What are the implications of this experience for today's poorer countries, including many in Africa, whose manufactured exports are a much smaller share of their total exports than in Asia? (The weighted average share of manufactures in total exports is 28 percent for Africa, 55 percent in Latin America, and 91 percent in Asia).

The simplest interpretation of this experience is that global markets should easily be able to absorb the magnitude of additional manufactured exports that can be expected from the poorer countries, because these are likely to be much smaller than the amounts already incorporated into markets of the larger and more dynamic among the developing countries. Consider the simple scale suggested by table 9.1. Aggregate manufactured exports for the 14 African nations amounted to about $27 billion in 2004 (at 2000 prices). In contrast, aggregate manufactured exports from Asia amounted to $1.5 trillion. Africa's manufactured exports would need to mushroom about sixfold just to reach one-tenth the size of Asia's. So African planners have much more relevant concerns, including governance in particular, than the risk of market closure from FC because their exports might be the straw that breaks the camel's back.

---

9 That is, $1 = 0.5\,e(1.1-1.0225)\,T$; $T = (\ln 2) / (1.1-1.0225) = 8.9$.

Sheer size suggests that it is worth considering possible strains on global markets that might arise from rapid growth in manufactured exports by India and by the next tier of populous poor nations: Bangladesh, Indonesia, Nigeria, and Pakistan. Once again, however, the numbers should allay such fears. Total manufactured exports for this group of six stood at $98 billion in 2004 (in 2000 prices), or only 6.6 percent of those from Asia.

To be sure, in the brief survey of FC literature presented here, there is some evidence that countries specializing in labor-intensive manufactures encountered greater terms-of-trade difficulties. Even in this dimension, however, the apparent pattern—movement of the G-4 toward more sophisticated goods, with China replacing some of their market share—would seem perfectly capable of being replicated by the next cohort of poor countries, which would expand labor-intensive manufactured exports as China moves toward more sophisticated goods.

The U.S. External Imbalance: A New Macro Fallacy of Composition?

The FC hypotheses of the past two decades have been primarily microeconomic in nature. The idea that import penetration would surpass critical thresholds and trigger protection is a sectoral question; so is the issue of falling terms of trade for labor-intensive manufactures, although the notion of a broader decline in terms of trade for all manufactures exported by developing countries would be a mixture of macroeconomic and microeconomic questions.

However, a new FC problem may be emerging that is more centrally macroeconomic: the seeming dependence of rapidly rising exports from developing countries on the U.S. market in a context of a large and widening U.S. current account deficit and net international liabilities.[10]

Consider the following propositions. (A) The U.S. market has been the principal destination for the rapid rise in developing countries' exports of manufactures in the past decade. (B) At about 7 percent of GDP, the U.S. current account deficit is unsustainably high. It would seem to follow that (C) in the future developing countries will no longer be able to rely on the United States as the principal market for further increases in their manufactured exports. If so, then it follows either that (D1) the developing countries will need to shift more toward their own domestic markets as the source of increased demand or that (D2) they will need to shift the locus of their export expansion toward the European Union, Japan, Canada, Australia, and New Zealand and, even then, may be unable to sustain the pace of export expansion that had been oriented toward the U.S. market.

---

10 From the vantage point of mid-2008, the risks represented by the U.S. external imbalance appear less acute than two years earlier when this study was completed. They nonetheless remain relevant, especially because the key East Asian economies, in particular, have not yet carried out the needed real appreciations necessary for consistency with full U.S. external adjustment.

Cline (2005a, 2005b) sets forth the case that the U.S. current account deficit is a growing problem that could jeopardize U.S. and global growth and stability if it is not resolved. The United States experienced a cycle of current account imbalance in the 1980s, when the sharp rise in the dollar through 1985 brought the current account deficit to a peak of 3.4 percent of GDP by 1987. The decline of the dollar following the 1985 Plaza Agreement for coordinated intervention and other measures to reduce the dollar against the yen and deutsche mark helped to reverse the imbalance, which was largely eliminated by 1990–91.

The present cycle of U.S. external imbalance began in earnest after the outbreak of the East Asian financial crisis in 1997, and from 1997 to 2005 the current account deficit soared from about 2 percent of GDP to 6.4 percent, almost twice the previous peak. The U.S. net international investment position (NIIP), which had fallen from +13 percent of GDP in 1980 to zero by 1988, then declined further to –23 percent of GDP by 2001 (BEA 2006a). Although changes in exchange rates and asset price valuations since then have so far kept the NIIP from falling further relative to GDP, despite large annual current account deficits, the long-term trend is for large further decline. Even before the recent additional increases in oil prices, my model projections in mid-2005 showed that, with the dollar at the real level of the first five months of that year and with likely future U.S. and foreign growth rates, the U.S. current account deficit would widen to 7.5–8 percent of GDP by 2010, 10 percent by 2015, and 14 percent by 2025. The NIIP would fall to about –75 percent of GDP by 2015 and to –140 percent by 2025 (Cline 2005b: 84–86; 180–81).[11]

No one knows what is a safe level for U.S. net international liabilities, but it would seem highly imprudent for policy makers to allow net international liabilities to rise beyond about 50 percent of GDP. The benchmark for danger for most developing countries has been in the range of 40 percent of GDP. Some allowance can be made for the lesser vulnerability of the United States thanks to the denomination of its liabilities in dollars rather than in foreign currency, but the external position of the United States is far more central to the international economy than that of any other country, so more rather than less caution seems to be in order. Simulations with my model suggest, however, that in order to bring the U.S. current account deficit back down to the range of about 3 to 3.5 percent of GDP by 2010 (a level consistent with eventual stabilization of the NIIP at about –50 percent of GDP), the trade-weighted average of foreign currencies would have to rise by about another 20 percent above the level of

---

11 However, by mid-2008 revised projections of my model showed the U.S. current account deficit on track to plateau at about 4 percent of GDP by 2010–12, rather than to continue on an ever-widening path. Substantial real effective depreciation of the dollar from mid-2006 to mid-2008 brought the change in outlook (despite higher oil prices). Even so, the U.S. external deficit remained excessive compared to a sustainable target of about 3 percent of GDP.

January–May 2005.[12] Exchange rate adjustment would need to be accompanied by either fiscal adjustment or a return to higher personal saving rates in the United States in order for the potential adjustment not to be thwarted by general-equilibrium feedbacks (for example, higher interest rates and thus a rebound in the dollar).

Delay in correction in the U.S. external imbalance would seriously raise the risks to the U.S. and international economies. A loss of confidence by international investors could trigger a cutback in the large capital inflows needed to finance the U.S. external deficit, which in turn would put upward pressure on interest rates and could precipitate a U.S. recession (the hard-landing scenario). The United States came close to such an outcome in 1979 and again in 1987. Even in the absence of a sudden hard landing, lengthy delay of adjustment would force much greater cutbacks in consumption (and investment) by households and businesses by the middle of the next decade than would otherwise be needed, adding to an already serious problem of postponing burdens to the future in the form of unfunded pension and health obligations.

U.S. external adjustment thus seems necessary and should be done sooner rather than later. Yet this adjustment could seriously challenge continuation of export-led growth in developing countries. Thus the trade surplus of developing countries as a group with the United States rose from 1 percent of their combined GDP in 1992 to 5.5 percent in 2004, so rising net exports to the U.S. market boosted demand for these economies by about 4.5 percent of their GDP (Cline 2006). The new macroeconomic fallacy of composition question is thus whether developing countries can continue their rapid expansion of manufactured exports (or total exports) even as the United States enters into an inevitable phase of reduction rather than further widening of its current account deficit.

Because the U.S. economy constitutes about 30 percent of global GDP at market exchange rates (World Bank 2006), a reduction in the U.S. current account deficit by about 3 percent of GDP would amount to a reduction in the current account position of other countries equivalent to about 1.3 percent of their combined GDP. If the adjustment were spread over three to four years, this would translate into a reduction in external demand amounting to about 0.3 to 0.4 percent of their GDP annually. This magnitude is by no means insurmountable. However, it would mean that instead of adding about 0.4 percent of GDP annually to demand for developing countries—the average in 1993–2004—the U.S. market would be subtracting about this much annually.

The developing countries will need to participate in the reduction of current account positions in the rest of the world that will be needed as the

---

12 Instead, by June 2006, the Federal Reserve's broad real exchange rate index for the dollar had risen about 1 percent (foreign exchange rates had fallen about 1 percent) from the January–May 2005 average. However, from June 2006 to June 2008, this broad real index fell by 12.1 percent (Federal Reserve 2008).

counterpart to reduction of the U.S. current account deficit. Including the G-4, the developing countries as a group swung sharply from being in an aggregate current account deficit position of about $100 billion in 1993, or 2.0 percent of their combined GDP, to being in aggregate surplus at $509 billion in 2005, or 4.3 percent of their combined GDP (IMF 2006b). This means that, instead of receiving net resources for investment from industrial countries—the more normal pattern for global capital flows and external accounts—the developing countries have become large net suppliers of capital to the industrial countries, mainly the United States.

As suggested above, a major further decline in the trade-weighted value of the dollar seems necessary to carry out the U.S. external adjustment. Many developing countries would appropriately experience real appreciation against the dollar as part of this process, although their trade-weighted appreciations would be much smaller because most of their trading partners would also be appreciating against the dollar. So far, however, relatively few developing countries have had substantial currency appreciations against the dollar. Instead, most of the exchange rate correction so far has been by industrial countries, especially those in the euro area as well as Canada, Australia, New Zealand, the United Kingdom, and, to a far lesser extent, Japan. Cline (2005b) develops a model of optimal exchange rate realignment that sets target current account adjustments by country as counterparts to the U.S. current account adjustment. The study then identifies changes in exchange rates that most closely yield the target current account adjustments subject to the constraint that the trade-weighted real foreign appreciation against the dollar meets the target for U.S. external adjustment (about 20 percent).

Many of the developing countries have not allowed their exchange rates to appreciate in response to market forces, but instead have intervened in the exchange markets and built up large foreign reserves. From 2001 to 2005, the period in which the dollar has staged some correction from its highest levels, the combined foreign reserves of developing countries rose from $1.3 trillion to $2.9 trillion. Although Japan's reserves also rose sharply (from $397 billion to $836 billion), reserves of the other industrial countries (excluding the United States, whose reserves are minimal) did not rise much at all (from $434 billion to only $469 billion; IMF 2006a). This pattern reflects the tendency to avoid exchange rate intervention in most industrial countries except Japan (which also stopped intervening after March 2004).

Among developing economies, in contrast, the increase in reserves was massive in China (from $217 billion to $823 billion); Korea (from $103 billion to $210 billion); India ($46 billion to $143 billion); and Taiwan, China ($123 billion to $254 billion). They were also large in economies such as Singapore ($76 billion to $116 billion), Malaysia ($31 billion to $70 billion), and Thailand ($33 billion to $51 billion).

Figure 9.2 shows the sharp contrast between major industrial countries, which, with the exception of Japan, have tended to allow their exchange

Figure 9.2. Appreciation against the U.S. Dollar and Change in Reserves Relative to Imports, End-2001 to End-2005

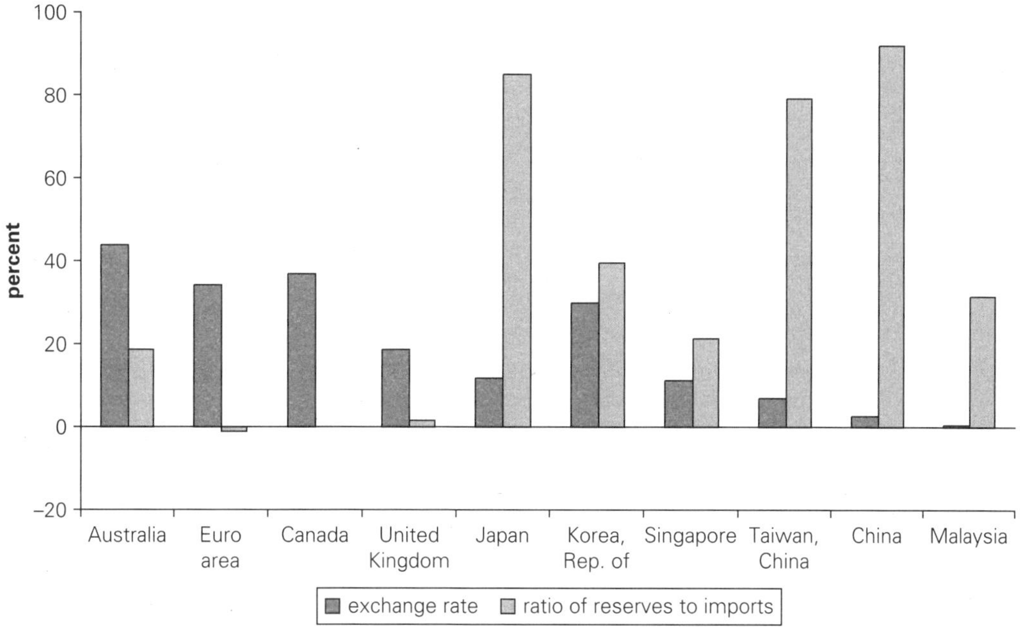

Source: IMF 2006a, 2006b; UNCTAD 2005.

rates to appreciate against the dollar rather than intervene in currency markets, and leading Asian emerging market economies, which have largely prevented market forces from bidding up their exchange rates by engaging in massive intervention and buildup of reserves (expressed as the change in reserves as a percent of 2005 imports).

Cline (2006) argues that because of the eventual damage of a disruptive global hard landing, it is in the developing countries' own interests to cooperate in helping to achieve an earlier, smoother U.S. external adjustment by ceasing to thwart the appreciation of their currencies against the dollar through intervention. To this end, Cline (2005a) calls for a Plaza 2 agreement among major economies, including the East Asian and other major emerging market economies, to orchestrate a coordinated package of exchange realignments and adjustments in fiscal and other demand-oriented policies to help to foster a smooth adjustment of the U.S. (and hence international) external imbalances. U.S. fiscal adjustment would be an indispensable component of the overall bargain in a Plaza 2. Based on the analysis of optimal currency realignment, Cline (2005b) indicates that there would need to be relatively large real appreciations against the dollar from the March 2005 level (about the average for January–May 2005) in several major developing economies, including a 45 percent appreciation by China, 59 percent by Malaysia, 79 percent by Singapore, and 44 percent by the Philippines. More moderate appreciations would also be appropriate in some Latin American countries (about 20 percent for Chile and Mexico,

14 percent for Argentina, but only 8 percent for Brazil). The Japanese yen would also rise sharply against the dollar, by 38 percent, whereas the euro would not move much more (5 percent), and the Australian and Canadian currencies would ease slightly against the dollar. Crucially, all of these currency appreciations would be much smaller when gauged in terms of real effective exchange rates against all trading partners. For China, for example, this increase would be only about half as large as the bilateral appreciation against the dollar, and for Korea, the real effective change would be a depreciation of 8 percent (compared to a bilateral appreciation of 14 percent).[13]

To recapitulate, the U.S. market has become like a global commons for the expansion of exports, especially by China as well as other developing countries. In a new macroeconomic fallacy of composition, these countries have been overexploiting this commons, analogous to overfishing an ocean region, and this commons faces an eventual collapse that would adversely affect the countries relying on it for their development strategy. A Plaza 2 or other coordinated effort, perhaps led by the new multilateral surveillance efforts of the International Monetary Fund, would seem desirable to ensure that this macroeconomic FC is addressed sooner rather than later.

One reason the new macroeconomic FC has arisen is that several major developing countries appear to have transited from the classical model of export-led growth to what amounts to a model of neo-mercantilism featuring ever-rising trade surpluses.[14] Instead, traditional export-led growth is premised on rapid growth in imports of raw material inputs and capital goods used for domestic growth. In this classical version, both exports and imports grow rapidly, either broadly maintaining a given trade balance or widening a trade deficit as inflows of financial capital from the North supplement domestic resources. Instead, the neo-mercantilist version features import growth lagging behind exports and the placement of excess export earnings into large and growing reserves. Although a building of reserves certainly made sense for some economies in the wake of the East Asian financial crisis of the late 1990s, by now this process has gone far beyond what can be justified by any prudential need for reserves.

Figures 9.3 and 9.4 show the increasing reliance of major economies on the U.S. market. The first indicates the path of U.S. imports from the

---

13 By mid-2008, several of the key East Asian currencies remained substantially undervalued. Realignments to reach fundamental-equilibrium exchange rates in a context of international adjustment continued to require appreciations on the order of 15 percent in real effective exchange rates for China and Singapore and 8 to 10 percent for Hong Kong, China; Taiwan, China; and Malaysia. These corrections would imply bilateral appreciations against the dollar on the order of 25–30 percent for the former two economies and 20–25 percent for the latter three. See Cline (2008).

14 Dooley, Folkerts-Landau, and Garber (2004) formalize this neo-mercantilist model into the Bretton Woods II regime, in which center countries float their exchange rates, but China and other countries in the periphery (curiously including Japan) intervene to fix their exchange rates against the U.S. dollar in order to sustain rising exports to absorb surplus labor. For a skeptical view of this framework, see Cline (2005b: 187–89).

Figure 9.3. U.S. Imports from Industrial, OPEC, and Other Developing Countries, 1991–2005

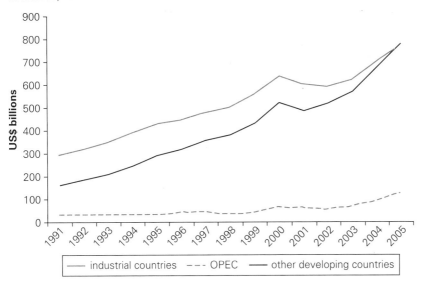

Source: BEA 2006a, 2006b.

industrial countries, Organization of the Petroleum-Exporting Countries (OPEC), and other developing countries over the past 15 years.[15] The non-oil developing countries have gained sharply in market share, as U.S. imports from this group have risen from only about half as large as U.S. imports from industrial countries to surpass imports from industrial countries by 2005. The cumulative average nominal growth of U.S. imports from non-oil developing countries from 1991 to 2005 was 11.2 percent, compared to just 6.9 percent from industrial countries. With a strong dollar after 1995, weak market growth in Japan, slower growth in Europe than in the United States, as well as devaluations in East Asia after the financial crisis in the late 1990s, U.S. exports have grown much more slowly than imports, at 7.3 percent annually to non-oil developing countries and at 4.4 percent annually to industrial countries. The gap between the import and export growth rates was higher for U.S. trade with the non-oil developing countries (3.9 percent annually) than for trade with the industrial countries (2.5 percent), again showing the rising role of developing countries in the U.S. external imbalance.

One shortcut way to see whether there might be a macroeconomic FC going forward is simply to consider what would happen if U.S. imports from non-oil developing countries continued at the average pace of the past 15 years. If these imports continued to grow at 11.2 percent in nominal terms, and U.S. GDP were to grow at a steady 5.5 percent (3 percent real, 2.5 percent for inflation), imports from non-oil developing countries

---

15 BEA (2006a, 2006b) data place South Africa in the industrial-country grouping.

would rise from 6.2 percent of U.S. GDP in 2005 to 10.6 percent in 2015 and to 17.9 percent by 2025. If at the same time U.S. exports to these countries grew at the same rate as in the past 15 years, they would only rise from 3.0 percent of U.S. GDP in 2005 to 3.6 percent by 2015 and to 4.3 percent by 2025. So the U.S. trade deficit with the non-oil developing countries would soar from 3.2 percent of U.S. GDP in 2005 to 7.0 percent by 2015 and to 13.6 percent by 2025.

These numbers alone cast doubt on the sustainability of ever-rising developing-country trade surpluses with the United States as an engine of development. They also highlight the fact that the macroeconomic FC is driven not just by high growth rates for U.S. imports from developing countries, but also by the substantially lower growth rates of U.S. exports to these countries. In a sense, the emphasis of the "general-equilibrium" school on an offsetting rise in demand for exports to these countries (the third variant of the FC issue) has not been validated for the United States, even if it were a plausible argument if the export growth rate had matched the import growth rate (which, again, ignores sectoral adjustment stresses).

Taking triangular trade into account would not alter this diagnosis. Whereas bilateral balances are inappropriate for most macroeconomic analysis, for groupings as broad as the three-way division in figure 9.3 the triangular trade missed in bilateral analysis largely disappears. Indeed, because the United States has a structural deficit with the OPEC economies, it might be expected to run a sizable trade surplus with all other developing countries, rather than a large and widening deficit.

Figure 9.4 shows detail on the evolution of U.S. imports by major trading partner. The figure reveals the striking rise in imports from China over the past decade. China's share in total U.S. imports soared from 6.5 percent in 1996 to 9.3 percent in 2000 and to 14.6 percent by 2005. In 2000 China ranked behind the European Union (of 15), Canada, Mexico, Japan, and the G-4 as a supplier to the U.S. market. By 2005 it ranked behind only the EU and Canada. The stagnation of U.S. imports from the G-4, in particular after 2000, reinforces the global pattern of deceleration in exports from this group as China moved rapidly ahead. Imports from Japan were also stagnant from 2000 to 2005, and Japan's share in the U.S. total fell from 14.5 percent in 1996 to 12.1 percent by 2000 and to only 9.3 percent in 2005. Essentially, Japan and China have switched places in their share of the U.S. import market over the past decade.

China's annual nominal growth rate of exports to the U.S. market over the past decade was 15.5 percent, almost twice the rate for the next-ranking developing-country partner (Mexico at 9.2 percent). Among the economies shown in figure 9.3, U.S. imports from developing countries other than China grew over the decade at an average of only 6.8 percent, and U.S. imports from industrial countries grew at only 5.6 percent. In other words, in an overall picture of U.S. imports from developing countries growing at rates so high as to be unsustainable over the longer term, China's stands

Figure 9.4. U.S. Imports from Principal Supplying Economies, 1996–2005

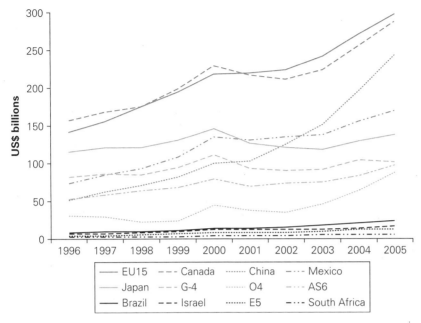

Source: USITC 2006.
Note: G-4: Hong Kong, China; Korea, Taiwan, China; Singapore; O4: Kuwait, Nigeria, Saudi Arabia, República Bolivariana de Venezuela; AS6: India, Indonesia, Malaysia, Pakistan, the Philippines, Thailand; E5: Czech Republic, Hungary, Poland, Slovak Republic, and Turkey.

out as the largest and most rapidly rising source of imports by far. It is no coincidence that U.S. officials have concentrated their attention on China as a trading partner whose exchange rate needs far more adjustment as part of the process of U.S. external adjustment.

To recapitulate, a new macroeconomic fallacy of composition has arguably arisen because of the unsustainability of the ever-widening U.S. current account deficit and the heavy dependence of developing countries' recent export growth on this widening deficit. The solution to this problem will require fiscal adjustment by the United States and a willingness among developing countries (especially China and other East Asian economies) to allow their exchange rates to appreciate. A shift toward domestic demand in several key developing countries will also be a necessary part of the solution.

Conclusions

This chapter has revisited the fallacy of composition argument after a quarter century of experience. It finds that buoyant growth of manufactured exports was in fact achieved and contributed vitally to economic growth over this period. However, this growth was at a pace that observed the "speed limits" of 10–15 percent suggested in Cline (1984). Over the past 25 years, manufactured exports from developing countries have grown at an annual average of about 10 percent (table 9.1). Although there was a modest tendency for these exports to shift direction toward the markets of other developing countries rather than industrial countries—a factor suggested by early critics of the FC hypothesis as a reason protection could be avoided—this shift has been only modest, from 59 percent in 1980 to 55 percent in 2003 for the top 20 manufacturing exporters (table 9.3). There is considerable evidence supporting the hypothesis of a shift in the direction of the original G-4 countries' exports away from industrial-country markets with replacement by other developing countries, especially China. Correspondingly, the G-4 has radically increased exports to China, from only 2 percent of their exports in 1980 (when trade with China was proscribed for two of the four G-4 economies) to 25 percent (table 9.4).

Despite remaining within safe speed limits in the aggregate, manufactured imports from developing countries into industrial countries have generated high import penetration ratios in several sectors, at levels that might have been expected to precipitate a protective response. Apparel imports from developing countries now stand at about half of consumption in the main industrial countries (table 9.8). However, although import penetration has reached remarkably high rates in a few sectors (79 percent for footwear, 69 percent for luggage and handbags, 68 percent for games and toys, and 63 percent for knitted and crocheted fabrics in the U.S. market), it has remained more moderate in a large number of other sectors. The median penetration ratio for the United States among the top 41 ISIC sectors shown in table 9.8 is 27 percent, and there are another 88 sectors not shown in the table.

At the same time, for some of the leading product sectors penetration is sufficiently high that there is some possibility of a new variant of the FC: market saturation. For the products just mentioned, as well as the important sector of office machinery (where penetration in the U.S. market is about 50 percent), high rates of penetration mean that the further growth of imports from developing countries will increasingly tend to be constrained by the underlying growth rate of domestic consumption. For products such as apparel that have relatively inelastic demand, this pace could be slow.

The lessons of the past two decades for today's poorer countries would seem to be that they should be able to expand manufactured exports without much fear of severe constraints from FC problems. The magnitudes they are likely to add to the market are simply too small to pose much of a problem.

Finally, a potentially serious new macroeconomic fallacy of composition seems to be emerging. Developing countries have relied heavily on rising exports to the U.S. market in the past decade, but much of this increase has reflected the widening of the U.S. current account deficit to unsustainable levels. The major developing countries will need to cooperate in allowing their exchange rates to adjust rather than intervening in foreign exchange markets and building up massive reserves, and the United States will have to take measures to carry out fiscal adjustment, if this new macroeconomic imbalance is to avoid winding up badly.

References

Balassa, Bela. 1978. "Exports and Economic Growth: Further Evidence." *Journal of Development Economics* 5 (2, June): 181–89.

BEA (Bureau of Economic Analysis). 2006a. "International Investment Position." U.S. Department of Commerce, Washington, DC. www.bea.gov.

———. 2006b. "U.S. International Transactions Accounts Data." U.S. Department of Commerce, Washington, DC. www.bea.gov.

BLS (Bureau of Labor Statistics). 2006. "Consumer Price Index: All Urban Consumers: Apparel." U.S. Department of Labor, Washington, DC. www.bls.gov.

Chenery, Hollis, and Moises Syrquin. 1975. *Patterns of Development, 1950–1970.* London: Oxford University Press.

China, DGBAS (Directorate-General of Budget, Accounting, and Statistics). 2005. *Statistical Yearbook of the Republic of China 2004.* Beijing: DGBAS. http://eng.dgbas.gov.tw.

Cline, William R. 1982. "Can the East Asian Model of Development Be Generalized?" *World Development* 10 (2): 81–90.

———. 1984. *Exports of Manufactures from Developing Countries.* Washington, DC: Brookings Institution Press.

———. 1985. "Reply." *World Development* 13 (4): 547–48.

———. 2005a. "The Case for a New Plaza Agreement." Policy Briefs in International Economics PB05-4 (December). Institute for International Economics, Washington, DC.

———. 2005b. *The United States as a Debtor Nation.* Washington, DC: Institute for International Economics.

———. 2006. "The U.S. External Deficit and Developing Countries." Working Paper 86 (March). Center for Global Development, Washington, DC.

———. 2008. "Estimating Consistent Fundamental-Equilibrium Exchange Rates." Working Paper WP 08-6 (June). Peterson Institute for International Economics, Washington, DC.

Dooley, Michael, David Folkerts-Landau, and Peter Garber. 2004. "A Map to the Revived Bretton Woods End Game: Direct Investment, Rising Real Wages, and the Absorption of Excess Labor in the Periphery." Deutsche Bank Global Markets Research, New York.

Faini, Riccardo, Fernando Clavijo, and Abdel Senhadji-Semlali. 1992. "The Fallacy of Composition Argument: Is It Relevant for LDCs' Manufactures Exports?" *European Economic Review* 36 (4): 865–82.

Federal Reserve. 2008. "Price-Adjusted Broad Dollar Index." Federal Reserve Board of Governors, Washington, DC. www.federalreserve.gov.

Havrylyshyn, Oli. 1990. "Penetrating the Fallacy of Export Composition." In *North-South Trade in Manufactures,* ed. Hans Singer, Neelamber Hatti, and Rameshwar Tandon. New Delhi: Indus Publishing.

IMF (International Monetary Fund). 2006a. Direction of Trade Statistics. CD-ROM (June). IMF, Washington, DC.

———. 2006b. International Financial Statistics. CD-ROM. IMF, Washington, DC.

———. 2006c. World Economic Outlook Database (April). IMF, Washington, DC. www.imf.org.

Martin, Will. 1993. "The Fallacy of Composition and Developing-Country Exports of Manufactures." *World Economy* 16 (2): 159–72.

Mayer, Jörg. 2003. "The Fallacy of Composition: A Review of the Literature." Discussion Paper 166 (February). United Nations Conference on Trade and Development, New York.

Ranis, Gustav. 1985. "Can the East Asian Model of Development Be Generalized? A Comment." *World Development* 13 (4): 543–45.

UNCTAD (United Nations Conference on Trade and Development). 2005. *UNCTAD Handbook of Statistics 2005.* New York: United Nations. http://stats.unctad.org/Handbook/.

UNIDO (United Nations Industrial Development Organization). 2006. Industrial Demand-Supply Balance Database: IDSB 2006. UNIDO, Vienna. www.unido.org/doc/3473.

USITC (United States International Trade Commission). 2006. "Interactive Tariff and Trade Dataweb." USITC, Washington, DC. www.dataweb.usitc.gov.

World Bank. 1983. *World Development Report 1983: World Economic Recession and Prospects for Recovery.* Washington, DC: World Bank.

———. 2005. World Development Indicators 2005. CD-ROM. World Bank, Washington, DC.

———. 2006. World Development Indicators 2006. CD-ROM. World Bank, Washington, DC.

CHAPTER 10
Industry Growth and the Case for Countercyclical Stimulus Packages

Philippe Aghion, David Hemous, and Enisse Kharroubi

Macroeconomic textbooks generally impose a strict separation between the long-term analysis of growth and the short-term analysis, which focuses on the effects of macroeconomic policies (fiscal and monetary) aimed at stabilizing the economy following a shock. Yet recently this view that short-run stabilization policies do not matter for long-run growth has been challenged. Ramey and Ramey (1995) were among the first to underline the negative correlation in cross-country regression between volatility and long-run growth.

More recently, Aghion and others (2008) have argued that higher macroeconomic volatility pushes toward more procyclical investments in research and development (R&D) in firms that are more credit constrained. This chapter goes one step further, looking at the effect of countercyclical fiscal policy on industry growth, depending on industry financial constraints. To this end, we carry out cross-industry, cross-country panel data regressions. Empirical evidence shows that industries with heavier financial constraints tend to grow faster in countries with more stabilizing fiscal policies.

We build on the methodology developed in the seminal paper by Rajan and Zingales (1998). Using cross-industry, cross-country panel data, we test whether industry growth is positively affected by the interaction between fiscal policy cyclicality (computed at the country level) and industry-level external financial dependence or asset tangibility (computed for each corresponding industry in the United States). This approach can be helpful to address the debate as to whether the cyclical pattern of fiscal policy indeed has a causal impact on growth: to the extent that macroeconomic policy affects industry growth, the opposite (industry growth affects macroeconomic policy) is much less likely to hold. A positive and significant interaction coefficient in the growth regressions can therefore help to deal with the causality issue.

Our main empirical finding is that the interaction between financial constraints in an industry and fiscal policy countercyclicality—measured as the sensitivity of a country's fiscal balance to changes in its output gap—in the country has a positive, significant, and robust impact on industry growth. More specifically, the higher the extent to which the corresponding industry in the United States relies on external finance, or the lower the asset tangibility of the corresponding sector in the United States, the more such industry benefits from a more countercyclical fiscal policy.

Moreover, based on the regression coefficients, we assess the magnitude of the corresponding difference-in-difference effect. The figures happen to be relatively large, especially when compared with the equivalent figures in Rajan and Zingales (1998). This suggests that, on top of being statistically significant, the effect of countercyclical fiscal policy is economically significant and cannot be discarded, considering it would be of second-order importance.

Overall, our results suggest a role for fiscal stimuli during recessions in economies where firms are credit constrained. However, our approach departs from alternative (more short-term) justifications based on the Keynesian multiplier.

The chapter details the methodology and the data used and presents the empirical results. A final section concludes. Appendix A presents estimation details.

Methodology and Data

Our dependent variable is the average annual growth rate of real value added in industry j in country k for the period 1980–2005. As explanatory variables, we introduce industry and country fixed effects $\{\alpha_j; \beta_k\}$ to control for unobserved heterogeneity across industries and across countries. The variable of interest, $(ic)_j \times (fpc)_k$, is the interaction between industry j's intrinsic characteristic and the degree of (counter) cyclicality of fiscal policy in country k over the period 1980–2005. As industry characteristics, we alternatively use external financial dependence or asset tangibility. Following

Rajan and Zingales (1998), we measure industry-specific characteristics using firm-level data in the United States. External financial dependence is measured as the average across all firms in a given industry of the ratio of capital expenditures minus current cash flow to total capital expenditures. Asset tangibility is measured as the average across all firms in a given industry of the ratio of the value of net property, plant, and equipment to total assets. Finally, we control for initial conditions by including the ratio of real value added in industry j in country k in 1980 to total real value added in the manufacturing sector in country k in 1980, (y_{jk}^{80}/y_k^{80}). Letting ε_{jk} denote the error term, our main estimation equation can then be expressed as follows:

$$\frac{\ln(y_{jk}^{05}) - \ln(y_{jk}^{80})}{25} = \alpha_j + \beta_k + \gamma(ic)_j \times (fpc)_k - \delta \log\left(\frac{y_{jk}^{80}}{y_k^{80}}\right) + \varepsilon_{jk} \qquad (10.1)$$

This methodology is predicated on the assumptions that (a) differences in financial dependence and asset tangibility across industries are driven largely by differences in technology; (b) technological differences persist over time across countries; and (c) countries are relatively similar in terms of the overall institutional environment faced by firms. Under those three assumptions, the U.S.-based industry-specific measure is likely to be a valid interactor for industries in countries other than the United States. We believe that these assumptions are satisfied especially given our restriction to a set of rich countries that all belong to the Organisation for Economic Co-operation and Development (OECD). For example, if pharmaceuticals require proportionally more external finance than textiles in the United States, this is likely to be the case in other OECD countries as well. Moreover, since little convergence has occurred among OECD countries over the past 20 ears, cross-country differences are likely to persist over time. Finally, to the extent that the United States is more financially developed than other countries worldwide, U.S.-based measures of financial dependence as well as asset tangibility are likely to provide the least noisy measures of industry-level financial dependence or asset tangibility.

Our measure of fiscal policy cyclicality, $(fpc)_k$, in country k is the marginal change in fiscal policy following a change in the domestic output gap. We use country-level data over the period 1980–2005 to estimate the following country-by-country "auxiliary" equation over the time period 1980–2005:

$$fb_{kt} = \eta_k + (fpc)_k z_{kt} + u_{kt}, \qquad (10.2)$$

where fb_{kt} is a measure of fiscal policy in country k in year t (for example, total fiscal balance or primary fiscal balance to gross domestic product, GDP); z_{kt} measures the output gap in country k in year t (that is, the percentage difference between actual and potential GDP) and therefore represents the country's current position in the cycle; η_k is a constant; and u_{kt} is an error term.[1]

Following Rajan and Zingales (1998), we estimate our main equation (10.1) with a simple ordinary least squares (OLS) procedure, correcting for heteroskedasticity bias whenever needed, without worrying much further about endogeneity issues. In particular, the interaction term between industry-specific characteristics and fiscal policy cyclicality is likely to be largely exogenous to the dependent variable. First, our external financial dependence variable pertains to industries in the United States, while the dependent variable involves countries other than the United States. Hence reverse causality, whereby industry growth outside the United States could affect external financial dependence or asset tangibility of industries in the United States, seems quite implausible. Second, fiscal policy cyclicality is measured at a macro level, whereas the dependent variable is measured at the industry level, which again reduces the scope for reverse causality as long as each individual sector represents a small share of total output in the domestic economy.

Our data sample focuses on manufacturing industries in a set of 15 industrial OECD countries. In particular, we do not include the United States, as this would be a source of reverse causality problems.[2]

Our data come from a set of different sources. Industry-level real value added data are drawn from the European Union (EU) KLEMS data set. The primary source of data for measuring industry financial dependence is Compustat, which gathers balance sheets and income statements for U.S. listed firms. We draw on Rajan and Zingales (1998) and Raddatz (2006) to compute the industry-level indicators for financial dependence. We draw on Braun (2003) and Braun and Larrain (2005) to compute industry-level indicators for asset tangibility. Finally, macroeconomic fiscal variables are drawn from the OECD Economic Outlook data set (OECD 2008).

Results

We estimate our main regression equation (10.1) using financial dependence or asset tangibility as industry-specific interactors. We consider two sets of fiscal policy indicators. The first set is built around the total fiscal

---

1   For example, if the dependent variable in equation 10.2 is total fiscal balance to GDP, a positive (negative) regression coefficient $(fpc)_k$ reflects a countercyclical (procyclical) fiscal policy as the country's fiscal balance improves in upturns (deteriorates in downturns). In appendix A, we provide two histograms reflecting the estimation results of the country-by-country "auxiliary" regression (10.2).

2   The sample consists of the following countries: Australia, Austria, Belgium, Denmark, Spain, Finland, France, Greece, Ireland, Italy, Japan, Netherlands, Portugal, Sweden, and United Kingdom. Industries included in the sample are those with 2-digit code ranging between 15 and 37 according to the ISIC rev. 2. See www.euklems.net for more details.

Table 10.1. Correlation between Growth in Real Value Added and the Interaction between Financial Dependence and Fiscal Policy Cyclicality: Total Fiscal Balance

Independent variable	Fiscal balance to GDP (1)	Fiscal balance to potential GDP (2)	Cyclically adjusted fiscal balance to GDP (3)	Cyclically adjusted fiscal balance to potential GDP (4)
Log of initial share in manufacturing value added	−0.784** (0.284)	−0.795** (0.282)	−0.772** (0.286)	−0.780** (0.285)
Interaction (financial dependence and fiscal policy countercyclicality)	6.724*** (1.526)	6.742*** (1.434)	7.847*** (1.604)	7.799*** (1.537)
Number of observations	521	521	521	521
R^2	0.569	0.571	0.573	0.575

Note: The dependent variable is the average annual growth rate of real value added for the period 1980–2005 for each industry in each country. Initial share in manufacturing value added is the ratio of beginning-of-period industry real value added to beginning-of-period total manufacturing real value added. Financial dependence is the fraction of capital expenditures not financed with internal funds for U.S. firms in the same industry for the period 1980–90. Fiscal policy countercyclicality is the coefficient of the output gap when the variable indicated in the column is regressed on a constant and the output gap for each country over the period 1980–2005. The interaction variable is the product of variables in parentheses. Estimated coefficients are in percentages. Standard errors—clustered at the country level—are in parentheses. All estimations include country and industry dummies.
*** Significant at the 1 percent level.
** Significant at the 5 percent level.

balance variable, which we consider as either cyclically adjusted or not and which we use as a ratio of GDP or potential GDP.[3]

The second set of fiscal policy indicators is built around the primary fiscal balance variable. As in the previous case, we consider it either as cyclically adjusted or not. Moreover, we use it as a ratio of GDP or potential GDP.

The empirical results show that growth in real value added is significantly and positively correlated with the interaction of financial dependence and fiscal policy countercyclicality (see table 10.1): a larger sensitivity to the output gap of total fiscal balance to GDP raises industry real value added growth, especially for industries with higher financial dependence. This result holds irrespective of whether total fiscal balance is cyclically adjusted or not and irrespective of whether the ratio considered is for actual or potential GDP. Table 10.2 provides a very similar picture: a larger sensitivity to the output gap of total fiscal balance to GDP raises industry real value added growth, especially for industries with lower asset tangibility. As in the previous case, this result holds independent of the precise measure of total fiscal balance.

Three remarks are worth making at this point. First, the estimated coefficients are highly significant, in spite of the relatively conservative standard-error estimates, which we cluster at the country level. Second, the pair-wise correlation between industry financial dependence and industry asset tangibility is around −0.6, which is significantly below −1. In other words, these two variables are far from being perfectly correlated, which, in turn, implies that the two tables (tables 10.1 and 10.2) do not just mirror

---

3 The cyclically adjusted balance is computed to show the underlying fiscal position when automatic movements are removed.

Table 10.2. Correlation between Growth in Real Value Added and the Interaction between Asset Tangibility and Fiscal Policy Cyclicality: Total Fiscal Balance

Independent variable	Fiscal balance to GDP (1)	Fiscal balance to potential GDP (2)	Cyclically adjusted fiscal balance to GDP (3)	Cyclically adjusted fiscal balance to potential GDP (4)
Log of initial share in manufacturing value added	−0.515 (0.350)	−0.517 (0.351)	−0.508 (0.351)	−0.508 (0.352)
Interaction (asset tangibility and fiscal policy countercyclicality)	−13.77*** (4.544)	−13.74*** (4.388)	−16.19*** (5.214)	−15.98*** (5.093)
Number of observations	521	521	521	521
R^2	0.550	0.550	0.551	0.552

Note: The dependent variable is the average annual growth rate of real value added for the period 1980–2005 for each industry in each country. Initial share in manufacturing value added is the ratio of beginning-of-period industry real value added to beginning-of-period total manufacturing real value added. Asset tangibility is the fraction of assets represented by net property, plant, and equipment for U.S. firms in the same industry for the period 1980–90. Fiscal policy countercyclicality is the coefficient of the output gap when the variable indicated in column is regressed on a constant and the output gap for each country over the period 1980–2005. The interaction variable is the product of variables in parentheses. Estimated coefficients are in percentages. Standard errors—clustered at the country level—are in parentheses. All estimations include country and industry dummies.
*** Significant at the 1 percent level.

each other, but instead convey complementary information. Finally, the estimated coefficients remain essentially the same whether the fiscal balance is considered as a ratio of actual or potential GDP. This suggests that we are capturing the effect of fiscal policy rather than just the effect of changes in actual GDP. Similarly, the estimated coefficients remain essentially the same whether the fiscal balance is considered as cyclically adjusted or not, which suggests that the effect we capture is not exclusively related to automatic stabilizers.

We now repeat the same estimation exercise, but take primary fiscal balance, not total fiscal balance, as our fiscal policy indicator (see tables 10.3 and 10.4). The difference between these two indicators is that the primary fiscal balance does not include net interest repayments to or from the government. The results are qualitatively similar in both cases: industries with larger financial dependence or lower asset tangibility tend to benefit disproportionately from a more countercyclical fiscal policy in the sense of a larger sensitivity of the primary fiscal balance to variations in the output gap.

Magnitude of the Effects

How large are the effects implied by the regressions? To get a sense of the magnitudes involved in these regressions, we compute the difference in growth between, on the one hand, an industry at the third quartile (seventy-fifth percentile) in terms of financial dependence located in a country at the third quartile in terms of fiscal policy countercyclicality and, on the other hand, an industry at the first quartile (twenty-fifth percentile) in terms of financial dependence located in a country at the first quartile in terms of

Table 10.3. Correlation between Growth in Real Value Added and the Interaction between Financial Dependence and Fiscal Policy Cyclicality: Primary Fiscal Balance

Independent variable	Primary fiscal balance to GDP (1)	Primary fiscal balance to potential GDP (2)	Cyclically adjusted primary fiscal balance to GDP (3)	Cyclically adjusted primary fiscal balance to potential GDP (4)
Log of initial share in manufacturing value added	−0.794*** (0.250)	−0.796*** (0.250)	−0.786*** (0.247)	−0.784*** (0.248)
Interaction (financial dependence and fiscal policy countercyclicality)	4.679*** 0.864)	4.700*** (0.846)	5.170*** (0.893)	5.183*** (0.872)
Number of observations	521	521	521	521 ·
R^2	0.569	0.569	0.571	0.572

Note: The dependent variable is the average annual growth rate of real value added for the period 1980–2005 for each industry in each country. Initial share in manufacturing value added is the ratio of beginning-of-period industry real value added to beginning-of-period total manufacturing real value added. Financial dependence is the fraction of capital expenditures not financed with internal funds for U.S. firms in the same industry for the period 1980–90. Fiscal policy countercyclicality is the coefficient of the output gap when the variable indicated in the column is regressed on a constant and the output gap for each country over the period 1980–2005. The interaction variable is the product of variables in parentheses. Estimated coefficients are in percentages. Standard errors—clustered at the country level—are in parentheses. All estimations include country and industry dummies. *** Significant at the 1 percent level.

fiscal policy countercyclicality. We then carry out a similar exercise, replacing financial dependence with asset tangibility.[4]

As it turns out, the approximate gain in real value added growth is between 1.7 and 2.4 percentage points a year when the industry characteristic considered is financial dependence, while the approximate gain in real value added growth is between 2.1 and 2.7 percentage points a year when the industry characteristic considered is asset tangibility.

These magnitudes are fairly large, especially when compared to the corresponding figures in Rajan and Zingales (1998). According to their results, the gain in real value added growth from moving from the twenty-fifth to the seventy-fifth percentile, both in a country's level of financial development and in an industry's level of external financial dependence, is roughly equal to 1 percentage point a year.

However, the following considerations are worth pointing out here. First, these are difference-in-difference (cross-country or cross-industry) effects, which are not interpretable as countrywide effects. Second, this result applies to manufacturing sectors, which represent no more than 40 percent of total GDP of countries in our sample. Third, irrespective of the

---

4 In this case, we compute the difference in growth between, on the one hand, an industry at the first quartile in terms of asset tangibility located in a country at the third quartile in terms of fiscal policy countercyclicality and, on the other hand, an industry at the third quartile in terms of asset tangibility located in a country at the first quartile in terms of fiscal policy countercyclicality. Given our difference-in-difference specification, it is impossible to infer the economic magnitudes of the estimated coefficients differently. In particular, the presence of industry and country fixed effects precludes investigating the impact of a change in the cyclical pattern of fiscal policy for a given industry or conversely the effect of a change in industry characteristics (financial dependence or asset tangibility) in a country with a given cyclical pattern of fiscal policy. Both these effects are absorbed with our country and industry dummies.

Table 10.4. Correlation between Growth in Real Value Added and the Interaction between Asset Tangibility and Fiscal Policy Cyclicality: Primary Fiscal Balance

Independent variable	Primary fiscal balance to GDP (1)	Primary fiscal balance to potential GDP (2)	Cyclically adjusted primary fiscal balance to GDP (3)	Cyclically adjusted primary fiscal balance to potential GDP (4)
Log of initial share in manufacturing value added	−0.492 (0.351)	−0.494 (0.351)	−0.485 (0.352)	−0.485 (0.352)
Interaction (asset tangibility and fiscal policy countercyclicality)	−9.228*** (2.878)	−9.336*** (2.812)	−10.230*** (3.136)	−10.330*** (3.072)
Number of observations	521	521	521	521
R^2	0.549	0.549	0.550	0.550

Note: The dependent variable is the average annual growth rate of real value added for the period 1980–2005 for each industry in each country. Initial share in manufacturing value added is the ratio of beginning-of-period industry real value added to beginning-of-period total manufacturing real value added. Asset tangibility is the fraction of assets represented by net property, plant, and equipment for U.S. firms in the same industry for the period 1980–90. Fiscal policy countercyclicality is the coefficient of the output gap when the variable indicated in the column is regressed on a constant and the output gap for each country over the period 1980–2005. The interaction variable is the product of variables in parentheses. Estimated coefficients are in percentages. Standard errors—clustered at the country level—are in parentheses. All estimations include country and industry dummies. *** Significant at the 1 percent level.

fiscal policy indicator considered, dispersion across countries in fiscal policy cyclicality is very large, given the limited number of countries in our sample. Hence moving from the twenty-fifth to the seventy-fifth percentile in fiscal policy countercyclicality corresponds to a radical change in the design of fiscal policy along the cycle, which, in turn, is unlikely to take place in any individual country over the time period we consider. Fourth, this simple computation does not take into account the possible costs associated with the transition from a steady state with low fiscal policy countercyclicality to a steady state with high fiscal policy countercyclicality. Yet the above exercise suggests that differences in the cyclicality of fiscal policy are an important driver of the observed cross-country, cross-industry differences in growth performance.

Conclusions

We have analyzed the extent to which macroeconomic policy over the business cycle can affect industry growth, focusing on fiscal policy. Following the Rajan and Zingales (1998) methodology, we have interacted industry-level financial constraints (measured with financial dependence or asset tangibility in U.S. industries) and fiscal policy cyclicality at the country level to assess the impact of this interaction on output growth at the industry level. Empirical evidence shows that a more countercyclical fiscal policy significantly enhances output growth in more financially constrained industries, that is, in industries whose U.S. counterparts are more dependent on external finance or display lower asset tangibility. This investigation also suggests that the growth impact of the cyclical pattern of fiscal policy is of comparable (or even greater) importance to that of more structural features.

More generally, our analysis in this chapter has far-reaching implications for how to conduct macroeconomic policy over the business cycle. Here we have focused on fiscal policy and argued that it should be more countercyclical the tighter the credit constraints. But the same applies to monetary policy and how the central bank makes decisions regarding interest rates and liquidity provision. Preliminary work not reported here, performed following a similar methodology and based on a similar sample as in this chapter, suggests that growth in industries that are "liquidity-dependent" in the sense that they either (a) rely disproportionally on short-term debt or (b) maintain a larger ratio of inventory to assets benefits more from more output-gap-sensitive short-term interest rates. This new approach to macroeconomics and growth allows us to go beyond the debate between supply-side and demand-side economists. While demand considerations can affect the market size for potential innovations, our effects are fundamentally supply-side driven, as they operate through their influence on innovation incentives. Thus a more countercyclical fiscal policy has both an ex ante and an ex post effect: ex ante it increases innovation incentives by reducing the risk that the innovation will fail in the future due to adverse macroeconomic shocks; ex post it helps to reduce the proportion of firms that will have to cut productivity-enhancing investments following a bad shock.

References

Aghion, Philippe, George-Marios Angeletos, Abhijit Banerjee, and Kalina Manova. 2008. "Volatility and Growth: Credit Constraints and Productivity-Enhancing Investment." NBER Working Paper 11349. National Bureau for Economic Research, Cambridge, MA.

Braun, Matías. 2003. "Financial Contractibility and Asset Hardness." Unpublished mss. Harvard University, Cambridge, MA.

Braun, Matias, and Borja Larrain. 2005. "Finance and the Business Cycle: International, Inter-Industry Evidence." *Journal of Finance* 60 (3): 1097–128.

OECD (Organisation for Economic Co-operation and Development). 2008. *OECD Economic Outlook* 84 (December).

Raddatz, Claudio. 2006. "Liquidity Needs and Vulnerability to Financial Underdevelopment." *Journal of Financial Economics* 80 (3): 677–722.

Rajan, Raghuram, and Luigi Zingales. 1998. "Financial Dependence and Growth." *American Economic Review* 88 (3): 559–86.

Ramey, Garey, and Valerie Ramey. 1995. "Cross-Country Evidence on the Link between Volatility and Growth." *American Economic Review* 85 (5): 1138–51.

Appendix A. Estimation Results of the Country-by-Country Fiscal Policy Regression (10.2)

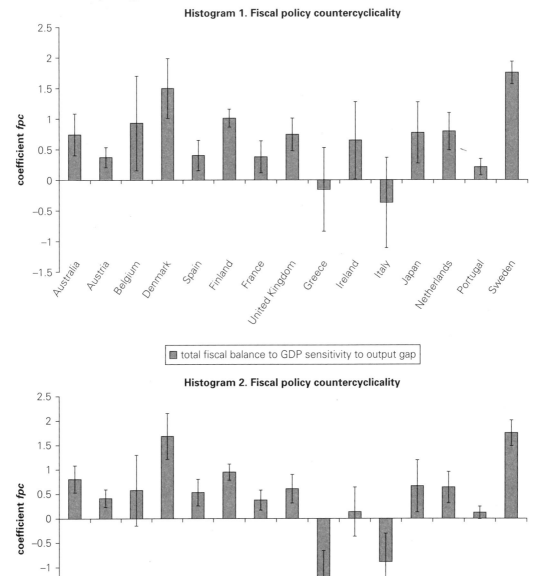

Histogram 1. Fiscal policy countercyclicality

total fiscal balance to GDP sensitivity to output gap

Histogram 2. Fiscal policy countercyclicality

primary fiscal balance to GDP sensitivity to output gap

Source: Authors' calculations.
Note: Bars represent the coefficient *fpc* estimated in the regression (10.2) for each country. Lines indicate the confidence interval at the 10 percent level around the mean estimate of *fpc*, based on the standard errors estimated in the regression (10.2).

Industry Growth and the Case for Countercyclical Stimulus Packages

PART 3
Long-Term Challenges to Growth

CHAPTER 11
Greenhouse Emissions and Climate Change: Implications for Developing Countries and Public Policy

David Wheeler

Among climate scientists, there is no longer any serious debate about whether greenhouse gas emissions from human activity are altering the earth's climate. According to the fourth assessment report of the Inter-governmental Panel on Climate Change (IPCC 2007), the likelihood of this effect is over 90 percent. Remaining debate in the scientific literature focuses on the size, timing, and impact of global warming, not its existence. Yet the controversy over climate change continues, the largest two carbon emitters—the United States and China—remain intransigent on mitigation, and we are far from reaching an international agreement that will supplant the Kyoto Protocol.

Although partisans frequently cite scientific issues, the real debate is no longer about the science. The controversies stem mostly from uncertainties

---

© 2010 Center for Global Development, 1800 Massachusetts Avenue, NW, Washington, DC 20036; www.cgdev.org. Used by permission.

regarding economic and technological forecasting, disputes about global and intergenerational equity, and political divisions over collective measures to combat climate change. Near-term closure seems unlikely on any of these fronts, but the science is sufficiently compelling that a global consensus supports concerted action. The interesting policy questions focus on appropriate measures to reduce greenhouse gas emissions, accelerate the development and diffusion of clean technologies, and support adaptation to the impacts of unavoidable climate change. Different positions on the nonscientific issues still drive very different conclusions about the scale, scope, and timing of the needed measures. In light of the scientific evidence, however, it would be difficult to defend complete inaction. The challenge is to develop an action strategy that supports moderate measures now, if the global consensus will support nothing stronger, while retaining the potential to undertake much more rigorous measures when they become politically feasible.

Climate change has catalyzed a global crisis for two main reasons. First, the international community has awakened to the possible existence of a critical threshold: an atmospheric carbon dioxide (CO_2) concentration, perhaps as low as 450 parts per million (ppm), beyond which large and irreversible damage from global warming is very likely.[1] We are already very late in the game. By mid-2007, the atmospheric concentration had increased from its preindustrial level, about 280 ppm, to a volume of 386 ppm. Under widely varying assumptions about future growth in current forecast scenarios (IPCC 2000),[2] we will almost certainly reach 450 ppm within 30 years in the absence of serious mitigation efforts. Avoiding this threshold will involve very rapid global adjustment, with unprecedented international coordination of efforts and a very strong focus on cost-effective measures.

Second, climate change presents a double-edged predicament for the billions who remain in poverty. If it is ignored, its impacts may undermine the development process because global warming will have its heaviest impact on the South.[3] If the South commits to carbon mitigation, the associated costs will be significant. This has created a crisis in North-South relations, as the South has seized on the idea that greenhouse gas emissions are a problem that the North must solve, while the South remains free to overcome poverty without worrying about carbon mitigation. Unfortunately, the evidence shows that this view is both wrong and dangerous for the South, because its own accumulating emissions are already sufficient to catalyze a climate crisis without any emissions from the North (Wheeler and Ummel 2007). The lesson is clear: global emissions are a global problem, and everyone must be at the table if we believe that carbon mitigation is necessary.

---

1 CO_2 is the primary greenhouse gas.
2 Scenario descriptions are available at www.grida.no/climate/ipcc/emission/089.htm.
3 North and South refer to developed and developing countries, respectively.

The chapter is organized as follows. It begins by reviewing the scientific evidence linking human activity to global warming and then describes the sources of controversy over the scope, scale, and timing of measures to combat climate change. This is followed by an explicit introduction of the North-South dimension, which shows why the evidence warrants serious mitigation in the South as well as the North. The chapter then summarizes recent research on climate change impacts, with a particular focus on impacts in the South, provides an overview of measures needed to confront climate change, and proposes concrete steps that could be taken immediately. A final section provides a summary and conclusions.

The Scientific Evidence on Climate Change

Climate scientists accept several basic propositions without question. First, human society exists because greenhouse gases trap heat in the atmosphere. Without them, the average global temperature would be about –18°C (degrees Celsius) instead of 14°C, its present level (NOAA 2007). To appreciate the significance of this 32°C differential, we need only note that a decline of 8–10°C was sufficient to produce the glaciers that covered much of North America and Europe during the last Ice Age.

The second universally accepted proposition, an obvious corollary of the first, is that a change in the atmospheric concentration of greenhouse gases will have thermal effects. Data from the Vostok Antarctic ice cores (Petit and others 2000) show that global mean temperatures and atmospheric CO_2 concentrations have been highly correlated through four interglacial (Milankovitch) cycles during the past 425,000 years (see figure 11.1). In each cycle, a change of about 100 ppm in the CO_2 concentration over the range 180–280 ppm has been associated with a corresponding change of about 10°C in global mean temperature.

Figure 11.1. Atmospheric CO_2 Concentration and Temperature: Four Ice-Age Cycles

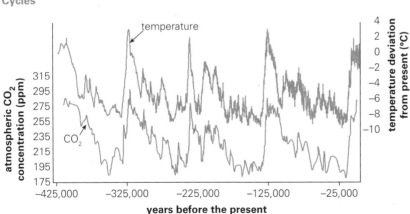

Source: Petit and others 2000.

Table 11.1. Cumulative Atmospheric CO$_2$ from the South and the North, 1850–2000
gigatons

	South			North		
Year	Land-use change	Fossil fuels	Total	Land-use change	Fossil fuels	Total
1850	19.38	0.00	19.38	25.68	4.83	30.52
1875	24.31	0.00	24.32	40.13	10.09	50.22
1900	33.93	0.14	34.08	54.05	25.83	79.88
1925	54.37	1.62	55.99	61.42	61.61	123.03
1950	82.07	5.32	87.39	62.33	106.51	168.83
1975	127.57	28.34	155.92	65.34	221.54	286.87
2000	180.17	115.13	295.30	58.29	371.73	430.02

Source: Wheeler and Ummel 2007.

But there was clearly no anthropogenic (human-induced) component in CO$_2$ changes during past Ice Age cycles. The consensus scientific explanation for the long-cycle correlation is as follows. Milankovitch cycles are driven by periodic changes in the earth's orbit and rotation that affect the global distribution of solar radiation. The cycles are highly asymmetric. As high-latitude radiation falls, the average temperature declines gradually over 100,000-year intervals in a cumulative process. Growing ice sheets reflect more solar radiation, which enhances the cooling effect, as does a simultaneous decline in the atmospheric CO$_2$ concentration. Once the solar cycle reverses, positive-feedback effects rapidly increase the average global temperature. These operate partly through decreased reflectivity from melting ice sheets and partly through an increasing atmospheric CO$_2$ concentration. We are currently near the top of a Milankovitch cycle, so the global temperature and CO$_2$ concentration should be near their cyclical maximums. But the atmospheric CO$_2$ concentration has risen far above the historical Milankovitch maximum since the eighteenth century. The resulting thermal effects are pushing the atmospheric temperature beyond the Milankovitch maximum as well.

The third proposition accepted by all atmospheric scientists is that cumulative anthropogenic emissions are increasing the atmospheric greenhouse gas concentration because terrestrial and oceanic sinks are insufficient to reabsorb the emitted carbon. Table 11.1 provides the most recent estimate of cumulative atmospheric CO$_2$ from human sources in the North and South during the period 1850–2000. Figure 11.2 shows the trend in the atmospheric concentration since 1744,[4] while figure 11.3 plots cumulative emissions against the atmospheric concentration (Wheeler and Ummel 2007). The data indicate that anthropogenic emissions since the mid-eighteenth century have increased the atmospheric concentration by about 40 percent, from 277 ppm in 1744 to 386 ppm in mid-2007.

---

4   Figure 11.2 combines observations from the Siple Ice Core (1744–1953) and the Mauna Loa Observatory, Hawaii (1959–2007); see Neftel and others (1994) and Keeling and others (2007), respectively.

Figure 11.2. Atmospheric CO_2 Concentration, 1744–2007

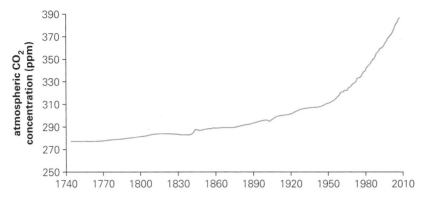

Source: Wheeler and Ummel 2007.

Figure 11.3. Atmospheric CO_2 Concentration and Cumulative Emissions, 1744–2007

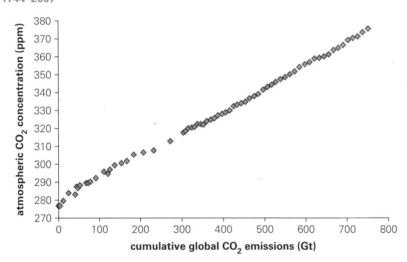

Source: Wheeler and Ummel 2007.

The fourth universally accepted proposition is that greenhouse gas emissions stay in the atmosphere for a long time. While carbon-cycle models differ in structure and sophistication, they all indicate similar long-duration effects. An example is provided by the Bern carbon-cycle model that is used for many estimates of cumulative emissions (Shaffer and Sarmiento 1995; Siegenthaler and Joos 2002). Figure 11.4 illustrates an application of the model to one ton of carbon emitted in 1850. Decay is relatively rapid during the first 40 years, with about 40 percent remaining in the atmosphere in 1890. However, rapid decline in the reabsorption rate leaves 25 percent of the original ton in the atmosphere in 2010. Such persistence is significant, because it ensures that current emissions will have very long-lived effects. To highlight the implication for emissions control policy, researchers frequently invoke a supertanker analogy. Given the sheer momentum

Figure 11.4. Fraction of One Ton of Carbon Emitted in 1850 Remaining in the Atmosphere, 1850–2010

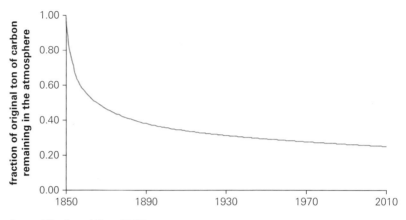

Source: Wheeler and Ummel 2007.

of a supertanker, safe, controllable docking requires cutting the engines 20–30 kilometers from port. Waiting until the last moment will guarantee a crash and cause tremendous damage. Carbon buildup in the atmosphere is like the tanker's momentum, and braking becomes harder as the accumulation continues.

To summarize, among climate scientists there is no meaningful dissent from the following propositions: heating from the naturally occurring greenhouse gas concentration in the atmosphere is the reason human society exists. Modern human activity has raised the atmospheric greenhouse gas concentration far above the maximum historical level observed over four major climate cycles during the past 425,000 years. The automatic result is a positive thermal effect, which will translate to global warming over an extended period of time.

Points of Scientific Contention

For climate scientists, projecting the impact of future greenhouse gas accumulation is complicated by two factors. The first is the existence of powerful adjustment systems that are not completely understood. These include thermal absorption by the oceans; associated thermal convection currents at global scale; absorption and expulsion of carbon by terrestrial sinks; changing absorption of solar radiation as melting polar ice yields darker waters and land masses; radiation blocking by cloud formations; and changes in carbon fixation by living biomass. The second factor is the existence of enormous, potentially unstable terrestrial and marine carbon deposits. A frequently cited example is the carbon sequestered in permafrost regions, which will escape into the atmosphere if global warming continues (Zimov, Schuur, and Chapin 2006). Another is the carbon sequestered in the deep oceans, which may be expelled into the atmosphere as global warming affects deep-sea circulation. Recent research suggests that such an expulsion occurred during the rapid temperature rise at the end of the most recent Ice Age (Marchitto and others 2007).

These factors make it difficult to forecast global warming with much precision. Some adjustment systems may have temperature-dampening effects (for example, radiation-blocking cloud formation from increased evaporation rates), while others have temperature-enhancing effects (for example, increased absorption of solar radiation as ice caps give way to darker open water or land; the escape of carbon from melting permafrost or the deep oceans; increased forest combustion as the atmosphere warms). All of these links are under intensive scientific study, and knowledge about them is increasing rapidly. At the same time, large-scale models of climate dynamics are improving steadily as computational power increases and supporting observational data become more plentiful. The overwhelming consensus is that temperature-enhancing feedbacks greatly outweigh countervailing mechanisms. Most climate scientists also believe that at least three elements of instability—ice cap melting, permafrost carbon, and deep-ocean carbon—are so large that they determine thresholds beyond which positive feedbacks would cause the atmospheric greenhouse gas concentration and temperature to increase rapidly over some range. Although scientists disagree about the timing of such "tipping" phenomena, few doubt that triggering them would have catastrophic implications because global society could not adjust rapidly enough to avoid enormous damage.

The Role of the IPCC

The scientific consensus on climate change is summarized periodically by assessment reports from the Intergovernmental Panel on Climate Change (IPCC). The IPCC is notable among global advisory bodies for the size and national diversity of its scientific representation, its scrutiny of the scientific literature, and the systematic process by which it assesses the evidence and identifies points of consensus among climate scientists. This chapter relies heavily on the IPCC's fourth assessment report (IPCC 2007) as an important source of information about global warming and its potential impacts.

However, certain features of the IPCC nearly guarantee that its reports will offer a conservative view of the problem. First, the IPCC's focus on consensus tends to exclude recent research that suggests larger-than-expected effects, because many of these results have not gained mainstream acceptance yet. A good example is provided by massive carbon release from melting permafrost. Some recent scientific evidence suggests that this has begun, but the IPCC's projections do not incorporate it. Another is the possibility of a rapid collapse of the Greenland ice sheet, which is again consistent with some recent research, but explicitly excluded from the IPCC projections. If such a collapse were to occur, the impact of the subsequent 7-meter sea-level rise on coastal populations would be enormous.

Second, climate science is progressing rapidly, but the extensive consultative requirements of the IPCC process make it difficult to incorporate scientific results published during the year prior to publication of an assessment. For the fourth IPCC report, the net impact of these requirements is undoubtedly conservative. The clear trend in recently published papers is toward more alarming conclusions about the magnitude of global warming and its potential impacts.

Finally, and most unfortunately, the IPCC process is vetted by governments' political representatives, some of whom (particularly those from the United States) have repeatedly demonstrated a strong inclination to discount evidence pointing to greater risks.

Nonscientific Sources of Contention

In the wake of the fourth IPCC report, scientific disputes no longer dominate the controversy over climate change. Even the well-known contrarian position of Lomborg (2001) has given way to acceptance of the need for concerted action on global warming and a focus on nonscientific elements of the controversy (Lomborg 2007).[5] The dramatic tension is supplied by three critical elements. Most climate change impacts will be experienced by future generations, there is a real possibility that unrestricted emissions will precipitate a climate catastrophe at some point in the future, and massive inertia in the global climate system[6] means that protecting future generations requires costly mitigation now. The points of contention are numerous, including economic and technological forecasts, mitigation costs, intergenerational distribution, risk assessment, national sovereignty, international distribution, emissions sources, and climate change impacts. This section discusses the first six issues, deferring the last two for more detailed treatment in later sections.

Economic and Technological Forecasts

Thinking about alternative policies in this context requires a backdrop—a long-run forecast of economic, technological, and demographic changes. IPCC (2007) acknowledges the inherent uncertainty by providing six forecast scenarios through 2100 (IPCC 2000). Table 11.2 and figure 11.5 provide comparative perspectives from these scenarios based on different models of economic, demographic, and technological change during the twenty-first century. In panel A of figure 11.5, scenario A1F1 reflects the

---

5   Lomborg (2007) employs benefit-cost analysis to support integrating mitigation and adaptation expenditures into a full assessment of global welfare impacts, with a particular focus on the implications for developing countries. He recommends modest carbon emissions charges and significant public support for clean-technology research and development, within the "moderate" range of measures discussed later in this chapter. Dasgupta (2007) argues that Lomborg's benefit-cost analysis and conclusions are flawed by an inappropriate specification of risk that discounts "tipping" thresholds. In contrast, the much more stringent conclusions and recommendations of Stern (2006) reflect the inclusion of such low-probability but potentially catastrophic risks.

6   This inertia arises from the long duration of carbon emissions in the atmosphere as well as the positive-feedback systems mentioned in previous sections.

Table 11.2. Global Surface Warming in Six IPCC Nonmitigation Scenarios
degrees centigrade: 2090–99 relative to 1980–99

Scenario	Low	Mean	High
B1	1.1	1.8	2.9
B2	1.4	2.4	3.8
A1T	1.4	2.4	3.8
A1B	1.7	2.8	4.4
A2	2.0	3.4	5.4
A1F1	2.4	4.0	6.4

Source: IPCC (2007: 749).
Note: B1 = a convergent world with the same low population growth as A1B, but with rapid changes in economic structures toward a service and information economy, with reductions in material intensity and the introduction of clean and resource-efficient technologies. The emphasis is on global solutions to economic, social, and environmental sustainability, including improved equity, but without additional climate initiatives. B2 = a world in which the emphasis is on local solutions to economic, social, and environmental sustainability. It is a world with continuously increasing global population at a rate lower than A2, intermediate levels of economic development, and less rapid and more diverse technological change than in B1 and A1. While the scenario is also oriented toward environmental protection and social equity, it focuses on local and regional levels. A1 = very rapid economic growth, global population that peaks in mid-century and declines thereafter, and the rapid introduction of new and more efficient technologies. Major underlying themes are convergence among regions, capacity building, and increased cultural and social interactions, with a substantial reduction in regional differences in per capita income. The A1 scenario family develops into three groups that describe alternative directions of technological change in the energy system. A1FI = fossil intensive. A1T = nonfossil energy sources. A1B = a balance across all sources. A2 = a very heterogeneous world, characterized by self-reliance and preservation of local identities. Fertility patterns across regions converge very slowly, which results in high population growth. Economic development is primarily regionally oriented, and per capita economic growth and technological change are more fragmented and slower than in other scenarios.

current aspirations of many developing countries: rapid economic growth in a globalizing economy; slow population growth; the rapid introduction of more efficient technologies; and an energy path, unconstrained by carbon mitigation, that is consistent with the current development strategies of countries with abundant domestic fossil fuel resources. In this scenario, northern CO_2 emissions continue growing to 37,000 megatons (Mt) by 2100 (about twice their current level), and southern emissions peak later in the century at about 73,000 Mt (over three times their current level).

In contrast, scenario B1 (figure 11.5, panel B) reflects rapid changes in economic structure toward services and information and the introduction of clean, resource-efficient technologies. In the North, emissions begin falling rapidly around 2020; by 2100, they have returned to a level not seen since the 1930s. In the South, emissions peak around mid-century at less than half of southern peak emissions in scenario A1F1 and then fall to their 1980s level by the end of the century.

Both scenarios are plausible, but their implications for atmospheric carbon loading and global warming are very different. Neither scenario assumes the existence of a global carbon mitigation regime. A significant part of the current dispute about stringency in climate policy stems from disagreement about whether the twenty-first century will look like A1F1, B1, or something in between.

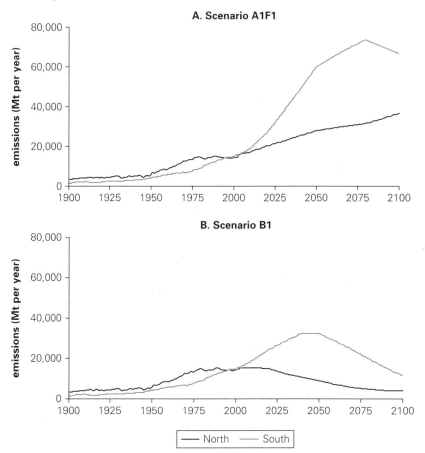

Figure 11.5. Emissions Attributable to the North and the South, by IPCC Scenario, 1900–2010

A. Scenario A1F1

B. Scenario B1

— North — South

Source: Wheeler and Ummel 2007.

Intergenerational Distribution

Economists continue to argue about the appropriate social discount rate—the weight that we should apply to our descendants' welfare in making benefit-cost decisions. This is extremely important for climate change policy, which must weigh large mitigation costs in the present against benefits that will accrue to people in the distant future. In brief, the social discount rate has two components. The first is a "pure" social rate of time preference, which reflects the response to the following question regarding values: If we know that our grandchildren's material status will be the same as our own, should we count their welfare equally with our own in making decisions about climate change policy? If the answer is yes, or nearly yes, then we should make significant sacrifices now to prevent adverse impacts on our grandchildren. If, however, we discount the fortunes of succeeding generations, then we will be inclined to let them fend for themselves. We will accept little or no sacrifice of consumption now to insure our successors against losses a century or two hence. The second component of the social discount rate reflects our assumptions about future progress. If world economic growth and technical progress continue at historical rates and are not undermined by global warming itself, then our grandchildren will be far richer and better endowed with technical options than we are. In this case, in fairness, it makes sense for us to minimize our sacrifices now, even if we value future generations' welfare the same as our own.

Much of the recent controversy over climate change policy among economists reflects different views about the appropriate social discount rate. Stern (2006) adopts a very low rate, tilting the benefit-cost calculus strongly in favor of future generations, while Nordhaus (2007a, 2007b) and others advocate a much higher rate. Quiggin (2006) provides a clear summary of the issues and determines that neither side has a conclusive case.

Mitigation Cost

Mitigation cost estimation is daunting in this context because of the long time horizon and uncertainty about the economic, technological, and demographic evolution of global society in the twenty-first century. It is useful to consider the total costs of mitigation by employing an identity that is a modified form of the Ehrlich equation (Ehrlich and Ehrlich 1991; Ehrlich and Holdren 1971):

$$G = P \times (Y/P) \times (G/Y), \tag{11.1}$$

where G = greenhouse gas emissions, P = population, and Y = total output (income).

In words, total greenhouse gas emissions are equal to the product of population (P), income (output) per capita (Y/P), and greenhouse gas emissions per unit of ouput (G/Y). There are clearly interdependencies on the right-hand side of this equation. For example, many econometric studies have analyzed the "Environmental Kuznets Curve" relationship between (G/Y) and (Y/P); see, for example, Dasgupta and others (2002); Stern (2004). If economic growth (increasing Y/P) remains an objective, then reducing greenhouse gas emissions requires a more-than-proportionate reduction in population (P) or emissions per unit of output (G/Y).[7] The latter is, in turn, a function of the structure of the economy (services are generally less carbon intensive than power generation or manufacturing, for example) and the sectoral technologies employed (hydropower generates no carbon emissions, while coal-fired power is highly emissions intensive). Each of these factors (population, sectoral composition, technology) can be altered at some cost on a schedule that is country specific, because the underlying cost functions are partly determined by local tradeoffs.

The complexities are obvious here, and the policy discussion has focused on very general results for P and G/Y. Birdsall (1992) finds that, under conditions prevailing in the early 1990s, investments in slowing population

---

7   This discussion simplifies the problem, since interdependencies among variables might well be an important factor. For example, the effect of policies to reduce population might be altered by their impact (positive or negative) on income per capita or carbon emissions per unit of output.

growth were generally more cost-effective in reducing carbon emissions than conventional investments in mitigation. This work needs updating, and new empirical research on the topic has begun.[8]

On the more conventional mitigation front (reduction in G/Y), recent work has contributed new insights about potential costs of mitigation. But it remains fraught with uncertainty, because computing the long-run cost of achieving an emissions target involves arbitrary assumptions about economic, technological, and demographic trends. As Dasgupta (2007) notes, it also rests on the assumption that continued anthropogenic carbon accumulation and heating will not breach one of the tipping thresholds that haunt the climate system.[9]

Stern (2006), Lomborg (2007), and Nordhaus (2007a, 2007b) have estimated the costs associated with various emissions targets. Stern and Lomborg focus on the cost of limiting the atmospheric CO_2 concentration to approximately 550 ppm. Lomborg estimates the global cost at approximately \$52 billion annually, or 0.11 percent of global income,[10] while Stern estimates the cost at 1 percent of income. Nordhaus (2007b) quantifies the costs associated with a variety of targets, using a social discount rate that is considerably higher than Stern's. Table 11.3 displays his results, which, given his modeling assumptions, show that when emissions restrictions are tightened, the costs increase faster than the benefits. Lowering the atmospheric concentration limit from 700 to 420 ppm, for example, increases discounted benefits (avoided damages) by \$7.4 trillion and increases discounted mitigation costs by \$25 trillion. While net benefits are positive for the 700 ppm limit relative to the no-control baseline (2.4 benefit-cost ratio), the converse is true for the 420 ppm limit (0.5 benefit-cost ratio). The same message about incremental benefits and costs recurs throughout table 11.3, which includes four temperature-increase limits, variations on the Kyoto Protocol, one version of the Stern Review results,[11] and a recent proposal for rapid emissions reductions by Al Gore.

At Nordhaus's discount rate, which tilts results more strongly toward the present than Stern's rate, near-term costs loom much larger than long-term benefits when sharp omissions reductions in the near future are needed to reach a target. As table 11.3 shows, Nordhaus's approach yields net negative benefits (benefit-cost ratios less than 1) for the Stern

---

8   The Center for Global Development has just launched a research program in this area.

9   As noted in a following section, carbon emissions from land clearing are a very important source of global warming. However, the cost calculations reported in this section focus principally on industrial emissions, primarily those from fossil fuel combustion. Introduction of population and deforestation effects generally relies on the assumption that the relevant variables change exogenously. For example, Nordhaus (2007b) imposes a logistic function on world population, roughly consistent with mid-range United Nations projections, that stabilizes global population at around 8.5 billion.

10 Based on global gross domestic product of \$48.2 trillion.

11 Nordhaus's results would not be acceptable to Stern, since Nordhaus's discount rate for the benefit-cost evaluation is much higher than Stern's. The consequences for the cost estimate are clarified by Nordhaus himself, who notes that his cost estimate for Stern's approach (1.5 percent of income) is 50 percent higher than Stern's own estimate.

Table 11.3. Estimated Benefits and Costs of Mitigation Relative to No Policies to Slow or Reverse Global Warming

US$ trillions (2005)

Policy option	Benefits (reduced damages)	Abatement costs	Benefit-cost ratio
Nordhaus/DICE optimal[a]	5.23	2.16	2.4
Greenhouse gas concentration limits			
420 ppm	12.60	27.20	0.5
560 ppm	6.57	3.90	1.7
700 ppm	5.24	2.16	2.4
Temperature-increase limits			
1.5°C	12.60	27.03	0.5
2.0°C	9.45	11.25	0.8
2.5°C	7.22	5.24	1.4
3.0°C	5.88	2.86	2.1
Kyoto Protocol			
With United States[b]	1.17	0.54	2.2
Without United States[c]	0.12	0.02	5.0
Strengthened[d]	6.54	5.82	1.1
Stern Review discounting[e]	13.53	27.70	0.5
Gore proposal[f]	12.50	33.86	0.4
Low-cost backstop[g]	17.63	0.44	39.9

Source: Nordhaus 2007b.

a. Yale DICE model sets runs to maximize the value of net economic consumption, assuming complete implementation efficiency and universal participation. Time discounting is at 1.5 percent pure time preference rate plus utility elasticity of 2.0.

b. Incorporates the Kyoto Protocol emissions limits (at least 5 percent below 1990 levels) for 2008–12 (all Kyoto Annex I countries, including the United States); no emissions reductions in nonparticipating countries.

c. Same as in note b, without the United States.

d. Sequential entry of the United States (2015), China (2020), and India (2030), with 50 percent emissions reductions within 15 years. Every region except Sub-Saharan Africa is assumed to reduce emissions significantly by 2050. The result is a global emissions reduction rate of 40 percent from the baseline by 2050 and a global emissions level somewhat above the level in 1990.

e. Emissions reduction path is determined by the DICE model using the Stern social discount rate. Then the model is rerun using this path, calculating benefits and costs with the standard DICE discount rate.

f. Global emissions control rate rises from 15 percent in 2010 to 90 percent in 2050; country participation rate rises from an initial 50 percent to 100 percent by 2050.

g. Emergence of a clean-technology or energy source that can replace all fossil fuels at current costs.

and Gore programs when they are compared to the baseline case (no explicit mitigation).

By far the best results in table 11.3 are for a hypothetical low-cost backstop technology that would utterly change the economic calculus if it emerged early in this century (benefit-cost ratio of 39.9). Although this result is not really comparable to the others, it emphasizes the potential payoff from more clean-energy research and development (R&D), a point also raised by Lomborg (2007).

Risk

A previous section described several "tipping" scenarios, considered likely by many climate scientists, that would have irreversible and potentially catastrophic effects. Scientists can attach relative probabilities to these scenarios, but they are inevitably somewhat arbitrary. Examples include disintegration of the polar ice sheets within decades rather than centuries, which would drown the world's coastal cities and infrastructure before there is time to adapt; shutdown of the Gulf Stream, which would make Europe's climate much more like Canada's; and an upsurge of catastrophic damage from violent "superstorms." We would undoubtedly invest heavily to avoid such catastrophes if we believed they were imminent. When they are deferred to the more distant future, however, the calculus becomes murkier.

IPCC (2007) acknowledges the possibility of such thresholds, but considers the science insufficient to incorporate them explicitly. Their treatment is critical for benefit-cost analysis, particularly if they threaten global catastrophe. Stern (2006) explicitly incorporates threshold effects, and the result is a strong tilt toward a stringent (and costly) mitigation policy. Lomborg (2007) does not incorporate such effects, and this moderates his conclusions about appropriate stringency. While criticizing Lomborg's approach, Dasgupta (2007) argues that traditional benefit-cost analysis is ill-equipped for such problems in any case.

National Sovereignty

Greenhouse gas emissions from any source make the same contribution to global warming, so confronting climate change will ultimately require concerted action by all countries and some limits on national sovereignty. This explains much of the politically polarized debate over climate change, particularly in the United States. Many ideological conservatives continue to discount global warming because they cannot accept evidence that legitimizes global regulation and limitation of American sovereignty. In their view, some risk of a future climate catastrophe is a small price to pay for avoiding measures that strengthen "collectivism" and restrain personal liberty. On the other side, many liberals seem almost eager to embrace worst-case climate-change scenarios and arguments for global regulatory intervention. In view of the stakes, this should be no more surprising than conservative intransigence.

International Distribution

The best scientific evidence suggests that the most severe impacts of global warming will be in low-latitude regions where the majority of people are poor. If they are to be spared the worst effects, the requisite resources for adaptation to climate change will have to come from the affluent North. As the endless debate over foreign aid reveals, citizens of the North have very different views about the desirability or the efficacy of aid as "charity." However, providing resources for adaptation looks less like charity than prevention of an epidemic, if we consider the potential for global disruption by climate change. Current political turbulence may pale in comparison with a possible future in which hundreds of millions of people are forced to flee from agricultural collapse and sea-level rise.

To summarize, nonscientific controversies dominate the current debate over climate change policy, and many of them will not be resolved in the near future. But movement on the scientific front, summarized in the IPCC's assessment report, has unquestionably altered the terms of the debate. Even many people who play "conservative" roles in the nonscientific controversies now advocate actions whose stringency would have been unthinkable two decades ago.

The Sources of Global Warming: North or South?

The perception that carbon emissions are the North's problem plays a critical role in the global policy dialogue.[12] Recently, a common southern view of global warming was expressed in a Security Council address by India's United Nations ambassador, who "told the developed nations that the main responsibility for taking action to lessen the threat of climate change rests with them . . . , while efforts to impose greenhouse gas commitments on developing nations would 'simply adversely impact' their prospects of growth."[13] This view implicitly holds that the South's contribution to global warming lags so far behind the North's that the South should defer worrying about its own emissions until it has vanquished extreme poverty.

Much turns on whether the evidence supports this view, which remains largely an article of belief. If the answer is yes, then the South should indeed defer costly mitigation, and a double burden should fall on the North, which should reduce emissions rapidly and compensate any mitigation undertaken by the South. If the answer is no, the converse is true: southern emissions are, by themselves, sufficient to damage the South. In this case, the South's interest dictates cost-effective action to reduce its own emissions, whatever the North has done or will choose to do in the future. And the case for active northern measures to assist southern mitigation becomes all the stronger.

Wheeler and Ummel (2007) test the conventional southern view using the most recent data on carbon emissions from combustion of fossil fuels, cement manufacturing, and land-use change (principally deforestation). They separate countries into the North and South, using regional identifiers

---

12 This section draws heavily on Wheeler and Ummel (2007).

13 Press Trust of India/Factiva, April 20, 2007. In fact, the ambassador was paraphrasing the original "understandings" in the Kyoto Protocol: (1) the largest share of historical and current global emissions of greenhouse gases has originated in the North; (2) per capita emissions in the South are still relatively low; (3) the share of global emissions originating in the South will grow to meet its social and development needs.

in the IPCC's projection scenarios.[14] Table 11.1 displays their estimates of cumulative atmospheric CO_2 in the two regions, separated into the combustion and land-use change components. As the table shows, the North has dominated cumulative emissions from fossil fuel combustion. In 2000, the volume of cumulative atmospheric CO_2 from fossil fuel emissions in the North and South was 372 and 115 gigatons (Gt, a billion tons), respectively. For land-use change, the converse has been true. Extensive deforestation in the South raised its cumulative CO_2 contribution to 180 Gt by 2000, while reforestation in the North led to carbon reabsorption and a decline from a peak in the early 1960s to 58 Gt by 2000. For fossil fuels and land-use change combined, cumulative CO_2 from the South in 2000 was 68.6 percent of cumulative CO_2 from the North: 295 Gt compared with 430 Gt.

To project conditions in the near future, Wheeler and Ummel compute annual CO_2 emissions for the North and South from the IPCC's A1F1 scenario (IPCC 2000). As previously noted, the A1F1 scenario reflects the current aspirations of many developing countries for rapid economic growth without explicit carbon mitigation. Figure 11.6 combines historical emissions from the South and North with scenario-based future emissions. Southern dominance is already emerging in 2007, and by 2025, only 18 years from now, the South's annual emissions are around 32 Gt, which is 32 percent higher than emissions from the North (21 Gt). Figure 11.7 displays cumulative emissions. By 2025 cumulative CO_2 from the South is 91 percent of the North's (555 Gt compared with 609 Gt), and the South takes the lead in about five more years.

Separating cumulative emissions from the North and South permits computing the atmospheric CO_2 concentrations that are attributable to each region. In the South, for example, the result is the preindustrial CO_2 concentration, plus the increment that has been produced by cumulative emissions from the South alone. Figure 11.8 provides an illuminating comparison between the historical global CO_2 concentration and the projected concentration attributable to the South alone. The South's isolated concentration in 2025 matches the measured global concentration in 1986 (350 ppm). By 1986, serious scientific concern about the greenhouse gas effect had already generated a crisis atmosphere that catalyzed the United Nations Conference on Environment and Development in 1992. Figure 11.9 reveals the implication of the South's continued rapid development on the IPCC's A1F1 track for the remainder of the century. Figure 11.9 displays the consequences of development in the South alone, with no historical or future emissions from the North. By 2040, the South passes the current global concentration; by 2060, it passes the 450 ppm threshold that the IPCC associates with large, irreversible impacts on developing countries (IPCC 2007); by 2090 it passes the Stern and Lomborg target (550 ppm); and by 2100 it approaches 600 ppm.

---

14 The North comprises Europe (including Turkey), the former Soviet Union, North America, Japan, Australia, and New Zealand. The South comprises Asia (excluding Japan and the former Soviet Union), Africa, the Middle East, Latin America, the Caribbean, and the Pacific Islands.

Figure 11.6. Annual CO$_2$ Emissions Attributable to the North and the South, 1965–2035

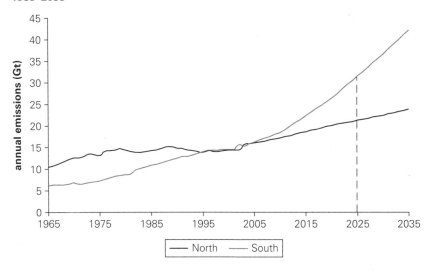

Source: Wheeler and Ummel 2007.

Figure 11.7. Cumulative Atmospheric CO$_2$ Emissions Attributable to the North and the South, 1965–2035

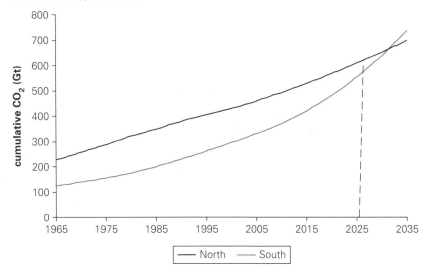

Source: Wheeler and Ummel 2007.

These results show that emissions from the South alone are enough to catalyze a climate crisis for the South. Why should the South have fallen into this trap when it remains much poorer than the North? On reflection, the answer is obvious. The South's population is more than four times greater than the North's, so it has been trapped by the sheer scale of its emissions at a much earlier stage of development.

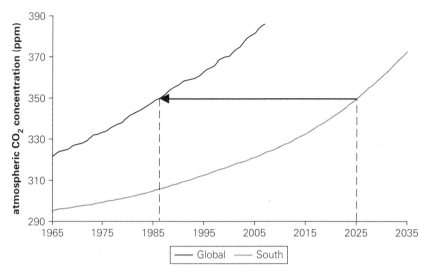

Figure 11.8. Global CO_2 Concentration and Projected Concentration Attributable to the South Alone (IPCC A1F1 Scenario), 1965–2035

Source: Wheeler and Ummel 2007.

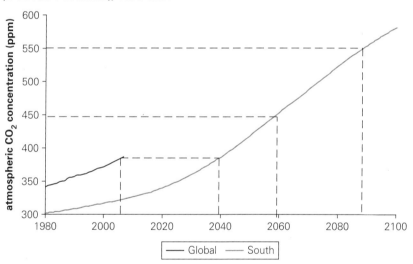

Figure 11.9. Atmospheric CO_2 Concentration Attributed to the South Alone (IPCC A1F1 Scenario), 1980–2100

Source: Wheeler and Ummel 2007.

By implication, the view that carbon emissions are the North's problem is misguided. Cumulative emissions from a carbon-intensive South have already reached levels that are dangerous for the South itself by the IPCC's scientific criteria. Since the South remains poor, this conclusion will undoubtedly be painful for the development community. But it does clarify and simplify the policy options, because it discredits the notion that climate negotiations must pit South against North. To use the analogy of a leaking lifeboat, either occupant is sufficiently bulky to sink the boat unless the leak is patched, and neither can do it alone. It makes no more sense for the South to stay on a carbon-intensive path than it does for the North, so the southern transition should start now, not two or three generations from now.

The Global Distribution of Climate Change Impacts

This year, the IPCC and the World Meteorological Organization (WMO) issued an urgent wake-up call: Global warming is not a future threat—it is here now. Drought conditions have caused unprecedented wildfires and serious agricultural losses in the American Southeast and Southwest, Southern Europe, Africa, and Australia (WMO 2007). William Cline, in his book *Global Warming and Agriculture* (2007), provides the best available country projections for changes in agricultural productivity through 2080. Cline uses the IPCC's A2 forecast, one of the no-mitigation scenarios described in table 11.2.

Cline portrays the impacts of projected temperature and rainfall changes, with and without countervailing effects from carbon fertilization (the impact of higher atmospheric CO_2 on plant growth rates). While the actual magnitude of the carbon fertilization effect remains controversial, both cases signify losses in the range of 15–60 percent, covering much of the southern United States, Central America, northern South America, Africa, the Middle East, South Asia, and Australia. A billion of the world's poorest people live in these areas. Figure 11.10 displays the distribution of projected losses for developing countries without carbon fertilization, by country and subregion. Countries are ordered from greatest to least productivity loss; most have significant losses, and more than 20 have losses greater than 30 percent.

Warmer seas and greater atmospheric moisture are increasing the power of hurricanes, compounding coastal impacts in the United States (Katrina being the most spectacular example), Central America, the Caribbean, East Asia, and South Asia (Emmanuel 2005; Webster and others 2006). The year 2007 also witnessed the first documented hurricane landfalls in Brazil and the Arabian Sea (WMO 2007). Coastal storm surges from hurricane-force winds are increased by sea-level rise, which many climate scientists believe will be accelerated by ice cap melting in this century. IPCC (2007) does not take a clear position on ice cap melting, but recent contributions to the scientific literature suggest that rapid melting in Greenland could raise the sea level by as much as 2 meters in this century (Hanna and others 2005; Lowe and others 2006; Dasgupta and others 2007; Rahmsdorf 2007). Even more extreme possibilities have been suggested by new information from the U.S. National Snow and Ice Data Center, which reports that the ice pack in the Arctic Ocean is melting far faster than previously expected (see figure 11.11; NSIDC

Figure 11.10. Projected Loss in Agricultural Productivity from Climate Change in Developing Countries

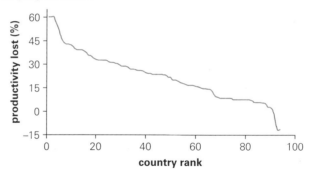

Source: Cline 2007.

Figure 11.11. Area of Arctic Ocean with At Least 15 Percent Sea Ice, 1979–2000 Average and September 2007

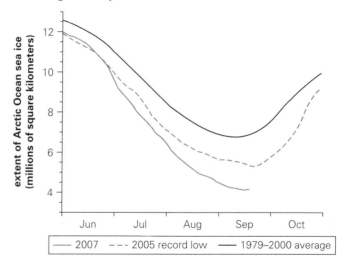

Source: NSIDC 2007.

2007).[15] Dasgupta and others (2007) use the latest digital elevation maps to assess the effects of sea-level rise and higher storm surges. For developing countries, they estimate the potential impact in inundation zones to be from 1 to 5 meters above sea level during the next century. With sea-level rise of 3 meters, major food-producing delta areas in countries

---

15 According to NSIDC (2007), "The minimum [sea ice cover] for 2007 shatters the previous five-day minimum set on September 20–21, 2005, by 1.19 million square kilometers (460,000 square miles), roughly the size of Texas and California combined, or nearly five United Kingdoms." Reacting to this development, Mark Serreze, an Arctic specialist at the NSIDC, is quoted in the *Guardian* (September 5, 2007) as saying, "It's amazing. It's simply fallen off a cliff, and we're still losing ice . . . If you asked me a couple of years ago when the Arctic could lose all of its ice, then I would have said 2100, or 2070 maybe. But now I think that 2030 is a reasonable estimate. It seems that the Arctic is going to be a very different place within our lifetimes and certainly within our children's lifetimes."

Figure 11.12. Projected Percentage of Population Displaced by a 3-Meter Sea-Level Rise in Coastal Developing Countries

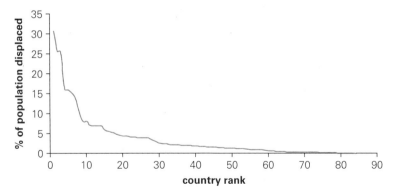

Source: Dasgupta and others 2007.

like the Arab Republic of Egypt, Bangladesh, and Vietnam would be inundated. More than 200 million people in developing countries live in the 5-meter impact zone and would become refugees from coastal flooding at a 3-meter sea-level rise. Figure 11.12 displays the distribution of impacts on coastal developing-country population for a 3-meter sea-level rise. The distribution is highly skewed: some coastal countries are heavily affected, but many have relatively low percentage impacts.[16]

A warmer world will also be a wetter world, as greater evaporation leads to more moisture and much heavier rainfall in some areas. Again, this is not a future threat. A WMO report issued in August 2007 notes unprecedented rainfall and flooding in Western Europe and South Asia as well as heavy flooding in China (WMO 2007). Although some departure from historical patterns will probably occur, the general expectation is that future problems from flooding will be like past problems, only more severe. In this context, recent work has quantified the relative severity of flood-related damage across countries (Wheeler 2007). Figure 11.13 displays the distribution of flood-damage risks across developing countries. It is tremendously skewed, with a few countries experiencing per capita damages that are far above the others. Wheeler's results also indicate that flood-damage risks are far higher in developing countries, even though flooding is only slightly more frequent than in developed countries (Wheeler 2007).

To summarize, recent impact projections for global warming indicate large but highly variable losses for developing countries. While the results presented in this section include significantly more country detail than the regional projections in IPCC (2007), they are basically consistent with those projections. Projections have shown that warming in this century may improve agricultural conditions in some northern-latitude countries. For the

---

16 Of course, relatively small percentage changes can translate into large absolute impacts. China provides the best example, with 4 percent of the population—51 million people—affected by a 3-meter sea-level rise.

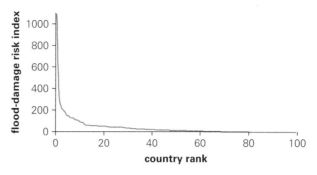

Figure 11.13. Flood-Damage Risk Index in Developing Countries, 1960–2000

Source: Wheeler 2007.

rest, however, the most likely prospects include increased droughts, wild-fires, floods, coastal storms and inundation, large-scale population displacements, and enormous financial losses. Although the benefit-cost analyses of Stern, Nordhaus, and others attempt to quantify these destructive impacts, the stark truth is that global society has not encountered anything like them since World War II.

Addressing the Problem

To summarize the previous two sections, the South is moving rapidly toward dominant status as both a source and a victim of global warming. The evidence suggests that the South's own cumulative emissions will soon reach crisis levels, regardless of northern emissions, and the converse is obviously true for the North. Confronting climate change therefore demands full participation and cooperation by both developed and developing countries.

Ultimately, there should be nothing to worry about if the global community is sensible and flexible. Encouraging evidence is provided by Vinod Khosla, who has been called the best venture capitalist in the world by *Forbes Magazine* (Pontin 2007). Khosla now focuses almost exclusively on scalable investments in solar power, and it is easy to see why. The sun annually bathes the earth in 80,000 terawatts of energy, while current human power consumption is about 15 terawatts. As figure 11.14 shows, current solar technology could power the whole United States from a small portion of Nevada.

What is true for the United States is also true for the world. With existing technologies, solar and other renewable energy sources can power most countries with room to spare. Recently, Buys and others (2007) have quantified renewable energy potentials for 200 countries, basing their calculations on technologies that can be implemented now. Their results show that renewable energy potential meets or exceeds total energy demand in almost

Figure 11.14. Area in Nevada Required to Power the Entire United States with Solar Energy

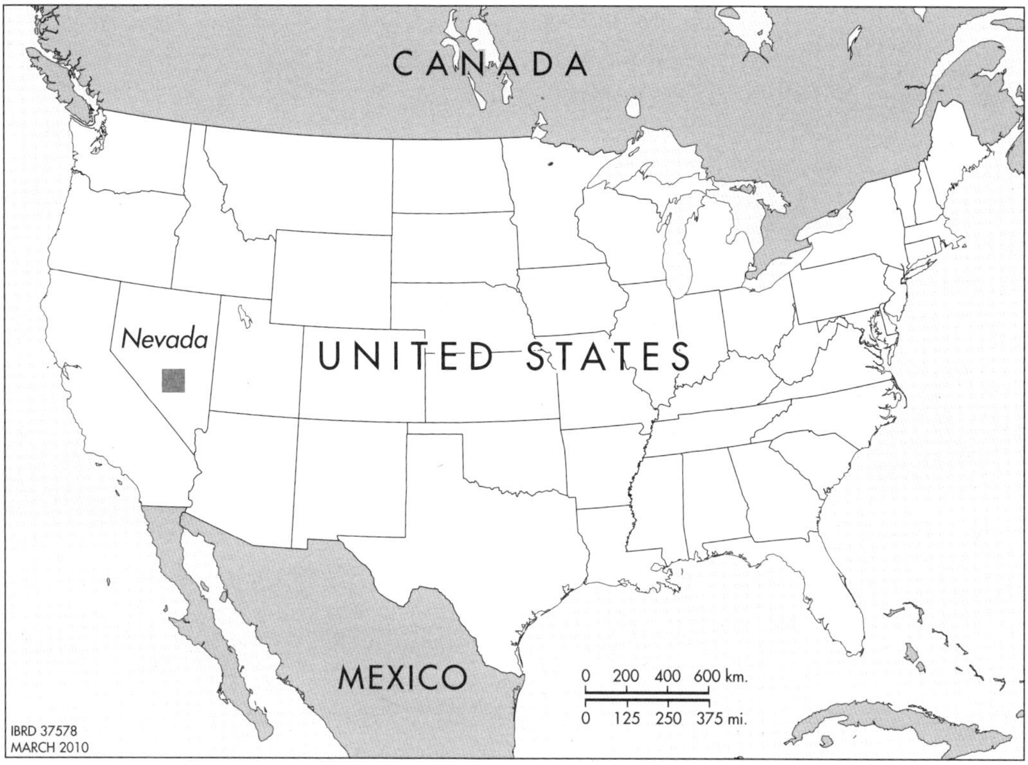

Source: Based on Khosla and O'Donnell 2006.

every country in the world's developing regions, including Brazil, China, and India. The global community can cooperate to harness this potential, in a collective exercise of will, imagination, and, not least, leadership. Politically, this will require a significant, probably simultaneous change of posture by the United States and China—the two largest emitters, each justifying recalcitrance by blaming the other. China invokes distributional arguments because the wealthy United States remains on the sidelines; the United States claims that costly mitigation would be useless as long as China does not act. This stand-off has to end before global cooperation on climate change can move to the next level.

Rapid change will come from programs that create strong incentives to reduce carbon emissions, lower the cost of clean energy, leverage private sector financing for a rapid transition, accelerate the transition in developing countries, and assist them with adaptation to the warming that is already inevitable. Mobilizing the global community for fast, efficient action will require unprecedented coordination of assistance; clear, evidence-based investment priorities; and commitment to honest trial-and-error learning as investments are scaled up.

Creating Incentives to Reduce Carbon Emissions

Creating effective incentives for carbon reduction will require some form of emissions regulation, which has developed in three "waves" since the 1960s (Tietenberg and Wheeler 2001; Wheeler and others 2000). In the first wave, until the 1980s for most countries, the focus was solely on command-and-control regulation. Polluters were given fixed regulatory limits (quantities, waste-stream intensities, or required technology installations) and subjected to escalating penalties as they progressively exceeded these limits. While this has remained the dominant approach to pollution regulation in most countries, its inherent inefficiency has been aptly criticized on several grounds. It does nothing to reward polluters who reduce pollution beyond compliance norms, it pays no attention to differences in pollution control costs, and it frequently entails burdensome technical specifications that must be updated constantly.

In reaction, the second wave focused on market-based regulatory instruments. Broadly, these instruments are separated into two classes. Pollution charges impose a charge on each unit of pollution and leave polluters free to decide how much to pollute. Charges have obvious, desirable efficiency properties, since they enable polluters to treat the environment as another "priced input" and optimize accordingly. They have achieved acceptance in some countries, particularly for water pollutants. However, their influence in many societies has remained limited because of inevitable uncertainty about the relationship between the charge and polluters' response. For dangerous pollutants, any given charge may prove insufficient to induce collective pollution reduction sufficient to reduce the hazard to a tolerable level. In principle, this can be handled through constant monitoring of the response and adjustment of the charge to move total pollution to the desired level (Baumol and Oates 1971). In practice, such adjustment has proven difficult because most political systems do not easily accommodate this kind of information-driven flexibility.

The other market-based approach addresses uncertainty about total pollution by imposing an overall limit on emissions, distributing unit emissions permits by some means, and then allowing polluters to buy and sell the permits as conditions warrant. Typically, marketable permit systems begin by accepting current total pollution and allocating permits to polluters in proportion to their emissions. From an efficiency perspective, it would be far better to auction the permits, just as governments auction broadcast spectrum, but this has rarely happened in the case of pollution. After initial permits are issued, total allowable pollution is periodically reduced, and polluters are allowed to trade permits as their economic circumstances warrant. Over time, total pollution falls, and economic efficiency is enhanced by the permits market. This approach is no panacea, however. Resolution of uncertainty about total pollution creates uncertainty about the price of polluting. This is the price of a unit emissions permit, which will vary over time in a complex trading system. Permit prices may prove inordinately high if overall reductions are too ambitious. In addition, marketable permit systems require the creation of a new and complex trading institution that requires constant oversight.

In response to such difficulties, a third wave of regulation emerged in the 1990s. The third wave is public disclosure, in which governments require firms to reveal their emissions to the public. Public disclosure systems arose to address problems with both command-and-control and market-based systems. They first emerged to address toxic pollution, because the sheer number of toxic pollutants exceeded the capacity of formal regulatory systems. Then they spread to other pollutants, particularly in developing countries, as their advantages became apparent. First, their transparency and relative simplicity enhance their appeal in weak institutional environments. Second, they introduce more flexibility than formal regulatory systems, by substituting multiple agents with multiple incentives for a single formal regulatory agent. Whatever the formal requirement (command-and-control regulation, tradable permit price, unit pollution charge), many stakeholders will prefer better environmental performance than the requirement. Public disclosure empowers these stakeholders to make their influence felt through many market and nonmarket channels (Tietenberg and Wheeler 2001; Wheeler and others 2000). Third, public disclosure demonstrably works. In both developing and developed countries, disclosure of plant-level pollution has led to rapid, significant reduction of pollution from many facilities (Dasgupta, Wang, and Wheeler 2006).

Which regulatory approach will work best for reducing carbon emissions? Both pollution charges and tradable permits have strong partisans, and debate about their relative merits continues. Meanwhile, the first step toward efficient regulation seems obvious, eminently practical, and highly desirable for many reasons: *global, mandatory public disclosure of emissions from all significant sources as soon as possible, with third-party vetting of the information.* This should have first priority for several reasons. First, it is a simple signal that participants are serious. Disclosure imposes no binding legal requirements, so it can be undertaken without imposing any direct costs on economic agents. Second, it is a necessary prelude to formal regulation. For command-and-control or market-based instruments to work credibly in the global arena, they will have to operate in a transparent, audited information environment. Starting disclosure now will work out the kinks in the information system, establish the principle of transparency, and develop generally accepted emissions benchmarks for formal regulation. Third, disclosure itself will activate many stakeholders who will, in turn, bring myriad pressures to bear on global polluters to reduce their emissions. If prior experience with other pollutants is any guide, the resulting emissions reductions will be surprisingly large. Disclosure offers particular promise at the current juncture, because global norms are clearly shifting toward insistence on the limitation of greenhouse emissions. It should begin immediately and continue once formal regulation begins. It is essential for transparency, credibility, and avoidance of corruption in regulatory monitoring and enforcement.

After public disclosure is well established, it will be possible to make a credible stab at formal regulation. Which system would be most feasible and desirable? [17] To date, tradable permit (cap-and-trade) systems have dominated the global discussion. They have the advantages of precedent (the Kyoto Protocol uses cap-and-trade) and relative certainty in the determination of overall emissions, particularly if public disclosure has established credible benchmarks. However, global cap-and-trade raises the prospect of large international financial transfers if the overall emissions limit has teeth. The magnitudes are potentially very large, and it seems unlikely that many national political systems could accommodate them very easily. In addition, the global institution needed to administer a cap-and-trade system would inevitably be large, complex, and charged with brokering the exceptions that haunt systems that control quantities. There is also the problem of the initial allocation of permits. Auctions have proven difficult to implement, because existing polluters organize to fight them politically. But giving initial permits to those polluters would reward them with a valuable property right and disadvantage newcomers. In summary, a truly global cap-and-trade system seems problematic. If operated efficiently, it could enforce an overall emissions reduction target, but the resulting permit price could not be predicted with any accuracy. Accordingly, a politically acceptable cap-and-trade program will have to include rules for adjusting the supply of permits as the price response is revealed.[18]

Emissions charges have several appealing characteristics in this context. First, they can be administered within each country on a fiscally neutral basis. Charge revenues can be used to reduce other taxes, some of which may be highly distortionary. Second, charges do not require the establishment of a complex institution to establish new property rights and monitor exchanges within the system. Third, revenues accrue to society, while tradable permits that are distributed without auctions deliver the potential revenue streams to existing polluters. Of course, the principal weakness of charge systems remains: their quantity effects are uncertain, and adjustments will be necessary as those effects become apparent.[19] And in some societies (particularly the United States), a deep aversion to new taxes might not be mollified by a guarantee of fiscal neutrality. Finally, at the global scale, a uniform charge system would collide with the same complexities that make a uniform cap-and-trade system problematic. Countries with very different initial conditions may simply refuse to accept a

---

17 Cogent support for charges can be found in Mankiw (2007); Nordhaus (2007c). For useful assessments of the European Union cap-and-trade system for carbon emissions, see Convery and Redmond (2007); Ellerman and Buchner (2007); Kruger, Oates, and Pizer (2007).

18 For discussion, see McKibbin and Wilcoxen (2002); Olmstead and Stavins (2006); Pizer (2002).

19 For elaboration of this approach as applied to conventional pollutants, see Baumol and Oates (1971).

globally uniform system that ignores the economic implications of those conditions.[20]

Given all these complexities, it seems likely that some countries will prefer charges, some will choose cap-and-trade, and some may choose inefficient quantity-based measures for political reasons (for example, progressive elimination of coal-based power through closure of mines, reduction of imports, and forced closure of coal-fired plants). In this hybrid setting, international negotiations will probably focus on target emissions for participating countries. Continued participation and at least rough compliance will be motivated by public pressure, the threat of sanctions in various economic arenas, the threat of punitive damages in an evolving international judicial system, the risk of severe political turbulence from environmental disasters, and the risk that recalcitrants will be shunned by their traditional allies.

Such a system will be far from perfect, but it would be unrealistic to expect a smoothly functioning system in a world where country stakes in the climate change problem are so diverse. In any case, the first and crucial step on the path forward is clear, doable, and necessary for all that follows. *We should move as quickly as possible to full, mandatory, third-party-audited public disclosure of greenhouse gas emissions from all significant sources. If the global community can accomplish that in the near future, it will be well positioned to move toward formal market-based instruments.*

Pricing Carbon

Nordhaus (2007b), Stern (2006), and others have estimated the carbon charges (or auctioned permit prices) consistent with different levels of emissions control. The underlying economic logic supports a charge that rises over time. At present, most damages are in the relatively distant future, and there are plentiful high-return opportunities for conventional investment. Investment should become more intensive in emissions reduction as climate-related damage rises, and rising charges will provide the requisite incentive to reduce emissions. The optimal "ramp" for charges depends on factors such as the discount rate, abatement costs, the potential for technological learning, and the scale and irreversibility of damage from climate change (Nordhaus 2007a). As we have seen, these factors remain contentious. It is therefore not surprising that different studies establish very different ramps. Nordhaus's preferred path begins at about $8 per ton of CO_2, rising to about $23 per ton by 2050. Stern's initial charge is 10 times higher—$82 per ton—and his ramp is steeper. IPCC (2007) cites a variety of studies whose initial values average $12 per ton, distributed across a range from $3–$95 per ton.

We are clearly a long way from reaching a consensus on pricing carbon, but it is critical to make a start, with all countries participating if possible. Even if initial carbon charges are at the modest end of the range, the revenue

---

20 For example, Brazil's energy sector relies heavily on hydropower and biofuels, which have zero net carbon emissions, while the U.S. energy sector is heavily dependent on carbon-intensive coal-fired plants.

implications are significant. Nordhaus's initial charge ($8 per ton of CO_2), if applied uniformly to current northern CO_2 emissions (16.5 Gt), would generate more than $130 billion. Some of this revenue could be earmarked for financing clean-technology R&D, rapid adoption of clean technology by developing countries, and assistance to those countries for adapting to the global warming that is inevitable. With such a revenue base, the annual clean-energy R&D budget recommended by Lomborg (2007)—$25 billion—could easily be financed.

Lowering the Price of Clean Energy

An international commitment to significant emissions reduction will probably not be sustainable without rapid expansion of low-cost, clean-energy options. To achieve this, the North should promote large-scale, cost-effective R&D and scale economies in the production of clean technologies. These should be understood to include energy-efficient designs for buildings, vehicles, and power transmission as well as direct carbon-saving designs. Once clean technologies have been developed, coordinated mass purchases can reduce their unit costs by exploiting learning curves.

Promoting Clean-Energy Investments

In developed countries, higher carbon prices and lower clean-technology prices should be sufficient to promote a rapid transition because capital markets work well. For developing countries, however, two additional elements will be necessary to promote a rapid transition: efficient financial and technical assistance and attractive conditions for private investment. Effective international assistance for a rapid transition will require unprecedented coordination among aid agencies, international financial institutions, and nongovernmental organizations (NGOs). And respecting the evidence will be critical for success. A uniform approach will not work because countries have vastly different portfolios of renewable resources. Recently, Buys and others (2007) have quantified renewable energy resources that can be exploited with existing technologies in more than 200 countries. To illustrate, the shares of renewable energy are very high by world standards in solar for Peru (61 percent) and Egypt (64 percent); biofuels for Mongolia (87 percent) and Uganda (83 percent); hydro for Nepal (53 percent) and Papua New Guinea (28 percent); wind for Cape Verde (71 percent) and China (21 percent); and geothermal for Turkmenistan (11 percent) and Indonesia (6 percent).

Supporting Adaptation to Global Warming

Global warming is well under way, and its consequences are already visible in many developing countries. According to some analysts, severe drought lurks behind the Darfur conflict (Faris 2007). A rising sea level is driving thousands of people off islands in the Sunderbans of India and Bangladesh (Sengupta 2007); and catastrophic flooding has accompanied torrential rains in China, India, and elsewhere (WMO 2007). The poorest countries are least capable of adapting to such impacts, and the poorest people in those countries are hardest hit. This situation is bound to get much worse before it gets better, even if the international community mobilizes a major assault on global warming. In fact, mass dislocation and impoverishment may threaten the international order, so the North has both humanitarian and self-interested reasons to promote international assistance for adaptation in developing countries.

Evidence-based allocations will be critical in this context. Conventional approaches based on standard per capita allocations or national political ties would be extremely wasteful, because countries face such different conditions. For example, Cline (2007) finds that agricultural productivity losses from global warming in Africa will vary from more than 50 percent in Sudan and Senegal to around 5 percent in Kenya. In Latin America, they will vary from more than 35 percent in Mexico to 11 percent in Argentina. As noted, projected patterns of inundation from sea-level rise show even more skewed patterns among coastal countries, with nearly one-third of the population displaced in some and very low percentages in others. As figure 11.13 shows, the skew is even more extreme for flood-damage risks.

While limiting climate change is a critical priority, it should not supersede programs that directly address other global priorities such as poverty reduction and communicable disease control. To meet this challenge, new financial resources will have to be mobilized from the private and public sectors. Most of the clean-energy revolution can be financed by massive capital infusions from the private sector, but only if the relative price of clean energy makes it an attractive investment. This transition will be accelerated by policies that put a high price on carbon, lower the price of clean energy, and maximize the efficiency of assistance for clean-energy development in poor countries.

A Program for Global Action

The international response to climate change should incorporate cost-effectiveness principles, the flexibility to accommodate changes in information and an evolving policy consensus, and universal participation. Although the details remain contentious, there is clearly some consensus on operating principles. There is widespread agreement that effective global action should incorporate four dimensions: emissions mitigation, clean-technology development, clean-technology diffusion, and adaptation to climate change. There is also agreement that market-based instruments will promote efficient mitigation, by confronting polluters with a uniform carbon price that is consistent with the overall mitigation goal.

Public Disclosure

This provides one keynote for immediate action, because implementation of any market-based instrument requires a monitoring-and-enforcement system based on accurate information about carbon emissions from all regulated sources. The global consensus supports carbon pricing via market-based instruments, but there is no agreement yet on the appropriate instrument or carbon price level. Nevertheless, agreement on the basic principles automatically implies acceptance of the supporting information system. This determines priority action 1: *Immediately establish an international institution mandated to collect, verify, and publicly disclose information about emissions from all significant global carbon sources. Its mandate should extend to best-practice estimation and disclosure of emissions sources in countries that initially refuse to participate.*

This institution will serve four purposes. First, it will lay the necessary foundation for implementing any market-based mitigation system. Second, it will provide an excellent credibility test, since a country's acceptance of full disclosure will signal its true willingness to participate in globally efficient mitigation. Third, global public disclosure will itself reduce carbon emissions, by focusing stakeholder pressure on major emitters and providing reputational rewards for clean producers. A large body of experience and research on pollution disclosure systems has shown that they significantly reduce pollution (Dasgupta, Wang, and Wheeler 2006). Fourth, disclosure will make it very hard to cheat once market-based instruments are implemented. This will be essential for preserving the credibility of an international mitigation agreement.

Some precedents already exist or soon will. The European Union's emissions trading system incorporates public information on European carbon emitters provided by the European Environment Agency.[21] To demonstrate the potential of global disclosure, the Center for Global Development has launched two Web sites: one publishes CO_2 emissions from more than 40,000 global power producers, and the other provides timely information on tropical forest clearing at a high level of spatial resolution.[22]

Global Consortia

The global response to climate change has four critical dimensions: reduction of greenhouse gas emissions, accelerated development of clean technologies, financing for their rapid diffusion in developing countries, and support for developing-country adaptation to the impacts of unavoidable climate change. Major stakeholders and implementation issues are different in each dimension. This defines priority action 2: *establish four collaborating global consortia—one for each dimension—that will set objectives and priorities using the best available scientific, technical, and economic assessments; avoid program overlaps where possible; and invest to achieve the most cost-effective global results.* Operations of the consortia will be transparent and independently audited for results.

---

21 European Pollutant Emission Register, available at http://eper.ec.europa.eu/eper/flashmap.asp. The register includes CO_2 emissions reports for several hundred major emitters in the European Union.

22 The power sector Web site, www.carma.org, was launched in mid-November 2007. The user interface permits detailed assessment of CO_2 emissions by individual power plants, their parent companies, and geographic areas. The forest-clearing Web site, www.cgdev.org/forest, was launched in mid-November 2009. All data on both sites are downloadable.

Consensus about the strength and direction of action in each dimension has yet to emerge, so the consortia should be initiated in "soft" form, with charters that permit hardening as the consensus develops. Operation in the soft spectrum will focus on building information systems that identify opportunities for cost-effective coordination of national and international programs in each sphere. Hardening will include endowment with extra-sovereign powers, mandated elimination of duplication among the efforts of individual agencies, rejection of political criteria in favor of benefit-cost assessment, and full public accountability.

Large-scale public sector financing for R&D and assistance to developing countries should come from programs that raise the price of carbon. As noted, emissions charges or auctioned tradable permits will generate significant resources, even if the initial carbon price is modest. International financial institutions, bilateral aid agencies, and NGOs can all play useful roles in channeling these resources, but only if they abandon their fragmented, overlapping, politicized approach to aid. New resources should only be provided to participating agencies that agree to a transparent, coordinated program that sets evidence-based priorities, operates with clear standards of accountability, and employs independent auditors to measure progress.

The "hard" versions of these consortia are obviously novel by traditional standards, but they will be necessary if global society decides that rapid adjustment is needed to avoid a critical climate threshold. The "soft" versions will provide a useful way station, in any case, if the international community decides to gear up for concerted action. So their establishment as collaborative, public-information-intensive groups seems warranted in any case. Once they are in place, it will be easier to adjust toward hard measures if the global community decides that they are needed. There can be little doubt that the successful operation of these consortia over many years would strengthen the institutional foundations of global governance and offer a useful precedent for other international collective-action problems.

Mitigation

The first consortium will address the global mitigation problem directly. In the soft version, it will develop indicative target paths for national emissions and provide in-depth public information so that the global community can judge countries' adherence to the target paths. In its hard version, the consortium will secure credible commitments to policies consistent with agreed adjustment paths, provide assistance to participants with weak implementing institutions, and enforce sanctions for noncompliance. Path-consistent policies will raise public revenues by implementing efficient market-based instruments (carbon charges or auctioned tradable permits). Revenues from implementation in high-income countries will provide financing for the activities of the other three consortia.

These three consortia will be charged with accelerating clean-technology development, promoting rapid diffusion of clean technologies to developing countries, and financing adaptation to unavoidable global warming. In their soft form, they will provide global coordination facilities and in-depth public information to promote collaboration among national and international agencies and NGOs. In their hard form, they will embody clear, progressive organizational principles: setting of evidence-based priorities, elimination of program overlaps, coordination of grants and low-cost loans, and independent, transparent accounting of results. The following discussion focuses on hard implementation, but many elements could be pursued on an indicative basis as part of a transparent system of international collaboration.

Clean-Technology R&D

To promote R&D, the G-8 and other developed nations should sponsor an international clean-technology development consortium committed to major increases in funding, minimum redundancy in national programs, rapid publication of results, and management of patenting to ensure competitive development of promising technologies. Consortium resources could also support very large monetary awards for development of clean technologies that meet prespecified criteria, as well as acceleration of cost reduction through guaranteed mass-purchase arrangements for promising technologies.

Clean-Technology Diffusion

The clean-technology diffusion consortium will operate principally in developing countries. This consortium will finance clean-energy systems on concessional terms that undercut fossil energy systems and sharply reduce traditional assistance costs by managing all resources from bilateral and multilateral agencies as parts of one portfolio. It will tailor the scale and sectoral composition of assistance to the conditions of individual countries, invest only in emissions-free technologies, and avoid political allocations.

What will prevent clean-energy assistance from foundering on the same shoals—red tape, corruption, political interference—that have haunted other forms of development assistance? To be successful, the clean-energy consortium and developing-country leaders will have to strike a grand bargain that has several elements. On the consortium side, these will include an unprecedented offer to promote rapid, large-scale energy development on very generous terms; an explicit, long-term commitment to maintain the systems that have been installed; and a single collaborative-assistance relationship instead of the current cross-agency babble. In return, recipient countries will make commitments to explicit emissions targets that are consistent with the assistance package; clear sanctions for noncompliance; strict accountability and transparency in the use of assistance; and openness to private investment in clean energy.

Adaptation

The adaptation consortium will use grants to finance developing-country adaptation to unavoidable climate change. Its operating principles will be similar to those of the clean-technology diffusion consortium: consolidation of bilateral and multilateral assistance in one portfolio, programs tailored to the conditions in individual countries, and avoidance of political allocations. Effective large-scale assistance will require unprecedented coordination among aid agencies, international financial institutions, and NGOs.

For efficient allocation, particular importance will attach to tailoring the scale and focus of allocation to the nature of the problems. For example, adaptive infrastructure and urbanization programs will be appropriate for Vietnam, Egypt, and Suriname, where inundation from sea-level rise will be massive. Adaptive agriculture and urban relocation should be the focus of assistance in countries facing huge agricultural productivity losses, such as Sudan, Senegal, India, and Mexico. Broader micro insurance coverage for the poor should also be part of these programs. Programs combining adaptive infrastructure and micro insurance should be the focus for countries facing high flood-disaster risks, such as Bangladesh, Cambodia, Benin, Mozambique, Jamaica, and Honduras.

Summary and Conclusions

This chapter has argued that among climate scientists, there is no longer any serious debate about whether greenhouse gas emissions from human activity are altering the earth's climate. There is also a broad consensus that efficient mitigation of emissions will require carbon pricing via market-based instruments (charges or auctioned tradable permits). The remaining controversies stem mostly from uncertainties regarding economic and technological forecasts, disputes about global and intergenerational equity, and political divisions over collective measures to combat climate change. Different positions on the nonscientific issues still drive very different conclusions about the scale, scope, and timing of the needed measures. Near-term closure seems unlikely on any of these fronts, but the science is now sufficiently compelling that a global consensus supports concerted action. The interesting policy questions focus on designing and implementing appropriate measures. Developing countries must be full participants, because they will be most heavily affected by global warming and because the scale of their emissions is rapidly approaching parity with that of developed countries. To meet the challenge, this chapter has advocated two priority actions that will lay the foundations for a cost-effective response to global warming.

The first priority is to undertake global emissions disclosure to support efficient carbon pricing. The United Nations should immediately establish an international institution mandated to collect, verify, and publicly disclose information about emissions from all significant global carbon sources. Its mandate should extend to best-practice estimation and disclosure of emissions sources in countries that initially refuse to participate. This institution will serve four purposes. First, it will lay the necessary foundation for implementing a market-based mitigation system. Second, it will provide an excellent credibility test, since a country's acceptance of full disclosure will signal its true willingness to participate in globally efficient mitigation. Third, global public disclosure will itself reduce carbon emissions, by focusing stakeholder pressure on major emitters and providing reputational rewards for clean producers. Fourth, disclosure will make it very hard to cheat once market-based instruments are implemented. This will be essential for preserving the credibility of an international mitigation agreement.

The second priority is to create consortia to orchestrate the global response to climate change in four critical dimensions: reducing greenhouse emissions, accelerating the development of clean technologies, financing their rapid diffusion in developing countries, and supporting developing countries in their efforts to adapt to the impacts of unavoidable climate change. Separate consortia seem warranted because major stakeholders and implementation issues are different in each dimension. To support the global response, the United Nations should establish four collaborating global consortia, one for each dimension, that will set objectives and priorities using the best available scientific and technical evidence, avoid program overlaps, and invest to achieve the most cost-effective global results. Their operations should be transparent and independently audited for results. Consensus about the strength and direction of action in each dimension has yet to emerge, so the consortia should be initiated in "soft" form, with charters that permit hardening as the consensus develops. Operation in the soft spectrum will focus on building information systems that identify opportunities for cost-effective coordination of national and international programs in each sphere. Hardening will include endowment with extra-sovereign powers, mandated elimination of duplication among individual-agency efforts, rejection of political criteria in favor of benefit-cost assessment, and full public accountability.

References

Baumol, William, and Wallace Oates. 1971. "The Use of Standards and Prices for Protection of the Environment." *Swedish Journal of Economics* 73 (1): 42–54.

Birdsall, Nancy. 1992. "Another Look at Population and Global Warming." Policy Research Working Paper 1020. World Bank, Washington, DC.

Buys, Piet, Uwe Deichmann, Craig Meisner, Thao Ton-That, and David Wheeler. 2007. "Country Stakes in Climate Change Negotiations: Two Dimensions of Vulnerability." Policy Research Working Paper 4300. World Bank, Washington, DC.

Cline, William. 2007. *Global Warming and Agriculture: Impact Estimates by Country*. Washington, DC: Center for Global Development and Peterson Institute for International Economics.

Convery, Frank, and Luke Redmond. 2007. "Market and Price Developments in the European Union Emissions Trading Scheme." *Review of Environmental Economics and Policy* 1 (1): 88–111.

Dasgupta, Partha. 2007. "A Challenge to Kyoto: Standard Cost-Benefit Analysis May Not Apply to the Economics of Climate Change." *Nature* 449 (13): 143–44.

Dasgupta, Susmita, Benoit Laplante, Craig Meisner, David Wheeler, and Jianping Yan. 2007. "The Impact of Sea-Level Rise on Developing Countries: A Comparative Analysis." Policy Research Working Paper 4136. World Bank, Washington, DC.

Dasgupta, Susmita, Benoit Laplante, Hua Wang, and David Wheeler. 2002. "Confronting the Environmental Kuznets Curve." *Journal of Economic Perspectives* 16 (1): 147–68.

Dasgupta, Susmita, Hua Wang, and David Wheeler. 2006. "Disclosure Strategies for Pollution Control." In *The International Yearbook of Environmental and Resource Economics 2006/2007: A Survey of Current Issues,* ed. Tom Tietenberg and Henk Folmer. Cheltenham, U.K.: Edward Elgar.

Ehrlich, Paul, and Anne Ehrlich. 1991. *Healing the Planet.* New York: Addison-Wesley.

Ehrlich, Paul, and John Holdren. 1971. "Impact of Population Growth." *Science* 171 (3977): 1212–17.

Ellerman, A. Denny, and Barbara Buchner. 2007. "The European Union Emissions Trading Scheme: Origins, Allocation, and Early Results." *Review of Environmental Economics and Policy* 1 (1): 66–87.

Emmanuel, Kerry. 2005. "Increasing Destructiveness of Tropical Cyclones over the Past 30 Years." *Nature* 436 (4): 686–88.

Faris, Stephan. 2007. "The Real Roots of Darfur." *Atlantic Monthly* (April). www.theatlantic.com/doc/prem/200704/darfur-climate.

Hanna, Edward, Philippe Huybrechts, Ives Janssens, John Cappelen, Konrad Steffen, and Ag Stephens. 2005. "Runoff and Mass Balance of the Greenland Ice Sheet: 1958–2003." *Journal of Geophysical Research* 110: D13108.

IPCC (Intergovernmental Panel on Climate Change). 2000. *IPCC Special Report: Emissions Scenarios.* Geneva: World Meteorological Association. www .ipcc.ch/pub/sres-e.pdf.

———. 2007. *Fourth Assessment Report.* Geneva: World Meteorological Association. www.ipcc.ch.

Keeling, Charles, Stephen Piper, Robert Bacastow, Martin Wahlen, Timothy Whorf, Martin Heimann, and Harro Meijer. 2007. "Exchanges of Atmospheric CO_2 and $13CO_2$ with the Terrestrial Biosphere and Oceans from 1978 to 2000." University of California, San Diego. Updated through 2007. http://scrippsco2.ucsd.edu/data/data.html.

Khosla, Vinod, and John O'Donnell. 2006. "Solar Flare: Making Coal Obsolete." www.khoslaventures.com/presentations/solarflare_final.ppt.

Kruger, Joseph, Wallace Oates, and William Pizer. 2007. "Decentralization in the EU Emissions Trading Scheme and Lessons for Global Policy." *Review of Environmental Economics and Policy* 1 (1): 112–33.

Lomborg, Bjorn. 2001. *The Skeptical Environmentalist: Measuring the Real State of the World.* Cambridge, U.K.: Cambridge University Press.

———. 2007. *Cool It: The Skeptical Environmentalist's Guide to Global Warming*. New York: Alfred A. Knopf.

Lowe, Jason, Jonathan Gregory, Jeff Ridley, Philippe Huybrechts, Robert Nicholls, and Matthews Collins. 2006. "The Role of Sea-Level Rise and the Greenland Ice Sheet in Dangerous Climate Change: Implications for the Stabilization of Climate." In *Avoiding Dangerous Climate Change*, ed. Hans Schellnhuber, Wolfgang Cramer, Nebojsa Nakicenovic, Tom Wigley, and Gary Yohe, 29–36. Cambridge, U.K.: Cambridge University Press.

Mankiw, N. Gregory. 2007. "One Answer to Global Warming: A New Tax." *New York Times*, September 17. www.nytimes.com/2007/09/16/business/16view.html?_r=1&adxnnl=1&oref=slogin&adxnnlx=1190059656-X9GgmU9Zm2LV7Q7Ebk415Q.

Marchitto, Thomas, Scott Lehman, Joseph Ortiz, Jacqueline Flückiger, and Alexander van Geen. 2007. "Marine Radiocarbon Evidence for the Mechanism of Deglacial Atmospheric CO_2 Rise." *Science* 316 (5830): 1456–59.

McKibbin, Warwick, and Peter Wilcoxen. 2002. "The Role of Economics in Climate Change Policy." *Journal of Economic Perspectives* 16 (2): 107–29.

Neftel, A., and others. 1994. "Historical Carbon Dioxide Record from the Siple Station Ice Core." University of Bern, Switzerland. Reported by the Carbon Dioxide Information Analysis Center at http://cdiac.esd.ornl.gov/ftp/trends/co2/siple2.013. Reported by the World Resources Institute at http://earthtrends.wri.org/searchable_db/index.php?theme=3&variable_ID=82&action=select_countries.

NOAA (National Oceanic and Atmospheric Administration). 2007. *Global Warming*. Washington, DC: NOAA. http://lwf.ncdc.noaa.gov/oa/climate/globalwarming.html#Q1.

Nordhaus, William. 2007a. "The Challenge of Global Warming: Economic Models and Environmental Policy." Department of Economics, Yale University (July 24).

———. 2007b. "Critical Assumptions in the Stern Review on Climate Change." *Science* 317 (July 13): 201–02.

———. 2007c. "To Tax or Not to Tax: Alternative Approaches to Slowing Global Warming." *Review of Environmental Economics and Policy* 1 (1): 26–44.

NSIDC (National Snow and Ice Data Center). 2007. "Overview of Current Sea Ice Conditions." NSIDC, Boulder, CO (September 20). http://nsidc.org/news/press/2007_seaiceminimum/20070810_index.html.

Olmstead, Sheila, and Robert Stavins. 2006. "An International Policy Architecture for the Post-Kyoto Era." *American Economic Review Papers and Proceedings* 96 (2, May): 35–38.

Petit, J. R., D. Raynaud, C. Lorius, J. Jouzel, G. Delaygue, N. I. Barkov, and V. M. Kotlyakov. 2000. "Historical Isotopic Temperature Record from the Vostok Ice Core." In *Trends: A Compendium of Data on Global Change*. Carbon Dioxide Information Analysis Center, Oak Ridge National Laboratory, U.S. Department of Energy, Oak Ridge, TN. http://cdiac.ornl.gov/trends/temp/vostok/jouz_tem.htm.

Pizer, William. 2002. "Combining Price and Quantity Controls to Mitigate Global Climate Change." *Journal of Public Economics* 85 (3): 409–34.

Pontin, Jason. 2007. "Vinod Khosla: A Veteran Venture Capitalist's New Energy." *MIT Technology Review* (March-April). www.technologyreview.com/Energy/18299/.

Quiggin, John. 2006. "Stern and the Critics on Discounting." School of Economics, School of Political Science and International Studies, University of Queensland, Australia (December 20).

Rahmstorf, Stefan. 2007. "A Semi-Empirical Approach to Projecting Future Sea-Level Rise." *Science* 315 (5810): 368–70.

Sengupta, Somini. 2007. "Sea's Rise in India Buries Islands and a Way of Life." *New York Times*, April 11. http://select.nytimes.com/gst/abstract.html?res=F60 C14FF395B0C728DDDAD0894DF404482.

Shaffer, Gary, and Jorge Sarmiento. 1995. "Biogeochemical Cycling in the Global Ocean: A New, Analytical Model with Continuous Vertical Resolution and High-Latitude Dynamics." *Journal of Geophysical Research* 100 (C2): 2659–72.

Siegenthaler, U., and F. Joos. 2002. "Use of a Simple Model for Studying Oceanic Tracer Distributions and the Global Carbon Cycle." *Tellus* 44B: 186–207.

Stern, David. 2004. "The Rise and Fall of the Environmental Kuznets Curve." *World Development* 32 (8): 1419–39.

Stern, Nicholas. 2006. *Stern Review Report: The Economics of Climate Change.* London: Her Majesty's Treasury.

Tietenberg, Tom, and David Wheeler. 2001. "Empowering the Community: Information Strategies for Pollution Control." In *Frontiers of Environmental Economics,* ed. Henk Folmer. Cheltenham, U.K.: Edward Elgar.

Webster, Peter, G. Holland, J. Curry, and H. Chang. 2006. "Frequency, Duration, and Intensity of Tropical Cyclonic Storms in a Warming Environment." Eighty-sixth annual American Meteorological Society meeting at the "Eighteenth Conference on Climate Variability and Change," Atlanta, GA. January 28–February 3.

Wheeler, David. 2007. "Will the Poor Be Flooded Out? The IPCC's Predicted Flood Disasters and Their Implications for Development Aid." CGD Note (April). Center for Global Development, Washington, DC.

Wheeler, David, and Kevin Ummel. 2007. "Another Inconvenient Truth: A Carbon-Intensive South Faces Environmental Disaster, No Matter What the North Does." Working Paper (September). Center for Global Development, Washington, DC.

Wheeler, David, and others. 2000. *Greening Industry: New Roles for Communities, Markets, and Governments.* Oxford, U.K.: Oxford University Press.

WMO (World Meteorological Organization). 2007. *World Weather Advisory Report.* Geneva: WMO.

Zimov, Sergey A., Edward Schuur, and F. Stuart Chapin III. 2006. "Permafrost and the Global Carbon Budget." *Science* 312 (5780): 1612 –13.

CHAPTER 12
Climate Change and Economic Growth

Robert Mendelsohn

There is no question that the continued buildup of greenhouse gases will cause the earth to warm (IPCC 2007c). However, there is considerable debate about what is the sensible policy response to this problem. Economists, weighing costs and damages, advocate a balanced mitigation program that starts slowly and gradually becomes more strict over the century. Scientists and environmentalists, in contrast, advocate more extreme near-term mitigation policies. Which approach is followed will have a large bearing on economic growth. The balanced economic approach to the problem will address climate change with minimal reductions in economic growth. The more aggressive the near-term mitigation program, however, the greater the risk that climate change will slow long-term economic growth.

It should be understood that climate is not a stable, unchanging phenomena even when left to natural forces alone. There have been several major glacial periods in just the last million years. Much of this period has been significantly colder than the climate in the last 20,000 years. Ice covered most of Canada and Scandinavia, and frozen tundra extended well into New Jersey and the Great Plains in the United States. These cold periods have been quite hostile, discouraging humans from living in much of the northern parts of the northern hemisphere. In addition, within these long glacial swings, there is increasing evidence that there have been many periods of abrupt climate change (Weiss and Bradley 2001). These natural changes have had major impacts on past civilizations, causing dramatic adaptations and sometimes wholesale migrations. Climate change is not new. Human-induced climate change is simply an added disturbance to this natural variation.

The heart of the debate about climate change comes from numerous warnings from scientists and others that give the impression that human-induced climate change is an immediate threat to society (IPCC 2007a, 2007c; Stern 2006). Millions of people might be vulnerable to health effects (IPCC 2007a), crop production might fall in the low latitudes (IPCC 2007a), water supplies might dwindle (IPCC 2007a), precipitation might fall in arid regions (IPCC 2007a), extreme events will grow exponentially (Stern 2006), and between 20 and 30 percent of species will risk extinction (IPCC 2007a). Even worse, there may be catastrophic events such as the melting of Greenland or Antarctic ice sheets, causing severe sea-level rise, which would inundate hundreds of millions of people (Dasgupta and others 2009). Proponents argue that there is no time to waste. Unless greenhouse gases are cut dramatically today, economic growth and well-being may be at risk (Stern 2006).

These statements are largely alarmist and misleading. Although climate change is a serious problem that deserves attention, society's immediate behavior has an extremely low probability of leading to catastrophic consequences. The science and economics of climate change are quite clear that emissions over the next few decades will lead to only mild consequences. The severe impacts predicted by alarmists require a century (or two, according to Stern 2006) of no mitigation. Many of the predicted impacts assume that there will be no or little adaptation. The net economic impacts from climate change over the next 50 years will be small regardless. Most of the more severe impacts will take more than a century or even a millennium to unfold, and many of these "potential" impacts will never occur because people will adapt. It is not at all apparent that immediate and dramatic policies need to be developed to thwart long-range climate risks. What is needed are long-run balanced responses.

In fact, the mitigation plans of many alarmists would pose a serious risk to economic growth. The marginal cost function of mitigation is very steep, especially in the short run. Dramatic immediate policies to reduce greenhouse gas emissions would be very costly. Further, by rushing into regulations in a panic, it is very likely that new programs would not be designed efficiently. The greatest threat that climate change poses to economic growth is that the world will adopt a costly and inefficient mitigation policy that places a huge drag on the global economy.

Efficient Policy

The ideal greenhouse gas policy minimizes the sum of the present value of mitigation costs plus climate damages (Nordhaus 1992). This implies that the marginal cost of mitigation should be equal to the present value of the marginal damages from climate change. The magnitude and severity of mitigation programs depend on the magnitude and severity of climate impacts. Mitigation also depends on how expensive it is to control greenhouse gas emissions.

Because marginal damages rise as greenhouse gases accumulate, the optimal policy is dynamic, growing stricter over time (Nordhaus 2008). Emission limits should be mild at first and gradually become more severe. Over the long run, cumulative emissions are strongly curtailed. But this optimal policy reduces emissions in the second half of the century more than in the first. Partly, this dynamic policy reflects the science of climate change; damages are expected to grow with the concentration of greenhouse gases. Partly, this dynamic policy reflects the discount rate; immediate costs and damages are expected to have a higher value than future costs and damages. Partly, this dynamic policy reflects the fact that technical change is going to improve our ability to control greenhouse gases over time. Resources that are saved for the future can be invested in better technologies that will be more effective at reducing tons of emissions.

Climate Change Impacts

Economic research on climate impacts has long revealed that only a limited fraction of the market economy is vulnerable to climate change: agriculture, coastal resources, energy, forestry, tourism, and water (Pearce and others 1996). These sectors make up about 5 percent of the global economy, and their share is expected to shrink over time. Consequently, even if climate change turns out to be large, there is a limit to how much damage climate can do to the economy. Most sectors of the global economy are not climate sensitive.

Of course, the economies of some countries are more vulnerable to climate change than the global average. Developing countries in general have a large share of their economies in agriculture and forestry. They also tend to be located in the low latitudes where the impacts on these sectors will be the most severe. The low latitudes tend to be too hot for the most profitable agricultural activities, and any further warming will further reduce productivity. Up to 80 percent of the damages from climate change may be concentrated in low-latitude countries (Mendelsohn, Dinar, and Williams 2006).

Some damages from climate change will not affect the global economy, but will simply reduce the quality of life. Ecosystem change will result in massive shifts around the planet. Some of these shifts are already reflected in agriculture and timber, but they go beyond the impacts on these market sectors. Parks and other conservation areas will change. Animals will change their range. Endangered species may be lost. Although these impacts likely will lead to losses of nonmarket goods, it is hard to know what value to assign to these effects. Another important set of nonmarket impacts involves health effects. Heat stress may increase. Vector-borne diseases may extend beyond current ranges. Extreme events could threaten lives. All of these changes could potentially affect many people if we do not adapt. However, it is likely that public health interventions could minimize many of these risks. Many vector-borne diseases are already controlled at relatively low cost in developed countries. Heat stress can be reduced with a modicum of preventive measures. Deaths from extreme events can be reduced by a mixture of prevention and relief programs. As the world develops, it is likely that these risks may involve higher prevention costs, but not necessarily large losses of life. Further, winters lead to higher mortality rates than summers, so warming may have little net effect on health.

Agricultural studies in the United States suggest that the impacts of climate change in mid-latitude countries are likely to be beneficial for most of the century and to become harmful only toward the end of the century (Adams and others 1990; Mendelsohn, Nordhaus, and Shaw 1994). In contrast, there will be harmful impacts on agriculture in African countries (Kurukulasuriya and Mendelsohn 2008c), Latin American countries (Seo and Mendelsohn 2008c), and China (Wang and others 2009) starting almost immediately and rising with warming. The overall size of these impacts is smaller than earlier analyses predicted because of the importance of adaptation. Irrigation (Kurukulasuriya and Mendelsohn 2008b), crop choice (Kurukulasuriya and Mendelsohn 2008a; Seo and Mendelsohn 2008b; Wang and others 2009), and livestock species choice (Seo and Mendelsohn 2008a) all play a role in reducing climate impacts. These studies document that farmers are already using all of these methods to adapt to climate in Africa, Latin America, and China.

Other sectors that were originally expected to be damaged include timber, water, energy, coasts, and recreation. Forestry models are now projecting small benefits in the timber sector from increased productivity as trees respond positively to a warmer, wetter, carbon dioxide (CO_2)–enriched world (Sohngen, Mendelsohn, and Sedjo 2002). Water models tend to predict damage as flows in major rivers decline. However, the size of the economic damages can be greatly reduced by allocating the remaining water efficiently (Hurd and others 1999; Lund and others 2006). Energy models predict that the increased cost of cooling will exceed the reduced expenditures on heating (Mansur, Mendelsohn, and Morrison 2008). Several geographic studies of sea-level rise have assumed that there will be large coastal losses from inundation (Dasgupta and others 2009; Nicholls 2004). However, careful economic studies of coastal areas suggest that most high-valued coasts will be protected (Neumann and Livesay 2001; Ng and Mendelsohn 2005). The cost of hard structures built over the decades as sea levels rise will be less than the cost of inundation to urban populations. Only less-developed coastal areas are at risk of inundation (Ng and Mendelsohn 2006). Initial studies of recreation measured the losses to the ski industry of warming (Smith and Tirpak 1989). Subsequent studies of recreation, however, noted that summer recreation is substantially larger than winter recreation and would increase with warming (Loomis and Crespi 1999; Mendelsohn and Markowski 1999). The net effect on recreation is therefore likely to be beneficial.

As economic research on impacts has improved, the magnitude of projected damages from climate change has fallen. Early estimates projected that a doubling of greenhouse gases would yield damages equal to 2 percent of gross domestic product (GDP) by 2100 (Pearce and others 1996). More recent analyses of impacts suggest that damages are about an order of magnitude smaller (closer to 0.2 percent of GDP; Mendelsohn and Williams 2004; Tol 2002a, 2002b). The reason that damages have been shrinking is that the early studies (a) did not always take into account some of the benefits of warming for agriculture, timber, and tourism, (b) did not integrate adaptation, and (c) valued climate change against the current economy. At least with small amounts of climate change, the benefits appear to be of the same magnitude as the damages. Only when climate change exceeds 2°C (degrees Celsius) will there be net damages. Many early studies assumed that victims would not change their behavior in response to sustained damages. More recent studies have shown that a great deal of adaptation is endogenous. If government programs also support efficient adaptations, the magnitude of damages will fall dramatically. Finally, by examining the effect of climate change on the current economy, early researchers made two mistakes. First, they overestimated the relative future size of sectors that are sensitive to climate, such as agriculture. Second, they underestimated the size of the future economy in general relative to climate effects.

Economic analyses of impacts also reveal that they follow a dynamic path, increasing roughly by the square of temperature change (Mendelsohn and Williams 2007; Tol 2002b). The changes over the next few decades are expected to result in only small net effects. Most of the damages from climate change over the next 100 years will occur late in the century. These results once again support the optimal policy of starting slowly with regulation of climate change and increasing the strictness of regulation gradually over time.

In contrast to the literature on economic impacts, the Stern report predicts large damages (Stern 2006). However, most of the losses detailed in the Stern report will occur in the twenty-second century. Stern argues that these damages are equivalent to losing 5 percent of GDP a year starting immediately. However, the argument is based on a false assumption that the discount rate is near zero. He argues that the only reason to discount for time at all is because there is a possibility that the earth will be destroyed by an asteroid. This assumption has been heavily criticized in the economics literature because it makes no economic sense (Dasgupta 2008; Nordhaus 2007). Stern also talks about the importance of adaptation, but gives little credence to any impact studies that include adaptation. In Stern's defense, he does take into account uncertainty and low-probability, high-consequence events. However, in general, he tends to overestimate the expected value of these impacts. For example, he assumes that climate change will cause extreme events to grow exponentially. This is a misinterpretation of data on historic damages from extreme events that are due to economic growth, not climate (Pielke and Downtown 2000; Pielke and Landsea 1998).

The consequences of catastrophic events are possibly quite severe. If there is large-scale melting of the Greenland ice sheets or West Antarctica, sea levels will rise dramatically, especially after several centuries. There is no question that mankind would be forced to retreat from rising seas and build new cities inland. However, given the long time frame involved, it is not clear that the cost of such a massive relocation would be as dramatic as it might at first seem. There is no question that the land along the coast would be lost. But new coastal land would appear, so what is actually lost is interior land. Buildings would not really be lost, as new cities would be built in anticipation of rising seas. Older cities along the old coast would gradually be depreciated until they are abandoned. Although this may seem like a huge loss, most of the buildings built 500 years ago no longer exist. Finally, it is uncertain whether catastrophic events will occur. These damages must be weighed by the low probability that they will occur.

Mitigation Costs

The literature on mitigation predicts a wide range of costs. On the more optimistic side, various bottom-up engineering studies suggest that mitigation may be inexpensive. Some studies argue that one could even stabilize greenhouse gas concentrations at negative costs (IPCC 2007b). The engineering studies suggest that one could reduce emissions by 20 to 38 percent by 2030 for as little as $50 per ton of CO_2 (IPCC 2007b). A super-optimistic technical change camp even argues that emissions could be cut 70 percent by 2050 for as little as $50 per ton of CO_2 (Stern 2006).

The empirical economic literature suggests that mitigation cost functions are price inelastic (Weyant and Hill 1999). Using today's technology, the average abatement cost for a 70 percent reduction in carbon in the energy sector is estimated to be about $400 per ton of CO_2 (Anderson 2006). The short-run mitigation function is very price inelastic. The long run is less clear. With time, it is expected that the short-run marginal cost curve for mitigation will flatten. However, whether it ever gets as flat as projected by the optimistic engineering models is not clear.

An inelastic short-run marginal cost function implies that large reductions of emissions in the short run will be very expensive. There simply is no inexpensive way to reduce emissions sharply in the short run. Renewable energy sources such as hydroelectricity have largely been exhausted. Solar and wind power are expensive except in ideal locations and circumstances.

Other strategies such as shifting from coal to natural gas can work only in the short run, as they cause more rapid depletion of natural gas supplies.

In the short run, a rushed public policy is likely to be inefficient. It will likely exempt major polluters, as Europe now does with coal. Very few national mitigation programs regulate every source of emissions. Most countries have sought to reduce emissions in only a narrow sector of the national economy. Rushed programs will likely invest in specific technologies that are ineffective, such as the United States has done with ethanol. Ethanol produces as much greenhouse gas as gasoline. The inelasticity of the marginal cost function implies that mitigation programs that are not applied universally will be very wasteful. Regulated polluters will spend a lot to eliminate a single ton, while unregulated polluters will spend nothing.

Universal participation also requires that all major emitting countries be included. The signatory countries that limit emissions under the existing international Kyoto agreement are responsible for only about one-quarter of global emissions. The United States and China generate another half of emissions, and all the remaining developing countries emit approximately the other quarter. Whereas Kyoto countries are beginning to spend resources on mitigation, non-Kyoto countries spend little to nothing. Even within the Kyoto countries, many countries are failing to reach their targets. By failing to get universal application of regulations, the current regulations are unnecessarily wasteful. Without near universal participation, the cost of mitigation doubles (Nordhaus 2008). In fact, the current Kyoto treaty is so ineffective that global emissions are rising at the pace predicted with no mitigation at all. Global CO_2 emissions in 2006 were 8.4 gigatons of carbon (GtC).

Stern and other climate advocates recommend immediately placing strict regulations on emissions. Stern recommends regulations that would increase the marginal cost of emissions to $300 per ton of CO_2. The stricter regulations would reduce emissions by 40 GtC a year (70 percent) by 2050. If the marginal cost does not fall, this program will cost $1.2 trillion a year by 2050. Of course, it is likely that long-term marginal costs will be lower as a result of technical change. Assuming that costs fall by 1 percent a year, the marginal cost would fall to $200 per ton of CO_2 by 2050. The overall cost of the Stern program would be $800 billion a year in 2050. The present value of mitigation costs in the Stern program is estimated to be $28 trillion (Nordhaus 2008).

The optimal regulations that minimize the present value of climate damages and mitigation costs are more modest. They would begin with prices closer to $20 per ton of CO_2 and then rise to $85 per ton by 2050 (Nordhaus 2008). That would lead to a 25 percent reduction in greenhouse gases by 2050 rather than the 70 percent reduction in the Stern program. The present value of the global mitigation costs of the optimal program this century is estimated to be $2 trillion (Nordhaus 2008). These costs are an order of magnitude less than the cost of the Stern program.

Conclusions

This chapter argues that the impacts from climate change are not likely to affect global economic growth over the next 40 years. The size of climate change during this period is projected to be too small to have much of a global net impact. In the second half of the century, warming will be large enough to detect, but even by 2100, the annual net market impacts are predicted to be between 0.1 and 0.5 percent of GDP. These impacts are simply not large enough to affect economic growth this century.

Catastrophic climate change could impose large annual losses on society. However, such events currently have a low probability and will occur far into the future. It is not self-evident that more dramatic mitigation policies are the most appropriate tool with which to address low-probability, high-consequence events. It is not clear how much mitigation would change the probabilities of these events occurring. Second, a tool that is more flexible and immediate would be more effective. What is needed is a tool that could be implemented once it is clear that a catastrophic event is actually under way. Geoengineering—seeding the upper atmosphere with particles—appears to be a better strategy for handling catastrophic events than mitigation. Society can choose to engage in geoengineering only if it is clear that a catastrophe is imminent. Geoengineering is relatively inexpensive. But most important, it is immediate and can reverse the consequences of decades of greenhouse gases in a matter of a few weeks. Finally, geoengineering is flexible. The particles will fall to earth in a matter of a few months. There are, of course, environmental concerns with intentionally managing the earth's climate. We need to learn more about what those consequences might be. However, faced with the possibility of a catastrophe, it seems that geoengineering is simply too good a policy tool not to develop.

Economically optimal mitigation policies would not pose a great threat to economic growth. Policies that balance mitigation costs and climate damages would lead to regulations that are not especially burdensome. The present value of mitigation costs of an optimal policy would be $2 trillion for the entire century.

Of course, not every country will be affected alike. Low-latitude countries will bear the brunt of climate damages (Mendelsohn, Dinar, and Williams 2006) and will likely see damages immediately. Low-latitude economies with large shares of rain-fed agriculture are especially vulnerable and may see reductions in agricultural income of 60 percent or more by 2100 (Seo and Mendelsohn 2008c). Similarly, some countries may face higher mitigation costs. Countries that are growing more quickly, are heavier energy consumers, and are more dependent on coal will face higher costs.

The biggest threat climate change poses to economic growth, however, is not from climate damages or efficient mitigation policies, but rather from immediate, aggressive, and inefficient mitigation policies. Immediate aggressive mitigation policies could lead to mitigation costs equal to $28 trillion (Stern 2006). This is 14 times higher than the mitigation costs of an optimal policy. If these policies were no more efficient than current policies, the costs could easily rise to $56 trillion. These misguided mitigation programs pose a serious threat to economic growth. They would impose heavy additional costs on the global economy that cannot be justified by the limited reductions in climate risk they offer.

References

Adams, Richard M., Cynthia Rosenzweig, Robert Peart, Joe Ritchie, Bruce McCarl, J. David Glyer, R. Bruce Curry, James Jones, Kenneth Boote, and L. Hartwell Allen. 1990. "Global Climate Change and U.S. Agriculture." *Nature* 345 (6272): 219–24.

Anderson, Dennis. 2006. "Costs and Finance of Abating Carbon Emissions in the Energy Sector." Supporting Documents for *Stern Review Report*. Her Majesty's Treasury, London.

Dasgupta, Partha. 2008. "Discounting Climate Change." *Journal of Risk and Uncertainty* 37 (2): 141–69.

Dasgupta, Susmita, Benoit Laplante, Craig Meisner, David Wheeler, and Jianping Yan. 2009. "The Impact of Sea-Level Rise on Developing Countries: A Comparative Analysis." *Climatic Change* 93 (3): 379–88.

Hurd, Brian, J. Callaway, J. Smith, and P. Kirshen. 1999. "Economic Effects of Climate Change on U.S. Water Resources." In *The Impact of Climate Change on the United States Economy*, ed. Robert Mendelsohn and James Neumann. Cambridge, U.K.: Cambridge University Press.

IPCC (Intergovernmental Panel on Climate Change). 2007a. *Climate Change 2007: Impacts, Adaptation, and Vulnerability.* Cambridge, U.K.: Cambridge University Press.

———. 2007b. *Climate Change 2007: Mitigation.* Cambridge, U.K.: Cambridge University Press.

———. 2007c. *Climate Change 2007: The Physical Science Basis.* Cambridge, U.K.: Cambridge University Press.

Kurukulasuriya, Pradeep, and Robert Mendelsohn. 2008a. "Crop Switching as an Adaptation Strategy to Climate Change." *African Journal of Agriculture and Resource Economics* 2 (1): 105–26.

———. 2008b. "Modeling Endogenous Irrigation: The Impact of Climate Change on Farmers in Africa." Policy Research Working Paper 4278. World Bank, Washington, DC.

———. 2008c. "A Ricardian Analysis of the Impact of Climate Change on African Cropland." *African Journal of Agriculture and Resource Economics* 2 (1): 1–23.

Loomis, John, and John Crespi. 1999. "Estimated Effects of Climate Change on Selected Outdoor Recreation Activities in the United States." In *The Impact of Climate Change on the United States Economy*, ed. Robert Mendelsohn and James Neumann. Cambridge, U.K.: Cambridge University Press.

Lund, Jay, Tingju Zhu, Stacy Tanaka, and Marion Jenkins. 2006. "Water Resource Impacts." In *The Impact of Climate Change on Regional Systems: A*

Comprehensive Analysis of California, ed. Joel Smith and Robert Mendelsohn. Northampton, MA: Edward Elgar.

Mansur, Erin, Robert Mendelsohn, and Wendy Morrison. 2008. "A Discrete Continuous Model of Energy: Measuring Climate Change Impacts on Energy." *Journal of Environmental Economics and Management* 55 (2): 175–93.

Mendelsohn, Robert, Ariel Dinar, and Larry Williams. 2006. "The Distributional Impact of Climate Change on Rich and Poor Countries." *Environment and Development Economics* 11 (2): 159–78.

Mendelsohn, Robert, and Marla Markowski. 1999. "The Impact of Climate Change on Outdoor Recreation." In *The Impact of Climate Change on the United States Economy,* ed. Robert Mendelsohn and James Neumann. Cambridge, U.K.: Cambridge University Press.

Mendelsohn, Robert, and Larry Williams. 2004. "Comparing Forecasts of the Global Impacts of Climate Change." *Mitigation and Adaptation Strategies for Global Change* 9 (4): 315–33.

————. 2007. "Dynamic Forecasts of the Sectoral Impacts of Climate Change." In *Human-Induced Climate Change: An Interdisciplinary Assessment,* ed. Michael Schlesinger, Haroon Kheshgi, Joel Smith, Francisco de la Chesnaye, John Reilly, Tom Wilson, and Charles Kolstad. Cambridge, U.K.: Cambridge University Press.

Mendelsohn, Robert, William Nordhaus, and Daigee Shaw. 1994. "Measuring the Impact of Global Warming on Agriculture." *American Economic Review* 84 (4): 753–71.

Neumann, James, and N. D. Livesay. 2001. "Coastal Structures: Dynamic Economic Modeling." In *Global Warming and the American Economy: A Regional Analysis,* ed. Robert Mendelsohn. Cheltenham, U.K.: Edward Elgar.

Ng, Wei-Shiuen, and Robert Mendelsohn. 2005. "The Impact of Sea-Level Rise on Singapore." *Environment and Development Economics* 10 (2): 201–15.

————. 2006. "The Impact of Sea-Level Rise on Non-Market Lands in Singapore." *Ambio* 35 (6): 289–96.

Nicholls, Robert J. 2004. "Coastal Flooding and Wetland Loss in the 21st Century: Changes under the SRES Climate and Socio-Economic Scenarios." *Global Environmental Change* 14 (1): 69–86.

Nordhaus, William D. 1992. "An Optimal Transition Path for Controlling Greenhouse Gases." *Science* 258 (5086): 1315–19.

————. 2007. "Critical Assumptions in the Stern Review Report on Climate Change." *Science* 317 (5835): 201–02.

————. 2008. *A Question of Balance: Economic Modeling of Global Warming.* New Haven, CT: Yale Press.

Pearce, David, William Cline, A. Achanta, S. Fankhauser, R. Pachauri, Richard Tol, and P. Vellinga. 1996. "The Social Cost of Climate Change: Greenhouse Damage and the Benefits of Control." In *Climate Change 1995: Economic and Social Dimensions of Climate Change.* Intergovernmental Panel on Climate Change. Cambridge, U.K.: Cambridge University Press.

Pielke, Roger Jr., and Mary W. Downtown. 2000. "Precipitation and Damaging Floods: Trends in the United States, 1932–97." *Journal of Climate* 13 (20): 3625–37.

Pielke, Roger Jr., and Christopher W. Landsea. 1998. "Normalized Hurricane Damages in the United States: 1925–95." *Weather and Forecasting* 13 (20): 621–31.

Seo, Niggol, and Robert Mendelsohn. 2008a. "An Analysis of Crop Choice: Adapting to Climate Change in Latin American Farms." *Ecological Economics* 67 (1): 109–16.

———. 2008b. "Measuring Impacts and Adaptation to Climate Change: A Structural Ricardian Model of African Livestock Management." *Agricultural Economics* 38 (2): 150–65.

———. 2008c. "A Ricardian Analysis of the Impact of Climate Change on South American Farms." *Chilean Journal of Agricultural Research* 68 (1): 69–79.

Smith, Joel, and Dennis Tirpak. 1989. *Potential Effects of Global Climate Change on the United States*. Washington, DC: U.S. Environmental Protection Agency.

Sohngen, Brent, Robert Mendelsohn, and Roger Sedjo. 2002. "A Global Model of Climate Change Impacts on Timber Markets." *Journal of Agricultural and Resource Economics* 26 (2): 326–43.

Stern, Nicholas. 2006. *The Stern Review Report: The Economics of Climate Change*. London: Her Majesty's Treasury.

Tol, Richard. 2002a. "New Estimates of the Damage Costs of Climate Change, Part I: Benchmark Estimates." *Environmental and Resource Economics* 21 (1): 47–73.

———. 2002b. "New Estimates of the Damage Costs of Climate Change, Part II: Dynamic Estimates." *Environmental and Resource Economics* 21 (1): 135–60.

Wang, Jinxia, Robert Mendelsohn, Ariel Dinar, Jikun Huang, Scott Rozelle, and Lijuan Zhang. 2009. "The Impact of Climate Change on China's Agriculture." *Agricultural Economics* 40 (3): 323–37.

Weiss, Harvey, and Raymond Bradley. 2001. "What Drives Societal Collapse?" *Science* 291 (5504): 609–10.

Weyant, John, and Jennifer Hill. 1999. "Introduction and Overview." *Energy Journal* 20 (special issue: The Costs of the Kyoto Protocol): vii–xliv.

CHAPTER 13
Population Aging and Economic Growth

David E. Bloom, David Canning, and Günther Fink

The world is entering substantially uncharted waters regarding the size of its elderly population. Recent declines in fertility rates and increases in life expectancy, combined with the dynamic evolution of past variations in birth and death rates, are producing a significant shift in the global age structure. The number of people over the age of 60 is expected to reach 1 billion by 2020 and almost 2 billion by 2050 (representing 22 percent of the world's population). The proportion of individuals age 80 or over (the so-called oldest old) is projected to rise from 1 to 4 percent of the global population by 2050.[1]

There is also mounting evidence that the elderly are healthier than before. In a phenomenon referred to by demographers and health specialists as the "compression of morbidity," the length of healthy old age appears to be increasing. Part of this increase is due to increases in the

The authors thank Robert Holzmann and Alain Jousten for their comments; Patrick Gerland and Rod Tyers for their helpful comments and assistance; and Neil Bennett, Jocelyn Finlay, Jennifer O'Brien, Larry Rosenberg, and Mark Weston for their assistance in the preparation of this chapter.

1   The United Nations makes several separate forecasts of population size, including ones based on low-, medium-, and high-fertility assumptions. This chapter uses the United Nations' medium-fertility scenario except where otherwise stated.

length of life and part to even greater increases in the length of life free of chronic illness. The net effect is a decline in the lifetime burden of illness (as measured in years unwell).

Since different age groups have different economic needs and productive capacities, a country's economic characteristics may be expected to change as its population ages. A standard approach to assessing these changes is to assume constant age-specific behavior with respect to earnings, employment, and savings and to assess the implications of changes in the relative size of different age groups for these fundamental contributors to national income. However, the simple application of this approach is likely to be misleading. Behavioral changes induced by changing expectations about the life cycle and by predictable demographic shifts are likely to influence the economic consequences of aging. For example, individuals' expectation of living longer than previous generations may induce them to remain in work for longer and to begin to draw down savings at a later age. In addition, the links between population aging and macroeconomic performance are mediated by the institutional context (for example, retirement policy, pension and health care finance, the efficiency of labor and capital markets, and the structure of regional and global economic systems). The policy environment may itself be influenced by population aging, depending on the voting and other political behavior of an aging electorate whose needs and interests may differ from those of younger people.

This chapter examines the effects of population aging on economic growth. It begins by presenting and analyzing descriptive statistics on the extent and pace of population aging. The chapter then explores the overall effect of population aging on economic growth as well as the effects operating via two main channels: labor supply and capital accumulation. Accounting effects of population aging on factor accumulation and economic growth are distinguished from behavioral effects. The final section highlights the important role played by the policy and institutional environment in mediating the effects of population aging on economic growth. This section also discusses a variety of demographic, behavioral, and policy forces pertinent to understanding and guiding the effect of population aging on economic growth.

Population Aging: Facts, Force, and Future

In this section, we lay out some of the key facts regarding past and projected future population aging and briefly consider some of the policy implications that these facts highlight. The data serve as anchors for the economic analyses that are developed in subsequent sections. First we look at United Nations (UN) population projections. Next we examine the factors underlying the rise in the elderly population. Then we take a brief look at how population trends will affect the options faced by policy makers.

Population Data and Projections

Population projections from the United Nations change as new estimates are published every two years. For example, forecasts of the total world population in 2050 declined from about 10 billion to 9 billion people between 1994 and 2006. One might have expected that projections of the number of people age 60 or above and 80 or above would be far more stable, since all those who will reach those ages in the next six decades have already been born, so unpredictable changes in fertility need not be taken into account. However, these projections have changed significantly, even in recent years, as shown in table 13.1. With each UN publication, the latest available data are taken into account. In some instances, a large amount of new census data is available, which can lead to significant differences in the estimate of future population size. The same is true of updated fertility and mortality data. The greatest proportionate differences shown here are for the forecasted size of the 80+ population in 2050. For the world, developed countries, and developing countries, the UN estimate of the size of this age group has risen by 20 percent or more since 1994. These figures show that population data are not sacrosanct; as the estimated sizes of current populations and age groups within them change and as fertility and mortality rates change in a manner that is different from earlier predictions, estimates of future population size will also change.

Demographic projections of population aging suggest that the world is experiencing a historically unprecedented phenomenon.[2] The 60+ and 80+ age groups' shares of the total population are higher than at any time in history, and their growth is accelerating. The number age 60 or over has increased from 200 million in 1950 to around 670 million today. By 2050, it is projected to reach 2 billion (see figure 13.1). The number age 80+ has risen from 14 million in 1950 to nearly 90 million today, and by 2050 it will have passed 400 million if current projections are borne out. Older age cohorts, moreover, are beginning to account for a substantial proportion of the total population. Indeed, all countries and other entities are forecast to see a higher share of people age 60+ in 2050 than in 2000, with the percentage-point increase ranging from 0.3 in Benin to 33 in Macao. (By contrast, numerous countries experienced large drops in this fraction between 1950 and 2000.)

These projections are based on the UN's medium-fertility scenario. If fertility rates in the coming decades are lower than the medium-scenario estimate, the share of elderly in the population will rise. Figure 13.2 shows how this source of uncertainty leads to a range of predictions regarding elderly share. The variation in 2050 is about one-third of the medium-scenario elderly share. This is not a huge range, and all three scenarios point in the same direction. But this source of uncertainty is in addition to that reflected by the change over time in UN estimates of the future size of the elderly population.

---

2   For a detailed analysis of several measures of population aging, see Lutz, Sanderson, and Scherbov (2008).

Table 13.1. UN Forecast of 2050 Elderly Population, 1994–2006
billions

Area and forecast year	Total	60+	80+
World			
1994	9.83	1.97	0.33
1996	9.37	1.94	0.32
1998	8.91	1.97	0.37
2000	9.32	1.96	0.38
2002	8.92	1.91	0.38
2004	9.08	1.97	0.39
2006	9.19	2.01	0.40
% change, 1994–2000	−5.2	−0.3	14.7
% change, 2000–06	−1.4	2.1	6.0
% change, 1994–06	−6.5	1.9	21.7
Developed countries			
1994	1.21	0.36	0.09
1996	1.16	0.36	0.09
1998	1.16	0.38	0.10
2000	1.18	0.40	0.11
2002	1.22	0.39	0.11
2004	1.24	0.40	0.12
2006	1.25	0.41	0.12
% change, 1994–2000	−2.2	9.5	21.2
% change, 2000–06	5.4	2.7	3.9
% change, 1994–2006	3.1	12.6	26.0
Developing countries			
1994	8.63	1.61	0.24
1996	8.20	1.58	0.23
1998	7.75	1.59	0.27
2000	8.14	1.57	0.27
2002	7.70	1.51	0.26
2004	7.84	1.57	0.28
2006	7.95	1.60	0.28
% change, 1994–2000	−5.6	−2.5	12.2
% change, 2000–06	−2.4	2.0	6.9
% change, 1994–06	−7.9	−0.5	20.0

Source: Authors' calculations based on data in United Nations 1994–2006.

Figure 13.3 is another way of viewing the change in the age structure of the world's population over time. Each shaded slice shows the age distribution at one point in time. The elderly share will be much higher in 2050 than it is now.

Figure 13.1. World Population, by Age Group, 1950–2050

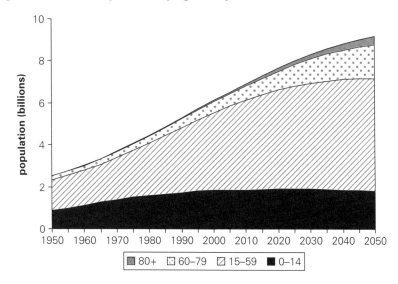

Source: United Nations 2006.

Figure 13.2. Share of Population At Least 60 Years Old, by UN Fertility Assumption, 2000–50

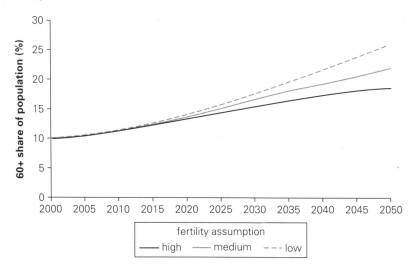

Source: United Nations 2006.

The phenomenon of population aging, of course, is not uniform across countries. In addition, the extent of aging varies considerably between the developed and the developing countries (see table 13.2 and figure 13.4) and across regions (see figure 13.5).

Much of the developed world already has large elderly cohorts. In developed countries, 20 percent of the population is over age 60 today, and this will rise to more than 30 percent in the next four decades (see figure 13.6). In the developing world, less than 10 percent of the population is over

Figure 13.3. World Population, by Five-Year Age Group, 1950–2050

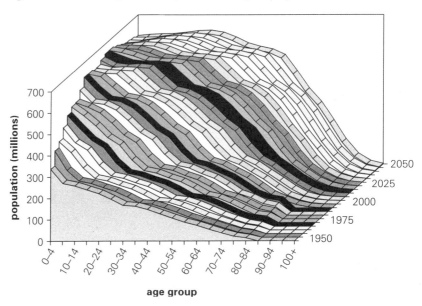

Source: United Nations 2006.

Table 13.2. Age Structure in Developed and Developing Countries' Populations, 1950–2050
millions

Region and age structure (years)	1950	2005	2050
World			
0–14	866	1,845	1,824
15–59	1,464	3,997	5,361
60–79	191	585	1,604
80+	14	88	402
Total	2,535	6,515	9,191
Developed countries			
0–14	223	207	190
15–59	496	764	650
60–79	87	200	289
80+	9	44	117
Total	814	1,216	1,245
Developing countries			
0–14	644	1,638	1,635
15–59	968	3,233	4,712
60–79	104	385	1,315
80+	6	43	284
Total	1,722	5,299	7,946

Source: Authors' calculations based on data in United Nations 2006.

Figure 13.4. Age Structure in Developed and Developing Countries, 1950–2050

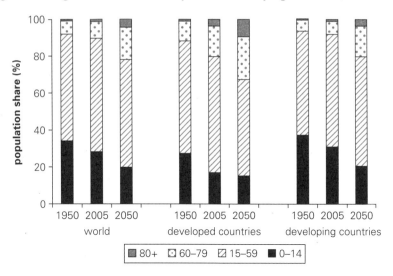

Source: Authors' calculations based on data in United Nations 2006.

Figure 13.5. Share of Population Aged 60+, by Region, 1950–2050

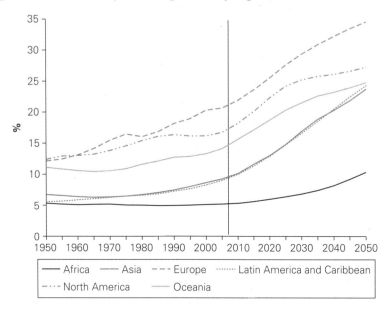

Source: United Nations 2006.

age 60. By 2050, however, the proportion is expected to more than double, and the 60+ age group will comprise 20 percent of India's population and 30 percent of China's—a total of more than 760 million people. Figure 13.7 offers another view of the same data.

Countries will also undergo aging at very different rates. Table 13.3 focuses on two sets of countries: those that are forecast to have the highest

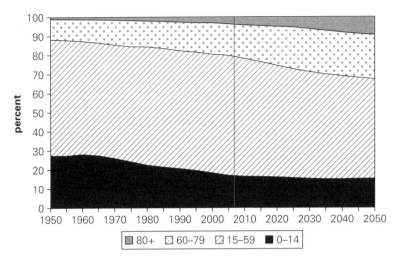

Figure 13.6. Share of Population in Developed Countries, by Age Group, 1950–2050

Legend: ■ 80+ ⊡ 60–79 ▨ 15–59 ■ 0–14

Source: United Nations 2006.

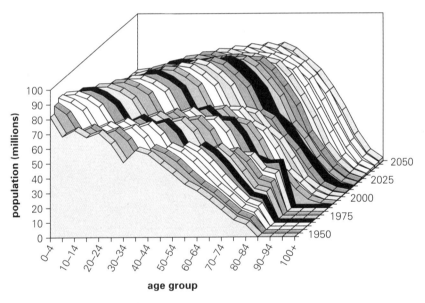

Figure 13.7. Population in Developed Countries, by Five-Year Age Group, 1950–2050

Source: United Nations 2006.

share of 60+ individuals in 2050 and those that are forecast to have the largest percentage-point increase in that share between 2000 and 2050. (Only countries with current populations greater than 2 million are considered.)

Figure 13.8 shows the expected growth of the elderly population for four large developing countries. In three of them, population aging will be a major demographic trend between now and 2050.

Table 13.3. Ten Countries with the Largest Share of Elderly in the Population in 2050 or the Largest Increase in Share of Elderly Population from 2000 to 2050

Countries with largest elderly share	Percentage of population 60+ in 2050	Countries with largest increase in elderly share	Percentage-point increase in 60+ share, 2000–50
Japan	44.0	Korea, Rep. of	30.7
Korea, Rep. of	42.2	Singapore	29.3
Slovenia	40.5	Cuba	24.5
Bulgaria	40.2	Poland	22.9
Singapore	39.8	Kuwait	22.3
Poland	39.6	Slovak Republic	22.2
Cuba	39.3	United Arab Emirates	22.1
Romania	39.1	Slovenia	21.1
Spain	39.0	China	21.0
Czech Republic	38.6	Japan	20.7

Source: Authors' calculations based on data in United Nations 2006.

Figure 13.8. Elderly Share in Select Developing Countries, 1950–2050

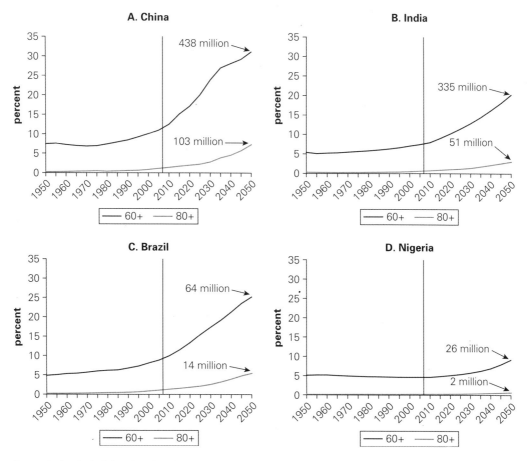

Source: Authors' calculations based on data in United Nations 2006.

Population aging will be accompanied by changes in the sex composition of the population. (Gerland 2005 notes that, in most countries, the decades-long divergence in adult survival between men and women has decreased since 1980, "caused by both a deceleration/leveling of female survival and an acceleration of male survival.") More male than female babies are born, but the death rate of male babies and adult men has long been higher than that of their female counterparts. This has led to the long-standing and widely recognized phenomenon of the predominance of women among the elderly. Better health at all ages is causing this disparity in longevity to diminish. Figure 13.9 compares the UN's forecasts of male-female ratios in 2050 with the present. In 2050, among individuals between the ages of 15 and 59, males will slightly outnumber females in both developed and developing countries. Among the elderly, females will continue to outnumber males, in both developed and developing countries.

The Drivers of Aging

There are three main factors behind the past and projected changes in the share of the global population ages 60+ and 80+. First, declining fertility rates in recent decades have reduced the number of young people and pushed up the share of the elderly. The total fertility rate fell from approximately 5 children per woman in 1950 to just over 2.5 in 2005. It is expected to fall to 2 children per woman by 2050 (United Nations 2005). Most of

Figure 13.9. Male-Female Ratio in Developed and Developing Countries, by Age, 2005 and 2050

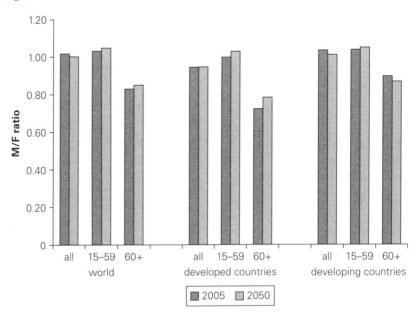

Source: Authors' calculations based on data in United Nations 2006.

Population Aging and Economic Growth

Figure 13.10. Share of Population in Developing Countries, by Age Group, 1950–2050

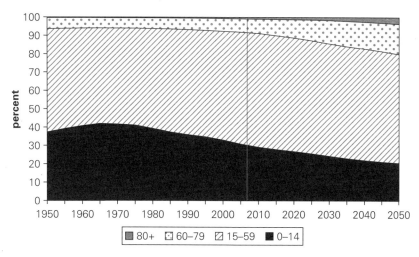

Source: United Nations 2006.

this decline occurred in the developing world. As figure 13.10 shows, this will contribute to a near halving of the share of children in the population of developing countries between 1965 and 2050.

The second key factor relates to recent increases in life expectancy. We calculate, for example, that one-fifth of the projected rise in India's 60+ population between 2000 and 2050 is due to rising life expectancy during that period. The corresponding figure for China is one-seventh.[3]

Global life expectancy has increased from 47 years in 1950 to over 65 today. It is projected by the UN Population Division to reach 75 years by 2045 (United Nations 2005). Both developed and developing countries are seeing rises in life expectancy, despite reversals of the trend in some low- and middle-income countries as a result of the HIV/AIDS (human immunodeficiency virus/acquired immune deficiency syndrome) (see figure 13.11). As many more people survive into their 60s and beyond, the absolute number of elderly will soar. Combined with fertility declines, this will also result in a sharp increase in the share of elderly in the overall population. And, as before, figure 13.12 gives a three-dimensional view of the same data.

There is much debate about whether there is a limit to increases in life expectancy (Oeppen and Vaupel 2002). Some have forecast that life expectancy in the wealthy industrial countries will surpass 100 years before 2100 as anti-aging and medical technologies become more widespread

---

3 This calculation was made by comparing projections of India's population and age distribution from 2000 to 2050 using (a) linearly interpolated values of the UN Population Division's assumptions of the total fertility rate and life expectancy in 2000 and 2050, and (b) linearly interpolated values of the UN Population Division's assumptions of the total fertility rate with life expectancy held constant at its 2000 level. A similar calculation was made for China, except that life expectancy for women was fixed at 80 beyond the year 2035, due to a restriction imposed by the software package DemProj.

Figure 13.11. Life Expectancy in Developed and Developing Countries, 1950–2040

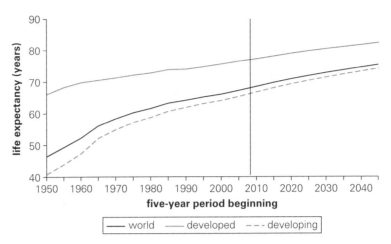

Source: United Nations 2006.

Figure 13.12. Share of Population in Developing Countries, by Five-Year Age Group, 1950–2050

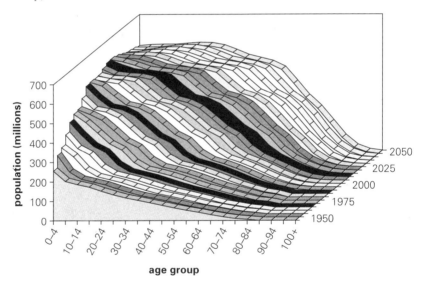

Source: United Nations 2006.

and sophisticated and as life styles become healthier, for example, via declines in smoking and alcohol abuse, improvements in diet, universal use of seatbelts, and so forth. Others are less optimistic, believing that life expectancy will plateau at 85 years. The latter school of thought holds that past increases are due mostly to declines in infant and child mortality that are not repeatable and thus will not contribute to further increases in life expectancy. It argues too that major new threats, such as avian flu, climate change, and obesity, will hold life expectancy down. Although the likely extent of increases is disputed, the fact that life expectancy will continue to rise is widely accepted.

Past variations in birth and death rates are the third factor behind population aging. For example, baby booms that occurred in rich countries after World War II are now shifting population structure as the swollen cohort of boomers, which resulted from increased (and not decreased) fertility, passes the age of 60. In parts of the developing world too, where fertility temporarily increased as health improvements reduced child mortality, elderly populations have been and will continue to be boosted as those high-fertility cohorts age.

Policy Implications

From a policy perspective, the aging of the world's population presents some major challenges. Its unprecedented nature, moreover, means that we cannot look to earlier historical episodes for guidance on how this demographic upheaval will play itself out or how best to manage it. However, population aging in most countries will not be noticeable for another 10 to 20 years. As the figures above show, the most rapid increase in aging has not yet occurred. This gives policy makers a window of opportunity in which to prepare for the change. Initiating action early can leave countries better positioned to deal with the social, economic, and political effects of an altered population structure in the future.

People age 60 or above tend to have different needs and different behaviors than younger generations. Older individuals, for example, tend to work and save less, meaning that less labor and capital will be available to economies. They also require more health care and, in many countries, rely on social pensions for a large part of their income. Politically, therefore, it might become more difficult to adopt certain policies, such as cutting health and pension benefits, as elder populations become politically more potent. Economically, there will be increased stress on working populations, whose taxes pay for the health care and pensions of their elders but whose numbers relative to those elders will be reduced.

Those age 80 or over also have different needs. Their health is generally weaker than that of people between the ages of 60 and 80, they have a greater need for full-time care, and their financial needs may be greater due to the costs of care and because they have had longer to draw down savings. As their numbers increase, they place further demands on government resources, familial resources, and personal savings.

That a greater share of elderly will put societies and economies under intolerable strain is not inevitable, however. Increased life expectancy has historically been strongly associated with increased per capita income (Preston 1975). Changes in age-specific health profiles are important for characterizing the phenomenon of population aging. If people moving into their 60s and 70s are healthier than preceding generations, the demands for health care will be less intense, and many will be able to work, and contribute to economies, for longer (Kulish, Smith, and Kent 2006). If they remain no healthier than earlier cohorts, they will have to endure more years of poor health, and their societies will be burdened with additional years of health care costs. Studies on whether increased life expectancy is accompanied by a "compression of morbidity," where the relative or absolute length of life spent in chronic ill health falls, have mainly focused on the United States. Most suggest that compression of morbidity does indeed occur, meaning that the burden of aging is reduced (Costa 2002; Crimmins 2004; Crimmins, Saito, and Ingegneri 1997; Fries 1980, 1989). Those over 60 can work more productively for longer and place fewer demands on public resources.

Cross-country differences in the timing of the aging process may also mitigate the negative impacts. Because rich countries are aging faster than poor ones, the former can draw on labor from the latter to compensate for the retirement of their own people. The large cohorts of working-age people in developing countries, in turn, are likely to be keen to fill the vacancies created.

Migration to the developed world could therefore theoretically slow the latter's shift toward an aged population and ease the pressure on economies. Migration, however, can bring with it social pressures and unrest, and many wealthy countries are already grappling with the difficult balance between the need for labor and the importance of taking account of immigration's social effects.

Some have observed the different—but highly complementary—age structures of developed and developing regions and suggested that "replacement migration" might serve the purposes of both sets of regions. Europe, for example, with a high percentage of elderly people and few children, needs workers, which Sub-Saharan Africa could readily supply. Figure 13.13 shows the ratio of working-age to non-working-age people in Europe and

Figure 13.13. Ratio of Working-Age to Non-Working-Age Population in Europe and Sub-Saharan Africa, 1950–2050

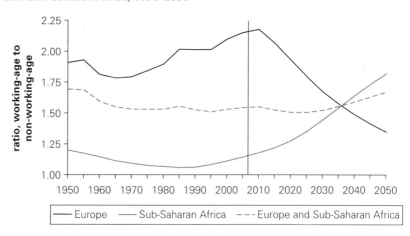

Source: United Nations 2004.

Sub-Saharan Africa separately, as well as the ratio for the two regions added together. The time path of the working-age ratio for the two regions taken together is steadier than that of either region alone.

Notwithstanding the theoretical soundness of the idea of replacement migration, we calculate that it would take more than a 30-fold increase in the current level of migration from Sub-Saharan Africa to Europe— which would need to last for 25 years—to achieve this smoothing (Bloom, Canning, and Sevilla 2002). This is hardly realistic, especially given the social and political tensions that even current rates of African migration to Europe raise. The goal of "replacement migration" thus appears to be much more interesting in theory than in practice. Given the massive increase in migration that would be needed to appreciably offset the impacts of population aging in Europe, international migration offers at best a partial solution to the problem—and one that comes with potentially great social and political costs.

Increased capital flows are an alternative way of addressing this same issue (that is, exporting jobs instead of importing workers), although the demand for services that require physical proximity (for example, gardeners, hair stylists, and security guards, as opposed to call center operators, investment analysts, and radiologists) would appear to place some limits on this market-based channel for adjusting to population aging.

In the next section of the chapter, we examine more closely some of the impacts of aging discussed above and in particular their implications for economic growth.

The Economic Impacts of Population Aging

The academic literature is overflowing with models and perspectives on the determinants of economic growth. Some frameworks highlight the importance of sectoral shift (that is, the reallocation of labor from the low-productivity agricultural sector to the higher-productivity industry and service sectors) and the improvement of productivity within all sectors. Others emphasize the contribution to growth of technological progress, human capital, institutions and governance, macroeconomic and trade policies, and random shocks. Still others stress feedback effects that run from economic growth to technical progress and human capital accumulation, which in turn influence economic growth.[4]

---

4 Tyers and Shi (2007) introduce demographics (population size and its age, sex, and skill composition) into a dynamic computable general-equilibrium model of the world economy with exogenously determined age patterns of labor force participation, consumption, and savings. Their work indicates that accelerated population aging (via lower fertility) tends to enhance real per capita income growth in regions with very young populations and slows it in regions with older populations and low rates of labor force participation among the elderly (for example, Western Europe). Based on a model that is similar in spirit, though demographically less fine grained, McKibbin (2006) reaches qualitatively similar conclusions, but also highlights the implications of global demographic change for international flows of trade and capital and therefore for domestic economic performance.

The key premise of this chapter is that changes in population age structure may exert a significant influence on economic growth. We adopt a life-cycle perspective, based on the fact that people's economic needs and contributions vary over the life cycle. Specifically, the ratio of consumption to production tends to be high for the young and the elderly and low for working-age adults. This means that aggregate labor supply, productivity, earnings, and savings—all key drivers of economic growth—will tend to vary depending on where most people are in the life cycle. Among these factors, it is well established that labor supply and savings are higher among working-age adults than among those age 60 or above. Other things equal, therefore, a country with large cohorts of youth and elderly is likely to experience slower growth than one with a high proportion of working-age people.

The value of this approach can be seen in an analysis of the impact of changing age structure on East Asia's remarkable economic growth in the second half of the twentieth century (Bloom and Williamson 1998). Rapid declines in infant and child mortality in the region began in the late 1940s. These declines triggered a subsequent fall in fertility rates—the crude birth rate dropped from over 40 births per 1,000 population in 1950 to just over 20 by 1980. During the lag between falling mortality and fertility, a "baby boom" generation was created, which was larger than the cohorts that preceded and followed it. As this generation reached working age, it boosted savings rates and also the size of the labor force; from 1965 to 1990, the working-age population grew by 2.6 percent annually and the dependent population grew by just 1.0 percent. Bloom and Williamson (1998) and Bloom, Canning, and Malaney (2000) estimate that this "demographic dividend" explains up to one-third of East Asia's economic miracle between 1965 and 1990.

Accounting Effects

If age-specific behavior with respect to labor supply and savings were fixed, labor supply and savings per capita—and hence income growth—would tend to decline with a rising elder share of the population. Based on this view of the link between population aging and economic growth, rapid aging has the potential to induce a correspondingly sharp reduction in the pace of growth. This frame of reference appears to underlie the rather alarmist views of commentators such as Peter Peterson (1999), who has argued, "Global aging could trigger a crisis that engulfs the world economy [and] may even threaten democracy itself." Ken Dychtwald (1999), too, has raised concerns that "we're going to have a self-centered generation just sucking down all the resources," and former U.S. Federal Reserve chairman Alan Greenspan (2003) has warned that aging in the United States "makes our Social Security and Medicare programs unsustainable in the long run."

In order to assess the potential magnitude of the impact of an increase in the share of elderly, we estimate the pure accounting effect of population aging on labor supply. We do this by applying International Labour

Organization (ILO) estimates of age- and sex-specific labor force participation rates to UN projections of the corresponding distributions of population by age and sex for 2040. We then compare these numbers to the actual labor force participation rate (LFPR) in 2000.[5] The results for the 174 countries in the ILO database are shown in figures 13.14 and 13.15, where we plot actual LFPR in 1960 versus actual LFPR in 2000 and actual LFPR in 2000 versus projected LFPR in 2040. For convenience, we show the 45-degree line, which corresponds to static rates of labor force participation.

Figure 13.14 shows that LFPR increased in slightly more countries than it decreased from 1960 to 2000, corresponding to the demographic transition in developing countries and the post–World War II baby boom in the developed countries. The scatter plot also reveals a demographic cycle of sorts, with high (low) LFPR in 1960 tending to correspond to lower (higher) LFPR in 2000. Rising rates of labor force participation create the potential for higher rates of economic growth.

However, the situation looks rather different going forward. Figure 13.15 projects that changes in the age distribution—and in the sex distribution—of the population will, under the assumption of constant age- and sex-specific LFPR, cause the aggregate LFPR to decrease in more countries than it will increase from 2000 to 2040. In Singapore and Hong Kong, China, for example, LFPR is projected to decline from around 60 percent to 45 percent. Spain, Austria, Germany, and the Netherlands are projected to experience similar declines.

For the 174 countries taken as a whole, LFPR is projected to decline from 66.4 percent in 2000 to 62.1 percent in 2040 (see table 13.4). Although this is a shift from the 1960–2000 experience (during which LFPR barely changed—from 67.4 to 66.4 percent), the 4.3 percentage-point decline represents less than half of a standard deviation (9.5 percent) in the cross-country distribution of LFPR for 2000.

To draw further attention to the small magnitude of the shift of demography from boon to bane with respect to economic growth, figure 13.16 plots ratios of labor force to total population (LFTP) in 2000 and 2040 (the numbers for 2040 again being projected under the assumption that age- and sex-specific LFPR will remain constant at their 2000 levels). The striking result here is that increases outnumber decreases with respect to LFTP. In other words, projected fertility declines imply that the fall in youth dependency is more than enough to offset the skewing of adults toward the older ages at which labor force participation is lower. For the

---

5   The calculations are carried out as follows. We use male and female labor force participation rates from the ILO for each five-year age group between 14–19 and 60–64 and an average for the population aged 65+. We match these data to the UN data on population stocks, which provide data on the number of males and females in each five-year age group. Multiplying each age group by the participation rate gives us the total number of people working. We then sum these and divide by the population aged 15+. For 1960 and 2000, we use actual participation rates. For 2040, we use the participation rates from 2000 and the age structure forecast from the UN *World Population Prospects 2006*.

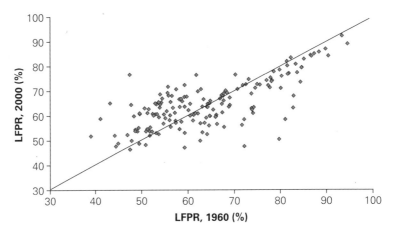

Figure 13.14. Labor Force Participation Rate, 1960 and 2000

Source: Authors' calculations based on United Nations Population Division data.

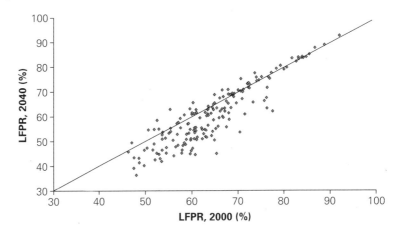

Figure 13.15. Labor Force Participation Rate, 2000 and 2040

Source: Authors' calculations based on United Nations Population Division data.

174 countries taken as a whole, the calculation of LFTP actually projects a rise from 46.5 to 48.6 percent between 2000 and 2040 (table 13.4).

Figure 13.17 plots actual annual growth rates of per capita income from 1960 to 2000 for 97 countries against counterfactual growth rates during that period. The counterfactual is constructed by taking note of the fact that income per capita equals income per worker times workers per capita. This means that the growth rate of income per capita equals the sum of the growth rates of income per worker and workers per capita.[6] The simulation makes the assumption that income per worker grew at

---

6 Using a logarithmic approximation, the growth in GDP per capita between period t and period $t + 1$ is given by $\ln(\text{GDP per capita}_t) - \ln(\text{GDP per capita}_{t-1})$. Since GDP per capita = GDP per worker $\times$ workers per capita, it is easy to show that growth can be expressed as $\ln(\text{GDP per worker}_t/\text{GDP per worker}_{t-1}) + \ln(\text{workers per capita}_t/\text{workers per capita}_{t-1})$.

Table 13.4. Global Labor Force, 1960, 2000, and 2004

Indicator	1960 (actual)	2000 (actual)	2040 (projected)[a]
LFPR (ratio of labor force to population aged 15+)	67.4	66.4	62.1
LFTP (ratio of labor force to total population)	42.4	46.5	48.6

Source: Authors' calculations based on United Nations Population Division data.
a. 2040 projections are based on medium-fertility population projection and age- and gender-specific participation rates in 2000. Averages are population weighted.

Figure 13.16. Labor Force per Capita, 2000 and 2040

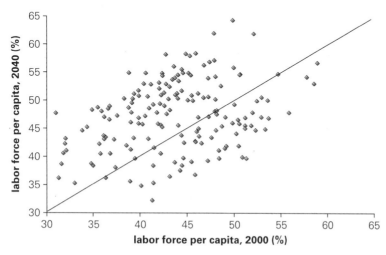

Source: Authors' calculations based on United Nations Population Division data.
Note: 2040 projections are based on medium-fertility population projection and age- and gender-specific participation rates in 2000.

the actual 1960–2000 rate, but that the growth rate of workers per capita followed the expected 2000–40 trajectory, instead of the actual growth rate in workers per capita observed during 1960–2000. Figure 13.17 thus provides a crude indication of the impact of demographic change on economic growth. The comparison is crude for a variety of reasons: it does not allow demographic change to affect behavior with respect to labor supply or savings, and it does not account for any changes in institutions or policies. Organisation for Economic Co-operation and Development (OECD) countries, whose populations are aging faster than the rest of the world, appear in green.

There are two key features of figure 13.17. First, the data points are evenly scattered around the 45 degree line, which implies that the shift in age structure will, on average for the world, have little effect on economic growth. Indeed, for the 97 countries for which the requisite income data are available for both 1960 and 2000, the average actual growth rate during 1960–2000 is 1.9 percent, which is identical to the average counterfactual growth rate. The largest deviation from the 45 degree line is for Singapore.

Figure 13.17. Actual and Counterfactual Annual Growth Rates of Income per Capita, 1960–2000

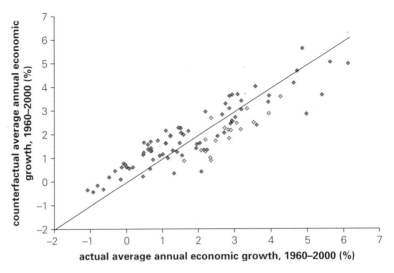

Source: Authors' calculations based on United Nations Population Division data.
Note: Counterfactual assumes 2000–40 growth rate of labor force per capita; original OECD countries are shown in gray.

Its actual growth rate of 5 percent from 1960 to 2000 occurred partly on the strength of an 18 percentage-point rise in labor force per capita from 33 to 51 percent. But in the counterfactual calculation, Singapore's labor force per capita will decline by 11 percentage points, a very pessimistic assumption. In fact, taking the period 1960 to 2000 as a whole, Singapore's labor force per capita is expected to rise from 33 to 40 percent, which means that the net demographic contribution to the growth in income per capita is actually positive over the full sample period.

Second, with the sole (not surprising) exception of Turkey, all of the OECD country points lie below the 45 degree line, indicating that the direction of population aging will be to depress economic growth. Yet even among the original OECD countries, the average actual growth rate during 1960–2000 is 2.8 percent, which is only modestly reduced to 2.1 percent in the counterfactual. It is worth stressing that the counterfactual is likely to overestimate the real effect of the demographic shifts, since it does not compare the projected growth rates to a demography-neutral benchmark, but rather compares economic growth under very favorable demographic conditions to that under very unfavorable demographic conditions. Taken as a whole, this very basic analysis implies that population aging does not represent an economic problem for the world economy. Rather, it is at most a modest issue for particular economies.

The Role of Behavioral Change

These calculations, however, reflect pure accounting effects, assuming constant age-specific behavior. They are likely to represent upper bounds on the magnitude of the effect of aging on labor supply and, since they neglect behavioral change in response to rising longevity, may be misleading.

Behavioral responses to population aging can occur in the form of higher savings for retirement, greater labor force participation, and increased immigration of workers (primarily from developing to developed countries). Countries with the institutional flexibility to facilitate these behavioral changes will be in a position to mitigate the adverse consequences of population aging.

Individuals faced with the prospect of increased life expectancy, where instead of dying in their 50s or 60s they can now expect to live well into their 80s, have several options to smooth their financial path. First, they can rely on social security payments, although these may be imperiled by demographically induced stress on government finances. Demographic change may force the reform of pay-as-you-go systems that become unattainable (Diamond 2002; Holzmann 2000).

Second, they can work longer to finance consumption in later years. Bloom, Canning, Mansfield, and Moore (2007) have shown that the theoretically optimal response to an exogenous rise in life expectancy is to increase working life proportionately, without increasing savings rates. In an environment where longer life expectancy is accompanied by compressed morbidity, people will have greater ability to work productively for longer, without decreasing the amount of years spent in retirement. According to Kulish, Smith, and Kent (2006), they also *desire* to work longer; individuals surveyed in Australia wish to spend a similar proportion of their lives in retirement as life expectancy increases. In practice, however, most countries with social security systems penalize those who wish to work beyond "retirement age." Mandatory retirement is the most extreme of these penalties, but, as Gruber and Wise (1998) have shown, there are many other social security arrangements that provide strong incentives to retire rather than to continue working. The large spike in retirement at age 62 in the United States (the earliest age at which social security benefits can be claimed) and another spike at age 65 (the age at which new retirees have access to even larger benefits) show that people respond to these incentives (Burtless and Moffitt 1985). This behavioral response to social security arrangements is evidenced in Bloom, Canning, Fink, and Finlay (2007a), which shows that institutional settings have strong effects on male labor supply for the 55+ age groups in a broad sample of countries.

The difficulty of working beyond national retirement ages and the precarious prospects for social security payments often mean that individuals resort to a third option—saving more to finance consumption later. Although the theoretically optimal response to longer life would be to work longer and not increase savings, the empirical evidence suggests that in fact people base decisions on the assumption of longer periods of retirement, and savings therefore rise. Bloom, Canning, and Graham (2003) find that increased life expectancy is associated with higher saving rates. More recent work suggests that saving rates increase with life expectancy in countries with universal pension coverage and retirement incentives, but not in countries with pay-as-you-go systems and high replacement rates (Bloom, Canning, Mansfield, and Moore 2007). Economic incentives to promote greater immigration are also likely to strengthen as populations age; outsourcing work is also likely to become an increasingly attractive option (Blinder 2006).

A fourth way for societies to adjust to aging is via increased labor force participation. The reduced fertility that contributes to the shift toward an older age structure allows more women to enter the labor force, as highlighted in Bloom, Canning, Fink, and Finlay (2007b), which can potentially compensate somewhat for the retirement of the elderly. We show the magnitude of these effects in table 13.5. The bottom row of the table shows the actual LFTP ratios in 2000 for females only (column 1), and the total population (column 2), respectively. The upper part of the table shows the predicted values of female and total LFTP between 2000 and 2040. As in table 13.4, age- and gender-specific participation rates are kept constant at their 2000 levels, and the resulting LFTP in 2040 is imputed. While the results displayed in table 13.4 are based exclusively on the medium-fertility population scenario, we now show results for the alternative low- and high-fertility scenarios. As can be seen in the upper part of table 13.5, fertility rates critically shape the LFTP in 2040. Under the low-fertility scenario, the fraction of workers to the total population rises from 0.465 in 2000 to 0.509 in 2040. Under the high-fertility scenario, the fraction declines slightly to 0.464. Higher fertility rates imply higher future youth dependency ratios and thus lower expected LFTP in 2040. This difference is even more pronounced when behavioral changes are taken into account. The second part of table 13.5 calculates "counterfactual" female labor force participation under the assumption that female labor supply responds to changes in fertility. Bloom,

Table 13.5. LFTP Ratios in 2000 (Actual) and 2040 (Predicted), with and without Female Labor Supply Response

Ratio and scenario	Labor force per capita		Additional annual growth (percentage points) in real GDP per capita
	Females	Males and females	
Predicted ratio (2040) assuming no behavioral response			
Low-fertility scenario	0.384	0.509	0.23
Medium-fertility scenario	0.369	0.486	0.11
High-fertility scenario	0.354	0.464	−0.01
Predicted ratio (2040) assuming behavioral response			
Low-fertility scenario	0.437	0.536	0.36
Medium-fertility scenario	0.401	0.502	0.19
High-fertility scenario	0.368	0.471	0.03
Actual ratio (2000)	0.373	0.465	

Sources: United Nations 2006; ILO Labor Statistics (http://laborsta.ilo.org/); authors' calculations.
Note: Based on 174 countries. All averages are population weighted.

Canning, Fink, and Finlay (2007b) estimate the labor supply response for each age group; we use their point estimate and then calculate female labor force participation based on the original 2000 rates plus the estimated adjustment to changing fertility rates. Under the low-fertility scenario, this behavioral response is largest, leading to an increase in LFTP from 46.5 percent in 2000 to 53.6 percent in 2040. Under the high-fertility scenario, this effect is less pronounced, but still implies an increase in LFTP relative to 2000, rather than the decrease expected in the absence of behavioral change.

The potential growth effects generated by changes in LFTP are relatively small. Under the assumption that output per worker stays constant (or is not affected by LFTP), an increase in LFTP from 46.5 to 53.6 percent, as predicted under the most optimistic low-fertility scenario with behavioral response, leads to an annual increase of 0.36 percentage point in real GDP per capita over the whole period. Under the high-fertility scenario, these effects are close to zero. For the OECD countries, the expected growth effects are slightly more negative, as summarized in table 13.6.

Since fertility rates are expected to stay low under all scenarios, little change in total labor force participation is generated by the behavioral response. Nevertheless, even under the most pessimistic high-fertility scenario, the decrease in annual real income growth is expected to be a relatively modest 0.39 percentage point.

Summary and Discussion

For most of the twentieth century the dominant issue in the field of demography was the explosion in population numbers caused by the lowering of mortality rates coupled with continuing high fertility rates. The predicted

Table 13.6. LFTP Ratios in OECD Countries in 2000 (Actual) and 2040 (Predicted), with and without Female Labor Supply Response

Ratio and response	Labor force per capita		Additional annual growth (percentage points) in real per GDP capita
	Females	Males and females	
Predicted ratio (2040) assuming no behavioral response			
Low-fertility scenario	0.375	0.448	−0.19
Medium-fertility scenario	0.368	0.436	−0.26
High-fertility scenario	0.360	0.424	−0.33
Predicted ratio (2040) assuming behavioral response			
Low-fertility scenario	0.385	0.453	−0.17
Medium-fertility scenario	0.363	0.433	−0.27
High-fertility scenario	0.341	0.414	−0.39
Actual ratio (2000)	0.411	0.484	

Sources: United Nations 2006; ILO labor statistics online (http://laborsta.ilo.org/); authors' calculations.
Notes: Based on the 30 current OECD member countries. All averages are country weighted.

negative consequences of high population densities and high population growth rates seem not to have been borne out. Many of the predictions made about the immiserizing effects of population growth seem in retrospect to have been unduly alarmist. For example, between 1960 and 1999, global population doubled, rising from 3 billion to 6 billion, but income per capita tripled, decisively refuting the predictions of population pessimists from Malthus to Ehrlich.[7]

Following the 1986 National Academy of Sciences' report on population growth, the nonalarmist position came to dominate economists' thinking on population (Kelley 2001). While rapid population growth poses problems, the report argues that market mechanisms and nonmarket institutions are usually sufficiently flexible to ameliorate those problems. In particular, projections of the effects of population growth based on unchanged behavior elsewhere in the economy might give a very bleak picture, but in general would be very misleading. Changing incentives through changes in prices and in nonmarket institutional arrangements to promote new behaviors could have large effects and produce responses that would alleviate the problems associated with population growth.

The population debate focused on population numbers and largely missed the issue of changes in age structure. Population growth caused by rising fertility and population growth caused by falling mortality are likely to have quite different economic consequences because they have different age structure effects. We have examined some of these consequences in this chapter. However, it is important to remember the lessons of the earlier debate. Analysis based on accounting effects, in particular on the assumption that age-specific behavior remains unchanged as the age structure evolves, may be misleading. When this type of analysis predicts large reductions in welfare, we should be particularly suspicious since these are exactly the conditions that will produce incentives for behavioral change.

This reasoning also applies to the implications for economic growth of continued improvements in health and reductions in mortality into old age, coupled with the aging of the baby boom generation. How well countries cope with the challenge of population aging will depend to a large extent on the flexibility of their markets and the appropriateness of their institutions and policies.

The preceding section explored the implications of population aging for economic growth. The key premise of the inquiry is that labor supply,

---

7   According to Malthus, who wrote around 1800, when world population first crossed the 1 billion mark, "Population growth appears . . . to be decisive against the possible existence of a society, all the members of which should live in ease, happiness, and comparative leisure; and feel no anxiety about providing the means of subsistence for themselves and families" (Malthus 1798). In a similar vein, Paul Ehrlich asserted in the late 1960s, "The battle is over. In the 1970s hundreds of millions of people are going to starve to death" (Ehrlich 1968). According to the Penn World Tables (version 6.2), total global GDP per capita was $7,565 (at 2000 purchasing power parity) in 2000, compared with $2,495 in 1960. This means that global GDP per capita increased 202 percent (or tripled) over the period 1960–2000, at the same time as the total population doubled. This corresponds to an average annual growth rate of 2.8 percent.

productivity, and savings vary over the life cycle. This implies that the age structure of a population may be consequential for its economic performance, as measured by income per capita. Large youth and elderly cohorts might slow the pace of economic growth, whereas large working-age cohorts might speed it. However, in addition to these accounting effects (assuming that age-specific behavior remains unchanged, we can simply calculate the consequences of a change in age structure), there are also behavioral effects. For example, increased longevity—a key driver of population aging—can change life-cycle behavior, leading to a longer working life or higher savings for retirement.

One view is that population aging in the developed countries is likely to have a large effect, reducing income per capita, mainly through the fall in labor supply per capita that will accompany the reduction in the share of working-age population. However, even if this occurs, it may not be as harmful as it at first appears for five reasons.

First, as seen in the previous section, rough estimates of the magnitude of the effect of population aging on the rate of labor force participation and the concomitant effect of changes in labor force participation on economic growth are, for most countries, of modest size.

Second, income per capita is not a welfare measure. Nordhaus (2003) estimates that over the twentieth century improvements in longevity made a contribution to increasing welfare in the United States of roughly the same magnitude as the rise in consumption levels. The longer life expectancies that lead to aging can be thought of as improving welfare directly by expanding the population's lifetime budget set. Even if rising life expectancy were to lead to reduced consumption levels per period, it is difficult to argue that the net effect of increased longevity on welfare will be negative.

Third, welfare depends on consumption, not income. Typically household income falls at retirement, but consumption may remain relatively high. It follows that we could have two populations, each enjoying the same consumption stream over the same lifespan, but the population with a larger elderly age cohort will have lower per capita income. For these populations, income per capita would vary with the age structure, but lifetime welfare would be equal. Thus aging-induced declines in income per capita are not necessarily indicative of corresponding declines in welfare.

Fourth, while the consequences of a fall in per capita income may not be all that bad for welfare, it is not even clear that population aging will lead to a fall in per capita income. Increases in life expectancy in the United States over the last two centuries have been associated with reductions in the age-specific incidence of disease, disability, and morbidity (Costa 1998a, 1998b; Fogel 1994, 1997). Mathers and others (2001) show that health-adjusted life expectancy (each life year weighted by a measure of health status) rises approximately one for one with life expectancy across countries. Other studies, mostly for the United States and other wealthy industrial countries, imply that the morbidity years are compressed—both relatively and absolutely—as life expectancy rises. Agents can respond to an expectation of longer healthy life spans by working longer or saving more (that is, consuming less). If they work longer, they can keep their consumption levels high and need only save for old age at the same rate as before. If they decide to take extra leisure and retire at the same age as before, they will have lower consumption levels throughout their life and will need higher saving rates while working. Bloom, Canning, and Graham (2003) and Bloom, Canning, and Moore (2004) examine this issue theoretically and argue that when health improves and longevity rises, the optimal response is likely to be a longer working life, without the need for higher savings.[8] To the extent that working lives lengthen in response to longer life spans, there is no reduction in income levels. Indeed, average income and consumption per capita can remain high. The assumption of fixed age-specific rates of labor force participation assumes no behavioral change when, in fact, such changes may occur.

Fifth, old age "dependency" is something of a misnomer. Lee (2000) shows that, in all preindustrial societies for which he was able to assemble evidence, the flow of transfers is from the middle-aged and old to the young. In developed countries, both the young and the old benefit from government transfers, and the net pattern of transfers is toward the elderly. However, at the household level in the United States, elderly households make significant transfers to middle-age households, undoing to some extent the effects of government policy. The dependency burden of the elderly is a function of the institutional welfare systems that are in place rather than an immutable state of affairs.[9]

Analysis of the effects of population aging on economic growth represents virgin territory. The size and nature of the current demographic shift is unprecedented, so past experience cannot provide a guide. Demographers and economists therefore need to rely on models.

Insofar as population aging leads to labor supply reductions that cause wages to rise, and given that different countries are in different phases of the demographic cycle, international migration flows are likely to be stimulated. Such flows will smooth the age distribution since working-age individuals account for a large proportion of international migrants. However, judging by historical experience, and in a context of widespread institutional and social constraints on immigration, the magnitude of the increases needed to smooth the age distribution is inordinately large and not, as a practical matter, likely to be a decisive response to population aging. Although migrants themselves benefit greatly, it is not yet well established whether immigration results in net economic benefits or losses to receiving countries. Lee and Miller (2000) find only very small net fiscal impacts of immigration to the United States over the next century.

---

8   The tendency toward early retirement is explained by an income effect, with people wanting more leisure time as incomes rise.

9   Mason and others (2006) propose and investigate a "national transfer accounts" methodology to aid in understanding the extent and effect of intergenerational transfers.

The Importance of Policy

The policy environment is crucial in determining the effect of aging on economic growth. The problem of population aging is more a problem of rigid and outmoded policies and institutions than a problem of demographic change per se. Policies are needed that account for the natural incentives individuals have to adjust their behavior in the face of population aging.

Among the most commonly proposed policy changes is to alter retirement incentives so that people can fulfill their expressed desires to work longer in response to expectations of greater longevity. More flexible old-age pension arrangements combined with increases in the official retirement age will encourage prolonged workforce participation. Legal and cultural efforts to discourage age discrimination by employers may also be required. Lifelong education programs could assist in these efforts, by helping people to adapt their skills and knowledge to the demands of a changing economy.

Investment in improving the health of those 60 years of age or older is a further policy option. Not only does this reduce the burden on health care and social security systems, but by compressing morbidity into fewer years late in life, it also enables people to work longer. While rising old age dependency may increase health care costs (Gray 2005), Zweifel, Felder, and Meiers (1999) have shown that health care costs appear to be concentrated in the last few years of life regardless of age, so population aging defers rather than increases costs. In addition to easing strains on state finances, the compression of morbidity enables older people to continue contributing their expertise and knowledge to economies.

Policy should also encourage increased labor force participation. Laws against sex discrimination have helped to open up the workplace to women in many wealthy countries; middle- and low-income countries with aging populations would likely benefit from similar measures. Upward pressure on wages is likely to increase women's participation in the workforce, and this can be complemented by policies that facilitate the ability of mothers to combine work and family, such as state-funded child care and more flexible working hours. The latter, of course, also incentivizes childrearing, with long-term impacts on the age structure.

The issue of immigration is also vital; policy makers in aging developed countries have not yet successfully made the case for increased immigration from the developing world, but demographic imbalances mean that demand by employers is likely to intensify in the coming decades. Compensating those who lose out from the process (such as low-skilled, receiving-country workers) might help to make opening up to migration more politically feasible.

A further important policy consideration is to address the funding gap caused by the intergenerational transfers implicit in pay-as-you-go health and pension systems (Poterba 2004). In an aging society, these imply that small cohorts of working-age people will make transfers to large cohorts of elderly. But, even under a pay-as-you-go system, it is not inevitable that the old must depend on transfers from younger generations. Adjusting premiums and benefits or making a transition to full funding or a system of private accounts, whereby individuals effectively draw at least part of their pensions from investments made during their time in work, could help to reduce old-age "dependency." Fully funded systems mean that older workers who continue in employment benefit by having a larger sum to draw on when they eventually retire. Moving toward such a system would require robust institutions that can both attract sufficient savings and invest them productively and safely. There are some concerns that the increases in savings required to move away from a pay-as-you-go system will mean scarcer investment opportunities and diminished returns. Although Poterba (2004) finds that the historic effect of demography on real rates of return has been small, Turner (2006) injects some major cautionary notes into this discussion: (a) higher saving rates will tend to lower returns on investments; (b) when new generations are smaller, both pay-as-you-go and fully funded pension systems will face falling asset prices, so the latter are not a cure-all for troubled pension systems; and (c) the performance of funded systems depends on global capital markets, not just those of any particular country. He concludes that fully funded systems will not necessarily provide a complete answer to demographic change and that pay-as-you-go systems can be adjusted to achieve "many of the supposed advantages of funded systems." Heller (2003) emphasizes the fact that the historically unprecedented commitments governments have already made to financial support of the elderly will play a major constraining role in future policy making in this area.[10]

An Uncertain Future

Of course, humility is required when making decisions based on future demographic projections. The sources of uncertainty remain considerable. Population projections, for example, are not cast in stone. The possibility of changes in fertility behavior or health shocks could tilt the balance between young and old in unforeseen ways. As discussed above, projections of population size and structure can change significantly even over short periods. Longevity projections are also precarious and hotly debated. Trends in diet and life style as well as medical and public health advances could combine to raise or lower life expectancy in the future. Technology has a crucial role to play. The compression of morbidity occurring today is driven partly by new health technology, but it is uncertain whether technological advance will continue, diminish, or accelerate in the future and what cost implications it will have. Trends such as the obesity "epidemic" could dampen the positive effects of technology. The World Health Organization projects that by 2025, 300 million people will be obese and that the health impacts of the rising prevalence of obesity could reverse the

---

10 Auerbach, Kotlikoff, and Leibfritz (1999) review the use of generational accounting as a means of studying these and broader questions about intergenerational transfers. Barr and Diamond (2006) systematically address many of the issues and controversies in the arena of pensions and their distributional effects, savings, and economic growth.

gains in life expectancy in some countries (Visscher and Seidell 2001). Non-health-related events such as climate change or war could also have an unpredictable effect on longevity.

It is not clear whether the economic impacts of aging will be uniform across societies. In the developed world, longer life spans have been accompanied by a shift in support for older generations from families to the state. In many developing countries, families remain pivotal to elder care; as life spans become longer, there may be disruption to family structures, leading to a similar move toward public transfer systems and savings as that experienced in wealthier parts of the world.

Although drawing lessons from the past may not be possible for an aging future, we know that some societies in the past century coped well with the major demographic shift represented by population growth. The world economy has had the flexibility to absorb and in general to benefit from dramatic increases in population numbers. If today's policy makers take prompt action to prepare for the effects of aging, the next major shift is likely to cause much less hardship than many fear.

References

Auerbach, Alan J., Laurence J. Kotlikoff, and Willi Leibfritz, eds. 1999. *Generational Accounting around the World*. NBER Books. Cambridge, MA: National Bureau of Economic Research.

Barr, Nicholas, and Peter A. Diamond. 2006. "The Economics of Pensions." *Oxford Review of Economic Policy* 22 (1): 15–39.

Blinder, Alan S. 2006. "Offshoring: The Next Industrial Revolution?" *Foreign Affairs* 85 (March-April): 113–28.

Bloom, David E., David Canning, Guenther Fink, and Jocelyn Finlay. 2007a. "Demographic Change, Institutional Settings, and Labor Supply." PGDA Working Paper 42. Harvard University, Cambridge, MA.

———. 2007b. "Fertility and Female Labor Force Participation." NBER Working Paper 13583. National Bureau of Economic Research, Cambridge, MA. www.nber.org/papers/w13583.

Bloom, David E., David Canning, and Bryan Graham. 2003. "Longevity and Life-Cycle Savings." *Scandinavian Journal of Economics* 105 (3): 319–38.

Bloom, David E., David Canning, and Pia Malaney. 2000. "Demographic Change and Economic Growth in Asia." *Population and Development Review* 26 (supplement): 257–90.

Bloom, David E., David Canning, Richard Mansfield, and Michael Moore. 2007. "Demographic Change, Social Security Systems, and Savings." *Journal of Monetary Economics* 54 (1): 92–114.

Bloom, David E., David Canning, and Michael Moore. 2004. "The Effects of Improvements in Health and Longevity on Optimal Retirement and Saving." NBER Working Paper 10919. National Bureau of Economic Research, Cambridge, MA.

Bloom, David E., David Canning, and Jaypee Sevilla. 2002. "The Demographic Dividend: A New Perspective on the Economic Consequences of Population Change." Paper 8808. Rand Corporation, Santa Monica, CA.

Bloom, David E., and Jeffrey G. Williamson. 1998. "Demographic Transitions and Economic Miracles in Emerging Asia." *World Bank Economic Review* 12 (3): 419–55.

Burtless, Gary, and Robert A. Moffitt. 1985. "The Effect of Social Security Benefits on the Labor Supply of the Aged." In *Retirement and Economic Behavior,* ed. Henry J. Aaron and Gary Burtless. Washington, DC: Brookings Institution Press.

Costa, Dora L. 1998a. *The Evolution of Retirement: An American Economic History, 1880–1990.* National Bureau of Economic Research Series on Long-Term Factors in Economic Development. Chicago: University of Chicago Press.

———. 1998b. "Unequal at Birth: A Long-Term Comparison of Income and Birth Weight." *Journal of Economic History* 58 (4): 987–1009.

———. 2002. "Changing Chronic Disease Rates and Long-Term Declines in Functional Limitation among Older Men." *Demography* 39 (1): 119–37.

Crimmins, Eileen M. 2004. "Trends in the Health of the Elderly." *Annual Review of Public Health* 25 (1): 79–98.

Crimmins, Eileen, Yasuhiko Saito, and Dominique Ingegneri. 1997. "Trends in Disability-Free Life Expectancy in the United States, 1970–90." *Population and Development Review* 23 (3): 555–72.

Diamond, Peter. 2002. *Social Security Reform.* New York: Oxford University Press.

Dychtwald, Ken. 1999. "Ken Dychtwald on the Future." *San Francisco Chronicle,* November 15. http://sfgate.com/cgi-bin/article.cgi?file=/gate/archive/1999/11/15/dychtwaldtalk.DTL.

Ehrlich, Paul. 1968. *The Population Bomb.* New York: Ballantine Books.

Fogel, Robert W. 1994. "Economic Growth, Population Theory, and Physiology: The Bearing of Long-Term Processes on the Making of Economic Policy." *American Economic Review* 84 (3): 369–95.

———. 1997. "New Findings on Secular Trends in Nutrition and Mortality: Some Implications for Population Theory." In *Handbook of Population and Family Economics,* Vol. 1A, ed. Mark Rosenzweig and Oded Stark. Amsterdam: Elsevier.

Fries, James. 1980. "Aging, Natural Death, and the Compression of Morbidity." *New England Journal of Medicine* 303 (3): 130–35.

———. 1989. "The Compression of Morbidity: Near or Far?" *Milbank Quarterly* 67 (2): 208–32.

Gerland, Patrick. 2005. "From Divergence to Convergence in Sex Differentials in Adult Mortality in Developed Countries." Poster #11—Session 1: Aging, Life Course, Health, Mortality, and Health Care. Population Association of America, Philadelphia, PA. March 31.

Gray, Alastair. 2005. "Population Ageing and Health Care Expenditure." *Ageing Horizons* 2: 15–20.

Greenspan, Alan. 2003. "Aging Global Population." Testimony before the Special Committee on Aging, U.S. Senate, Washington, DC. February 27.

Gruber, Jonathan, and David Wise. 1998. "Social Security and Retirement: An International Comparison." *American Economic Review* 88 (2): 158–63.

Heller, Peter S. 2003. *Who Will Pay? Coping with Aging Societies, Climate Change, and Other Long-Term Fiscal Challenges.* Washington, DC: International Monetary Fund.

Holzmann, Robert. 2000. "The World Bank Approach to Pension Reform." *International Social Security Review* 53 (1): 11–34.

Kelley, Allen C. 2001. "The Population Debate in Historical Perspective: Revisionism Revised." In *Population Matters: Demographic Change, Economic Growth, and Poverty in the Developing World,* ed. Nancy Birdsall, Allen C. Kelley, and Steven W. Sinding, 24–54. New York: Oxford University Press.

Kulish, Mariano, Kathryn Smith, and Christopher Kent. 2006. "Ageing, Retirement, and Savings: A General-Equilibrium Analysis." Research Discussion Paper 2006-06. Reserve Bank of Australia, Sydney, Australia.

Lee, Ronald. 2000. "A Cross-Cultural Perspective on Intergenerational Transfers and the Economic Life Cycle." In *Sharing the Wealth: Demographic Change and Economic Transfers between Generations,* ed. Andrew Mason and Georges Tapinos, 17–56. New York: Oxford University Press.

Lee, Ronald, and Timothy Miller. 2000. "Immigration, Social Security, and Broader Fiscal Impacts." *American Economic Review* 90 (2): 350–54.

Lutz, Wolfgang, Warren Sanderson, and Sergei Scherbov. 2008. "The Coming Acceleration of Global Population Ageing." *Nature* 451 (January 20): 716–19.

Malthus, Thomas R. 1798. *An Essay on the Principle of Population as It Affects the Future Improvement of Society, with Remarks on the Speculations of Mr. Godwin, M. Condorcet, and Other Writers.* London: J. Johnson.

Mason, Andrew, Ronald Lee, An-Chi Tung, Mun-Sim Lai, and Tim Miller. 2006. "Population Aging and Intergenerational Transfers: Introducing Age into National Accounts." NBER Working Paper 12770. National Bureau of Economic Research, Cambridge, MA. www.nber.org/papers/w12770.

Mathers, Colin D., and others. 2001. "Healthy Life Expectancy in 191 Countries, 1999." *Lancet* 357 (9269): 1685–91.

McKibbin, Warwick J. 2006. "The Global Macroeconomic Consequences of a Demographic Transition." CAMA Working Paper 6/2006. Australian National University, Centre for Applied Macroeconomic Analysis, Canberra, Australia. http://cama.anu.edu.au/Working%20Papers/Papers/2006/McKibbin_62006.pdf.

Nordhaus, William. 2003. "The Health of Nations: The Contribution of Improved Health to Living Standards." In *Measuring the Gains from Medical Research: An Economic Approach,* ed. Kevin H. Murphy and Robert H. Topel. Chicago: University of Chicago Press.

Oeppen, Jim, and James W. Vaupel. 2002. "Broken Limits to Life Expectancy." *Science* 296 (5570): 1029–31.

Peterson, Peter G. 1999. "Gray Dawn: The Global Aging Crisis." *Foreign Affairs* 78 (January-February): 42–56.

Poterba, James. 2004. "The Impact of Population Aging on Financial Markets." In *Symposium Proceedings, Global Demographic Change: Economic Impacts and Policy Challenges*. Federal Reserve Bank of Kansas City, Jackson Hole, WY. August 26–28. www.kc.frb.org/ Publicat/sympos/2004/sym04prg.htm.

Preston, Samuel H. 1975. "The Changing Relation between Mortality and Level of Economic Development." *Population Studies* 29 (2): 231–48.

Turner, Adair. 2006. "Pension Challenges in an Aging World." *Finance and Development* 43 (3): 36–39.

Tyers, Rod, and Qun Shi. 2007. "Global Demographic Change, Policy Responses, and Their Economic Implications." *World Economy* 30 (4): 537–66.

United Nations. 1994–2006. *World Population Prospects*. New York: UN Population Division.

Visscher, Tommy L., and Jacob C. Seidell. 2001. "The Public Health Impact of Obesity." *Annual Review of Public Health* 22 (May): 355–75.

Zweifel Peter, Stefan Felder, and Markus Meiers. 1999. "Ageing of Population and Health Care Expenditure: A Red Herring?" *Health Economics* 8 (6): 485–96.

Index

Figures, notes, and tables are indicated by f, n, and t following the page number.

Agreement on Subsidies (WTO), 144–45, 145*n*4
agricultural impact of climate change, 265, 266*f*, 275, 279, 286, 288
Akerlof, George, 111, 112
Albala-Bertrand, José, 159
Alt-A mortgages, 51
American International Group (AIG), 77, 78, 86
Andres, Luis, 182
Angola, manufactured exports from, 205
antidumping, 8
arbitrage, 47, 47*n*1, 48, 75, 77, 79
architecture of networks, 72, 77
Argentina
    bank capital standards, 57
    climate change impact, 275
    exchange rate adjustments, 228
    investment risk in, 100
    offshore savings, 10
    population density, 208
    private sector infrastructure investments, 174, 178*n*31, 179*n*32
Aschauer, David, 160, 166, 167
Asia
    See also specific countries
    aging population, 303*f*
    economic growth, 128
    manufactured exports, 207, 207*f*
    population density, 208
    urban population growth, 17
Asian financial crisis (1997–98), 70, 76, 85, 134
asset-backed securities. *See* securitization of assets
asset bubbles, 59, 76, 77
asset tangibility, 237
asymmetry of risks, 85
audit trails, 89
Auerbach, Alan J., 324*n*10
Australia
    climate change impact, 265
    debt instrument yields, 101
    exchange rate corrections, 226, 227*t*, 228
    export expansion to, 223

foreign ownership of assets, 104
retirement age, 317
Austria
    centralized wage bargaining, 146
    labor force participation rate, 313
auto industry, 43, 44

B

bailouts, 11–12, 16, 40, 43, 53
Banco Nacional de Desenvolvimento Economico e Social (Brazil), 13
Bangladesh
    climate change impact, 279
    manufactured exports, 223
Bank Holding Company Act of 1956 (U.S.), 52, 64
Bank of England, 11
Bank of Spain, 83
bankruptcy process for large banks, 54
banks
    bailouts for, 11–12, 16, 40, 43, 53
    capital risk weighting of loans, 185
    development banking, 131
    ecological system parallels to, 80
    equity ratios, 61, 62
    management compensation systems, 52, 84–86
    in networks, 71
    public sector, 13
    risk management, 55
    state development banks, 9
    stockholder discipline, 52, 63–64
Barabási, Albert-László, 73
Bardhan, Pranab, 184
Barr, Nicholas, 16, 324*n*10
Barth, James R., 55
Basel Capital Accords, 48, 59, 82
Bear Stearns, 53
benefit-cost analysis for climate change mitigation, 254*n*5, 268
Benin, climate change impact on, 279
Bennathan, Esra, 159, 163
Bern carbon-cycle model, 251, 252*f*
Bertolini, Lorenzo, 183
Besley, Timothy, 111, 112, 113
Bevan, David, 170
Bhagwati, Jagdish, 5, 6, 20

biofuels, 273*n*20, 274, 291

Birdsall, Nancy, 257

Blinder, Alan, 6–7, 7*nn*4–5, 20

Bloom, David E., 15, 27, 297, 312, 317, 318, 319, 322

Boccanfuso, Dorothee, 170

Bolivia

    investment risk in, 100

    manufactured exports, 205

    private sector infrastructure investments, 179*n*32

Bookstaber, Richard, 79

Bordo, Michael, 81

Borio, Claudio, 60, 61

Bougheas, Spiros, 163

Bourguignon, François, 19

Braun, Matías, 238

Brazil

    aging population, 305*f*

    climate change impact on, 265

    domestic saving as growth constraint, 135

    exchange rate adjustments, 228

    income inequality in, 19

    infrastructure investments, 166, 166*n*17

    manufactured exports, 206*t*, 209, 210*t*

    private sector infrastructure investments, 179*n*32

    public sector banks, 13

    renewable energy, 269, 273*n*20

    spatial development, 168

breakpoints, 80

Briceño, Cecilia, 158

"bridge bank" plans, 54, 62–63, 66

Brunnermeier, Markus, 61

budget constraints

    infrastructure and, 166–67

    in poverty-targeted programs, 113–14, 115–16

business cycles, 38, 39, 59

Buys, Piet, 268, 274

C

Cadot, Olivier, 162

Calderon, Cesar, 158, 160

Calomiris, Charles W., 21–22, 47, 49, 61

Cambodia, climate change impact on, 279

campaign contributions, 43

Canada

    debt instrument yields, 101

    exchange rate corrections, 226, 227*t*, 228

    export expansion to, 223

    import trends, 212–22, 213–21*t*

    income inequality in, 19

Canning, David, 15, 27, 159, 161, 163, 297, 312, 317, 318, 319, 322

cap-and-trade systems, 272, 273, 276

Cape Verde, wind power in, 274

capitalism, 11, 39, 40, 42

capital outflows, 134–36, 135*f*

capital regulations, 48, 59, 76

capital risk weighting of bank loans, 185

Caprio, Gerard, Jr., 55

carbon-cycle models, 251, 252*f*

carbon emissions

    See also climate change

    North-South breakdown, 248, 250*t*

    reduction incentives, 270–73

carbon fertilization effect, 265

carbon pricing, 273–74

    See also cap-and-trade systems

carbon sequestration, 252–53

Case-Shiller index, 63*n*3

Castells, Manuel, 70

CCCs (contingent capital certificates), 58

CDOs (collateralized debt obligations), 83

CDSs. *See* credit default swaps

Census Bureau, U.S., 9, 99

Center for Global Development, 258*n*8, 276

Central America, climate change impact on, 265

    See also specific countries

central banks

    asset bubbles and, 60

    countercyclical stimulus packages and, 243

    foreign exchange reserves and, 85

    in networks, 71

    purchases of dollar-denominated assets, 102

Central Europe, private sector foreign capital investments in, 101

    See also specific countries

centralized networks, 72, 73f
centralized wage bargaining, 146
Chenery, Hollis, 197
Chile
   exchange rate adjustments, 227
   industrial policies in, 132
   infrastructure impact on
      productivity, 159
China
   aging population, 99, 100, 303,
      305f, 305t, 307, 307n3
   climate change and, 247, 267,
      269, 274, 288
   currency valuation, 105, 133,
      227, 228, 228n13, 231
   economic growth, 127–28, 128f
   foreign exchange reserves held by,
      10, 226, 227t
   industrial policies, 129, 132
   manufactured exports, 204, 205,
      206t, 207, 210–11, 210–11t
   private sector infrastructure
      investments by, 175, 180
   public sector banks, 13
   renewable energy, 269
   reproduction ratio, 99
   trade surplus, 126, 133, 134
   wind power in, 274
Claessens, Stijn, 3, 3n1
clean energy
   diffusion of technology, 248, 278
   investments in, 274
   price reductions, 274
   research and development, 254n5,
      259, 274, 277, 278
climate change, 247–83
   adaptation support, 274–75, 278–79
   carbon emissions reduction
      incentives, 270–73
   carbon pricing, 273–74
   clean energy development, 248, 254n5,
      259, 274, 277, 278
   economic forecasts, 254–61, 255t,
      256f, 287–90
   economic growth and, 18–19, 285–95
   energy infrastructure and, 157
   health impacts of, 286, 288

impact distribution, 265–68, 266–67f
intergenerational distribution, 256–57
interventions, 268–75
IPCC role, 253–54
mitigation, 257–59, 259t,
   277–78, 290–91
national sovereignty and, 260
policies for, 286–87
program for global action, 275–79
risks, 260
scientific evidence on, 249–54,
   249f, 250t, 251f
sources of, 261–65, 263–64f
technological forecasts, 254–61
transport infrastructure and, 157
Cline, William R., 25, 195, 204, 214,
   224, 226, 227, 265, 275
cluster effect of knowledge
   hubs, 73
coastal areas and climate change, 288
collective bargaining, 146
Collier, Paul, 4
Colombia
   investment needs analysis, 165n15
   macro prudential regulation, 60–61
collateralized debt obligations (CDOs), 83
command-and-control regulation, 270
commercial banks
   "bridge bank" plans and, 62
   capital regulations, 48
   regulation of, 52
Commission of Experts (UN), 13
common standards, 72, 75, 89
community-driven participatory
   projects, 119
compensation systems, 52,
   84–86, 90
competitive nature of networks, 75
complexity of networks, 77, 79, 89
compression of morbidity, 297, 310, 321
concession contracts, 178
conditional cash transfers, 110
conduits, 83
connection costs, 173
consumer demand, 44, 106
Continental Bank bailout, 53
contingent capital certificates (CCCs), 58

exchange rate

   See also currency valuation

   adjustment recommendations, 225, 226, 227–28, 231

   capital inflows impact on, 135

   depreciation, 132

   industrial policies and, 126

   infrastructure investments and, 170

   tradable goods market equilibrium and, 141, 142*f*

   U.S. dollar, 226–27, 227*f*

exchange risk, 101–2

expectational trap, 44

export-processing zones, 143

exports, 136–39, 137*t*, 199

   See also manufactured exports

external financial dependence, 237, 238, 239, 240

F

Faguet, Jean Paul, 184

Faini, Riccardo, 168

fair-value accounting, 84, 89

fallacy of composition (FC) problems, 195–234

Fannie Mae, 50, 51, 63, 66

Farmer, J. Doyne, 89

Fay, Marianne, 24, 151, 163

Federal Deposit Insurance Corporation Improvement Act of 1991 (FDICIA, U.S.), 53, 62

Federal Home Loan bank system, 50, 63, 66

Federal Housing Administration (FHA), 50, 63, 66

Federal Reserve

   asset bubbles and, 60

   bailouts by, 11

   interest rate policy, 49

   moral hazard potential in, 53

   on total U.S. financial assets, 104

Federal Reserve Bank of New York, 74, 82

Fedwire interbank payment network, 74

feedback loop interactivity, 77, 82–83, 88, 90

Fernald, John, 159, 161

fertility rate, 98–99, 297, 299, 306, 319

FGT alpha (degree of poverty aversion), 111

FHA. *See* Federal Housing Administration

financial dependence, 237, 238, 239, 240

financial engineering, 76

financial networks, 69–93

   characteristics of, 72–75, 73*f*

   global economic crisis and, 76–87

   overview, 71–76

   topology of, 72–73, 73*f*

financial regulation, 47–68

   See also regulatory framework

   reform, 54–65

   subprime crisis errors and, 49–54

financial sector

   bailouts for, 43

   "bridge bank" plans, 54, 62–63, 66

   deregulation of, 70, 76

   derivatives transactions, 64–65

   reallocation and, 44

   regulatory reform, 54–65

   securitization of assets, 48

Financial Stability Forum, 15, 89

fine targeting, 113, 114–15, 116, 117–18, 120

Fink, Günther, 15, 27, 297, 317, 318, 319

Finland, income inequality in, 19

Finlay, Jocelyn, 317, 318, 319

fire-sale externalities, 80–81

firewalls, 90

fiscal consolidation, 105

fiscal incidence policy, 5

Fisman, Raymond, 184

fixed-effect approach, 160

Flannery, Mark, 58

flight to quality, 70, 107, 134

flooding, 267, 268*f*, 274, 279

Folkerts-Landau, David, 228*n*14

foreclosure mitigation protocols, 50

foreign exchange reserves, 85, 101–2, 226

foreign ownership of assets, 104

formal sector wages, 146

Foster, James, 111

Foster, Vivien, 173

France

   foreign ownership of assets, 104

   import trends, 212–22, 213–21*t*

France (*continued*)
  income inequality in, 19
  political influence on infrastructure
      investments, 162
  spatial development policy, 168
Freddie Mac, 50, 51, 63, 66
Freund, Caroline, 3n1, 4n2

G
G-8 (Group of Eight), 6, 8, 278
G-20 (Group of Twenty), 8, 14, 17
Garber, Peter, 228n14
Gasmi, Farid, 182
Gatti, Roberta, 184
Gelbach, Jonah, 113
General Agreement on Tariffs and Trade
      (GATT), 132, 196, 219
general-equilibrium model
  aging population, 311n4
  infrastructure investments, 166,
      166n17, 169–70
  manufacturing exports, 200
geoengineering, 292
geothermal power, 274
Germany
  aging population in, 99
  currency valuation, 105
  current account surplus, 99
  foreign ownership of assets, 104
  import trends, 212–22, 213–21t
  income inequality in, 19
  labor force participation rate, 313
  reproduction ratio, 99
  saving rates, 99
global economic crisis
  financial networks and, 76–87
  financial regulation and, 49–54
  government errors in, 49–54
  growth after, 125–50
  network characteristics of, 76–87
  poverty-targeted programs and, 109–22
Global Economic Prospects (World Bank,
      2007), 7
global imbalances, 95–108
  demographics and, 98–100
  investment in U.S., 100–104
  savings-investment balance, 98–100

Global Warming and Agriculture
      (Cline), 265
Goldin, Claudia, 20
Goldman Sachs, 53
Goodhart, Charles, 83
Gore, Al, 258
governance, 6, 78–87
governance arbitrage, 75, 77
Government Financial Statistics
      (IMF), 156–57
government-sponsored enterprises
      (GSEs), 50–51, 63
Graham, Bryan, 317, 322
Gramm-Leach-Bliley Act of 1999 (U.S.), 57
"gravity model" for world financial
      flows, 97–98
greenhouse gas emissions.
      See climate change
Greenspan, Alan, 57, 81, 312
Greer, Joel, 111
Group of Thirty, 78
growth
  after global economic crisis, 125–50
  aging population and, 297–328
  climate change and, 285–95
  countercyclical stimulus packages
      and, 235–45
  cross-border lending reduction and,
      134–36, 135f
  current account balances and, 139–46,
      140t, 142f
  historical overview, 127–33, 128f
  industrial policy and, 129–33, 130f,
      133t, 138–46, 139f
  input costs reduction and, 145
  trade and, 136–39, 137t
  wage restraints and, 146
Gruber, Jonathan, 317
Guasch, José Luis, 182

H
headcount ratio, 111
health care
  aging population and, 309, 323
  climate change impact on, 286, 288
  obesity epidemic and, 324–25
  redistributive nature of, 110

Kuncoro, Ari, 168
Kuwait, investing of oil revenues by, 98
Kyoto Protocol, 258, 261*n*13, 272, 291

L

labor costs, 146
labor force participation rate (LFPR),
    311*n*4, 313, 313*n*5, 314*f*, 315*t*, 323
labor force to total population (LFTP),
    313–14, 315*t*, 318–19
labor unions, 146
Lall, Somik, 163, 167
land-use change, 258*n*9, 262
Larrain, Borja, 238
Latin America
    See also specific countries
    aging population, 303*f*
    climate change impact, 275, 288
    cost of capital, 177*n*30
    economic growth, 128
    exchange rate adjustments, 227
    import substitution, 197
    income inequality in, 19
    infrastructure
        access, 155
        affordability, 171, 172
        private sector investments,
            175, 176, 178
        public sector investments, 177
    manufactured exports, 207, 207*f*, 208
    population density, 208
    regulatory agencies, 182
    subsidies, 173
Lawrence, Robert Z., 20, 20*n*11
leakages in poverty-targeted programs,
    112, 113, 115
learning spillovers, 131, 141
Lee, Ronald, 322
Lehman Brothers, 22, 53, 70, 77
Leibfritz, Willi, 324*n*10
Leipziger, Danny, 5, 19, 20
leverage, 84, 85
leverage subsidies, 63
Levin, Simon A., 80, 89
Levine, Ross, 55
LFPR. *See* labor force participation rate
LFTP. *See* labor force to total population

LGD (loss given default), 58, 66
life-cycle saving behavior model, 98, 312
life expectancy, 98–99, 297, 307, 308*f*, 317
Lin, Justin, 13
liquidity requirements, 58, 86
    See also capital regulations
livestock species choice, 288
Lo, Andrew, 75, 89
loan-provisioning requirements, 82
loan-to-asset ratios, 61
location theory, 168
logistics costs, 145
Lomborg, Bjorn, 254, 254*n*5,
    258, 259, 260, 274
London in global financial market
    network, 74
loss allocation, 78, 79
loss-avoidance behavior, 81–82, 107
loss given default (LGD), 58, 66
loss leaders, 73

M

macro prudential capital regulation,
    59–62, 86
Mahler, Vincent, 9*n*6
maintenance costs, 152, 164, 164*t*, 166
Malaney, Pia, 312
Malaysia
    exchange rate adjustments, 227, 228*n*13
    foreign exchange reserves held by,
        226, 227*t*
    manufactured exports, 205, 206*t*
Malthus, Thomas R., 320, 320*n*7
Mamatzakis, Emmanuel, 159
Mamuneas, Theofanis, 163
management compensation systems,
    52, 84–86, 90
management information systems
    (MISs), 82
mandatory retirement age, 317
Mansfield, Richard, 317
Mansuri, Ghazala, 184
manufactured exports, 195–234
    to China, 210–11, 211*t*
    growth strategy and, 128–29
    import penetration and, 212–22, 213–21*t*
    literature review on, 197–200

National Snow and Ice Data Center,
U.S., 265, 265*f*
national sovereignty and climate
change, 260
national transfer accounts, 322*n*9
negative externalities of bank risk
management, 55
negative feedback mechanisms, 77, 82
neo-mercantilist model, 228*n*14
Nepal, hydropower in, 274
Netherlands
current account surplus, 99
labor force participation rate, 313
net international investment position
(NIIP), 102–4, 107, 224
network altruism principle, 73
networks
applied to financial markets, 75–76
characteristics, 72–75, 73*f*
complexity, 79, 89
externalities, 80–81
feedback loop interactivity, 82–83
hub-and-spoke transport, 168
incentives, 84–86
information overload, 83–84
infrastructure and, 158–59
interconnectivity, 81–82, 90
labor division between home and
host regulators, 86–87
systemwide view, 78–79
in telecommunication sector, 158–59
transparency, 83–84
in transport sector, 158–59, 168
New York Stock Exchange/Euronext, 74
New Zealand
exchange rate corrections, 226
export expansion to, 223
NGOs. *See* nongovernmental organization
Nigeria
aging population, 305*f*
manufactured exports, 205, 223
NIIP. *See* net international
investment position
nodes, 71, 72, 81–82, 81*f*
no-doc mortgages, 51
nongovernmental organization (NGOs),
274, 277, 278, 279

Nordhaus, William, 257, 258, 258*n*9,
258*n*11, 268, 273, 274, 321
North Africa. *See* Middle East and
North Africa
North American Free Trade Agreement
(NAFTA), 205
North-South relationship
See also developing countries
climate change and, 248, 250*t*, 255,
256*f*, 261–65, 263–64*f*
trade and, 197
Norway
economic growth, 127–28, 128*f*
income inequality in, 19
investing of oil revenues by, 98
NRSROs. *See* nationally recognized
statistical rating organizations

O

obesity epidemic, 324–25
OECD countries
infrastructure impact on growth, 158
labor force participation, 315
population aging, 316
private sector infrastructure
investments, 175, 178
Office of Thrift Supervision, 78
offshoring, 6, 7, 7*n*4
off-take agreements, 180
oil-exporting countries, 98, 99
Olken, Benjamin A., 184
opportunity cost of time, 112–13
outsourcing, 318
over-the-counter (OTC) transactions,
64–65, 86

P

Pakistan, manufactured exports
by, 206*t*, 223
Panagariya, Arvind, 6
Papua New Guinea, hydropower in, 274
PD (probability of default), 58, 66
Pedroni, Peter, 161
pension systems, 15–16, 323–24
perfect targeting, 112, 113
permanent shocks and poverty
targeting, 114–16

for carbon emissions, 270–73
competition in, 78
for derivatives transactions, 64–65, 84, 88
global economic crisis lessons for, 44–45
industrial policies and, 141
labor division between home and
    host regulators, 86–87
for public infrastructure services,
    182–83, 183t
reform, 54–65
for securitization of assets, 48
Reinhart, Carmen, 3n1
renewable energy, 268–69,
    269f, 274, 290–91
replacement investment, 96
replacement migration, 310–11
repo finance, 48, 48n2
repression of finance, 131
reproduction ratio, 99
República Bolivariana de Venezuela
    investment risk in, 100
    private sector infrastructure
        investments, 179n32
Republic of Korea
    economic growth, 127–28, 128f, 198
    exchange rate adjustments, 228
    foreign exchange reserves
        held by, 226, 227t
    industrial policies in, 132
    infrastructure investments, 12
    manufactured exports, 205–6,
        206t, 210, 210t
Repullo, Rafael, 59
research and development
    clean energy, 254n5, 259, 274, 277, 278
    as form of savings, 96
    procyclical investments in, 235
retirement age, 98, 317, 322n8, 323
retirement location, 106
return on equity, 177n28
reverse causation, 160, 160n8
Rioja, Felix K., 163, 166, 166n17
The Rise of the Network Society
    (Castells), 70
risk
    asymmetry of, 85
    climate change and, 260

counterparty risk, 64, 65
diversification via derivatives
    activities, 88
exchange risk, 101–2
measurement of, 56–59, 66
modular network systems and, 90
systemic, 80, 82, 85
tolerance, 87
underestimation of, 49, 50, 52
warnings, 83
risk-adjusted yield differential, 100–101
risk management, 55, 76–77
risk-spillover externalities, 80–81
Rodrik, Dani, 4n3, 6, 10, 12, 23–24,
    125, 129, 131, 132, 135
Rogoff, Kenneth, 3n1
Röller, Lars-Hendrik, 159, 161, 162
Romania and EU accession
    requirements, 164n14
Romer, Paul, 13
Romp, Ward, 158
rural areas
    in China, 100
    informal sector wages in, 146
    infrastructure investments in, 169–70
    public works schemes in, 118–19
Russian Federation, investment risk in, 100

S
Saltzman, Cynthia, 162
sanitation
    access to, 170–71, 171t
    affordability of, 171–72
    EU accession requirements, 164n14
    network effects in, 159n7
    private sector investments, 175, 175t
    public sector investments, 180–82, 181t
    regulatory agencies and, 183t
    status of, 154–57, 154t
Sapir, Andre, 9n7
Savard, Luc, 170
savings-investment balance, 76, 95,
    98–100, 225, 317, 324
scale-free networks, 69n1, 74, 79
Schelling, Thomas, 18
Schumpeter, Joseph, 39
Schur, Michael, 175

manufactured exports, 207,
207f, 208, 209
replacement migration and, 310, 310f
subsidies
cross-subsidies, 172, 173
housing finance, 63
industrial policies and, 131,
141, 142f, 143, 145n4,
146, 149–50
in poverty-targeted programs, 110, 115
Sudan, climate change impact on, 275, 279
Sugihara, George, 80, 89
Summers, Lawrence, 57
supervisory failures, 87
Sweden
centralized wage bargaining, 146
income inequality in, 19
Switzerland, current account surplus in, 99
Syrquin, Moises, 197
systemic risk
discounting of, 80
home and host regulators for, 86
leverage and, 85
loss-avoidance behavior and, 82

T

Taiwan, China
exchange rate adjustments, 228n13
foreign exchange reserves
held by, 226, 227t
industrial policies in, 132
manufactured exports, 205, 206,
206t, 207, 210, 210t
tariffs
cost-recovery levels, 156, 172, 173
deregulation of, 76
infrastructure needs of poor and, 170
input cost reductions and, 145
taxation arbitrage, 75, 77
taxes
industrial policies and, 131, 143
infrastructure financing with, 153
optimal framework, 111, 115
as redistributive, 110
"Taylor rule" approach, 49
technological forecasts for climate
change, 254–61

technology, 42, 76–77
See also information and
communication technology
telecommunications
See also information and
communication technology
access to, 170–71, 171t
information gap in, 156, 157n5
network effects in, 158–59
private sector investments, 174–75,
175t, 176, 176f
public sector investments, 180–82, 181t
regulatory agencies and, 182, 183t
status of, 154–57, 154t
temporary shocks and poverty
targeting, 117–20
Terrones, Marco E., 3, 3n1, 136
TFP (total factor productivity), 160
Thailand
foreign exchange reserves
held by, 226
manufactured exports, 206, 206t
Thatcher, Margaret, 174
Thorbecker, Erik, 111
thresholds in complex networks, 80
timber industry, 288
tipping points, 80
Togo, manufactured exports by, 205
too-big-to-fail problem, 53,
58, 62–63, 64, 80
total factor productivity (TFP), 160
tradable goods and services
in growth strategy, 126
infrastructure investments
and, 170
market equilibrium for, 141,
142f, 149–50
profitability of, 126, 135
tradable permit systems, 272, 273
trade
costs, 145
deficit, 106, 126, 133, 223, 225, 230
global regulation of, 79
growth and, 136–39, 137t
industrial policies and, 132
surpluses, 139–40, 140t
trade protection, 13, 131, 145, 196, 197

ECO-AUDIT

Environmental Benefits Statement

The World Bank is committed to preserving endangered forests and natural resources. The Office of the Publisher has chosen to print *Globalization and Growth* on recycled paper with 50 percent post-consumer waste, in accordance with the recommended standards for paper usage set by Green Press Initiative— a nonprofit program supporting publishers in using fiber that is not sourced from endangered forests. For more information, visit www.greenpressinitiative.org.

Saved:

- 25 trees
- 8 million British thermal units of total energy
- 683 pounds of solid waste
- 11,255 gallons of waste water
- 2,337 pounds of net greenhouse gases (CO_2 equivalent)